The Government of Self and Others

MICHEL FOUCAULT

The Government of Self and Others

LECTURES AT THE COLLÈGE DE FRANCE

1982-1983

Edited by Frédéric Gros
General Editors: François Ewald and Alessandro Fontana

English Series Editor: Arnold I. Davidson

TRANSLATED BY GRAHAM BURCHELL

Liberté • Égalité • Fraternité
RÉPUBLIQUE FRANÇAISE

This book is supported by the
French Ministry of Foreign Affairs,
as part of the Burgess programme
run by the Cultural Department of
the French Embassy in London.
(www.frenchbooknews.com)

FOREWORD

MICHEL FOUCAULT TAUGHT AT the Collège de France from January 1971 until his death in June 1984 (with the exception of 1977 when he took a sabbatical year). The title of his chair was "The History of Systems of Thought."

On the proposal of Jules Vuillemin, the chair was created on 30 November 1969 by the general assembly of the professors of the Collège de France and replaced that of "The History of Philosophical Thought" held by Jean Hyppolite until his death. The same assembly elected Michel Foucault to the new chair on 12 April 1970.[1] He was 43 years old.

Michel Foucault's inaugural lecture was delivered on 2 December 1970.[2] Teaching at the Collège de France is governed by particular rules. Professors must provide 26 hours of teaching a year (with the possibility of a maximum of half this total being given in the form of seminars[3]). Each year they must present their original research and this obliges them to change the content of their teaching for each course. Courses and seminars are completely open; no enrolment or qualification is required and the professors do not award any qualifications.[4] In the terminology of the Collège de France, the professors do not have students but only auditors.

Michel Foucault's courses were held every Wednesday from January to March. The huge audience made up of students, teachers, researchers and the curious, including many who came from outside France, required two amphitheaters of the Collège de France. Foucault often complained about the distance between himself and his "public" and of how few exchanges the course made possible.[5] He would have liked a seminar in which real collective work could take place and made a number of attempts to bring this about. In the final years he devoted a long period to answering his auditors' questions at the end of each course. This is how Gérard Petitjean, a journalist from *Le Nouvel Observateur*, described the atmosphere at Foucault's lectures in 1975:

> When Foucault enters the amphitheater, brisk and dynamic like someone who plunges into the water, he steps over bodies to reach his chair, pushes away the cassette recorders so he can put down his papers, removes his jacket, lights a lamp and sets off at full speed. His voice is strong and effective, amplified by the loudspeakers that are the only concession to modernism in a hall that is barely lit by light spread from stucco bowls. The hall has three hundred places and there are five hundred people packed together, filling the smallest free space...There is no oratorical effect. It is clear and terribly effective. There is absolutely no concession to improvisation. Foucault has twelve hours each year to explain in a public course the direction taken by his research in the year just ended. So everything is concentrated and he fills the margins like correspondents who have too much to say for the space available to them. At 19.15 Foucault stops. The students rush towards his desk; not to speak to him, but to stop their cassette recorders. There are no questions. In the pushing and shoving Foucault is alone. Foucault remarks: "It should be possible to discuss what I have put forward. Sometimes, when it has not been a good lecture, it would need very little, just one question, to put everything straight. However, this question never comes. The group effect in France makes any genuine discussion impossible. And as there is no feedback, the course is theatricalized. My relationship with the people there is like that of an actor or an acrobat. And when I have finished speaking, a sensation of total solitude..."[6]

Foucault approached his teaching as a researcher: explorations for a future book as well as the opening up of fields of problematization were formulated as an invitation to possible future researchers. This is why the courses at the Collège de France do not duplicate the published books. They are not sketches for the books even though both books and courses share certain themes. They have their own status. They arise from a specific discursive regime within the set of Foucault's "philosophical activities." In particular they set out the program for a genealogy of knowledge/power relations, which are the terms in which he thinks of his work from the beginning of the 1970s, as opposed to the program of an archeology of discursive formations that previously orientated his work.[7]

The course also performed a role in contemporary reality. Those who followed his courses were not only held in thrall by the narrative that unfolded week by week and seduced by the rigorous exposition, they also found a perspective on contemporary reality. Michel Foucault's art consisted in using history to cut diagonally through contemporary reality. He could speak of Nietzsche or Aristotle, of expert psychiatric opinion or the Christian pastoral, but those who attended his lectures always took from what he said a perspective on the present and contemporary events. Foucault's specific strength in his courses was the subtle interplay between learned erudition, personal commitment, and work on the event.

With their development and refinement in the 1970s, Foucault's desk was quickly invaded by cassette recorders. The courses—and some seminars—have thus been preserved.

This edition is based on the words delivered in public by Foucault. It gives a transcription of these words that is as literal as possible.[8] We would have liked to present it as such. However, the transition from an oral to a written presentation calls for editorial intervention: at the very least it requires the introduction of punctuation and division into paragraphs. Our principle has been always to remain as close as possible to the course actually delivered.

Summaries and repetitions have been removed whenever it seemed to be absolutely necessary. Interrupted sentences have been restored and faulty constructions corrected. Suspension points indicate that the recording is inaudible. When a sentence is obscure there is a

one

5 JANUARY 1983

First hour

[
Remarks on method. ᔓ *Study of Kant's text: What is
Enlightenment?* ᔓ *Conditions of publication: journals.* ᔓ *The
encounter between Christian* Aufklärung *and Jewish* Haskala:
freedom of conscience. ᔓ *Philosophy and present reality.* ᔓ *The
question of the Revolution.* ᔓ *Two critical filiations.*
]

FIRST OF ALL I would like to tell you how much I appreciate your
regular attendance. I would also like to say that it is often rather
difficult giving a series of lectures like this without the possibility
of comebacks or discussion, and not knowing whether what one is
saying finds an echo in those who are working on a thesis or a master's
degree, whether it provides them with possibilities for reflection and
work. On the other hand, you know that in this institution, where
the rules are very liberal, we cannot give closed seminars, reserved for
just a few auditors. So I won't be doing that this year. All the same,
what I would like, not so much for you but selfishly for myself, is to
be able to meet, Off-Broadway, outside of the lectures, with those of
you who could possibly discuss the subjects I will be talking about
this year, or that I have talked about elsewhere and previously. So,
maybe we can wait until one or two lectures have taken place before
organizing this small group, or at any rate this small informal meeting external to the lectures themselves and to the institution strictly
speaking. Either next week or in two weeks' time I will suggest a time

We can say that the work I tried to do after this consisted in studying each of these three areas in turn in order to see what further work needed to be done on the methods and concepts for analyzing them, first as dimensions of an experience, and then insofar as they were to be linked together.

First of all I tried to study the formation of forms of knowledge with particular regard to seventeenth and eighteenth century empirical sciences like natural history, general grammar, and economics. For me, these were only an example for the analysis of the formation of forms of knowledge (*savoirs*).[3] It seemed to me that if one really wanted to study experience as the matrix for the formation of forms of knowledge, one should not analyze the development or progress of particular bodies of knowledge, but rather one should identify the discursive practices which were able to constitute the matrices of possible bodies of knowledge, and study the rules, the game of true and false, and, more generally, the forms of veridiction in these discursive practices. In short, it was a matter of shifting the axis of the history of the contents of knowledge towards the analysis of forms of knowledge, of the discursive practices that organize and constitute the matrix element of these forms of knowledge, and studying these discursive practices as regulated forms of veridiction. For some time I have tried to bring about a shift from the contents of knowledge to forms of knowledge, and from forms of knowledge to discursive practices and rules of veridiction.

Second, it was then a matter of analyzing, let's say, the normative matrices of behavior. Here the shift did not consist in analyzing Power with a capital "P", or even institutions of power, or the general or institutional forms of domination. Rather, it meant studying the techniques and procedures by which one sets about conducting the conduct of others. That is to say, I tried to pose the question of norms of behavior first of all in terms of power, and of power that one exercises, and to analyze this power as a field of procedures of government. Here again the shift consisted in passing from analysis of the norm to analysis of the exercise of power, and passing from analysis of the exercise of power to the procedures of, let's say, governmentality. In this case my example was criminality and the disciplines.[4]

Finally, the third area involved analyzing the constitution of the subject's mode of being. Here, instead of referring to a theory of the subject, it seemed to me that one should try to analyze the different forms by which the individual is led to constitute him or herself as subject. Taking the example of sexual behavior and the history of sexual morality,[5] I tried to see how and through what concrete forms of the relation to self the individual was called upon to constitute him or herself as the moral subject of his or her sexual conduct. In other words, once again this involved bringing about a shift from the question of the subject to the analysis of forms of subjectivation, and to the analysis of these forms of subjectivation through the techniques/technologies of the relation to self, or, if you like, through what could be called the pragmatics of self.

Replacing the history of knowledge with the historical analysis of forms of veridiction, replacing the history of domination with the historical analysis of procedures of governmentality, and replacing the theory of the subject or the history of subjectivity with the historical analysis of the pragmatics of self and the forms it has taken, are the different approaches by which I have tried to define to some degree the possibility of the history of what could be called "experiences." The experience of madness, the experience of disease, the experience of criminality, and the experience of sexuality are, I think, important focal points of experiences in our culture. This then is the route I have tried to follow and that quite frankly it was necessary to try to reconstruct for you, if only to take a bearing on where we are. But you knew this already.*

---

* The manuscript contains an argument at this point which Foucault did not present in his lecture:

"What meaning is this enterprise to be given?

There are above all its immediately apparent 'negative,' negativist aspects. A historicizing negativism, since it involves replacing a theory of knowledge, power, or the subject with the analysis of historically determinate practices. A nominalist negativism, since it involves replacing universals like madness, crime, and sexuality with the analysis of experiences which constitute singular historical forms. A negativism with a nihilistic tendency, if by this we understand a form of reflection which, instead of indexing practices to systems of values which allow them to be assessed, inserts these systems of values in the interplay of arbitrary but intelligible practices.

Faced with these objections, or to tell the truth, 'reproaches,' we should adopt a very firm attitude. For there are 'reproaches,' that is to say objections, such that in defending oneself from them one inevitably subscribes to what they maintain. Under these different objections/reproaches, a sort of implicit contract of theoretical decision is assumed or imposed, a contract whose terms disqualify historicism, nominalism, and nihilism from the start: no-one dares to declare themselves such and the trap consists in not being able to do anything but accept a challenge, that is to say, subscribe…

Having explored these three dimensions somewhat, it was natural that in the course of these explorations, which I systematize rather arbitrarily since I will come back to them, certain things were dropped or left to one side which nevertheless appeared to me to be interesting and maybe posed new problems. What I would like to do this year is retrace some of the paths already followed, taking up again a few points, such as, for example, what I said to you last year about *parrēsia*, true discourse in the political realm. It seemed to me that this study would make it possible to see, to tighten up a bit, the problem of the relations between government of self and government of others, to see the genesis, the genealogy, if not of political discourse in general, the object of which is essentially government by the Prince, at least of a certain form of political discourse whose object would be government of the Prince, of the Prince's soul by the counselor, the philosopher, the pedagogue responsible for forming his soul. True discourse, discourse of truth addressed to the Prince and the Prince's soul will be one of my first themes. I would also like to take up the things I said, two or three years ago I think, concerning the art of government in the sixteenth century.[6] I am not sure exactly what I will do, but I would like to take up again these still open dossiers. I say "dossiers," a very solemn term, but it is really a matter of tracks which I have just come across and followed for a while, and then left to one side, poorly marked out.

This week I would like to start with, how to put it, not exactly an *excursus*: a little epigraph (*exergue*). As epigraph, I would like to study a text which may not be situated exactly within the reference points I will choose for most of this year. Nevertheless, it appears to me to be

---

Now what is striking first of all of course is that historicism, nominalism, and nihilism have been around for a long time as objections, and above all that the form of the discourse is such that the givens have not even been examined.
1. The question of historicism is: what have been and may be the effects of historical analysis in the field of historical thought?
2. The question of nominalism is: what have been the effects of nominalist criticism in the analysis of cultures, knowledge, institutions, and political structures?
3. The question of nihilism is: what have been and what may be the effects of nihilism in the acceptance and transformation of systems of values?
To objections that postulate the disqualification of nihilism/nominalism/historicism, we should try to reply by undertaking a historicist, nominalist, nihilist analysis of this current. By this I mean: not construct this form of thought in its universal systematic character and justify it in terms of truth or moral value, but rather seek to know how the constitution and development of this critical game, this form of thought, was possible. There is no question of doing that this year, but only of indicating its general horizon."

very exactly in line with, and to formulate in rigorous terms, one of the important problems that I would like to talk about, which is precisely this relationship between the government of self and the government of others. And, on the other hand, it seems to me that it not only talks about this subject itself, but it does so in a way with which—without too much, [or rather], with a little vanity—I can associate myself. It is a text which is something of a blazon, a fetish for me, which I have already spoken about several times, and which I would like to examine a bit more closely today. This text, if you like, bears some relation to what I am talking about, and I would really like the way in which I talk about it to have some connection with it. The text is, of course, Kant's *Was ist Aufklärung?*

As you know, Kant wrote the text in September 1784 and it was published in the *Berlinische Monatsschrift* in December 1784. First of all I would just like to recall very briefly the conditions and dates of its pub-lication. There is absolutely nothing extraordinary in Kant publishing a text like this in a journal. You know that a large part of his theoreti-cal activity consisted in publishing articles, reviews, and contributions in certain journals. It was in the *Berlinische Monatsschrift* that, the pre-vious month, November 1784, he published a text which, somewhat expanded, became the *Idea for a Universal History from a Cosmopolitan Point of View.*[7] The following year, 1785, he published his *Definition of the concept of race*[8] in the same journal; in 1786 he also published his *Conjectural Beginning of Human History* in this journal.[9] He also wrote in other journals: in the *Allgemeine Literaturzeitung* he published a review of a book by Herder;[10] in the *Teutsche Merkur* in 1788 he published *On the Use of Teleological Principles in Philosophy,*[11] and so on.

However, the reason we should keep in mind the fact that the text was published in a journal is that, as you will see, the text on the *Aufklärung* brings into play, as one of its central concepts, or as one of the sets of concepts, the notion of public, of *Publikum*. This notion of *Publikum* means, first of all, the concrete, institutional, or at any rate established relationship between the writer (the qualified writer, translated in French as *savant*; *Gelehrter*; man of culture), and the reader (considered as any individual). The function of this relation-ship between reader and writer, the analysis of this relationship—the conditions under which this relationship can and should be established constantly progressing? With regard to this question, which for him is the most important question of the relationships between philosophy and law, his reasoning is as follows. In the fifth section of this essay he says: If we want to answer the question—"is the human race constantly progressing?"—we must of course determine the possibility of progress and the cause of a possible progress. But, he says, once we have established that there is a cause of a possible progress, in fact we will only be able to know that this cause is actually at work if we can identify an event which shows that cause in action. In short, what Kant means is that designating a cause can only ever determine possible effects, or more precisely the possibility of effects. The reality of an effect can be established only if we isolate an event that we can attach to a cause. So we will not be able to answer this question through the process by which we analyze the teleological structure of history, but through a process which is the opposite of this. Thus, we should not follow the teleological thread which makes a progress possible, but isolate an event in history which will have, Kant says, the value of a sign. A sign of what? A sign of the existence of a cause,[23] of a permanent cause which has guided men down the road of progress throughout history. A constant cause which must be shown to have acted in the past, to be active now, and that will act in the future. Consequently the event which will enable us to decide whether there is progress will be a sign which is "*rememorativum, demonstrativum, pronosticum,*"[24] that is to say, a sign which indicates that it really was always thus (rememorative sign); that it really is thus now (demonstrative sign); and finally a prognostic sign which shows us that it will always be thus. This is how we can be sure that the cause which makes progress possible has not just acted at a given moment but really is a matter of a tendency, and that it confirms a general tendency of the entire human race to advance in the direction of progress. This then is the question: Is there around us an event which would serve as a rememorative, demonstrative, and prognostic sign of a constant progress which carries along the whole of the human race? You will be able to guess Kant's answer from what I have said, but I would like to read to you the passage through which he introduces the Revolution as the sign of this event. At the start of the sixth section he says: "Do not expect this event [with rememorative, demonstrative, and prognostic value; M.F.] to consist in the lofty deeds or major crimes of men by which what was thought great is made small or what was thought small is made great, nor in ancient and magnificent political structures which disappear as if by magic, while others arise in their place as if from the depths of the earth. No, none of this."[25]

There are two things to note in this text. First, of course, Kant alludes here to forms of analysis which it was customary to refer to in the debate on whether or not the human race is progressing. That is to say: the overthrow of empires, great catastrophes which cause the best established states to disappear, the reversals of fortune which make the great become small and the small become great. He refutes all this, but at the same time says: Take note, it is not to great events that we should look for the rememorative, demonstrative, and prognostic sign of progress. We should look for it in events which are almost imperceptible. That is to say, we cannot analyze our own present in its significant values without engaging in a hermeneutics or decipherment which will enable us to endow what is apparently of no significance and value with the significance and value we are looking for. Now what is this event which is therefore not a great event? Well, it is the Revolution. The Revolution…But after all, we can hardly say that the Revolution is not a resounding, striking event. Is it not precisely an event which overturns everything and makes small what was great and great what was small, and which abolishes and engulfs what seem to be the most solid structures of society and of states? But, Kant says, it is not the Revolution in itself which is significant. What is significant and constitutes the event with demonstrative, prognostic, and rememorative value is not the exploits and gesticulations of the revolutionary drama itself. What is significant is the way in which the Revolution exists as spectacle, the way in which it is greeted everywhere by spectators who are not participants, but observers, witnesses, and who, for better or worse, let themselves be caught up in it. The gesticulations of revolution do not constitute progress. Not only is it not, in the first place, revolutionary gesticulation which constitutes progress, but, to tell the truth, if the Revolution was to be made again, we would not go through with it. There is an extremely interesting text on this: "No matter whether the revolution of a gifted people, which we have seen carried out in our time [Kant is therefore referring to the French Revolution; M.F.],

situate it for you both for the context in which it was placed, its relationship to the public, to Mendelssohn's *Aufklärung*, for the type of questions it raises, and for the fact that in a way it is at the origin, the point
of departure of a whole dynasty of philosophical questions. Because
it seems to me that these two questions—"What is *Aufklärung*?" and
"What is the Revolution?"—which are the two forms in which Kant
poses the question of his own present reality, have continued to haunt,
if not all of modern philosophy since the nineteenth century, then at
least a large part of this philosophy. After all, the *Aufklärung*, both as
singular event inaugurating European modernity and as a permanent
process which manifests itself in the form of the history of reason, the
development and establishment of forms of rationality and technology,
the autonomy and authority of knowledge, all of this, this question of
the *Aufklärung*—or of reason and the use of reason as a historical problem—seems to me to have run through all philosophical thought from
Kant up to now. The other present reality encountered by Kant, the
Revolution—the Revolution as at once an event, rupture, and upheaval
in history, as failure, and almost necessary failure, but with at the same
time a value, an operational value in history and the progress of the
human species—is also another great question of philosophy. I would
be tempted to say that basically Kant seems to me to have founded the
two great traditions which have divided modern philosophy.

Let's say that in his major critical œuvre—that of the three *Critiques*
and above all the first *Critique*—Kant set out and founded that tradition of critical philosophy which posed the question of the conditions
of possibility of a true knowledge. And we can say that a whole part of
modern philosophy since the nineteenth century presented itself and
developed from this as the analytic of truth. This is the form of philosophy that you now find in the form of, say, Anglo-Saxon analytical
philosophy.

But within modern and contemporary philosophy there is another
type of question, of critical questioning whose birth we see precisely
in the question of *Aufklärung* or in Kant's text on the Revolution. This
other critical tradition does not pose the question of the conditions
of possibility of a true knowledge; it asks the question: What is present reality? What is the present field of our experiences? What is the
present field of possible experiences? Here it is not a question of the

analytic of truth but involves what could be called an ontology of the present, of present reality, an ontology of modernity, an ontology of ourselves. It seems to me that the philosophical choice confronting us today is the following. We have to opt either for a critical philosophy which appears as an analytical philosophy of truth in general, or for a critical thought which takes the form of an ontology of ourselves, of present reality. It is this latter form of philosophy which, from Hegel to the Frankfurt School, passing through Nietzsche, Max Weber and so on, has founded a form of reflection to which, of course, I link myself insofar as I can.*

There you are. So, if you like we will take a five minutes rest and then I will move on to a closer reading of this text on *Aufklärung* whose surroundings I have simply tried to outline.

---

* With regard to Kant and his opuscule, the manuscript speaks of a "point at which a certain form of reflection takes root to which the analyses I would like to make are linked."

1. "On the 30th [November 1969], the assembly of the professors of the Collège de France voted for the transformation of chair of the history of philosophical thought, previously held by Jean Hippolite, into the chair of the history of systems of thought" (Daniel Defert, "Chronologie" in M. Foucault, *Dits et Écrits, 1954-1988*, ed. D. Defert and F. Ewald, with the collaboration of J. Lagrange, 4 volumes, Paris: Gallimard, 1994, vol. 1, p. 35). On the problematization of a "history of thought," see more precisely "Préface à l'*Histoire de la sexualité*" in ibid., vol. 4, pp. 579-580.

2. M. Foucault, *Histoire de la folie à l'âge classique* (Paris: Plon, 1961); English translation by Jonathan Murphy, *History of Madness* (London: Routledge, 2006).

3. Michel Foucault, *Les Mots et les Choses* (Paris: Gallimard, 1966); English translation by A. Sheridan, *The Order of Things* (London: Tavistock and New York: Pantheon, 1970).

4. M. Foucault, *Surveiller et Punir* (Paris: Gallimard, 1975); English translation by A. Sheridan, *Discipline and Punish. Birth of the Prison* (London: Allen Lane and New York: Pantheon, 1977). On governmentality, see M. Foucault, *Sécurité, Territoire, Population*, éd. Michel Senellart (Paris: Gallimard-Le Seuil, 2004); English translation by Graham Burchell, *Security, Territory, Population*, ed., Michel Senellart, English series ed., Arnold I. Davidson (Basingstoke and New York: Palgrave Macmillan, 2007).

5. See the second and third volumes of the History of Sexuality, M. Foucault, *L'Usage des plaisirs* and *Le Souci de soi* (Paris: Gallimard, 1984); English translations by R. Hurley, *The Use of Pleasure* and *The Care of the Self* (New York: Random House, 1985 and Harmondsworth: Viking, 1986).

6. *Sécurité, Territoire, Population*; *Security, Territory, Population*.

7. French translation by S. Piobetta in I. Kant, *La Philosophie de l'histoire* (Paris: Gonthier, 1947) pp. 26-45; English translation by Lewis White Beck as "Idea for a Universal History from a Cosmopolitan Point of View" in I. Kant, *On History*, ed. Lewis White Beck (Indianapolis: The Bobbs-Merrill Company, 1963) pp. 11-26, and also by H.B. Nisbet as "Idea for a Universal History with a Cosmopolitan Purpose" in Hans Reiss, ed., *Kant's Political Writings* (Cambridge: Cambridge University Press, 1970) pp. 41-53.

8. French, ibid., pp. 88-109 (originally published in November 1785).

9. French, ibid., pp. 110-127; English translation by Emil L. Fackenheim in Kant, *On History*, pp. 53-68; (originally published in January 1786).

10. French translation as "Compte rendu de l'ouvrage de Herder: 'Idées en vue d'une philosophie de l'histoire de l'humanité'" in ibid., pp. 56-88; English translation by Robert E. Anchor as "Reviews of Herder's *Ideas for a Philosophy of the History of Mankind*" in Kant, *On History*, pp. 27-52; (originally published in January 1785 in the *Jenaische allgemeine Literaturzeitung*).

11. French ibid., pp. 128-162 (originally published in January-February 1788).

12. On this movement see M. Pelli, *The Age of Haskala: Studies in Hebrew Literature of the Enlightenment in Germany* (Leyde: Brill, 1979); G. Scholem, *Fidélité et Utopie. Essais sur le judaïsme contemporain*, trans. B. Dupuy (Paris: Calmann-Lévy, 1978); A. Altmann, *Moses Mendelssohn: A Biographical Study* (London: Routledge & Kegan Paul, 1973); and D. Bourel, "Les réserves de Mendelssohn, Rousseau, Voltaire et le juif de Berlin," *Revue internationale de philosophie*, Brussels, 1978, vol. 24-25, pp. 309-326.

13. Moses Mendelssohn, *Philosophische Gespräche* (Berlin: C.F. Voss, 1755).

14. Moses Mendelssohn, *Jérusalem ou Pouvoir religieux et Judaïsme*, trans. D. Bourel, with a preface by E. Levinas (Paris: Presses d'Aujourd'hui, 1982).

15. The letter was addressed to Johann Peter Uz, 12 February 1756. A more complete version reads: "The author of the philosophical dialogues and of the short work on the sensations is not an imaginary Jew but a very real Jew, still very young and remarkably brilliant who, without teachers, has penetrated deeply into the sciences, does algebra in his spare time like we write poetry and who, since he was young, has earned his living in a Jewish enterprise. This, at least, is what Lessing tells me. His name is Moses. Maupertius joked about him saying that he lacks nothing to be a great man except a bit of foreskin." Quoted in D. Bourel, *Moses Mendelssohn. La naissance du judaïsme moderne* (Paris: Gallimard, 2004) p. 109.

16. I. Kant, Letter of 16 August 1783, XIII, 129, French translation by J.L. Bruch, Paris, 1969, quoted in *Jérusalem*, p. 48.

17. See above note 9.

18. See above note 8.
19. See above note 7.
20. See above note 11.
21. J.G. Fichte, *Considérations destinées à rectifier le jugement du public sur la Révolution française* [Contribution to the Rectification of the Public's Judgment of the French Revolution], trans. J. Barni (Paris: Payot-Rivages, 1989).
22. Foucault uses the translation by S. Piobetta, in I. Kant, *La Philosophie de l'histoire*, pp. 163-179; English translation (of second essay only) by Robert E. Anchor as "An Old Question Raised Again: Is the Human Race Constantly Progressing?" in I. Kant, *On History*, pp. 137-154, and by H.B. Nisbet as "The Contest of the Faculties. A Renewed Attempt to Answer the Question: Is the Human Race Continually Improving?" in Hans Reiss, ed., *Kant's Political Writings*, pp. 176-190.
23. "We must therefore look for an event which indicates the existence of such a cause": ibid., French p. 169; English p. 143, and p. 181.
24. Ibid., Fr. p. 170; Eng. p. 143, and p. 181.
25. Ibid., Fr. p. 170; Eng. p. 143, and p. 182.
26. Ibid., Fr. p. 171; Eng. p. 144, and p. 182.
27. Ibid.
28. Ibid.
29. Ibid., Fr. p. 173; Eng. p. 147, and p. 184.
30. Ibid., Fr. pp. 173-174; Eng. p. 147, and pp. 184-185.

two

5 JANUARY 1983

Second hour

[
*The idea of tutelage (*minorité*)*: neither natural powerlessness nor authoritarian deprivation of rights.* ∽ *Way out from the condition of tutelage and critical activity.* ∽ *The shadow of the three* Critiques. ∽ *The difficulty of emancipation: laziness and cowardice; the predicted failure of liberators.* ∽ *Motivations of the condition of tutelage: superimposition of obedience and absence of reasoning; confusion between the private and public use of reason.* ∽ *The problematic turn at the end of Kant's text.*
]

AFTER SOME GENERAL REMARKS on this text [concerning] *Aufklärung*, I would like to start a rather more precise analysis of at least some of its important points. I will leave aside a whole section of the text which refers specifically to problems of religious legislation

---

* [The German word *Unmündigkeit*, translated in French as *minorité*, has been variously rendered in English as "tutelage" by Lewis White Beck ("What is Enlightenment" in Kant, *On History*, p. 3), "immaturity" by H.R. Nisbet ("An Answer to the Question: 'What is Enlightenment?'" in Hans Reiss, ed., *Kant's Political Writings*, p. 54) and James Schmidt ("An Answer to the Question: What is Enlightenment?" in James Schmidt, ed., *What is Enlightenment? Eighteenth-Century Answers and Twentieth-Century Questions*, Berkeley: University of California Press, 1996, p. 58), and as "minority" by Mary J. Gregor ("An Answer to the Question: What is Enlightenment?" in Immanuel Kant, *Practical Philosophy*, trans. and ed. Mary J. Gregor, Cambridge: Cambridge University Press, 1999, p. 17). Although Kant's use of the term evokes both the legal sense of minority (the condition of being a minor) and the developmental physical and/or psychological sense of immaturity (in the sense of a lack of ability), I have opted for tutelage as capturing better than either of these the sense of the condition of being under instruction, guidance, and guardianship. However, see James Schmidt's useful note to his translation, pp. 63-64—G.B.]

ask ourselves what this man is who comes out in this way. Should man be understood to mean the human race as a species? Or should man be understood to mean human society as the universal element within which different individual reasons join together? Are only some human societies the bearers of these values? Is it a matter of individuals, and if so, what individuals, and so on? The text just says "man's way out."

Finally, the third remark, the third question concerns the end of the paragraph. On the one hand, if we look at the start of the paragraph, the start of the definition, then Enlightenment is "*man's way out from his self-incurred tutelage.*" In reading this we get the impression that Kant here is designating a movement, a movement of getting out, of release which is being carried out and which constitutes precisely the significant element of our present reality. Now at the end of the paragraph a different type of discourse appears. The discourse is no longer descriptive, but prescriptive. Kant no longer describes what is happening but says: "*Sapere aude!* Have the courage to use your own understanding. That is the motto of Enlightenment." Finally, I said that this is a prescription, but it is a bit more complicated than that. Kant employs the word "*Wahlspruch*," which is motto, blazon. The *Wahlspruch* is actually a maxim, precept, or order given to others and to oneself, but at the same time—and this is what makes the precept of the *Wahlspruch* a motto, a blazon—it is something by which one identifies oneself and enables one to distinguish oneself from others. The use of a maxim as a precept is therefore at once an order and a distinctive mark. As you can see, what all this means is that what Kant means when he speaks of Enlightenment as "man's way out from his tutelage" is not at all clear or easy to see.

These are some general questions. Now let us try to go a bit more deeply into the text to see: how this description can be at the same time a prescription; what the man who must come out is; and in what this coming out consists, since these are the three questions encountered straightaway.

The first point to clarify is what Kant understands by the condition of tutelage from which, he says, man is in the process of emerging, and from which he says it is necessary that man emerge, since he gives man the order to get out from this condition. First of all, we should not confuse this condition of tutelage with that of natural powerlessness; it is not something like humanity's childhood. A bit further on in the text he employs an expression which the French translators (there are two French translations) have not translated well.[6] This is the German word *Gängelwagen*, which designates those little kinds of vehicles used in the eighteenth century to train children: they were put in a sort of trapezoid frame on wheels, which made them walk. He says that men today are in a sort of *Gängelwagen* (which is not at all the "*brancard*" [shaft of a cart to which the horse or animal is attached] or the "*parc*" [pen] to which the French translators refer),[7] and this does suggest that man is in his childhood. But at the beginning of the second paragraph Kant says that actually the condition of tutelage in which man finds himself is not in any way a natural powerlessness inasmuch as men are, in fact, perfectly capable of taking charge of their own conduct. They are perfectly able to do so, it is just that something—which must be defined: a flaw, a shortcoming, or a form of will—makes them incapable. So, we must not confuse this condition of tutelage with what some philosophers designated as the condition of the natural childhood of a humanity which has not yet acquired the means and possibilities of autonomy.

Second, if this notion of tutelage is not a matter of natural powerlessness, are we then dealing with a juridical or political-juridical notion referring to the fact that men are currently denied the legitimate exercise of their rights due to the circumstance of their having effectively given up their rights voluntarily in an initial founding act, or else because they have been deprived of their rights by some stratagem or violence? But here again we must note that this is not what Kant is talking about. He says so moreover: If men are in this condition of tutelage, if they are subject to direction by others, it is not because these others have seized power, or that it has been handed over to them in an essential, founding and instituting act. He says it is because men are unable or do not wish to conduct themselves, and others have obligingly come forward to conduct them.[8] He refers to an act, or rather to an attitude, a mode of behavior, a form of will which is general, permanent, and does not create any right, but simply a sort of state of affairs in which it turns out that, through connivance and, as it were, an obligingness slightly tinged with cunning and shrewdness, some people have taken upon themselves the direction of others. But what demonstrates much more clearly that this is not a matter of the deprivation of a right, that it is absolutely not a condition of legal minority others by virtue of their own autonomy, some of these people, aware of their value to others, as well as "of the vocation (*Beruf*) of every man to think for himself,"[12] decide to play the role of liberators. So, they think for themselves and rely on this autonomy to assume authority over others. But they use this authority in such a way that awareness of their worth will somehow spread and become the acknowledgement and affirmation of the will of every man to do the same, that is to say, think for himself. Now, he says, in reality these individuals, who are like spiritual or political leaders, cannot get humanity out of its tutelage. Why is this? Precisely because they began by placing others under their authority, so that these others, being thus accustomed to the yoke, cannot bear the freedom and emancipation they are given. They force, they constrain precisely those who want to free them because they have freed themselves to come back under the yoke, the yoke which they accepted from the other out of cowardice and laziness and under which they now wish to bring back those who want to free them. Consequently, he says, the law of all revolutions—this was written in 1784—is that those who make them necessarily fall back under the yoke of those who wanted to free them.

So, since it is not men themselves, or some men, who will carry out this process of transformation, of this way out from the condition of tutelage into a condition of majority, then, Kant says, in order to see how *Aufklärung*, liberation and leaving the condition of tutelage must take place, we must see exactly how this condition of tutelage functions. And he says that the condition of tutelage is characterized by the constitution of two unjustified and illegitimate couples: [first] the couple formed by obedience and the absence of reasoning; second the couple formed by, or at least the confusion between two things that should be distinguished: the private and the public.

The first couple, then, is this. In the societies we know, it is accepted—this is what governors would have the governed believe, but it is also what the governed believe out of cowardice and laziness—that there can only be obedience where there is absence of reasoning (*raisonnement*). Kant gives three examples of this:[13] officers who say to their soldiers: Do not argue (*raisonnez*), obey; the priest who says to the faithful: Do not argue, believe; and the tax collector who says: Do not argue, pay. The word, the term used here is *Räsonnieren*, which as you know, in the *Critiques*, but especially in the *Critique of Pure Reason*, has a very particular sense of "quibbling,"[14] but which we should take here in the sense of "using one's faculty of reason." So, in this structure of the condition of tutelage we have this affiliation of obedience and the absence of *Räsonnieren*, of the use of the faculty of reason. And, Kant says, there is only one being in the world—he does not say who—one "ruler in the world,"[15] who says: Argue (*raisonnez*) as much as you like, but obey. And, of course, the question arises of the identity of this sole ruler in the world who says: Argue as much as you like, but obey. Is it God, reason itself, or the Prussian king? You will see that it is certainly not the first, but the second, a bit, and especially the third.

The second couple which characterizes the condition of tutelage is that formed by the two domains of the private and public, *Privat* and *Publikum* (the famous public that we have just been talking about). When Kant distinguishes between what is private and what is public he is not in any way, or not mainly, setting his sights on two domains of activity, one which would be public for certain reasons, and the other which would be private for opposite reasons. The characterization "private" is not applied to a domain of things but to a use, precisely to a use of our own faculties. And what he calls "public" is less a precise domain of things or activities than a certain way of putting to work and using our own faculties.

What is the private use of the faculties? In what way do we make what Kant calls a private use of the faculties? We make private use of our faculties in our professional activity, in our public activity as functionaries, when we are components of a society or government whose principles and objectives are those of the collective good. In other words—and there is an ingenious little trick here, a little discrepancy with regard to our use of these words—what he calls private is in fact what we call public, or at any rate professional. Why does he call it private? Quite simply he does so for the following reason. What are we in all these forms of activity, in the use we make of our faculties when we are functionaries, when we belong to an institution, to a political body? We are, he says, just "parts of a machine."[16] We are parts of a machine, placed in a given spot, [with] a precise role to play, with other parts of the machine having to play different roles. To that extent we do not function as a universal subject but as an individual. We have to make a particular and precise use of our faculty within a system which is charged with an overall and collective function. This is private use. What then is public use? It is precisely the use we make of our understanding and our faculties inasmuch as we place ourselves in a universal element in which we can figure as a universal subject. Now it is quite clear that no political activity, administrative function, or form of economic practice puts us in this situation of universal subject. We constitute ourselves as a universal subject when as rational beings we address all other rational beings. It is simply here, precisely and par excellence in that activity of the writer addressing the reader, that we encounter a dimension of the public which is at the same time the dimension of the universal. Or rather, we encounter a dimension of the universal and the use we make of our understanding at this point can and must be a public use.

Consequently, we can now see what tutelage and the way out from tutelage are in substance. There is tutelage whenever the principle of obedience—confused with non-reasoning—is made to coincide with, is superimposed on not only the private, but also the public use of our understanding. There is tutelage when obedience is confused with non-reasoning, and when, in this confusion of obedience and non-reasoning, we suppress what should be the public and universal use of our understanding. On the other hand, we will have attained our majority when we have re-established, as it were, the right connection between these two couples: when obedience, clearly separated from *Räsonnieren* (using one's reason), is wholly, absolutely, and unconditionally good in private use (that is to say, when as citizen, functionary, soldier, member of a religious community, etcetera, we obey), and when, on the other hand, *Räsonnieren* (the use of reason) takes place in the dimension of the universal, that is to say in opening to a public in which there is no obligation, or rather no relationship of obedience or authority. In the condition of tutelage one obeys whatever the case, in private and public use, and consequently one does not reason. In the condition of majority, reasoning and obedience are disconnected. Obedience is emphasized in private use and the total and absolute freedom of reasoning is emphasized in public use. And you can see that we have here the definition of what is *Aufklärung.* You can see that *Aufklärung,* and Kant says this, is the exact opposite of "*tolerance.*"[17] What is tolerance in fact? Tolerance is precisely what excludes reasoning, discussion, and freedom of thought in its public form, and only accepts it—tolerates it—in a personal, private and hidden use. *Aufklärung*, on the contrary, gives freedom the dimension of the greatest publicity in the form of the universal, and it maintains obedience only in this private role, let's say in this particular, defined individual role within the social body.

So this is what the process of *Aufklärung*, the new dividing up, the new distribution of government of self and government of others consists in. Now how is this operation to be carried out; what will its agent be? It is here, if you like, that the text turns round in such a way that, up to a point, most of the principles on which its analysis was based are put into question and, up to a point, this calls for, or marks out the possible place of the text on the Revolution. How in actual fact, says Kant, is the *Ausgang* going? Is this *Ausgang*, this way out, being accomplished; where are we in the process? What is the present point in this process of the way out? He gives an answer to this question which is absolutely tautological and says nothing more than the question. He says: We are *"moving towards Enlightenment."*[18] The German text says very precisely: We are in the period, in the *Zeitalter*, in the age of *Aufklärung*. To the question: "What is *Aufklärung* and where are we in this process of *Aufklärung*?" he confines himself to giving the answer: We live in the age of *Aufklärung*.

But in fact, to give the question this content Kant introduces a number of heterogeneous elements which, once again, call the very operation of his analysis into question. First he says: There are today some signs which foreshadow this process of liberation and these signs show that some "obstacles,"[19] which previously were opposed to man making use of his reason, have now been removed. Now we know that there are no obstacles to man making use of his reason but man's own cowardice and laziness. Here, then, Kant emphasizes the existence of these obstacles. Second, after having stated and demonstrated at some length that there cannot be an individual agent or individual agents of this liberation, he now introduces precisely the King of Prussia. He brings in Frederick of Prussia who, he says, has not prescribed anything in questions of religion, and this is what makes Frederick an agent, the agent of *Aufklärung*. In this domain—as in the domain of the arts and sciences,[20] but Kant, who has a precise problem to deal

1. French translation by S. Piobetta, "Qu'est-ce que les Lumières?" in I. Kant, *La Philosophie de l'histoire*, p. 46; English translations by: Lewis White Beck, "What is Enlightenment?" in I. Kant, *On History*, p. 3; H. B. Nisbet, "An Answer to the Question: 'What is Enlightenment?'" in Hans Reiss, ed., *Kant's Political Writings*, p. 54; James Schmidt, "An Answer to the Question: What is Enlightenment?" in James Schmidt ed., *What is Enlightenment? Eighteenth-Century Answers and Twentieth-Century Questions* (Berkeley: University of California Press, 1996) p. 58; and Mary J. Gregor, "An Answer to the Question: What is Enlightenment?" in Immanuel Kant, *Practical Philosophy*, trans. and ed. Mary J. Gregor (Cambridge: Cambridge University Press, 1999) p. 17.

2. Ibid.

3. French translation by J. Michelet, J.B. Vico, *Principes de la philosophie de l'histoire* (Paris: Armand Colin, 1963).

4. Ibid., p. 358 (Vico writes "widespread" rather than "taking hold").

5. Ibid., p. 360.

6. Apart from S. Piobetta's translation, which he uses for the lectures, Foucault was able to consult the translation by J. Barni in I. Kant, *Éléments de métaphysique de la doctrine du droit* (Paris: A. Durand, 1855).

7. Piobetta translation, p. 47; English translations have: Lewis White Beck, "harness of the cart to which they are tethered," p. 3; H.B. Nisbet, "leading-strings to which they are tied," p. 54; James Schmidt, "leading strings of the cart to which they are tethered," pp. 58-59; Mary J. Gregor, "walking cart in which they have confined them," p. 17.

8. Ibid., French p. 46; English p. 3; p. 54; p. 58; p. 17.

9. Ibid.

10. Ibid.

11. Ibid. [Where the French translation has "*majorité*," "*tuteurs*," and "*direction*," the English translators have: Lewis White Beck, "competence," "guardians," "superintendence"; H.B. Nisbet "maturity," "guardians," "work of supervision"; James Schmidt, "maturity," "guardians," "oversight"; Mary J. Gregor, "majority," "guardians," "supervise"; G.B.].

12. Ibid., French p. 47; English p. 4; p. 55; p. 59; p. 18.

13. Ibid., French p. 48; English p. 5; p. 55; p. 59; p. 18.

14. The word *Räsonnieren* is not found in the *Critique of Pure Reason*. However, this term does have the sense of "quibbling" in Hegel, particularly in the *Phenomenology of Mind*: "...the process of raisonnement (*Das Räsonnieren*), is...detachment from all content, and conceited superiority to it." G.W.F. Hegel, *Phénoménologie de l'esprit*, trans., J.B. Baillie (London: George Allen & Unwin; New York: Humanities Press, 1949) p. 117.

15. Kant, *Qu'est ce que les Lumières*, p. 48; English: *What is Enlightenment?* p. 5; *An Answer to the Question: "What is Enlightenment?"*, p. 55; *An Answer to the Question: What is Enlightenment?* p. 59; *An Answer to the Question: What is Enlightenment?* p. 18.

16. Ibid., French p. 49; English p. 5; p. 56; p. 60; p. 18.

17. Ibid., French pp. 53-54; English p. 9; p. 58; p. 62; p. 21.

18. Ibid., French p. 53; English pp. 8-9; p. 58; p. 62; p. 21.

19. Ibid.

20. Ibid., French p. 54; English p. 9; p. 59; p. 63; p. 21.

21. Ibid., French p. 54; English p. 10; p. 59; p. 63; p. 22.

22. "Argue as much as you like and about whatever you like, but obey!" ibid., French p. 53; English p. 10; p. 59; p. 63; p. 22.

three

12 JANUARY 1983

First hour

[*Reminders of method.* ∽ *Definition of the subject to be studied this year.* ∽ Parrēsia *and culture of self.* ∽ *Galen's* On the Passions and Errors of the Soul. ∽ Parrēsia: *difficulty in defining the notion; bibliographical reference points.* ∽ *An enduring, plural, and ambiguous notion.* ∽ *Plato faced with the tyrant of Syracuse: an exemplary scene of* parrēsia. ∽ *The echo of* Oedipus. ∽ Parrēsia *versus demonstration, teaching, and discussion.* ∽ *The element of risk.*]

LAST WEEK I BRIEFLY reminded you of the general project, which is to try to analyze what may be called the focal points or matrices of experience like madness, criminality, and sexuality, and to analyze them according to the correlation of the three axes which constitute these experiences: the formation of forms of knowledge (*savoirs*), the normativity of behavior, and the constitution of the subject's modes of being. I also tried to indicate the theoretical shifts involved in this kind of analysis when one is studying the formation of forms of knowledge, the normativity of behavior, and the subject's modes of being in their correlation. It seems to me in fact that when one tries to delineate the formation of forms of knowledge in this perspective, the analysis should be conducted not so much as the history of bodies of knowledge, but on the basis of and from the point of view of the analysis of discursive practices and forms of veridiction. The first theoretical displacement to be made was this transition, this shift from the development of bodies of knowledge to the analysis of forms of veridiction. The second theoretical displacement to be carried out consists in freeing oneself from any would-be general Theory of Power (with all the capital letters), or from explanations in terms of Domination in general, when analyzing the normativity of behavior, and in trying instead to bring out the history and analysis of procedures and technologies of governmentality. Finally, the third displacement consists, I think, in passing from a theory of the subject, on the basis of which one would try to bring out the different modes of being of subjectivity in their historicity, to the analysis of the modalities and techniques of the relation to self, or again to the history of this pragmatics of the subject in its different forms, some examples of which I tried to give you last year. So: analysis of forms of veridiction; analysis of procedures of governmentality; and analysis of the pragmatics of the subject and techniques of the self. These, then, are the three displacements that I have outlined.

I have indicated that this year I would like to take up some of the questions that were left hanging in this itinerary, by laying stress precisely on some aspects, some questions, which give a better idea of the correlation of these three axes. I have, if you like, devoted myself mostly to studying each of these three axes in turn: that of the formation of forms of knowledge and practices of veridiction; that of the normativity of behavior and the technology of power; and finally that of the constitution of the subject's modes of being on the basis of practices of self. I would now like to see how we can establish the correlation, how in actual fact the correlation is established, and try to grasp some points, elements, notions, and practices which indicate this correlation and show how in fact it can be carried out. And, [...] in posing the question of the government of self and others, I would like to try to see how truth-telling (*dire-vrai*), the obligation and possibility of telling the truth in procedures of government can show how the individual is constituted as subject in the relationship to self and the relationship to others. This is what I would like to say something about this year: truth-telling in procedures of government and the constitution of [an] individual as subject for himself and for others. So the lectures this year will no doubt be a bit discontinuous. Still, I would like to try to study some aspects of this general problem by considering some notions and particular practices.

So the first domain, the first dossier I would like to open is one that we came across last year in relation to spiritual direction and practices of self in Antiquity, in the first and second centuries C.E. You recall that we came across this rather interesting notion of *parrēsia*[1] [...*]. One of the original meanings of the Greek word *parrēsia* is to "say everything," but in fact it is much more frequently translated as free-spokenness (*franc-parler*), free speech, etcetera. You recall that this notion of *parrēsia*, which was important in practices of spiritual direction, was a rich, ambiguous, and difficult notion, particularly insofar as it designated a virtue, a quality (some people have *parrēsia* and others do not); a duty (one must really be able to demonstrate *parrēsia*, especially in certain cases and situations); and a technique, a process (some people know how to use *parrēsia* and others do not). And this virtue, duty, and technique must characterize, among other things and above all, the man who is responsible for directing others, and particularly for directing them in their effort, their attempt to constitute an appropriate relationship to themselves. In other words, *parrēsia* is a virtue, duty, and technique which should be found in the person who spiritually directs others and helps them to constitute their relationship to self. You recall that last year we saw how, from the classical epoch of Antiquity to Late Antiquity, and particularly in the first two centuries C.E., a certain culture of self developed which assumed such dimensions that we could talk of a veritable golden age of the culture of self.[2] In this culture of self, in this relationship to self we saw the development of a whole technique, an art that was taught and practiced. We saw that this art of oneself required a relationship to the other. In other words: one cannot attend to oneself, take care of oneself, without a relationship to another person. And the role of this other is precisely to tell the truth, to tell the whole truth, or at any rate to tell all the truth that is necessary, and to tell it in a certain form which is precisely *parrēsia*, which once again is translated as free-spokenness (*franc-parler*).

With regard to this general theme, you may particularly recall a text, Galen's *On the Passions and Errors of the Soul*,[3] which we looked at for a while. It is a very interesting text in which we saw, first of all,

---

* M.F.: Maybe you would like me to write it on the board? [*the sound of chalk can be heard*].

the old traditional theme, or rather the double theme of care of self and self knowledge; the obligation for every individual to care about himself, which is immediately linked to its condition, self knowledge. One cannot take care of oneself without knowing oneself. This put us on the track of the interesting fact that the well-known and, for us, fundamental principle of *gnōthi seauton* (self knowledge), rests on and is a component of what is basically the more general principle of caring for oneself.[4] In Galen's text we also found the idea that one can only take care of oneself in a continuous and permanent fashion, and not, as in Plato's *Alcibiades*, at the adolescent's point of entry into public life and responsibility for the city; one must in fact take care of oneself throughout one's life, from youth to the culmination of old age.[5] So, in Galen's text we saw that this care of self, which must be developed and practiced laboriously and continuously throughout life, cannot dispense with the judgment given by others. Those who wish to dispense with this judgment in the opinion they form of themselves, Galen says, frequently fall—a phrase which will be frequently taken up again in a very different context: Christian spirituality will say that those who dispense with guidance from others fall like the leaves in autumn.[6] Well, Galen had already said: In the opinion we have of ourselves we frequently fall when we dispense with the judgment made by others. On the other hand, Galen says, those who submit the declaration of their own worth to others are rarely deceived.

So, starting from this principle, Galen said that clearly we need to appeal to someone to help us to form our opinion of ourselves and to establish an appropriate relationship to self. We need to appeal to someone else. What should this other person be? Here was one of the surprising elements in the text. You recall that Galen does not present the person to whom we must resort as a technician; he is not presented as a technician of the medicine of the body or as a technician of the medicine of souls, neither as a doctor nor as a philosopher. According to Galen's text we should appeal to a man who has reached a certain age, has a sufficiently good reputation, and who possesses, in addition, a certain quality. This quality was *parrēsia*, free-spokenness. A man of a certain age, who has a good reputation, and who possesses *parrēsia* are the three necessary and sufficient criteria for the person we need for us to have a relationship to self. So we have, if you like, a whole structure, a whole bundle of important notions and themes: care of self, knowledge of self, art and exercise of oneself, relationship to the other, government by the other and truth-telling, and the obligation to speak the truth on the part of the other. You can see that with *parrēsia* we have a notion which is situated at the meeting point of the obligation to speak the truth, procedures and techniques of governmentality, and the constitution of the relationship to self. Truth-telling by the other, as an essential component of how he governs us, is one of the essential conditions for us to be able to form the right kind of relationship to ourselves that will give us virtue and happiness.

This was the general theme, if you like, that we found in Galen in the second century C.E. I would like to take this as my starting point, noting straightaway that this notion of *parrēsia*, which we came across in this and similar texts devoted to individual spiritual direction, extends far beyond the use and meaning picked out in this way. We can say that *parrēsia* is something of a spidery kind of notion which, it must be said, has not been studied a great deal. It is a spidery kind of notion because, in the first place, [although the] Ancients themselves often refer to it (we will see a whole set of texts concerning *parrēsia*, and the set I will use is obviously far from exhaustive), there is nonetheless no, or anyway very little direct reflection on the notion. It is a notion which is used and referred to, but it is not considered directly or thematized as such. Among the texts which have come down to us, there is practically only one treatise actually devoted to *parrēsia*, and this is in a fragmentary condition. This is the treatise of the most important Epicurean of the first century C.E. It is a treatise by Philodemus, some fragments of which have been published and can be found, in Greek and without translation, in the Teubner collection.[7] Apart from this we possess no direct reflection by the Ancients on this notion of *parrēsia*. And on the other hand, it is a notion which, if you like, is not integrated in a clearly identifiable and localizable way within a particular conceptual system of philosophical doctrine. It is a theme which runs from one system to another, from one doctrine to another, so that it is quite difficult to define its meaning precisely or identify its precise system.

A bibliographical point on this notion of *parrēsia*. Apart, of course, from this text by Philodemus, there is hardly anything, or at any rate

I know of hardly anything apart from, first, an article devoted to
"*parrēsia*" in the *Realencyclopädie* (the Pauly-Wissowa),[8] written a long
time ago (in 1938-1939), just before the war I think, by Philippson.[9]
Then there is an important book written in Italy by Scarpat, published in 1964,[10] in which there is an interesting and careful record
of the notion of *parrēsia*, with a very strange elision of precisely all the
meanings, values, and uses of the notion for individual guidance. While
everything concerning its political and religious use is well covered,
[the work] is extremely incomplete for individual spiritual direction.
Finally, in the proceedings of the eighth congress of the Association
Guillaume Budé, from 1968, there is an article in French by Marcello
Gigante devoted precisely to Philodemus and his treatise on *parrēsia*.[11]

What, from my point of view, is worth our attention in this notion
of *parrēsia* is first of all—and I am going to say some very elementary
things—its very long life, its use throughout Antiquity, since—obviously
we will come back to this in more detail today and next week—the use
of the notion is already well-established, well-defined in the great classical texts, whether of Plato or Euripides, and then in a whole series of
other texts (Isocrates, Demosthenes, Polybius, Philodemus, Plutarch,
Marcus Aurelius, Maximus of Tyre, Lucian, and so on). Then you
find this notion at the very end of Antiquity in Christian spirituality, in Saint John Chrysostom, for example, in his *Letters to Olympias*,[12]
the *Letter from exile*,[13] or the *Treatise on Providence*.[14] You also find a very
important, rich, and to a certain extent very new use of this notion of
parrēsia in Doretheus of Gaza.[15] The theme is, of course, found in Latin
texts, although the translation of the term *parrēsia* is not entirely stable and somewhat fluctuating. It is found in Seneca,[16] in the historians
also, of course, and in theorists of rhetoric like Quintilian.[17] And then
there are many translations with words like *licentia*, *libertas*, *oratio libera*,
etcetera. So, the notion has a very long life.

Second, the notion is found on a number of different levels, since it
has been possible to find it quite clearly and well-defined in the practice of individual guidance, but also in the political field. And here
too it has a multiplicity of interesting meanings which undergo a significant evolution from Athenian democracy to the Roman Empire.
And—this is one of the things I will try to study in the lectures—it is
used on the borders of what could be called individual guidance and

the political field, and specifically around the problem of the Prince's soul: How should one guide the Prince's soul, and what form of true discourse does the Prince need, as an individual, to form an appropriate relationship to himself that will guarantee his virtue, and also such that, thereby and through this teaching, he is formed as a morally worthy individual, as a governor who takes responsibility for and care of others as well as himself? What then is the type of discourse which is such that the Prince will be able to take charge of himself, to take care of himself as well as those he governs? How can one govern the Prince in such a way that he will be able to govern himself and others? This is one of the points I would like to stress. And then this notion is also found in the field of religious experience and the religious theme where there is a very strange and interesting change, a slippage, almost a reversal of the poles of this notion of *parrēsia*. To start with we find *parrēsia* meaning that the master is obliged to tell the disciple all the truth that is necessary, and then we find it again with the idea that it is possible for the disciple to tell the master everything about himself. That is to say, we pass from a meaning of the notion in which *parrēsia* refers to the master's obligation to tell the disciple what is true, to a meaning which refers to the disciple's obligation to tell the master the truth of himself.

Finally, a third source of the richness of this notion is that however general and constant its valorization (I have said that it is a virtue, a quality), it is in fact surrounded by a great deal of ambiguity, and its valorization is not entirely constant or homogeneous. We will see, for example, that Cynic *parrēsia*, Cynic free-spokenness, is far from being an absolutely univocal notion or value. And we will see that in Christian spirituality *parrēsia* may well have the sense of indiscretion, in the form of chattering about everything concerning oneself.

All this must seem to you to be at once abstract, imprecise, rough, and loose. So let's try to make some headway and be a bit more precise. I don't want to go over the history of this notion in detail here today. I will take an average text, if you like, an average case, an average example of *parrēsia* from almost exactly mid-way between the classical age and the great Christian spirituality of the fourth to fifth century C.E., in which we see this notion of *parrēsia* at work in a traditional but very well-defined field of philosophy. I take this example of *parrēsia* from a text by Plutarch, an average author in every sense of the term. There are a great many texts by Plutarch, and we will come back to this, which are devoted, [or rather] which use this notion of *parrēsia*, since as I have said it is rarely considered for itself. Plutarch's text is found in the *Lives*, in *Dion*, paragraph v, page 960a. You can see more or less who Dion is: he is the brother of Aristomache. But you probably do not know who Aristomache was. Aristomache was one of the two official wives of Dionysius, the tyrant of Syracuse. Dionysius had two wives. One of these was Aristomache, and Dion was her younger brother. Dion, who, in relation to Dionysius the Elder, and especially in relation to Dionysius the Younger, will play an important part in the life of Syracuse, will be Plato's disciple, correspondent, sponsor, guarantor, and host when Plato comes to Sicily. Plato's real, effective relationship with the political life of Syracuse and the tyranny of Dionysius comes about through Dion.

So, in this text devoted to Dion, Plutarch recalls that this young brother of Aristomache was a boy endowed with fine qualities: generosity of spirit, courage, and the ability to learn.[18] However, living as a young man at the court of a tyrant like Dionysius, he had gradually become accustomed to fear, "servility," and pleasure. As a result, he was "full of prejudices," that is to say—clearly referring to Stoic or Stoicizing themes—while the quality of his nature had not been undermined, some false opinions had been deposited in his soul, until the day when, by chance—a benevolent "spirit (*daimōn*)," Plutarch says[19]—brought Plato to the shores of Sicily. It is there that Dion meets Plato, becomes his pupil, and benefits from his master's lessons. At this point his true and good nature reappears and, he says—and here we come to it—"in his soul's youthful ingenuousness," Dion expected that "under the influence of the same lessons" as those he had received from Plato, his uncle, the tyrant Dionysius, might experience "the same feelings" and "might easily let himself be improved in the good. In his enthusiasm, he set about doing all he could that Dionysius might enter into a relationship with Plato and hear his lessons."[20] And now Plato, Dion, and Dionysius arrive on the scene. "Their conversation having got under way, the basic theme of the discussion was virtue, but more especially courage. Plato showed that tyrants were anything but courageous; then, moving away from this subject, he elaborated on justice and showed that the life of the just man was happy and that the unjust man was unhappy [a lesson, then, on virtue and its different elements, its different components, its different forms: courage, justice; M.F.]. The tyrant could not bear these remarks [concerning the fact that the life of the just was happy and that of the unjust was unhappy; M.F.], which he thought were directed at him, and he did not conceal his displeasure at seeing the other admiring auditors being charmed by the discourse of the great man. Finally, filled with anger and exasperation, Dionysius asked Plato: 'What have you come to Sicily for?' And Plato replied: 'I am looking for a good man.' The tyrant replied: 'By the gods, it is clear that you have not yet found one!' Dion thought that Dionysius' anger would end there, and he put Plato, who was in a hurry to leave, on a trireme taking Pollis, the Spartan, back to Greece. But Dionysius secretly asked Pollis to kill Plato on the journey, if it was possible, and if not, at least sell him into slavery. 'This will do him no harm,' he said, 'and insofar as he is a just man, he will be just as happy, even as a slave.' It is said that Pollis hastened to sell Plato in Aegina, for Aegina was then at war with Athens and according to an Aeginetan decree any Athenian taken on their territory was to be sold. These incidents did not diminish Dion's enjoyment of the favor and confidence of Dionysius. He was charged with important missions and when he was sent to Carthage he attracted extraordinary admiration. He was pretty well the only person whose *parrēsia* Dionysius tolerated and was allowed to speak his mind boldly, as is evidenced by their discussion concerning Gelon [Gelon was a Syracusan who exercised power before Dionysius; M.F.]. It seems that one day Dionysius ridiculed Gelon's government, which he said had been the laughing stock of Sicily [actually, this is a play on words: in Greek, to laugh is *gelan*, hence Gelon: *Gelōn/gelan*; so Dionysius made some silly puns on Gelon and said he had been the laughing stock of Sicily; M.F.]. The courtiers seemed to admire this play on words and Dion was the only one to show his disapproval. 'Nevertheless', he said, 'you are tyrant thanks to Gelon, who inspired a confidence from which you have benefited; but after having seen you at work, no one will be trusted again'. [And Plutarch comments on Dion's parrhesiastic statement to Dionysius, and says:] For it is clear that Gelon made a town governed by a monarchy the most beautiful sight, whereas Dionysius made it

Since we cannot situate *parrēsia* in an end envisaged by the discourse, where can we situate it?

Let's consider the scene again, or the two scenes of *parrēsia*, and try to isolate the elements from which it is composed. Plato and Dion are people endowed with *parrēsia*, who employ *parrēsia*, who make use of *parrēsia* in very different forms, in lessons, aphorisms, replies, advice, judgments. But whatever the forms in which this truth is spoken, whatever the forms employed when one resorts to *parrēsia*, there is always *parrēsia* when telling the truth takes place in conditions such that the fact of telling the truth, and the fact of having told it, will, may, or must entail costly consequences for those who have told it. In other words, if we want to analyze the nature of *parrēsia*, I do not think we should look to the internal structure of the discourse, or to the aim which the true discourse seeks to achieve vis-à-vis the interlocutor, but to the speaker, or rather to the risk that truth-telling opens up for the speaker. We should look for *parrēsia* in the effect that its specific truth-telling may have on the speaker, in the possible backlash on the speaker from the effect it has on the interlocutor. In other words, telling the truth to the tyrant Dionysius, who gets angry, opens up a space of risk for the person who tells the truth; it opens up a danger, a peril, in which the speaker's very life will be at stake, and it is this that constitutes *parrēsia*. *Parrēsia*, therefore, is to be situated in what binds the speaker to the fact that what he says is the truth, and to the consequences which follow from the fact that he has told the truth. In these scenes Plato and Dion are people who practice *parrēsiazesthai*, who practice *parrēsia*, inasmuch as they actually, presently, tell the truth, and in telling the truth lay themselves open to the risk of having to pay the price, or a certain price, for having done so. And it is not just any price that they are ready to pay and that in telling the truth they affirm they are ready to pay: the price is death. We have here, if you like—and this is why I take this scene as a matrix, exemplary scene for *parrēsia*—the point at which subjects willingly undertake to tell the truth, while willingly and explicitly accepting that this truth-telling could cost them their life. Parrhesiasts are those who, if necessary, accept death for having told the truth. Or more precisely, parrhesiasts are those who undertake to tell the truth at an unspecified price, which may be as high as their own death. Well, this seems to me to be the crux of *parrēsia*. Obviously,

I would not want us to stop at this somewhat pathetic formulation of the relationship between truth-telling and the risk of death, but this is what we should now start to disentangle.

I'm bothered. Without acting like Pierre Bellemare and introducing a commercial break,[25] there is all the same something of a natural scansion in what I want to say. So if you like, we will take a five minutes rest and then continue. Because unless we do so I risk running on for half or three quarters of an hour and this may be a bit tiring. We will come back in five minutes.

1. See the lectures of 10 March 1982 in *L'Herméneutique du sujet. Cours au Collège de France, 1981-1982*, éd. F. Gros (Paris: Gallimard-Le Seuill, 2001) pp. 355-394; English translation by Graham Burchell, *The Hermeneutics of the Subject. Lectures at the Collège de France 1981-1982*, English series editor, Arnold I. Davidson (New York: Palgrave Macmillan, 2005) pp. 371-411.

2. See the lecture of 3 February 1982, ibid., French pp. 172-174; English pp. 179-181.

3. Galien, *Traité des passions de l'âme et de ses erreurs*, trans. R. Van der Elst (Paris: Delagrave, 1914); English translation by P.W. Harkins, *On the Passions and Errors of the Soul* (Columbus: Ohio State University Press, 1963). For Foucault's analysis of this text, see *L'Herméneutique du sujet*, pp. 378-382; *The Hermeneutics of the Subject*, pp. 395-399.

4. On the relationship of "care of self" and "self knowledge," see the lectures of January 1982 in *L'Herméneutique du sujet*; *The Hermeneutics of the Subject*.

5. For the extension of care of self to the whole of life, see ibid., the lecture of 20 January 1982.

6. The metaphor of dead leaves comes from *Isaiah* (64:6): "We wither, all of us, like leaves, and all our misdeeds carry us off like the wind."

7. Philodēmos, *Peri parrēsias*, ed., A. Olivieri (Leipzig: Teubner, 1914). For an analysis of this text, see *L'Herméneutique du sujet*, pp. 370-372; *The Hermeneutics of the Subject*, pp. 387-389.

8. The *Paulys Realencyclopädie der classischen Alertumswissenschaft* (Stuttgart: 1894-1975) is a basic German encyclopedic dictionary. It is sometimes abridged to PW, that is to say, Pauly-Wissowa, after the name of the first editors. There are two new and more manageable editions: *Der Kleine Pauly. Lexikon der Antike* (Stuttgart, 1964-1975) 5 volumes; *Der Neue Pauly. Enzyklopädie der Antike* (Stuttgart: 1996-2002).

9. Nothing like this can be found in the complete bibliography of the works of Robert Philippson in, R. Philippson, *Studien zu Epikur und den Epikureern* (Hildesheim: Olms, 1983) pp. 339-352. It is likely that Foucault is referring to the article "Philodemos" (*Realencyclopädie*, 19, 2, 1938, 2444-2482) which concerns the treatise on *parrēsia* by Philodemus.

10. G. Scarpat, *Parrhesia. Storie del termine et delle sue traduzioni in Latino* (Brescia: Paideia, 1964).

11. M. Gigante, "Philodème et la liberté de parole," in *Association Guillaume Budé, Actes du VIIIe congrès, Paris 5-10 avril 1968* (Paris: Les Belles Lettres, 1970). See the analysis of this text in *L'Herméneutique du sujet*, pp. 371-374; *The Hermeneutics of the Subject*, pp. 387-391.

12. Jean Chrysostome, *Lettres à Olympias*, introduction, translation, and notes by A.-M. Malingrey (Paris: Éditions du Cerf, coll. "Sources chrétiennes" 103, 1947); English translation by W.R.W. Stephens as *Letters of St. Chrysostom to Olympias* (New York: New York Christian Literature Publish Co., 1886) [also available on line at http://mb-soft.com/believe/texug/chryso11.htm].

13. Jean Chrysostome, *Lettre d'exil*, introduction, translation, and notes by A.-M. Malingrey (Paris: Éditions du Cerf, coll. "Sources chrétiennes" 103, 1964), here in the sense of confidence (*la confiance*): 3-55 p. 72, 16-51 p. 138, 17-9 p. 140.

14. Jean Chrysostome, *Sur la Providence de Dieu*, introduction, translation, and notes by A.-M. Malingrey (Paris: Éditions du Cerf, coll. "Sources chrétiennes" 79, 1961). According to Malingrey (note 2, pp. 66-67) in the triple sense of a confident assurance (XI-12 p. 67), a free speech which transmits the word of God (XIV-6 p. 205), or of a courageous assurance in the face of persecution (XIX-11 p. 241, XXIV-1 p. 272).

15. *Œuvres spirituelles par Dorothée de Gaza*, introduction, Greek text, translation and notes by L. Regnault and J. de Préville (Paris: Éditions du Cerf, coll. "Sources chrétiennes" 72, 1963). *Parrēsia* has the sense of either confident assurance (1613B, p. 112, or 1661C, p. 226), or culpable impudence (1665A-D, pp. 235-236).

16. For an analysis of *libertas* in Seneca, see *L'Herméneutique du sujet*, pp. 385-388; *The Hermeneutics of the Subject*, pp. 401-406.

17. For Quintilian's definition of *parrēsia* (*libertas*), see below, note 23.

18. Plutarque, *Vies parallèles*, t. III, "Dion," 959d, ch. IV, trans. B. Latzarus (Paris: Classiques Garnier, 1999) p. 110; English translation by Bernadotte Perrin, "Dion" in *Plutarch's Lives*, vol. 6 (Cambridge, Mass. and London: Harvard University Press and William Heinemann Ltd., "Loeb Classical Library," 1961) p. 9.

19. Ibid.: "C'est un génie (*daimōn tis*), semble-t-il, qui, jetant de loin les bases de la liberté Syracusains et préparant la chute de la tyrannie, amena Platon d'Italie à Syracuse"; English, ibid.: "some heavenly power, as it would seem, laying far in advance of the time a foundation for the liberty of Syracuse, and devising a subversion of tyranny, brought Plato from Italy to Syracuse."

20. Ibid.; English, ibid.: "since he very artlessly and impulsively expected, from his own ready obedience to the call of higher things, that the same arguments would have a like persuasive force with Dionysius, he earnestly set to work and at last brought it to pass that the tyrant, in a leisure hour, should meet Plato and hear him discourse."

21. Ibid., pp. 110-111; English, ibid., pp. 11-13: "At this meeting the general subject was human virtue, and most of the discussion turned upon manliness. And when Plato set forth that tyrants least of all men had this quality, and then, treating of justice, maintained that the life of the just was blessed, while that of the unjust was wretched, the tyrant, as if convicted by his arguments, would not listen to them, and was vexed with the audience because they admired the speaker and were charmed by his utterances. At last he got exceedingly angry and asked the philosopher why he had come to Sicily. And when Plato said that he was come to seek a virtuous man, the tyrant answered and said: 'Well, by the gods, it appears that you have not yet found such a one.' Dion thought that this was the end of his anger, and as Plato was eager for it, sent him away upon a trireme, which was conveying Pollis the Spartan to Greece. But Dionysius privily requested Pollis to kill Plato on the voyage, if it were in any way possible, but if not, at all events to sell him into slavery; for he would take no harm, but would be quite as happy, being a just man, even if he should become a slave. Pollis, therefore, as we are told, carried Plato to Aegina and there sold him; for the Aeginetans were at war with the Athenians and had made a decree that any Athenian taken on the island should be put up for sale.

  In spite of all this, Dion stood in no less honour and credit with Dionysius than before, but had the management of the most important embassies, as, for instance, when he was sent to Carthage and won great admiration. The tyrant also bore with his freedom of speech, and Dion was almost the only one who spoke his mind fearlessly, as, for example, when he rebuked Dionysius for what he said about Gelon. The tyrant was ridiculing the government of Gelon, and when he said that Gelon himself, true to his name, became the *laughing-stock* ('gelos') of Sicily, the rest of his hearers pretended to admire the joke, but Dion was disgusted and said: 'Indeed, thou art now a tyrant because men trusted thee for Gelon's sake; but no man hereafter will be trusted for thy sake.' For, as a matter of fact, Gelon seems to have made a city under absolute rule a very fair thing to look upon, but Dionysius a very shameful thing."

22. Sophocle, *Œdipe-roi*, 584-602, in *Tragédies*, t. 1, trans. P. Mazon (Paris: Les Belles Lettres, 1958) p. 230; English translation by David Grene, *Oedipus The King*, in *Sophocles I*, ed., David Grene and Richard Lattimore (Chicago and London: University of Chicago Press, 1991, 2nd ed.) p. 36.

23. Quintilien, *Institution oratoire*, Books VIII-IX, t. V, trans. J. Cousin (Paris: Les Belles Lettres, 1978) p. 177; English translation by H.E. Butler, Quintilian, *The Institutio Oratoria of Quintilian*, *III* (London and New York: Heinemann and Putnam's Sons, Loeb Classical Library, 1976) Book IX, 2.27, pp. 388-389: "The same is true of free speech, which Cornificius calls *licence*, and the Greeks *parrēsia*. For what has less of the *figure* about it than true freedom (*quid enim minus figuratum quam vera libertas*)?"

24. This term designates an art of disputation and debate (from the Greek *eris*: argument, quarrel; Eris is the goddess of Discord) developed especially by the Megarian school (fifth and sixth century B.C.E.). In a famous text (ch. 2 of *Sophistical Refutations*), Aristotle distinguishes between didactic, dialectical, critical, and eristical arguments, the latter being defined as arguments which arrive at a conclusion starting from premises which are only apparently probable.

25. This is an allusion to a well-known television program of the time on TF1 ("C'est arrivé un jour") in which P. Bellemare kept his audience in suspense by recounting breathless stories, always introducing a commercial break at the most critical point of the narrative.

four

12 JANUARY 1983

Second hour

[
Irreducibility of the parrhesiastic to the performative utterance: opening up of an unspecified risk/public expression of a personal conviction/bringing a free courage into play. ∿ Pragmatics and dramatics of discourse. ∿ Classical use of the notion of parrēsia*: democracy (Polybius) and citizenship (Euripides).*
]

SO, IN ORDER TO try to begin to disentangle the general and rather shaky formula I have just put forward—by [taking as] a limit-situation [that] of the parrhesiast who stands up, speaks, tells the truth to a tyrant, and risks his life—I will take as a point of reference (it has become an old chestnut, but maybe it's handy), as a counter example, as a form of enunciation which is exactly the opposite of *parrēsia*, and which has been called for some years now the performative utterance.[1] You know that a performative utterance requires a particular, more or less strictly institutionalized context, an individual who has the requisite status or who is in a well-defined situation. Given all this as the condition for an utterance to be performative, [an individual] then makes this statement. The utterance is performative inasmuch as the enunciation itself effectuates the thing stated.* You are familiar with the extremely banal example: the chairman of the meeting sits down

---

* The manuscript clarifies: "The performative is carried out in a world which guarantees that saying effectuates what is said."

and says: "The meeting is open." Despite its appearance, the statement "the meeting is open" is not an assertion. It is neither true nor false. What is essential is simply that the formulation "the meeting is open" opens the meeting. Or again, in a much more weakly institutionalized context, but one which nevertheless implies a set of rituals and a well-defined situation, when someone says, "I apologize," he has in fact apologized, and the enunciation "I apologize" effectuates what is stated, namely that someone has apologized to someone else. So, on the basis of this example, let us now take up the different elements of *parrēsia* again, of the statement of truth and especially of the scene in which *parrēsia* is effectuated. In Plutarch's text—and to some extent there is an element in common with performative utterances here—we find ourselves in a typical, familiar, and institutionalized situation of the sovereign. The text clearly shows this situation: the sovereign surrounded by his courtiers. The philosopher arrives to give his lesson, and the courtiers applaud the lesson. The other scene in the text is very similar, hardly different: it is still the tyrant Dionysius in his court. The courtiers present are laughing at Dionysius' puns and someone, Dion, stands up and speaks. It is a classical scene of sovereign, courtiers, and the person who tells the truth (the scene also, you recall, of *Oedipus the King*).

However, there is a major and crucial difference. In a performative utterance, the given elements of the situation are such that when the utterance is made, the effect which follows is known and ordered in advance, it is codified, and this is precisely what constitutes the performative character of the utterance. In *parrēsia*, on the other hand, whatever the usual, familiar, and quasi-institutionalized character of the situation in which it is effectuated, what makes it *parrēsia* is that the introduction, the irruption of the true discourse determines an open situation, or rather opens the situation and makes possible effects which are, precisely, not known. *Parrēsia* does not produce a codified effect; it opens up an unspecified risk. And this unspecified risk is obviously a function of the elements of the situation. When one finds oneself in a situation like this, the risk is in a way extremely open, since Dionysius' character, his unlimited tyrannical power, and his excessive temperament, the passions which drive him, may lead to the worst effect, and, as actually happens, to him wanting to kill the person who has told the truth. But you see that even when the situation is not as extreme as this, even when it does not involve a tyrant with the power of life and death over the person who speaks, what defines the parrhesiastic statement, what precisely makes the statement of its truth in the form of *parrēsia* something absolutely unique among other forms of utterance and other formulations of the truth, is that *parrēsia* opens up a risk. Although it states the truth, there is no *parrēsia* in the progressive steps of a demonstration taking place in neutral conditions, because the person who states the truth in this way does not take any risk. The statement of the truth does not open up any risk if you envisage it only as an element in a demonstrative procedure. But, whether the truth is internal—think of Galileo—or external to a demonstrative procedure, we can say there is *parrēsia* when the statement of this truth constitutes an irruptive event opening up an undefined or poorly defined risk for the subject who speaks. In a sense, therefore, it is the opposite of the performative, in which the enunciation of something brings about and gives rise to a completely determined event as a function of the general code and institutional field in which the utterance is made. Here, on the contrary, it is a truth-telling, an irruptive truth-telling which creates a fracture and opens up the risk: a possibility, a field of dangers, or at any rate, an undefined eventuality. This is the first thing, the first characteristic.

Second—still comparing *parrēsia* with the performative—you know that the subject's status is important in a performative utterance. The person who opens the meeting simply by saying "the meeting is open" must have the authority to do so and be the chairman of the meeting. The person who says "I apologize" only makes a performative utterance when he is actually in a situation of having offended his interlocutor or one in which he could or should apologize to him. The person who says "I baptize you" must have the status that permits him to baptize, namely, he must at least be a Christian, etcetera. But although this status is indispensable for the effectuation of a performative utterance, there does not have to be an, as it were, personal relationship between the person making the utterance and the utterance itself for the latter to be performative. In other words, purely as a matter of fact, it does not matter whether the Christian who says "I baptize you" and makes the appropriate signs does not believe in God or the Devil.

When he has actually made the gesture and uttered the words, he will have baptized, and the utterance will have been performative. It does not matter whether the chairman who says "the meeting is open" is really bored by the meeting or if he dozes off; he will have opened the meeting. The same goes for the apology: what makes "I apologize" performative is not at all the subject's sincerity when he says "I apologize." It is just that he utters the sentence, even if he says to himself: I'll wait for my chance, and then you'll see. In *parrēsia*, on the other hand, and what makes it *parrēsia*, is that not only is this indifference not possible, but that *parrēsia* is always a sort of formulation of the truth at two levels. A first level is that of the statement of the truth itself (at this point, as in the performative, one says the thing, and that's that). The second level of the parrhesiastic act, the parrhesiastic enunciation is the affirmation that in fact one genuinely thinks, judges, and considers the truth one is saying to be genuinely true. I tell the truth, and I truly think that it is true, and I truly think that I am telling the truth when I say it. This doubling or intensification of the statement of the truth by the statement of the truth of the fact that I think this truth and that, thinking it, I say it, is what is essential to the parrhesiastic act. In Plutarch's text these two levels are not, of course, explicitly distinguished, as is the case most of the time moreover, the second level (the affirmation of the affirmation) frequently being implicit. Nevertheless, it remains the case that if you look at the elements of the scene which constitutes *parrēsia*, it is quite clear that something in them indicates this affirmation of the affirmation. This is essentially the public character of the affirmation, and not only the public character, but the fact that here—and this will not always be the case—*parrēsia* takes place in the form of a scene in which there are: first, the tyrant; then, confronting him, the person who speaks, who stands up or gives his lesson and tells the truth; and then, around these two, the courtiers, whose attitude varies according to the moment, the situation, who is speaking, and so forth. What this kind of joust or challenge shows is this solemn ritual of truth-telling in which the subject commits what he thinks in what he says and attests to the truth of what he thinks in the enunciation of what he says. In other words, I think that there is something in the parrhesiastic utterance that could be called a pact: a pact of the speaking subject with himself. It is a pact which has two levels: that of the act of enunciation and then [that], explicit or implicit, by which the subject binds himself to the statement he has just made, but also to the act of making it. This is what makes the pact double. On the one hand, the subject in *parrēsia* says: This is the truth. He says that he really thinks this truth, and in this he binds himself to the statement and to its content. But he also makes a pact in saying: I am the person who has spoken this truth; I therefore bind myself to the act of stating it and take on the risk of all its consequences. *Parrēsia* therefore [includes] the statement of the truth, and then, on top of this statement, an implicit element that could be called the parrhesiastic pact of the subject with himself, by which he binds himself both to the content of the statement and to the act of making it: I am the person who will have said this. And this pact is demonstrated here [through] the joust, the challenge, the great scene of the man standing up to the tyrant and telling the truth before the eyes and ears of the whole court.

Third difference between the performative and the parrhesiastic utterance: a performative utterance assumes that the person speaking has the status which permits him to carry out what is stated by making his utterance; he must be the chairman really to open the meeting, he must have suffered an offense to be able to say "I forgive you" and for "I forgive you" to be a performative utterance. What characterizes a parrhesiastic utterance, on the other hand, is not the fact that the speaking subject has this or that status. He may be a philosopher, the tyrant's brother-in-law, a courtier, or anyone whomsoever. So status is not important or necessary. What characterizes the parrhesiastic utterance is precisely that, apart from status and anything that could codify and define the situation, the parrhesiast is someone who emphasizes his own freedom as an individual speaking. After all, if Plato, by virtue of his status, had to teach his own philosophy—this is what he was asked to do—then when Dionysius asked him a question he was entirely at liberty not to reply: I have come to Sicily in search of a good man (and—by implication—I have not found him). In a way, this reply was supplementary to Plato's statutory teaching function. In the same way, Dion's function as the tyrant's courtier and brother-in-law, etcetera, was to give advice and good counsel to Dionysius so that the latter could govern properly. After all, only Dion's freedom was involved in his decision to say: When Gelon governed things were fine; now that you are governing the town is in a disastrous state. Whereas the performative utterance defines a definite game in which the status of person speaking and the situation in which he finds himself determine precisely what he can and must say, *parrēsia* only exists when there is freedom in the enunciation of the truth, freedom of the act by which the subject says the truth, and freedom also of the pact by which the subject speaking binds himself to the statement and enunciation of the truth. To that extent, it is not the subject's social, institutional status that we find at the heart of *parrēsia*; it is his courage.

Parrēsia—and I am summarizing here, asking you to forgive me for having been so slow and plodding—is therefore a certain way of speaking. More precisely, it is a way of telling the truth. Third, it is a way of telling the truth that lays one open to a risk by the very fact that one tells the truth. Fourth, *parrēsia* is a way of opening up this risk linked to truth-telling by, as it were, constituting oneself as the partner of oneself when one speaks, by binding oneself to the statement of the truth and to the act of stating the truth. Finally, *parrēsia* is a way of binding oneself to oneself in the statement of the truth, of freely binding oneself to oneself, and in the form of a courageous act. *Parrēsia* is the free courage by which one binds oneself in the act of telling the truth. Or again, *parrēsia* is the ethics of truth-telling as an action which is risky and free. To that extent, if we give this rather broad and general definition to the word "*parrēsia*"—which was rendered as "free-spokenness" (*franc-parler*) when its use was limited to spiritual direction—I think we can propose to translate it as "veridicity" (*véridicité*). The parrhesiast, the person who uses *parrēsia*, is the truthful man (*l'homme véridique*), that is to say, the person who has the courage to risk telling the truth, and who risks this truth-telling in a pact with himself, inasmuch as he is, precisely, the enunciator of the truth. He is the truth-teller (*le véridique*). And (maybe we will be able to come back to this, I don't know if I will have the time) it seems to me that Nietzschean veridicity (*véridicité*) is a way of putting to work this notion whose distant origin is found in the notion of *parrēsia* (truth-telling) as a risk for the person who states it, a risk accepted by the person who states it.

Forgive these delays, the question of *parrēsia* had to be put in the triple context which form the starting point from which I would like to approach it. First of all, you see of course that a fundamental philosophical problem arises if we adopt this definition of *parrēsia*. At any rate, we see that *parrēsia* brings into play a fundamental philosophical question, which is no more or less than that of the connection between freedom and truth. This is not the familiar question of how far the truth limits or constrains the exercise of freedom, but is in a way the opposite of this: how and to what extent is the obligation of truth— the "binding oneself to the truth," "binding oneself by the truth and by truth-telling"—at the same time the exercise of freedom, and the dangerous exercise of freedom? How is [the fact of] binding oneself to the truth (binding oneself to tell the truth, binding oneself by the truth, by the content of what one says and by the fact that one says it) actually the exercise, the highest exercise, of freedom? I think that the whole analysis of *parrēsia* should basically be developed around this question.

Second, there is an even tighter and closer methodological context of the analysis, which I would like to condense or summarize very schematically in the following way. If we adopt this general definition, starting from the example from Plutarch, we see that *parrēsia* is therefore a certain way of speaking such that the statement and the act of enunciation will produce some kind of "retroactive effects" on the subject himself, but not of course in the form of the consequence. Maybe I have not been clear enough on this point, but, if you like, *parrēsia* does not exist as a result of the fact that [Dionysius] wanted to kill Plato for what he said. There is *parrēsia* from the moment Plato actually accepts the risk of being exiled, killed, sold, etcetera, in telling the truth. So *parrēsia* is really that by which the subject binds himself to the statement, to the enunciation, and to the consequences of this statement and enunciation. So, if this is *parrēsia*, you can see that we have here perhaps a whole stratum of possible analyses concerning the effect of discourse. What is it that we call, or anyway what we could call the pragmatics of discourse? Well, it is the analysis of what it is in the real situation of the person speaking that affects and modifies the meaning and value of the utterance. To that extent, as you can see, analyzing or locating something like a performative falls squarely in the domain of a pragmatics of discourse. You have a situation, and a status of the subject speaking such that the statement "the meeting is open" will have a certain value and meaning, and a value and meaning which will not be the same if the situation and the subject speaking are different. If a journalist in the corner of the room says "the meeting is open," he is observing that the meeting has just been opened. If it is the chairman of the meeting who says "the meeting is open" then you know full well that the utterance does not have the same value or meaning. It is a performative utterance which actually opens the meeting. All this is known. You can see that the analysis of the pragmatics of discourse is the analysis of the elements and mechanism by which the situation of the enunciator modifies the value of meaning of the discourse. The discourse changes meaning as a function of this situation, and the pragmatics of this is: How does the situation or the status of the subject speaking modify or affect the meaning and value of the statement?

With *parrēsia* we see the appearance of a whole family of completely different facts of discourse which are almost the reverse, the mirror projection of what we call the pragmatics of discourse. In fact, *parrēsia* involves a whole series of facts of discourse in which it is not the real situation of the person speaking which affects or modifies the value of the statement. In *parrēsia*, in one way or another both the statement and the act of enunciation affect the subject's mode of being and, taking things in their most general and neutral form, quite simply mean that the person who said something has actually said it, and by a more or less explicit act binds himself to the fact that he said it. I think it is this retroaction—such that the event of the utterance affects the subject's mode of being, or that, in producing the event of the utterance the subject modifies, or affirms, or anyway determines and clarifies his mode of being insofar as he speaks—that characterizes a type of facts of discourse which are completely different from those dealt with by pragmatics. The analysis of these facts of discourse, which show how the very event of the enunciation may affect the enunciator's being, is what we could call—removing all pathos from the word—the "dramatics" of discourse. It seems to me that *parrēsia* is exactly what could be called one of the aspects and one of the forms of the dramatics of true discourse. *Parrēsia* involves the way in which by asserting the truth, and in the very act of this assertion, one constitutes oneself as the person who tells the truth, who has told the truth, and who recognizes oneself in and as the person who has told the truth. The analysis of *parrēsia* is the analysis of this dramatics of true discourse which brings to light the contract of the speaking subject with himself in the act of truth-telling. In this way I think one could make an analysis of the dramatics of true discourse and its different forms: the prophet, the seer, the philosopher, the scientist. In fact, whatever the social determinations defining their status, all of these involve a dramatics of true discourse, that is to say they have a way of binding themselves as subjects to the truth of what they say. And it is clear that the subject does not bind himself to the truth of what he says in the same way in each of these different ways of speaking as seer, prophet, philosopher, or scientist in a scientific institution. I think this very different mode of the subject's bond to the enunciation of the truth opens the field for possible studies of the dramatics of true discourse.

And so I come to what I would like to do this year. Taking the philosophical question of the relationship between the obligation of truth and the practice of truth as the general background, and taking what could be called the general dramatics of true discourse as the methodological point of view, I would like to see whether, from this double, philosophical and methodological point of view, we might not undertake the history, the genealogy, etcetera, of what could be called political discourse. Is there a political dramatics of true discourse, and what different forms, what different structures of the dramatics of political discourse might there be? In other words, when someone stands up, in the city in front of the tyrant, or when courtiers approach the person who exercises power, or when the politician mounts the tribune and says: "I am telling you the truth," what type of dramatics of true discourse is he putting to work? So what I would like to do this year is a history of the discourse of governmentality which would follow the thread of this dramatics of true discourse, which would try to locate some of the major forms of the dramatics of true discourse.

As a starting point I would like to take the way we see this notion of *parrēsia* taking shape: how can we locate in Antiquity the formation of a particular dramatics of discourse in the political domain; that of the counselor? How did we pass from a *parrēsia* which, as you will see in a moment or next week, characterizes the public orator, to a conception of *parrēsia* which characterizes the dramatics of the Prince's counselor, speaking and telling him what he must do? These are the first two figures that I would like to study. Second, I would like to study the figure of what I will call simply, somewhat schematically—obviously

all these words are somewhat arbitrary—the dramatics of the minister, that is to say, that new dramatics of true discourse in the political
order which appeared around the sixteenth century, when the art of
governing began to acquire its eminence and autonomy and to define
its own technique in terms of the nature of the State. What is this true
discourse addressed to the monarch by his "minister"* in the name
of something called *raison d'État* and in terms of a particular form of
knowledge, that is to say, knowledge of the State? Third, we could, but
I do not know if I shall have time, see the appearance of a third figure
of the dramatics of true discourse in the political domain, which is
the figure of, let's say, "critique": what is the critical discourse in the
political domain that we see forming, developing, or anyway assuming
a certain status in the eighteenth century and on through the nineteenth and twentieth centuries? And finally, of course, we could locate
a fourth major figure in the dramatics of true discourse in the political
domain, which is the figure of the revolutionary. What is this person
who arises within society and says: I am telling the truth, and I am
telling the truth in the name of the revolution that I am going to make
and that we will make together?

This is, if you like, something of the general framework of this year's
studies. Then I am both behind and ahead. I am behind with regard to
what I wanted to say, and ahead if I wanted to finish at this point. [...]†
So, the first set of studies, or first considerations of the way in which
this personage is formed, this genre of dramatics of discourse exemplified by Dion in Plutarch's text. The scene I am talking about dates
from the fourth century B.C.E. (but Plutarch wrote it at the beginning
of the second century C.E.). We see the figure of the Prince's counselor,
close to him, his relative even, coming forward and telling him the

---

* Foucault clarifies: between quotation marks.
† M.F. adds: Before beginning this history of *parrēsia* and of the first figure, that of the counselor,
I would like to take up again, not a question, but well something that I broached last week; the
possibility, if you want, of a meeting with those of you who are studying. Once again, this is not
so as to exclude others, but we may in fact have some questions, some work relationships a bit
different from the purely spectacular relationships that are possible within the lectures. I don't
know, possibly, for those who are working, who would like to discuss their work, or who would
like to ask me some question about what I am saying, but in terms of their own work, what
about next Wednesday, around a quarter to twelve? We will take a half hour for coffee, and then
I will try to reserve the room next to this one, that is to say room 3 I think. We will meet again
like that, twenty, thirty, well, a small number...Agreed, do you want us to do this?

truth. And he tells the truth in a mode of discourse that Plutarch calls precisely *parrēsia*. I have tried to give you a general idea of the notion and of the types of problem it may raise. But, nevertheless, when we take up the diachronic history of the notion of *parrēsia*, we should not forget that in the classical texts of the fourth century B.C.E., the word does not have the meaning that Plutarch gives it when he employs it with reference to Dion. The use of the word *parrēsia* in the classical texts is a bit more complex and rather different. Today and next week I would like to indicate some of these usages.

First, whereas in Plutarch's text—and in terms of what I told you when I tried to elucidate this notion—*parrēsia* seems to be linked to a virtue, a personal quality, a courage (courage in freely telling the truth), the use of the word *parrēsia* in the classical epoch does not include, at least not primarily, fundamentally, and essentially this dimension of personal courage, but is much more a concept related to two things: first, a particular, characteristic political structure of the city-state; and second, the social and political status of some individuals within this city-state. First, *parrēsia* as a political structure. I will make just one reference, which is not from the fourth century moreover, since it is from Polybius, but which helps us situate the problem. In the text by Polybius (Book II, chapter 38, paragraph 6), the Achaean regime [is defined] by three major characteristics. He says that the Achaeans have city-states in which one finds *dēmokratia* (democracy), *isēgoria*; and *parrēsia*.[2] *Dēmokratia*, that is to say, the participation, not of everyone, but of all the *dēmos*, that is to say, all those who are qualified as citizens, and so as members of the *dēmos*, to participate in power. *Isēgoria* is related to the structure of equality which means that right and duty, freedom and obligation are the same, are equal, once again for those who are part of the *dēmos* and so have citizen status. And finally, the third characteristic is that there is *parrēsia* in these states. We find *parrēsia*, that is to say, the freedom for citizens to speak, and of course to speak in the political field, understood as much from the abstract point of view (political activity) as very concretely: the right, even of someone who does not hold any particular office and is not a magistrate, to get up and speak in the meeting of the Assembly, tell the truth, or claim and assert that one is telling the truth. This is *parrēsia*: a political structure.

Now, [as] is quite clear from several texts by Euripides, there is a whole series of other uses of the word *parrēsia* which are related less to this general structure of the city-state than to the status of individuals. First, in the tragedy *Ion*, 668-675, you find the following text: "If I do not find she who bore me, my life is impossible; And if I might permit myself a wish, may this woman [the woman who bore me and whom I seek; M.F.] be Athenian, so that through my mother I have the right to speak freely [*hōs moi genētai mētrothen parrēsia*: so that *parrēsia* comes to me from my mother's side; M.F.]. If a stranger enters a town where the race is without stain, the law may make him a citizen, but his tongue will remain servile; he does not have the right to say everything [*ouk ekhei parrēsian*: he does not have *parrēsia*; M.F.]."[3] So, what is this text and what do we see in it? We see someone in search of his birth, who does not know his mother, and so who wants to know what city and community he belongs to. Why does he want to know this? He wants to know precisely so that he knows if he has the right to speak. And since he is searching for this woman in Athens, he hopes that the mother he will eventually discover will be Athenian and thus belong to this community, this *dēmos*, etcetera, and that, by virtue of this birth, he himself will have the right to speak freely, to have *parrēsia*. For, he says, in a town "without stain," that is to say, precisely in a town which keeps the traditions, in a town in which the *politeia* (the constitution) has not been debased by tyranny or despotism, or by the abusive integration of people who are not truly citizens, so in a town which has remained without stain and in which the *politeia* has remained what it should be, only those who are citizens have *parrēsia*. Beyond this general theme which structures the search for this single personage's mother and which links the right to speak to membership of the *dēmos*, it is worth keeping hold of two things. The first is that the right to speak, *parrēsia*, is transmitted in this case by the mother. Second, you see too that the stranger's status is defined and appears in contrast with that of citizens who have the right to speak, and, so far as the town is without stain, his tongue is servile. Exactly: *to ge stoma doulon*—his mouth is slave. That is to say, the right to speak, the restriction on the freedom of political discourse is total. He does not possess this freedom of political discourse; he does not possess *parrēsia*. So: membership of a *dēmos*; *parrēsia* as right to speak, inherited through the maternal line; and finally exclusion of non-citizens whose tongue is servile. This is what appears.

Listen, I would like to stop there now, although I have not completely finished, but I am very aware that if I launch myself into the comparison between these and other texts in Euripides...So, I will resume next week, thank you.

1. The two essential references are: J.L. Austin, *How To Do Things with Words*, ed., J.O. Urmson and Marina Sbisà (Oxford: Oxford University Press, 1980 [1962]) and John Searle, *Speech Acts: An Essay in the Philosophy of Language* (Cambridge: Cambridge University Press, 1969).

2. "One would not be able to find a regime and an ideal of equality, liberty, in a word of democracy, more perfect than that among the Achaeans (*isēgorias kai parrēsias kai katholou dēmokratias alēthinēs sustēma kai proairesin eilikrinesteran ouk an heuroi tis tēs para tois Akaiois huparkhousēs*)" Polybe, *Histoires*, Book II, 38, 6, trans. P. Pédech (Paris: Les Belles Lettres, 1970) p. 83; English translation by W.R. Paton as Polybius, *The Histories*, vol. 1, Books I and II (Cambridge, Mass.: Harvard University Press, "Loeb Classical Library," 1922) p. 337: "One would not find a political system so favourable to equality and freedom of speech, in a word so sincerely democratic, as that of the Achaean league."

3. Euripides, *Ion*, 671-675, in *Tragédies*, vol. III, trans H. Grégoire (Paris: Les Belles Lettres, 1976) p. 211; English translation by Philip Vellacott, *Ion*, in Euripides, *The Bacchae and Other Plays* (Harmondsworth: Penguin Books, 1973) pp. 61-62: "I care nothing for all this...unless I can find my mother. And, if I might choose, I would like her to be an Athenian; then I should have free speech in my blood! A foreigner, coming to a city of unmixed race, must curb his speech: the law can enfranchise his name, but not his tongue."

five

19 JANUARY 1983

First hour

TODAY I WOULD LIKE to continue with the study of this notion of *parrēsia* which, as a first approximation, seems to cover a fairly wide domain since the term refers on the one hand to "saying everything," and on the other to "telling the truth," and third to "free-spokenness." These are the three axes of the notion. You recall that I brought up this notion in the particular context of spiritual direction. This year I would like to study it in the broader context of the government of self and others.

In the last lecture I tried to define some aspects of this notion of *parrēsia* as it appears in an, as it were, average text, in Plutarch's text, in which he stages, first Plato's, and then Dion's parrhesiastic confrontation with the tyrant Dionysius. Now I would like to go back a bit from this first sketch and try to follow in more detail the history, or anyway different stratifications in the history of this notion of *parrēsia*, essentially from the perspective of its political meanings. It seemed to me that some of the most important classical texts concerning this notion of *parrēsia* are found in Euripides, and in particular in four of his plays: *Ion, The Phoenicians, Hippolytus,* and *The Bacchae.* Last week I spoke to you very rapidly about a passage in *Ion* in which we see the principal character, Ion, explaining that, not knowing his mother, he has a powerful need to know who she is. Not only does he need to know who she is, but he would really like her to be Athenian so that from his mother's side (*mētrothen*) he will have the right to speak freely, so that he will obtain *parrēsia* through her. For, he says: "If a stranger enters a town where the race is without stain, the law may make him a citizen, but his tongue will remain servile [his mouth will remain slave: *stoma doulon*; M.F.]; he does not have the right to say everything [he does not have *parrēsia*; M.F.]."[1] This is the text I pointed out to you last week.

So, obviously we can say a number of things regarding this text. In the Budé edition of Euripides, Grégoire, the author of the note—which is very interesting, moreover, and I think historically correct and well-documented, since notwithstanding the age of the edition (it dates from 1925 or 1930), I have found that literary historians do not change much to what is [established] from the historical point of view—says: Ion is a very decent, laudable, and honorable young man who displays "rigorous piety" and "tender affection," who has the "impulsive intelligence" and "joyful activity of youth," and who "values speaking out freely (*franc-parler*)."[2] Well, it seems to me that this problem of free-spokenness is somewhat different and has more than just the psychological dimensions Grégoire points out in his note. If I am interested in this text from *Ion* it is because it is inserted precisely in the middle, or let's say at the end of the first third of a tragedy which I really think we can say is entirely devoted to *parrēsia*, or at any rate which is permeated from end to end by this theme of *parrēsia* (of saying everything, telling the truth, and free-spokenness).

Let us go back a bit again, if you like, to the history which serves as background to the tragedy. Ion is a character who does not belong to any of the major mythical sets of the Greek heritage and who does not have a place in any of the known cultic practices. He is a late, artificial character who seems to have first appeared with a very discreet existence in the scholarly genealogies which were used above all from the seventh century and which were frequently revived in the fifth century. As you know, these scholarly genealogies involved establishing and justifying the political and moral authority of some major family groups. Or else they sought to provide a city with ancestors, asserting the city's rights, justifying a policy, etcetera. In these political, artificial, and late genealogies, Ion appears (I was going to say: as his name indicates) as the ancestor of the Ionians. That is to say, even the name Ion was fabricated in order to give an ancestor to the Ionians, who had been called by this name for a long time. Herodotus explains that when the Ionians lived in the Peloponnese—that is to say, in the part of the Peloponnese called the *Achaïe*—they were not called Ionians. They were called Pelasgians. But in the time of Ion, son of Xuthus, they took the name of Ionians.[3] So Ion is the eponymous hero of the Ionians, their common ancestor. This is, if you like, the general theme of the genealogies which speak of Ion.

I will skip the different versions and successive developments of this genealogy. I would just like to indicate the following: Ion, ancestor of the Ionians, was thus located first of all in Achaea. But as the strength of Athens increased, as the opposition between Sparta and Athens became more pronounced, and also as Athens laid claim to and moreover exercised leadership* over Ionia, Athens was increasingly inclined to present itself as the city of the Ionians and to claim Ion as an Athenian, or at any rate as one of the principal actors in the history of Athens. We see Ion gradually migrate, so to speak, from Achaea to Athens, where, in some versions of the legend, he arrives as an immigrant, but as an important, decisive immigrant, since the first great revolution or reform of the Athenian constitution is attributed to him. The following change is attributed to him: after the first foundation of Athens, there would have been a sort of new foundation, or anyway an internal reorganization, which would have divided the Athenian people into four tribes. These four tribes would be at the origin of Athens and its political organization. This is the version given in the *Constitution of Athens*, in which Aristotle lists the eleven revolutions or great reformations of the Athenian city. The first is Ion founding the four tribes.[4] But in Aristotle Ion is someone who migrates to Athens and who reorganizes Athens. Only, we can see what type of problems

---

* In English in original.

and difficulties this type of legend could give rise to, at a time when Athens was claiming its autochthony, that is to say, that the inhabitants of Athens, unlike many other Greeks, were not people who came from elsewhere, but had been born on their own soil. At the time then when Athenians want to distinguish themselves from other Greeks by asserting this original autochthony, at a time when they claim to exercise political domination over the Ionian world, how can they accept the idea that it was an Ionian immigrant who reformed Athens? Hence, if you like, a tendency, a constant inclination of this legend is to integrate or insert Ion as strictly as possible in Athenian history. Euripides' tragedy, and [also] a lost tragedy by Sophocles, which was called *Creusa* and seems to have been written shortly before Euripides' *Ion*, are situated in the framework of this movement, this tendency in the elaboration of the legend.[5] It is likely that Sophocles' tragedy, and anyway certainly Euripides' *Ion*, try to give the elaboration of the legend an acceptable meaning. That is to say, the stake of this tragic elaboration of the legend will be: how can one preserve the ancestral and founding function of Ion in relation to all the Ionians by inscribing and rooting Ion's history in Athens itself, and, contrary to the original form of the legend, by making Ion a native of Athens? Ion must be reinstated in Athens, retaining his function as ancestor of all the Ionians. This reversal, placing Ion's birth at Athens and making him the ancestor of all the Ionians, is fully carried out and taken to its extreme limits by Euripides, since he adopts a plot in which Ion is fully Athenian, or more precisely, of both Athenian and divine blood. He will be the child of Creusa, on the maternal side, and Apollo, on his paternal side. So he will be Athenian. Through his four sons Ion will be the source of the four original Athenian tribes. Through his four sons he will be the ancestor of all the Ionians. And on another side, he will be given half-brothers, Achaeus and Dorus, the sons of Creusa, his mother, and Xuthus. Achaeus, as of course his name indicates, is the ancestor of the Achaeans, and Dorus, as his name indicates too, is the ancestor of the Dorians. So that Ionians, Achaeans, and Dorians are thus related, thanks to the bond of kinship between Creusa, Xuthus, etcetera, all characters found at Athens itself.*

* The manuscript concludes in the following way: "In short, all those who populate Greece have a root in Athens."

This elaboration of the legendary framework of Ion, this transformation of an immigrant into a native, this sort of genealogical imperialism which will mean that ultimately all Greeks (Achaeans, Dorians, and Ionians) will come from the same stock, all this—as well as other information scattered in the text—has enabled historians, and Grégoire in particular, to date the play exactly. The date proposed by Grégoire has been maintained until now. It is accepted that [the play] is from 418, and very probably from the second half of 418, definitely during the brief period called the Nicias peace, at the end of the first part of the Peloponnesian War between Spartans and Athenians. You know that all in all, after various episodes, victory had rather fallen to Athens. In any case the Nicias peace was signed under conditions such that Athenian power was not yet broken (the disaster of Sicily will take place after the breakdown of the Nicias peace). Athenian power is not broken, its empire especially has not been touched, and Athens tries to take advantage of this truce to strengthen its alliances, assert its supremacy, and above all to form a sort of alliance of Ionians, bringing them together under Athenian direction. This consolidation of the Ionians was one of the main components of Athenian strategy for some time. Certainly, more intensely than ever this is Athenian strategy during the Nicias peace when the confrontation with Sparta is not yet over, but only in its first phase. We should also take into account, and this has an important role in the play, of the fact that Delphi—the Amphictyons of Delphi, the whole movement of pan-Hellenism which revolved around Delphi, during the first part of the Peloponnesian War, before the Nicias peace—inclined much more towards Sparta than towards Athens. Throughout the first part of the Peloponnesian War the Delphic center displayed quite violent hostility towards Athens. The Nicias peace represented a sort of compromise, an appeasement between Delphi and Athens. Delphi had Laconized [and] one of the elements of the Nicias peace was a sort of reconciliation between Athens and Delphi. Euripides constructs his play on the basis of this legendary framework on the one hand, and this precise political strategy on the other, and he adopts the following schema for his plot, which is set out at the beginning of the play by Hermes, following a procedure found in many of his plays, and in many other tragedies as well: a character, sometimes a god—in this case, Hermes—comes on stage and explains where we are in the plot, recalling the legendary background which will be used in the play.

So what Euripides explains through the mouth of Hermes is the following.[6] Erechtheus—of Athenian stock, of course, born on Athenian soil, and consequently guaranteed that autochthony to which Athenians attach such value—has had a daughter called Creusa, who is therefore of Athenian stock, linked directly to the soil of Athens through her father who was born there. The young girl, Creusa, is seduced by Apollo. She is seduced by Apollo and taken by him in the caves of the Acropolis, very close therefore to the temple and the sacred place reserved for the cult of Athena. She is seduced, taken by Apollo on the slopes of the Acropolis, and she conceives a son whom, from shame, and to hide her dishonor, she exposes, abandoning him. This son disappears without trace. In fact, Hermes has removed the son born from the affair of his brother, Apollo, and Creusa. Hermes takes him away on the order of Apollo himself, carries the child in his cradle to Delphi, where he is placed, still through the ministrations of Hermes, in the temple. Apollo's priestess, the Pythia, seeing this child and, despite being the Pythia, not knowing it is Apollo's child, taking him to be a foundling, nevertheless takes him in, feeds him and makes him a temple servant. And so the son of Apollo and Creusa becomes a humble servant who sweeps the temple. The son is, of course, Ion. Creusa meanwhile, no one around her knowing that she was seduced by Apollo and that she has had a son, is married to Xuthus by her father, Erechtheus. Now Xuthus is a foreigner. He was not born at Athens. He comes from Achaea, that is to say, from a part of the Peloponnese, but Erechtheus has given him Creusa. For in the course of a war of conquest of Euboea, Xuthus had helped the Athenian army, had helped Erechtheus. Xuthus receives Creusa and her dowry as reward for this aid. This is the situation given by Euripides, or that he gets Hermes to give, at the beginning of the play.

Before entering into the analysis of the different elements of the play and their mechanism, I would like to pause for a moment. You can see straightaway that the play will consist in the discovery of a truth; the truth of Ion's birth. The play will consist in the revelation that the anonymous slave of Apollo's temple is not an anonymous child found at Delphi, but someone who, conceived at Athens, born at Athens, will be able to return to Athens where he will accomplish the historical and political mission of the city's reorganization and, even better, the foundation of the long human dynasty of the Ionians. This revelation of the truth of Ion's birth is a dramatic framework found in many Greek plays. If the text had been preserved, we would have been able to find it in another play by Euripides, *Alexander,*[7] which recounts how the Trojan sovereigns, Hecuba and Priam, having learned through a prophecy that their son, Paris or Alexander, was in danger of unleashing the disaster of Troy, decide to abandon him, expose him, and believe that he has disappeared. And then one day they meet him. And the identity and birth of Paris-Alexander is revealed. Hence the disasters of Troy will be able to take place. So there is a familiar schema. But what should be noted is, first, that this coming to light of the truth, this coming to light of the truth of the birth, will be brought about in a precise place. It will not take place at Athens, in fact, but at Delphi, since that is where Ion is found, hidden in the form of a temple servant. The truth is revealed precisely at Delphi, where, as everyone knows, the truth is told. The truth is told in an oracular form, in the oracular form of a truth-telling which, as you know, is always reticent, enigmatic, and difficult to understand, and yet which ineluctably says what is and what will be. The oblique god, the god who, as Heraclitus said, only speaks through signs,[8] resides precisely at Delphi, and it is at Delphi, better, it is very close to the temple, better still, it is on the very parvis of the temple that this truth will be told. You will see that it is not told through the power of the oracle, but is told very close to the oracle, as near as can be to the oracle, in front of the oracle, and to a certain extent against the oracle. Anyway, we are at the essential site of oracular truth-telling in Greek culture. Second, you note that this alethurgy,* this discovery of the truth, this production of the truth, can only take place if the two secret and hidden partners of the union—Creusa the mother, Apollo the father and god—tell the truth about their secret union. They must say what they have done and they

---

* [Frédéric Gros adds the following note to the Collège de France lecture of 1 February 1984, *Le courage de la vérité. Le gouvernement de soi et des autres II. Cours au Collège de France (1983-1984),* ed. Frédéric Gros (Paris: Seuil/Gallimard, 2009) p. 20 n5: "On the concept of alethurgy, see the Collège de France lectures of 23 and 30 January 1980 ('by creating the fictional word *alē thourgia* from *alēthourgēs,* we could call "alethurgy" (manifestation of truth) the set of possible procedures, verbal or otherwise, by which one brings to light what is posited as true, as opposed to the false, the hidden, the unspeakable, the unforeseeable, or the forgotten. We could call "alethurgy" that set of procedures and say that there is no exercise of power without something like an alethurgy,' lecture of 23 January)"; G.B.]

must say it to their offspring. The union of the woman and the god, the conception and birth of the child, the mother's exposure of the child, and Apollo's rescue of the child, is all unknown to the characters, and all of it will have to be told. Third, this unveiling of the truth must also lead to Ion's return to the Athens where he was conceived and born and it must enable him to exercise a fundamental political right there: the right to speak, to speak to the city and address it with a language of truth and reason, which will be precisely one of the essential armatures of the *politeia*, of the political structure, the constitution of Athens. As a result, the play will go from the place where the god tells the truth through oracular and enigmatic words—Delphi—to the political stage where the leader uses his right to speak freely through a constitution which is that of *logos*—Athens. And this passage, from the place where the truth is spoken in oracular form to the political stage where the reasonable language of government is spoken, can only take place if the god and the woman, the man and the woman, the father and the mother, tell the truth of their son's birth in the confession of what they have done.

The play recounts this series of three truth-tellings: of the oracle, of confession, and of political discourse. It involves the foundation of true discourse in the city through a double operation, or in a double reference, first to oracular speech—which, you will see, has a role to play, but a very enigmatic and ambiguous one—and then [to] the speech of the confession of the father and the mother, of the god and the woman. I think this series constitutes the play's main theme. And to the extent that *Ion* is a tragedy of truth-telling, a drama of truth-telling, then it seems to me that it is the most striking representation, the most striking development of that dramatics of true discourse, of truth-telling that I talked about last week and which seemed to me to be the framework in which we can understand the nature of *parrēsia*. *Ion* is truly the dramatic representation of the foundation of political truth-telling in the field of the Athenian constitution and of the exercise of power at Athens. This is the first aspect.

The second thing I would like to pause over before beginning the reading of *Ion* is this. You can see that this play contains, of course, a number of analogies with many other plays by Euripides. It seems to me that it also contains some fairly precise analogies with another play not by Euripides, but by Sophocles. And it seems to me that we can make use of this proximity in order to analyze a bit more closely how things take place and how the truth is told in *Ion*. [...]*

The play by Sophocles that I would like to put alongside Euripides' play is one which, of course, also involves the god at Delphi who tells the truth and hides the truth. It is a play which also involves parents who expose their children, in which a child disappears, is taken for dead, and then reappears. There is no need to tell you that the play that *Ion* inevitably brings to mind is *Oedipus*. *Oedipus* is also a play of truth-telling, of the unveiling of the truth, of the dramatics of truth-telling, or, if you like, of alethurgy. And I think it will be easy to find many elements common to both *Ion* and *Oedipus*.

Some elements of direct symmetry. There is a small, unobtrusive scene...I don't want to over interpret, but very quickly, almost at the start of *Ion*, we see the first meeting of Ion and Xuthus, who, in good faith, honestly believes himself to be Ion's father. They meet each other, and there is a somewhat ambiguous scene. Once again, no doubt we should not over interpret it, but a number of elements give the impression that Xuthus, who honestly believes he is greeting his son in the person of Ion, throws himself on him, embraces him, and covers him with paternal flattery. Ion defends himself, he defends himself with what is manifestly the modesty of a young man who finds himself somewhat assailed by a bearded gentleman, and he says to him: Keep calm (*eu phroneis*),[9] be reasonable. And since Xuthus, in his paternal fervor, continues to display his affection, Ion gets angry and threatens to kill him. I think we can recognize here a sort of echo of the famous scene of Laius and Oedipus, which you know, in many versions (not in that of Sophocles, but in many others), was a seduction scene.[10] Laius wanted to seduce the young Oedipus who crossed his path, and Oedipus responded by killing him. So there is this element.

But other elements are much more convincing, and in particular some elements of reversed symmetry. Ion, in fact, not knowing who he is, lives in Apollo's temple. That is to say, he lives in his father's home

---

* M.F.: There seems to be a noise in the mike no, a whistling?
  —It must be one of these machines that isn't working.
  —Oh dear, how can we find out which it is...Does it bother you a lot, too much? Good, it's stopped.

unaware that Apollo is his father, just as Oedipus lived in the home of a woman, his wife, not knowing that she was his mother. Ion lives in Apollo's home as Oedipus lives in his mother's home. Second, we then see an absolutely explicit scene in which, for a number of reasons, through episodes I will recount or summarize for you, Ion, at a given moment, wants to kill his mother, without, of course, knowing that she is his mother. And in this I think we have the exact reproduction of Oedipus' murder of Laius, but this time transferred to the mother.

I also think we can pick out some analogies between these two plays at the level of the mechanism of the search for the truth, [which] takes place by halves as it were. In *Oedipus*,[11] you recall, in the first part of the play, the truth of the murder of Laius is discovered. Then, in the second part, the truth of the birth of Oedipus is discovered. And then the murder of Laius can itself be divided in two insofar as one part of the story of Oedipus recounts how he killed an unknown man on the road, and then there is the story which teaches us that this unknown man can only be Laius. In the same way, the truth of the birth advances by halves; there is the paternal half, and then the maternal half, until the set of these elements reconstitute the whole of the truth.

Only, if there are many common elements and analogies in the episodes as well as in the structure of the play, it seems to me that there is a difference, even an opposition, between the dramatics of truth-telling in *Oedipus* and the dramatics of truth-telling in *Ion*. In *Oedipus*, in fact, first of all it is Oedipus himself who brings truth-telling into play. It is Oedipus who wants to know the truth. As sovereign, and in order to restore peace and happiness in his town, he needs to know the truth. And what is this truth revealed to be? First of all it comes out that he has done away with his own father and thereby created a hole, as it were, in the sovereignty exercised over the city and in the palace of Laius itself. And he rushes into this empty place, marrying his mother and taking power. It is the discovery of this that finally leads to him being excluded and to him excluding himself from the city. He says so himself at the end of the play: "As long as I shall live, never let this town, the town of my fathers, be my dwelling place."[12] He is obliged to leave therefore, by the very discovery of the truth whose process of discovery he set in motion. Henceforth all that remains is for him to wander through the world in the night of his blindness, since he has put out his own eyes. And what is left to guide him as he passes through this world without shelter or homeland? He says this too very clearly at the end of the play: he has only the voice of his daughters who guide him, and his own voice that he hears floating in the air without being able to place it, not knowing where he is, not knowing where it is. And through this wandering, guided only by the exchange of voices between father and daughters, Oedipus returns to Greek soil, where he will find, precisely at Athens, his final resting place.[13]

With *Ion*, on the other hand, we have a process of discovery of the truth in which, on the one hand, and first of all, we see that it is not Ion himself who seeks the truth, but his parents. Second, this truth which Ion discovers, or rather, which is discovered about Ion, is not, of course, that he has killed his father. He discovers that he has, in a way, two fathers, and at the end of the play he finds himself with two fathers: a sort of legal father who will continue to believe right to the end that he, Xuthus, is the real father; and then a second father. This second father is Apollo who, through Ion's real paternity, establishes that Ion was indeed conceived entirely at Athens. It is thanks to this double paternity of Xuthus and Apollo that, exactly the opposite of Oedipus, Ion will be able to return to his native land, settle there, and regain all his rights. And thanks to finding this fundamental bond in this way, thanks to this re-insertion in the very soil of Athens, he will be able to exercise the legitimate right of speech, that is to say, to exercise power in Athens. And so, in these two processes of the alethurgy of the birth, of the discovery of the truth of the birth, you see that in fact there are two different processes which lead to exactly opposite results. One had a father less and finally is obliged to leave his homeland and to wander, without land, guided by a voice. The other discovers that he has two fathers and, thanks to this double paternity, will be able to insert his speech, the speech of someone who commands, in the land to which he has a right. This, if you like, is the framework of the play.

I would like now to show you how this process of truth-telling, and this unveiling of the truth through the different procedures of truth-telling, unfolds through the events I have recalled and which Hermes points out right at the start of the play, namely: Ion's secret birth; the later marriage of Creusa to Xuthus; the fact that Ion lives hidden as the god's servant at Delphi without anyone knowing his identity; and the fact that at the start of the play Creusa and Xuthus do not yet have the two sons, Achaeus and Dorus, who will be born after the play and are referred to in the final verses.[14] They have no descendants therefore, and it precisely for this reason that they, who live in Athens—Xuthus, an immigrant, but married to Creusa, and Creusa, daughter of Erechtheus—come to Delphi to consult the god and ask him if they will ever have descendants who will be able to ensure the historical and territorial continuity founded by Erechtheus when, born on Attic soil, he founded the Athenian city. So this is the first point: Creusa and Xuthus come to consult the god. They come to consult the god because they do not have any children and they want to establish this continuity.

Actually, you see that the consultation is not exactly the same for the two of them. On the one hand, Xuthus comes to consult Apollo. He comes to consult Apollo according to the usual rules in order to know if he really will have no descendants. This is the question put to the oracle. Creusa too apparently comes to put the same question: Will I have no descendants? But in fact she asks another question at the same time. Because she knows full well that she has had a child. And she knows full well that she had this child by Apollo. She comes to put the question: What then has become of the son you gave me, the son you made and I exposed? Is he still alive or is he dead? But whereas the first consultation, that of Xuthus, is, if you like, both a standard question—the consultation of the common consultant—and a public question, Creusa's question (What have you done with the son you gave me?) is a private question that the woman puts to the man, or rather to the god.

By coming to Delphi for this double question—the official question and the secret question—by coming to make this double demand, Creusa and Xuthus, presenting themselves at Apollo's temple, meet this young man who is sweeping the temple porch with laurel branches, and who is sprinkling the lustral water because, he says, he has the right to do so, having always been chaste. And of course, Ion does not know his own identity so cannot recognize his parents, any more than his parents can recognize him. So we have three ignorant people, each of whom has the answer to their question in front of them: Xuthus is looking for an heir, and in fact he has one before him without knowing it; Creusa is looking for a son, the son she bore, and she too has him before her; and as for Ion, he complains, without much insistence moreover, of being an abandoned child, of not having a homeland, and of not having a mother and father. Now he has his mother in front of him, and he has two fathers: he has the one who will become his legal father, Xuthus, and then beside him, behind him, he has his real father, the god. So, if you like, we have the following: on the one hand, at the back of the stage, the temple of the god who knows everything and who must tell the truth in answer to the questions put to him; and then in front of the stage, the public amphitheater which, at the start of the play, was informed by Hermes of the whole truth of the matter. Between these two instances which know—the public which has been informed by Hermes, and Apollo who, of course, knows—between these two instances of the truth, are the three ignorant characters. They do not recognize each other and the whole play will be precisely the unveiling of the truth for these three characters there on the space of the stage. Alethurgy of the truth therefore.

What will be the mainspring of the drama? Well, it is the difficulty [in] telling the truth; it is an essential reticence. To what is this essential reticence due? Well, it is due to two things, and this is what I think makes the play *Ion* important and interesting. On the one hand there is, if you like, the essential, fundamental, permanent, I was going to say structural reason, which means that when men question the gods, nothing forces the gods, if they reply, to do so in such a way that their answer is clear. On the contrary, it is part of oracular truth-telling that the answer is such that men may or may not understand it. In any case, the god is never forced by men to tell the truth. His answer is ambiguous, and he is always free to give it if he wants. So there is reticence in the very clarity of the enunciation. There is also reticence in the god's freedom to speak or not to speak. This is part of the stock in trade if you like. It is the common, permanent feature of every oracular game of questions and answers. The text frequently refers and alludes to this essential reticence peculiar to the oracular structure of all truth-telling by the gods, and by the god of Delphi in particular. For example, from 374, we see Ion saying to Creusa: "How can one draw from the God the oracle he wishes to conceal?", "you cannot consult disregarding the gods."[15] This refers to the fact that the god is always free to be silent if he so wishes. Elsewhere Ion says to Xuthus, who has brought him an answer from the god: You are mistaken in your interpretation of the riddle.[16] The answer is a riddle, and so one may always be mistaken. So all of this refers to known elements.

But there is a specific reason in the play which is peculiar to the plot, which means that the god's reticence is in a way sealed by another clause. For it turns out that it is not just because he is free not to speak that the god remains silent, and it is not just because it is part of the oracular answer to be enigmatic and to speak only through signs, as Heraclitus said.[17] It is quite simply because Apollo has done wrong by taking Creusa by force and then abandoning her on the slopes of the Acropolis. He is guilty, and the theme of the god's guilt is found throughout the entire play, from beginning to end. [When] Ion learns—I am now skipping the details of the plot—that Apollo has seduced a girl and abandoned her, he is still completely unaware that this girl is his mother; he does not know that she is Creusa. He just hears of this seduction, and he, Ion, who is nevertheless the god's faithful servant, and also his chaste servant, is indignant and says: "The God is indeed guilty and the mother to be pitied."[18] And in the same dialogue where he is speaking with Creusa, we hear the following. Ion asks: "How can one draw from the God the oracle he wishes to conceal?"[19] Creusa replies: "On this tripod, he must reply to every Greek."[20] Ion replies: "He blushes for his action, ah! don't press him...—Creusa: If he blushes for it, she groans, the poor woman."[21] Ion concludes: "No one will be found to communicate such an oracle to you: convicted of an offense in his own dwelling place, Apollo would justly blame the one who makes him announce it to you."[22] You see the clash of the two words and so the problem that is posed. Apollo has been unjust (*adikos*), he has committed an offense. And it is "*dikaiōs*" (justly)[23] that he will refuse to speak and designate himself as guilty. Consequently, the answer cannot come from the god, not because of the very structure of oracular truth-telling, but because the god, who has acted wrongly, would have to confess that he had done so and overcome the shame of his bad action. The god's shame for his bad action is one of the main themes of the play. And right at the end—when the alethurgy will at last be complete and come to an end, when all the truth will be told—is the truth told by the god, by Apollo, by the one who, [according to] the text, owes the truth to all the Greeks? Not at all. The divinity who tells the truth at the end, who appears above Apollo's temple, covering it and dominating it—for political reasons, of course, but also for reasons to do with what I am in the process of explaining—is Athena. It is Athena, the goddess of Athens, who will found the whole history in truth, who will found the political structure of Athens through her own discourse of truth. She will intervene and tell the truth that the god Apollo cannot say, and she explains moreover why it is she who comes and not Apollo. She says: Apollo does not want to appear before you in person, for he fears the public reproaches for the past and sends me to declare that...[24] The whole function, both foundational and prophetic at the same time, will be assured by Athena, for it must be Athena, again, for political reasons, but also because Apollo cannot tell the truth himself.

It seems to me that we have here one of the basic, characteristic features of this tragedy: the truth-telling of a god speaking to men and, in accordance with the oracle's function, revealing to them what is and what will be, must also be, in the case of *Ion*, the truth-telling of the god about himself and his misdeeds. The oracle's reticence is also the hesitation to confess. And the superimposition of the oracular riddle on the difficulty of confessing, of the truth-telling of the oracle and the truth-telling of confession, a superimposition which is carried out in the god and in his own words, is, I believe, one of the basic mainsprings of the play. Consequently, since we are dealing with a situation in which the one who must tell the truth, whose function is to tell the truth, the one whom one consults to tell the truth, is the one who cannot tell the truth, since the truth would be a confession concerning himself, how will the truth make its way, how will truth-telling be established and at the same time establish the possibility of a political structure within which one will be able to tell the truth in *parrēsia*? Well, it has to be [through] men. Men must flush out this truth and practice truth-telling. And it is in fact in the god's deficiency in telling the truth, in this double reticence of the oracle and the confession that humans will try to unravel the truth. How will they break the double seal of the oracular riddle and the shame of confession? I think we may summarize the play, or bring together its elements, by saying that there are two major moments.

The first moment is what we could call that of the double half-lie. For one of the essential points also of this play—we will have to come back to this—is precisely that, unlike what takes place in *Oedipus*, in this play the truth is not told without bringing with it a dimension, I would say a double, of illusion, which is at once its necessary accompaniment, its condition, and its shadow. There is no truth-telling without illusions. Let's see anyway how this takes place. So the first part, the two half-lies. These are the following: first, the half-lie on the mother's side; and then, the half-lie on the father's side, since, as in *Oedipus*, things proceed by halves. First, on Creusa's side. So, Creusa the woman and Xuthus the man arrive at Delphi. Xuthus wants to ask if he will have a son. Creusa wants to ask what has become of her son. Creusa is the first to appear on the stage and who first encounters the young man who is sweeping the temple porch with laurel branches. She meets this young man and tells him that she would like to consult the god. And Ion asks her the nature of her consultation, but obviously she dare not tell Ion the truth of her question. She dare not tell him: I have committed an offense with the god and I come to ask him what he has done with my son. So she will tell a half-truth or a half-lie. She will say what anyone would say in this situation: I have a sister who has committed an offense with a god.[25] She had a son by this god and would really like to know what has become of him. At this point—honestly believing, moreover, Creusa's story (but it does not really matter whether it is Creusa or her sister, in either case the answer for Ion is clear, or rather the god's non-answer is necessary)—Ion says to her: Since the god has committed an offense, an offense with your sister, have no fear, the god will not speak. Humans cannot force the god to speak against his will. And since he has committed an offense, since he has been *adikos*, he will remain silent *dikaiōs* (justly).[26] To have committed an injustice founds the justice of not speaking. Therefore he will not speak.

But during, or a little after this dialogue between Ion and Creusa, Xuthus puts his, much more direct, simple, and clear question: Will I have a son? And in a way, while Creusa says only half the truth to Ion when she consults him, the god answers Xuthus, who asks him a sincere and clear question, with a half-truth. That is to say, neither father nor mother, neither Apollo nor Creusa, will dare to tell the truth, and they will only say half-truths or half-lies. [...] To Xuthus, who asks

him: Will I have a son? Apollo replies: It's very simple, when you leave
the temple, the first person you meet (*iōn*: a play on words, for sure)[27]
will be your son. Recognize him as your son. And leaving the temple,
Xuthus meets the young man who is there of course to serve the god
and who hangs round the temple over which he has to keep watch.
This young man is Ion. And it is at this point that the scene takes place
in which Xuthus throws himself on Ion and embraces him, telling
him: You are my son. And Ion, a bit uneasy, says: Hold on there, control yourself, or else I will kill you. Actually, the non-truth or half-lie
uttered by the god was not just a matter of his reluctance to confess. Or
rather, the reluctance to confess is translated here into normal, run of
the mill, if I may say so, oracular ambiguity; the god said [to Xuthus]:
I give you, "*dōron*,"[28] I give you as a gift the young man you will meet
when you leave the temple. Giving him as a gift does not exactly mean:
this will be your son. But Xuthus understands that, since he came in
search of a son, what will be given to him as a gift will be his real son.

Through the god's indication, telling Xuthus that the first person
he meets will be his son, Ion now finds himself provided with a father.
Now if he is somewhat reluctant to let himself be embraced by this
bearded gentleman, when Xuthus tells him: But you know, it is the
god who gave me this answer and told me that I would have as *dōron*
the young man I would meet when leaving the temple, Ion is clearly
obliged to yield and to acknowledge, with some hesitation: Yes, this
is my father. So now Ion, thanks to the god's half-truth or half-lie, is
provided with a family, or anyway with a father. But he has received
this family in the wrong way, I would almost say in false kinship, since
he actually believes—as does Xuthus—that they are father and son,
whereas in reality the truth is that there is no relation between Xuthus
and Ion. The true kinship relation is between Creusa and Ion, and this
does not emerge. To the distorted question of the true mother, who
pretends not to be the mother but the sister of the mother, the god
has thus responded by distorting the answer that he gives to the man:
he gives him a false son. But after all, things could well remain there,
since thanks to this Ion will be able to return to Athens. Xuthus is not
entirely his father, but all in all he can serve as his father. And then he
will be able to live with Creusa, whom he does not know is his mother,
but it could be worked out. *Grosso modo*, we are close enough to the

truth for it to work. And this is, moreover, how Xuthus understands it. He is perfectly happy with this solution, which, in any case, he genuinely thinks is a good one. He says to Ion: Now things are clear. You are no longer the abandoned child you thought you were. I was looking for a son, and now I have one. "Leave this temple and your miserable existence. Leave for Athens, in full agreement with your father [*koinophrōn patri*[29]—and here, of course, as in *Oedipus*, as in all these tragedies, you have the amphibological phrase: in full agreement with your father. Xuthus thinks he is the father, but in fact it is with Apollo that the agreement is made, should be made; M.F.]. There the illustrious scepter and immense wealth of your father awaits you, thus escaping the double disgrace of poverty and lowly origins; you will be both noble and rich."[30]

So the problem seems to be resolved. Ion has found parents—well, a father. Xuthus has found a son and proposes he return to Athens and exercise that famous power which will be able to assure some kind of continuity with the founding dynasty of Athens—some kind of continuity, of course, because, you can see, the situation is only approximate, and if it is to be accepted one must not be too demanding. One must not be too demanding—and this is actually the case with Xuthus, who is not very demanding about this truth, in short this half-lie that he received in good faith from the god and which he takes to be the whole truth. All the same, he is not very demanding, because when he says to Ion: I am your father, you are my son, Ion says to him: Let's see then, from what union was I born?[31] Was it with Creusa? No, no, says Xuthus, it wasn't Creusa. But from whom was I born, for you did not beget me on your own? And at this point Xuthus answers: Listen, don't worry. In the first place, don't worry about an ignoble birth, because I, Xuthus, am the son, well, the descendant of Zeus, so there is nobility on that side. As for your mother...You know, I committed some youthful misdeeds before marrying, some youthful follies. And as Ion, for reasons that you will quickly understand, still wants to know exactly who his mother is, who gave birth to him, the nature of his birth, his nobility, and his land of origin, insists and says: But if you conceived me in one of your youthful follies, how is it that I am here at Delphi? And now Xuthus evokes a visit he once made to Delphi for the celebrations of Bacchus, when he would have been with one of the god's

Maenads, in a sort of hierogamy which corresponds, but in the form of illusion and lie, to the true hierogamy which took place between Apollo and Creusa. And so the solution that Xuthus proposes is: Well, there it is, I have made a child through one of the god's Maenads, in the course of a ceremony, a festivity, and a drunken ritual. Now this explanation, which is only very approximate from the point of view of the truth, is disastrous from the legal point of view. Why is it disastrous from the legal point of view? Quite simply because Xuthus comes from Achaea, he is foreign to Athens and received there only as an ally who was given Creusa in payment for his alliance with Erechtheus and the aid he gave him. If then he returns with a son, but a son who would have been conceived with some girl or other, be she one of the god's Maenads, then the son of a non-Athenian father and a non-Athenian mother cannot in any way exercise that founding function in the town which is precisely Ion's function, his vocation. He cannot exercise that function, and the approximate nature of Xuthus' truth is translated in fact into a sort of juridical ban or juridical impossibility. Ion himself realizes that it won't do and that, being the son of Xuthus and a foreign girl, he won't be able to found his power, and it is precisely at this point that he makes that famous declaration I have talked about in which he says: But I cannot return to Athens if I do not know what mother gave birth to me. I cannot receive the power you offer me; I cannot sit on the throne and receive the scepter. I cannot speak and exercise speech that commands if I do not know who my mother is.[32] It is this text, and this declaration by Xuthus* that I would like to take up shortly in a bit more detail. [...]†

---

* [This seems to be a slip. It is Ion's declaration that Foucault examines in the next hour; G.B.]

† M.F.: If you like, we will take five minutes rest. I wanted to tell you something. Last year at the time of the events in Poland, the Collège de France had the good idea to invite some Polish professors here to give some lectures, some being in a situation of non-freedom, others being in a rather marginal situation. There have been several no-answers to these invitations and one positive answer. One of the professors has been able to come here and, to tell the truth, he began his lectures last Monday. His course, his series of lectures are on the history of Polish nationalism from the nineteenth to the twentieth century. Unfortunately—it is my fault, and also some organizational things which are absolutely nothing to do with the Collège administration, but various circumstances that you can imagine—it has therefore been a bit hurried. But I do not think it matters very much if you missed the first lecture. If you like, if you are interested in this subject, his name is M. Kieniewicz and he lectures on Polish nationalism on Mondays at 10 a.m. That's it. So in five minutes I will come back and we will continue.

1. Euripides, *Ion*, 671-675, French p. 211; English pp. 61-62.

2. "The young hierodule has the rigorous piety of his profession, a tender and jealous affection for the God who nourishes him, the impulsive intelligence, the joyful activity of his youth (…). Athenian without knowing it, he values above all free-spokenness." "Notice" to *Ion*, by H. Grégoire, in ibid., pp. 177-178.

3. "These Ionians, as long as they were in the Peloponnese dwelling in what is now called Achaia, before Danaus and Xuthus came to the Peloponnese, as the Greeks say, were called Aegialian Pelasgians; they were named Ionians after Ion the son of Xuthus." *Herodotus*, Vol. III, Book VII, 94, trans. A.D. Godley (London: William Heinemann, and New York: G.P. Putnam's Sons, 1922) pp. 397-399 (quoted by H. Grégoire, ibid., pp. 177-178).

4. "This was the eleventh change which had taken place in the constitution of Athens. The first modification of the primaeval condition of things was when Ion and his companions brought the people together into a community, for then the people were first divided into the four tribes, and the tribe-kings were created." Aristotle, *Constitution of Athens*, 41, translated by F.G. Kenyon, in *The Complete Works of Aristotle*, The Revised Oxford Translation, ed. Jonathan Barnes (Princeton: Princeton University Press/Bollingen Series LXXI 2) Vol. 2, p. 2366.

5. On this point, see the "Notice" to *Ion* by H. Grégoire, pp. 161-163.

6. Euripides, *Ion*, 1-81, French pp. 183-186; English pp. 41-43.

7. On this tragedy, of which only fragments survive, see the note by F. Jouan and H. Van Looy in Euripides, *Œuvres*, vol. VIII: *Fragments 1ère partie* (Paris: Les Belles Lettres, 1998) pp. 39-58.

8. *Les Écoles présocratiques*, B XCII, ed., J.-P. Dumont (Paris: Gallimard, 1991) p. 87: "The prince whose oracle is at Delphi does not speak or hide, but signifies (*signifie*)"; English translation by Jonathan Barnes, *Early Greek Philosophy* (Harmondsworth: Penguin, 1987) [B 93] p. 118: "…the king whose is the oracle at Delphi neither speaks nor conceals but indicates."

9. Euripides, *Ion*, 520, French p. 204: "*Eu phroneis men* (keep cool)"; English p. 57: "behave sensibly."

10. On the different versions of the most famous parricide and on the character of Laius more generally, see T. Gantz, *Early Greek Myth: A Guide to Literature and Artistic Sources* (Baltimore and London: Johns Hopkins University Press, 1993) pp. 487-502.

11. Foucault proposed an analysis of Oedipus on a number of occasions: in 1971 (unpublished lectures at the Collège de France, "La Volonté de savoir"); in 1972 (unpublished lecture at Buffalo on "Le Savoir d'Œdipe"); in 1973 (lectures in Brazil on "Les Formes juridiques de la vérité," in *Dits et Écrits*, vol. III, pp. 553-570; English translation by Robert Hurley, "Truth and Juridical Forms" in Michel Foucault, *Essential Works of Foucault 1954-1984: vol. 3, Power* (New York: New Press, 2000); in January 1980 (unpublished lectures at the Collège de France, "Le Gouvernement des vivants"); and May 1981 (series of unpublished lectures at Louvain entitled "Mal faire, dire vrai. Fonctions de l'aveu"). He was very quickly aware of this structure of "interlocking halves (*emboîtement par mopitiés*)."

12. Sophocle, *Œdipe-roi*, 1450, trans. P. Mazon, p. 269; English translation by David Grene, Sophocles, *Oedipus the King* in *Sophocles I*, ed., David Grene and Richmond Lattimore (Chicago and London: University of Chicago Press, 1991) pp. 72-73: "For me—never let this my father's city have me living a dweller in it."

13. Sophocles, *Oedipus at Colonus*, 84-93, English translation by David Grene in *Sophocles I*, p. 83.

14. Euripides, *Ion*, 1590-1593, French p. 246: "Xuthus and yourself will have descendants, Dorus through whom will spring the famous Dorians (*Doride*) in the Peloponnese; then, a second son, Achaeus, future king of the coastal land, near Rhium; a people will get their name from him"; English p. 87: "Moreover, you and Xuthus too shall have sons: first Dorus, from whom shall spring the celebrated Dorian State; then Achaeus, who shall be king of the sea-coast by Rhium in Peloponnese, and set the seal of his name upon a nation."

15. Ibid., 365 and 375, French p. 198; English p. 53: "is Apollo to reveal what he intends should remain a mystery?"; "We must not accuse Apollo in his own court. That is what our folly would amount to, if we try to force a reluctant god to speak.…"

16. Ibid., 533, French p. 205: "Its obscure content has mislead you"; English p. 57: "You heard some riddle and misunderstood it."

17. See above, note 8.
18. Euripides, *Ion*, 355, French p. 197; English p. 52.
19. Ibid., 365, French p. 198; English p. 53: "Is Apollo to reveal what he intends should remain a mystery?"
20. Ibid., 366, French p. 198; English p. 53: "Surely his oracle is open to every Greek to question?"
21. Ibid., 368, French p. 198; English p. 53: "ION: No. His honour is involved; you must respect his feelings.—CREUSA: What of his victim's feelings? What does this involve for her?"
22. Ibid., 369, French p. 198; English p. 53: "There is no one who will ask this question for you. Suppose it were proved in Apollo's own temple that he had behaved so badly, he would be justified in making your interpreter suffer for it."
23. Ibid., 370. Actually Ion employs the adjective *kakos* to designate Apollo's injustice: "Convicted of an offence (*kakos phaneis*) in his own dwelling place, Apollo, justly would blame the one who makes him announce it to you" ibid., 370-371, French p. 198; English p. 53, has "behaved so badly."
24. Ibid., 1557-1559, French p. 245; English p. 86.
25. Ibid., 338, French p. 197 (Creusa speaks simply of a friend: "I have a friend who says she has been with Phoebus"); English p. 52 ("She says—this friend—that Apollo lay with her…").
26. See above, note 23.
27. Euripides, *Ion*, 535, French p. 205: "*Domōn tōn d'exionti tou theou* (on leaving this divine temple)"; English p. 57: "…whoever met me as I came out of the temple." There is an explicit play on words at 802, French p. 216: Xuthus' son, the Chorus says, is called "Ion, for, he will be the first to meet his father"; English p. 65: "Yes, he is calling him 'Ion', because he was the first to meet him." And at 831, French p. 217: "and this completely new name, Ion, was made up afterwards: on the grounds that *Ion* was met on the road (*Iōn, ionti dēthen hoti sunēnteto*); English p. 66: "and his name, Ion, after all this time he passes off as a new name given because of the way he met him."
28. Ibid., 536-537, French p. 205; English p. 57.
29. Ibid., 577, French p. 207; English p. 59: "But meanwhile you must not live in the temple on charity any longer. Come with me to Athens, and take the position that I plan for you as the son of a rich and powerful king."
30. Ibid., 578-580, French p. 207; English p. 59: "Come with me to Athens, and take the position that I plan for you, as the son of a rich and powerful king. It is true there is a cloud over your birth; but at least no one shall call you poor. Your wealth will establish your blood as royal."
31. The discussion develops from 540 to 560, French pp. 205-207; English pp. 58-59.
32. Ibid., 669-676, French p. 211; English pp. 61-62.

by the tirade which we will consider for a while—he wants the truth
because he wants to justify the right. He wants to justify his right,
his political right at Athens. He wants the right to speak there, to say
everything, speak the truth, and speak freely. In order to justify his
parrēsia he needs the truth finally to be told, a truth which will found
this right. This then is why, after Xuthus has warmly embraced him
and more or less convinced him that, all in all, he is more or less his
son, Ion says: Yes, but it's not enough. "Things, father, have a different
aspect depending upon whether they are seen from afar or from nearby
[I think "nearby" should be understood in the sense of very local: at
Athens; at Delphi you may say, in short, that I am your son and then
that I will return to exercise power, but at Athens [this is something
else]; M.F.]; certainly, I am grateful that chance has led me to find a
father in you; but listen to the thought that comes to mind."[1] And then
the question is precisely that of the place where power must be exercised: Athens. "It is said that the autochthonous and glorious people of
Athens is free of any foreign mixture. Now this is where I fall down,
afflicted by the double misfortune of being both the son of a foreigner
and a bastard. Branded as such, if I do not have power, I will remain, as
the saying goes, a *Nobody, son of Nobody*. If, on the other hand, I seek to
occupy the front rank, if I aspire to become somebody, I will be hated
by the crowd of those without ability; superiority is always unbearable.
And those who are good and able, who wisely keep silent and avoid
politics, will find me quite foolish and ridiculous for not keeping quiet
in the troubled town. Finally, those who combine politics and reason
will vote against me all the more if I achieve honors; for that is the way
things are father. Those with the advantage of both power and position
are the most determined against their rivals. Then, having arrived as
an intruder in another's home, that of a childless woman who for long
has shared your pain and who, disappointed and alone, will not support her destiny without bitterness, I will justly be the victim of her
hatred."[2]

I shall come back to this passage. I would like to re-read the first
part of the text and of the rejoinder. What do we see in Ion's objections to his quasi-father, his pseudo-father Xuthus? First of all, he
says, Athens is autochthonous. This is Athens' old claim: unlike other
Greek peoples, the Athenians have always inhabited Athens, they are

born from its very soil, and Erechtheus, born from the soil of Athens, is the guarantee of this. Second, not only is Athens autochthonous, it is also pure of any foreign element. This also refers to an important theme in Euripides—for example, in a fragment of a lost play called *Erechtheus*. In other cities, Euripides says, one lives like pieces moved around in the game of jackstraws, of backgammon; new elements are constantly being introduced like poorly fixed pegs in a piece of wood.[3] Actually this refers to a quite precise piece of legislation. From the middle of the fifth century, from 450-451, legislation peculiar to Athens, which is not found in most other Greek cities, refused the right of citizenship to children with an Athenian father and a non-Athenian mother.[4] In other words, from the middle of the fifth century both parents had to be Athenian. The aim of this extremely strict legislation, again, typical of Athens, was to avoid a marked increase in the number of citizens. Its effect was also, of course, to reduce their number. And precisely, in the second part of the Peloponnesian War when, weakened by plague, war, and defeats, Athens needs citizens, the legislation is overturned. But in 418, when Euripides is writing *Ion*, it has not yet come to this and the law is still in force. And, following a procedure which is usual with these legendary re-elaborations, the ancient nature of the law is emphasized, although it is actually a very recent law. And here Ion is supposed to refer to an absolutely original tradition of Athens and say: Athens is pure of any foreign mixture, that is to say, every citizen must be born of a mother and father who are both citizens. Instead he says: "Now this is where I fall down, afflicted by the double misfortune of being both the son of a foreigner and a bastard."[5] That is to say, he is not even the son of an Athenian and a foreign woman. He is the son of a non-Athenian, Xuthus, and a girl from who knows where. So: "Branded as such, if I do not have power, I will remain...a *Nobody, son of Nobody*."[6] Nobody, son of no one: he will be nothing at all.

And this is where the second development begins. I do not think the translation does full justice to and does not clearly reconstruct a text whose discursivity is quite legible. He says: If I wish to arrive at the front rank (*eis to prōton zugon*: for the front rank)[7]—note that [it is not a question] of exercising tyrannical, monarchical power, the power of a single individual; occupying the front rank is being one of those who are in the front rank of the town—then he says, I will find myself

(I am schematizing, but this is how the text is constructed) facing three categories of citizens. The text says: "I will be hated by the crowd of those without ability. And those who are good and able, who wisely keep silent and avoid politics, will find me quite foolish and ridiculous for not keeping quiet in the troubled town. Finally, those who combine politics and reason...."[8] In fact, three categories of citizens are evoked. In another text by Euripides, *The Suppliant Women*, there are also three categories of citizen: the rich, the poor, and those in the middle.[9] We also have a distinction between three terms, but here it is completely different. For it is a matter of three categories of citizen who are divided up, not by reference to wealth, but in relation to what Ion defines as his objective, or his hypothetical objective: to be in the front rank of the town. [With regard to] the distribution of power, authority, and effective influence in the town, there are three categories of citizen. Now what I think has to be understood is that it is not a matter of three, if you like, legal categories of citizens who do not have the same poll tax status. We are dealing with Athenian democracy. It is a question of the effective distribution of political authority, of the exercise of power among and within the mass or set formed by legal citizens. It is not even a question of those who lack certain rights, either as slaves, of course, metics, or foreigners. No, we are dealing with citizens, and among these citizens there are three categories.

Tōn men adunatōn:[10] with regard to those who are *adunatōn* ("powerless"). I think we should clarify this text through another text which is also in *The Suppliant Women* and where it is a question of citizens who have ability and are powerful, who by themselves and through their wealth can do something for the city.[11] The first category evoked by Ion here is those who do not even have this ability, this power to do something, by themselves or through their wealth, for the city. That is to say, they do not even have the wherewithal to buy weapons and armor in order to take part in war, and they do not belong to those who bring wealth into the city or who make it prosperous. Faced with someone like Ion who, arriving as an intruder and branded as a bastard, would like to take power, this crowd without ability, this mass of citizens, who are full legal citizens but lack that something "more" which characterizes political authority, all of this group could display only envy and anger. At any rate, these people always detest those who are stronger, whoever they may be. So, [Ion says], I will be exposed to the hostility of the powerless, or of those who have no political authority in our land. I will come up against their hostility, an even stronger hostility, because of my birth.

The second category of citizen—and then this is very interesting—is those who are *khrēstoi* and *dunamenoi*. *Dunamenoi*,[12] that is to say: those who can do something, those whose birth, status, and wealth give them the means to exercise power. *Khrēstoi*, that is to say they are "good," morally estimable people. In short, this is the elite, and it is indeed this term *khrēstoi* that Xenophon, for example, or rather the pseudo-Xenophon uses to designate the elite in *The Constitution of the Athenians*.[13] Anyway, among these people, these *dunamenoi* and *khrēstoi*, there are those who are also *sophoi* (who are wise). And these, "*sigōsin kai ou speudosin eis ta pragmata*";[14] these people keep quiet and do not concern themselves with *ta pragmata* (the affairs of the city). So we have this second category of citizens who belong to the good people, to the powerful people, to the people who have wealth, birth, and status, but whose wisdom means that they do not concern themselves with politics. To not be concerned with politics, with affairs, is also to remain silent. How will these people react when they see a bastard intruder try to push himself to the front rank? Well, quite simply they will find it ridiculous. They will find it ridiculous that this bastard intruder does not keep quiet in the city (*hēsukhazein*).[15] So here we clearly have a philosophical theme concerning that form of belonging to a city which, while being rich, powerful, well-born, etcetera, consists in being a *sophos*,[16] someone wise who does not concern himself with affairs and who keeps himself in *hēsukhia*, in peace and quiet, in idleness, in what the Latins will call *otium*.

The citizens of the third category are also rich and powerful citizens, good people. But unlike the *sophoi* (the wise), who keep quiet and concern themselves with their own affairs, these "*logō to khrōmenōn te tē polei*,"[17] they deal with politics and reason (*khrōmenōn*, from the verb *khrēstai*: make use of, practice, be concerned with; both *logos* and *polis*: they deal with both *logos* and *polis*; and these, of course, are the ones who represent political authority). You can see that this third category is absolutely opposed on every point to the preceding category, but they also belong to the category of good people. There is the category of good people who keep quiet and do not concern themselves with *pragmata*, and there is the category of people who make use of, concern themselves with, manipulate, have to do with, and practice both *logos* (that is to say they do not keep quiet, they speak) and the *polis* (they are concerned with the affairs of the town). I think there is an exact, term for term opposition. The latter category, says the text moreover, have the town, they possess the town, they control the town and have the honors. These are the people one would risk coming up against in the form of rivalry: they, he says, would not put up with competition and with their votes would try to condemn or exclude those who offend them.

So in the city and in relation to these three categories of characters who are, once again, three categories of legal citizens—the poor without power; then, within the powerful, those who keep quiet and do not concern themselves with city affairs; and those who make use of *logos* and *polis*—the bastard intruder Ion will be too much, he will be in the way. With [what] consequences? [The answer is found in] the text I have begun reading to you.[18] As the bastard son of a foreign father he will be unwelcome in the very family in which he will live, that is to say the family of Xuthus and Creusa. Creusa, who on the one hand is Athenian by birth, the daughter of Erechtheus, and, on the other, the legitimate wife, will not tolerate it. There will therefore be hatred in the home of the sovereigns, in the home of the king, of the monarch and his wife, anyway in the home in which harmony is absolutely indispensable to the city's harmony. Either Xuthus will take the part of his illegitimate son against his wife, and this will mean the destruction of peace in the household, or he will take the part of his wife against his son and thereby betray Ion. In any case, Ion will be too much in relation to the structure of the chief's house whose harmony is indispensable to the public good and the peace of the entire city. And on the other side, on the public stage, he will be unwelcome. For coming from outside, forcibly imposed with his illegitimate birth, the only power he will be able to exercise—and this is what appears at the end of the text—will be that of tyranny. He will be like those tyrants who were imposed on Greek cities from outside, who came under the protection of Zeus. Now Xuthus happens to be, precisely a descendant of Zeus, so the reference to tyrannical power is fairly clear. [Ion] could arrive in

Athens, and remain there, only as a tyrant. Now the tyrant's existence, he says, is detestable, and in no way does he want to lead that life.[19] He prefers to remain near the god where he lives a calm and quiet life. This is why, after having accepted the paternity offered to him by Xuthus, Ion finishes by saying: No, in the end I do not want to go to Athens for the reasons I have given.

At this point Xuthus insists and emphasizes that things can still be arranged (with Xuthus we are always in this realm of arranging things), and he says: It's very simple, we will not say straightaway that you are my son, or that you are my heir, or that I will grant you power, but we will do it all softly and gradually. We will choose the right moment to tell Creusa so that she accepts it without grief or difficulty. And Ion accepts this arrangement.[20] He accepts it with the result that he agrees to go with Xuthus to take part in a feast to thank the god for the revelation (in reality the deceptive revelation) he has made. And then, after, they will leave for Athens and Ion's presence will gradually be imposed in the household of Creusa and Xuthus. Ion accepts, but not without adding this, which is the text I wanted to explain to you: I will go then, but destiny (*tukhē*) has not yet given me everything.[21] He agrees to go to Athens, but "if I do not find she who bore me, my life is impossible [*abiōton hēmin*: it is impossible for us to live; M.F.] and, if I am permitted to make a wish, may this woman be Athenian, so that through my mother I have the right to speak freely. If a stranger enters a town where the race is without stain, the law may make him a citizen, but his tongue will remain servile."[22] He will not have *parrēsia: ouk ekhei parrēsian.*[23] So why does he want *parrēsia* so much? Why does the absence of *parrēsia* wreck the vague scheme constructed by Xuthus, why anyway, when Ion accepts this vague scheme, is he not satisfied and still wants to know who his mother is so as to obtain *parrēsia*? It seems to me that in this lack of *parrēsia* which is shown in this way and so bothers Ion, we can see a [...].*

You can see very clearly that *parrēsia* is not exactly the same as the exercise of power. For Xuthus possesses power itself, authority over the city, sovereignty—a monarchical or tyrannical type of sovereignty—and he is ready to pass it on to his son. The magnificent ancestry that goes

---

* Inaudible.

back to Zeus, the real power he exercises at Athens, and the wealth
he has accumulated are not and will not be enough to give Ion *parrēsia*.
Parrēsia is not therefore the exercise of power itself.* But you can also
see that it is not just the status of citizen. Certainly, with Athenian
legislation—that of 451, but supposed to be in force already—he cannot
be a citizen because his mother is not Athenian. But what is interesting in the text is precisely that he says: Even if the law made someone
a citizen, even if he is therefore legally a citizen, he still does not have
parrēsia. In other words, he cannot get *parrēsia* through his father, who
gives him power, or through the law, if it existed, which would give him
the status of citizen. He demands this *parrēsia* from his mother. Does
this mean that we are dealing here with the survival or expression of
some matrilineal right? I really don't think so. We should recall Ion's
particular situation. He has a father who was welcomed on Athenian
soil but who is not of Greek origin. Second, he does not know who his
mother is. And third, he wants to exercise a power, he wants to be
in the front rank of the city. He could receive his father's tyrannical
power, but this would not suffice for what he wants to do. What he
wants to do, therefore, is to be in the front rank of the city. And to be in
the front rank in the city—or rather, to be involved in the city by being
in its front rank, being bound to it—he needs *parrēsia*. This *parrēsia* is
therefore something other than the pure and simple status of citizen,
and it is not given by tyrannical power. What is it?

I think *parrēsia* is, in a way, a discourse spoken from above, which
comes from a source higher than the status of the citizen, and which is
different from the pure and simple exercise of power. It is a form of discourse which will exercise power in the framework of the city, but of
course in non-tyrannical conditions, that is to say, allowing others the
freedom to speak, the freedom of those who also wish to be in the front
rank, and who may be in the front rank in this sort of agonistic game
typical of political life in Greece and especially in Athens. It is then a
discourse spoken from above, but which leaves others the freedom to
speak, and allows freedom to those who have to obey, or leaves them
free at least insofar as they will only obey if they can be persuaded.

---

* The manuscript clarifies: "*Parrēsia* is not the language of command; it is not speech which
places others under its yoke."

What constitutes *parrēsia* is, I think, the exercise of a form of discourse which persuades others whom one commands and which, in an agonistic game, allows freedom for others who also wish to command. With, of course, all the effects associated with such a struggle and situation. First: that the words one utters fail to persuade and the crowd turns against you. Or that the discourse of others, to which one leaves space alongside one's own, may prevail over your discourse. What constitutes the field peculiar to *parrēsia* is this political risk of a discourse which leaves room free for other discourse and assumes the task, not of bending others to one's will, but of persuading them. What is making use of this *parrēsia* within the framework of the city if not, precisely, and in accordance with what has just been said, handling, dealing with both *logos* and *polis*? *Parrēsia* consists in making use of *logos* in the *polis—logos* in the sense of true, reasonable discourse, discourse which persuades, and discourse which may confront other discourse and will triumph only through the weight of its truth and the effectiveness of its persuasion—*parrēsia* consists in making use of this true, reasonable, agonistic discourse, this discourse of debate, in the field of the *polis*. And, once again, neither the effective exercise of tyrannical power nor the simple status of citizen can give this *parrēsia*.

Who, then, can give this *parrēsia*? It is here that Euripides emphasizes, if not his solution, at least his suggestion. He says: it must come from the mother. But, once again, in no way is this a reference to some matrilineal right; it is a function of Ion's very situation until now that, while he has a brilliant father, since he comes from Zeus, and an all-powerful father, since he exercises power at Athens, he was not born at Athens. It is simply belonging to the land, autochthony, being rooted in the soil, this historical continuity based on a territory, which alone can give *parrēsia*. In other words, the question of *parrēsia* corresponds to an historical problem, to an extremely precise political problem at the time when Euripides writes *Ion*. The situation is that of democratic Athens, of the Athens in which Pericles has been dead for a dozen years, of that democratic Athens in which all the people, of course, had the right to vote, while the best of them and the best of all (Pericles) in fact exercised authority and political power. In this post-Periclean Athens the problem arises of who will really exercise power within the framework of legal citizenship. Given that the law is equal for all (the principle of *isonomia*), and given that everyone has the right to vote and to give his opinion (*isēgoria*), who will have the possibility and the right of *parrēsia*, that is to say, to stand up, speak, try to persuade the people, and try to prevail over his rivals, at the risk, moreover, of losing the right to live in Athens, as happens when a political leader is exiled or ostracized, and possibly of his own life? Anyway, who must take this risk of political discourse and exercise the authority bound up with it? This was the debate at Athens at this time, between Cleon, the democrat, the demagogue, etcetera, who claimed that everyone should be able to have this *parrēsia*, and, on the other hand, let's say the movement of an aristocratic tendency around Nicias, who thought that *parrēsia* should in fact be reserved to an elite. Different solutions will be tried in the great crisis in Athens provoked by the second part of the Peloponnesian War. When Euripides is writing, the crisis has not yet clearly broken out, but the problem arises. And it is at this time or around this time that we see new constitutional projects being formulated in Athens. Euripides has no desire to put forward a constitutional solution in *Ion* which would say who should exercise *parrēsia*, but we can clearly see the context in which he formulates the question: this context is one in which, as the text clearly shows, *parrēsia* cannot be inherited as a violent, tyrannical power, and no more is it simply entailed purely by the status of the citizen; it must be reserved only for some and cannot be obtained as a matter of course. And what Euripides suggests is that belonging to the land, autochthony, this being historically rooted in a territory will assure the individual of the exercise of this *parrēsia*.

I am not deducing what I am saying here about the immediate political context of this problem and theme of *parrēsia* in *Ion* from what I said earlier about the fundamental character of this tragedy as a drama of truth-telling, and as a sort of founding representation of truth-telling. I think that this play immediately corresponds, in fact, to a precise political problem, [and] that at the same time it is the Greek drama about the political history of truth-telling, about the foundation, both legendary and true, of truth-telling in the realm of politics. That the main, fundamental part of history takes place through the fine, slender thread of events is something [to which] I think we should reconcile ourselves, or rather that [we should] bravely confront. History, and the main part of history, passes through the eye of a needle. It is then in this small constitutional conflict over the exercise of power at Athens that the great drama, *Ion*, is formulated as the drama of the formulation of the truth, and of the foundation of political truth-telling, in terms of oracular truth-telling. How can we pass from this oracular truth-telling to political truth-telling?

This is what emerges even more clearly in the second part of the play. The god who must tell the truth is present. I have shown you why and how he refused to tell the truth. How can we get beyond the approximate truth that Xuthus proposed to Ion, and which Ion was so hesitant to accept, how can we surmount the secret kept by the god, owing to his oracular ambiguity, and also because he is ashamed to confess his offense? Well, it is precisely to humans that we must turn, for the god will remain mute, ambiguous, and ashamed. Humans will forge the path to truth-telling, to the truth-telling about Ion's birth which will finally be able to establish his right to tell the truth in the city.

How do things work out? I would like to try to speed up a little; I will at least start the analysis of the second part. Just as the truth is revealed by halves in *Oedipus*, here too there is a game of halves, or rather two games of halves. We have had a first game of halves: Creusa putting her distorted question; Xuthus putting his innocent question; and the god giving a distorted answer. This is the first point. Now, Ion has practically agreed to play this game of distorted truth or of semi-lie. He has half accepted it, but he is not entirely satisfied. He still has this remainder, this need to justify the *parrēsia* that he has not managed to establish. The final stretch will also be covered in two parts: on the woman's side on the one hand, and the god's truth-telling on the other—and you will see how reticent and allusive this is.

First, the woman's side. For Ion's birth to be revealed in its truth, the two partners responsible for his birth, Creusa and Apollo, must tell the truth. This, then, is what happens on Creusa's side: Ion, having accepted willy-nilly the solution proposed by Xuthus, decides to go with him to take part in the thanksgiving banquet. So he leaves the stage, with Xuthus warning the chorus to remain silent, since, according to their agreement, it is understood that Ion will just return to Athens, and gradually, so as not to hurt Creusa, the truth will be told and it will be said that Ion really is Xuthus' heir. Everyone therefore

1. Euripides, *Ion*, 585-588, French pp. 207-208; English p. 60: "Things have one appearance when far away, and quite another when looked at closely. I welcome the chance that has discovered you as my father; but there are certain facts that I realize now."

2. Ibid., 586-611, French p. 208; English p. 60: "The Athenians, I am told, are not settlers, but a race born from their own soil; and I shall arrive among them with two disadvantages—my father a foreigner, and myself born, as you say, under a cloud. So long as I remain without power, this disgrace will brand me as a nobody. If, on the other hand, I struggle to be somebody in politics, and reach the front rank, I shall be hated by those who have no ability—success is always unpopular; while those who have ability, and could rise, will be clever enough to sit back and look on, and laugh at me for a busy fool inviting the slander of the city. Established politicians will use their brains and influence to frustrate my ambition. It is always so: place and power have no mercy on a rival. Then, your home is not mine: I am an alien. Your wife has no child; now instead of sharing her sorrow with you as before, she must bear it alone in bitterness of heart. She will hate me, and rightly."

3. "Other cities, like pieces set out on a board, are formed of elements imported from every origin. Whoever comes from a foreign town to settle in a different town is like a poor peg stuck in a beam: he is a citizen in name, in fact he is not" in Euripide, *Œuvres*, t. VIII-2, *Fragments*, trans., F. Jouan and H. Van Looy (Paris: Les Belles Lettres, 2000), "Érechthée," 14, 9-14, fr. 360, 5, p. 119. Foucault uses the translation of the fragment proposed by H. Grégoire, in *Ion*, note 1, p. 208.

4. In 451, on the proposal of Pericles, the Assembly voted a decree restricting the conditions of access to Athenian citizenship (Aristotle, *Constitution of Athens*, 46). Previously, it was enough to have an Athenian father. Henceforth, in the terms of the law, it will be necessary to have both a free Athenian father and a free Athenian mother to be a fully-fledged citizen. In 411, after serious military defeats, a first coup d'État (of the Four Hundred, *hoi tetrakosioi*) overturned the democratic regime and restricted the body of citizens to the wealthiest.

5. Euripides, *Ion*, 592, French p. 208; English p. 60.

6. Ibid., 594.

7. Ibid., 595, "*ēn d'es to prōton poleōs hormēteis zugon*"; French: "If, on the other hand, I seek to arrive at the front rank"; English: "If, on the other hand, I...reach the front rank."

8. Ibid., 597-602.

9. Euripides, *The Suppliant Women*, 238-245. French translation by H. Grégoire, *Les Suppliantes* in Euripide, *Tragédies*, t. III, p. 112: "There are, in fact, three classes in the State. First of all, the rich, useless citizens endlessly concerned with increasing their wealth. Then the poor, lacking even the bare necessities. These are dangerous, for inclined to envy, seduced by the discourse of perverted demagogues, they assail the wealthy with cruel gibes. Of the three classes, in short, it is the middle class which saves cities; it is this class which maintains the institutions of the State"; English translation by Phillip Vellacott, *The Suppliant Women* in *Orestes and Other Plays* (Harmondsworth: Penguin, 1972) p. 201: "Citizens/Are of three orders. First, the rich; they are useless, and/Insatiable for more wealth. Next, the very poor,/The starving; these are dangerous; their chief motive is/Envy—they shoot their malice at those better off,/Swallowing the vicious lies of so-called champions./The middle order is the city's life and health;/They guard the frame and system which the state ordains."

10. Euripides, *Ion*, 596, French p. 208, "the incompetent crowd"; English p. 60, "those who have no ability."

11. In the long tirade of Theseus, the importance of the best (*aristoi*) appears negatively, when he emphasizes that the tyrant hates them whereas a city in which the people govern favors them. *The Suppliant Women*, 442-446, French p. 119; English pp. 207-208.

12. "*Hosoi de khrēstoi dunamenoi te*." Euripides, *Ion*, 598, French p. 208: "the good and the capable"; English p. 60: "those who have ability, and could rise."

13. Pseudo-Xenophon [The Old Oligarch], *The Constitution of the Athenians*, trans. Hartvig Frish in H. Frish, *The Constitution of the Athenians: A Philological-Historical Analysis of Pseudo-Xenophon's Treatise De Re Publica Atheniensium* (Copenhagen: Glydedalske Boghandel-Nordisk Forlage, 1942) ch. 1, §1-6, pp. 13-15: "Indeed, as to the constitution of the Athenians my opinion is that I do not at all approve of their having chosen this form of constitution because by

making this choice they have given the advantage to the vulgar people at the cost of the good (*khrēstous*)...Then there is the thing at which several people wonder, that they everywhere give the vulgar and the poor and the common people the preference to the aristocrats (*khrēstois*)...For if [only] the aristocracy (*khrēstoi*) were allowed to speak and took part in the debate, it would good to them and their peers, but not to the proletarians."

14. Euripides, *Ion*, 599, French p. 208; English p. 60.
15. Ibid., 601: "*oukh hēsukhazōn en polei phobou plea*"; French, "for not keeping quiet in the troubled town"; English, "laugh at me for a busy fool inviting the slander of the city."
16. Ibid., 598, "*ontes sophoi*."
17. Ibid., 602.
18. Ibid., 607-647, French pp. 208-210; English p. 60.
19. Ibid., 621-622, French p. 209: "And then, beneath a pleasant exterior, the kingship (*turannidos*) that is idly praised, is a sad thing"; English p. 60: "As for being a king, it is overrated. Royalty conceals a life of torment behind a pleasant facade."
20. Ibid., 650-667, French pp. 210-211; English p. 61.
21. Ibid., 678, French p. 211; English p. 62.
22. Ibid., 669-675.
23. Ibid., 675.
24. Ibid., 725-726, French p. 213; English p. 63.

seven

26 JANUARY 1983

First hour

[
Continuation and end of the comparison between Ion *and* Oedipus:
*the truth does not arise from an investigation but from the clash of
passions.* ∽ *The rule of illusions and passions.* ∽ *The cry of confession and accusation.* ∽ *G. Dumézil's analyses of Apollo.* ∽
Dumézil's categories applied to Ion. ∽ *Tragic modulation of the
theme of the voice.* ∽ *Tragic modulation of the theme of gold.*
]

SO, IF YOU LIKE, we will continue reading *Ion*, and I would like to
pursue it in the following way: to read this tragedy as a tragedy of
truth-telling, of *parrēsia*, of the foundation of free-spokenness. As you
know, this tragedy tells the story of the secret son born of Creusa's
secret lovemaking with Apollo, a son who is abandoned, exposed,
disappears, is thought to be dead, and that his mother, now accompanied by Xuthus, her lawful husband, comes to ask for her son again
from the Apollo at Delphi. And when she comes, accompanied by
Xuthus, to ask Apollo for her son again, or to find out from Apollo
what could have become of this disappeared son, the son is there in
front of her. He is in front of her in the guise of a temple servant, but
she does not know that he is her son. And he, not knowing his own
identity, does not know that he is looking at his mother. Such then,
you can see, is the somewhat oedipal story of the exposed son who
is lost and then finds himself in front of his parents, or his mother,
but not knowing who she is. It is an oedipal story except for the

fact that Oedipus—you recall I tried to emphasize this—precisely in discovering who he was, was driven from his land, whereas the situation is exactly the reverse in Ion's case, since he needs to know who he is in order to be able to return home with authority, and to exercise there the fundamental rights of speech. And it is when he has discovered who he is that he will be able to return home. So there is, if you like, an oedipal framework, but with an exactly opposite meaning, polarity, and orientation.

I am aware that in telling you this story of the young man who can only gain access to the truth and to truth-telling at the price of having to drag out the secret of his birth, it may be thought, as I reminded you last week, that we are dealing with an invariant: for the child, access to the truth involves discovering the secret of his birth. But I am obviously not interested in the play *Ion* for the purpose of extracting this kind of invariant (one always needs a mommy in order to speak). Rather, I want to try to see the particular determinations in this play by Euripides,* and we can say in classical Athens, of a juridical, polit-ical, and religious principle, namely, that the right and duty of telling the truth—a right and duty intrinsic to the exercise of power—can only be based on two conditions: one, that a genealogy, in the double sense of historical continuity and territorial belonging, is brought out and truthfully told; and the other, that this truth-telling of the genealogy, this truthful revelation of the genealogy has a certain relationship to the truth spoken by the god, even if this truth is violently dragged out of him.

The play recounts this extraction of the truth and genealogy, and I would like to return to the point we reached in the plot last week. You recall what has happened: Xuthus and Creusa had come to consult Apollo. Creusa, for her part, had said what she had come in search of, which was not exactly the same thing as Xuthus. She had invented the half-lie that she had come in her sister's name to ask what had become of this sister's illegitimate son. A half-lie in order to get the truth. Meanwhile, Xuthus, conducting his own consultation, had asked the god if he would ever have a descendant. And the god had replied

---

* Foucault pronounces the name here "Euridipe." [The French for Oedipus is, of course, "Œdipe"; G.B.]

through a half-lie, which is in a way symmetrical to Creusa's half-false question, saying to Xuthus: I will give you the first person you meet. And the first person Xuthus meets on leaving the temple is, of course, Ion. The god had therefore given an answer which was only very partially true. He had in fact given Xuthus and Creusa someone who could serve as a son to them, but in short the god's truth-telling was, to say the least, inexact. Let's say, in the strict sense of the term, the god had proposed a hybrid (*bâtarde*) solution. Now this hybrid solution—Ion, son of Creusa and Apollo, who Apollo falsely represents as the illegitimate son of Xuthus—is clearly lacking something, because if Ion really is the son of Xuthus, then, since Xuthus is in reality a foreigner to Athens who was integrated into the Athenian city only as a result of helping the Athenians carry off a victory, and then by marrying Creusa who was given to him in reward, it follows that his son will not be able to benefit from the ancestral rights of the exercise of political power. And Ion is perfectly aware of this. When Xuthus recognizes him, or believes he recognizes him as his son, Ion is very reticent, very hesitant, and says: But if I return to Athens as Xuthus' bastard, either I will be nothing at all ("*A nobody, son of no-one*"), or I will be a tyrant. In any case, under these conditions he will not be able to benefit from that extra something which enables one to occupy the front rank ("*prōton zugon*") and thereby exercise power over the city using rational and true language. He will not be given this common use of *logos* and *polis*, this government of the *polis* by *logos*, legitimately. To be granted *parrēsia*, the use of the town and of rational and true language, it is necessary to move forward, go beyond this hybrid and illusory solution initially proposed by the oracle, take a new plunge to get to the very heart of the truth.

Today I would like to analyze this second part of the play, which is as complex, troubled ("full of sound and fury"), and shot through with passions and events as the first part was calm, hieratic, simple, and rather Sophoclean. Here again, if you like, we can make a bit of a comparison between *Ion* and *Oedipus the King*. As you know, it is not the oracle who tells the secret of the birth in *Oedipus the King*. The oracle has simply caught Oedipus in a kind of pincer movement: first there are the very ancient prophetic words pronounced by the god, which Oedipus escapes just as his parents wished, and then there are the present day signs sent by the god, which are first the plague, and then Creon's answer. Between these two sets of expressions, verdicts, decrees, and signs sent by the god, Oedipus can only question others and himself. Spurred on by these different signs, issued by the god in the past and again now, Oedipus decides to conduct the inquiry himself. You recall that Sophocles' text shows with what tenacious determination Oedipus decided to get to the heart of the truth whatever the cost to himself, and he says so from the start. Unlike *Oedipus*, and despite the analogies of situation I have spoken about, the process of disclosing the truth in *Ion*, the alethurgic procedure, does not have a principal agent or central actor. In fact, the truth will be brought to light through successive fragments, somewhat as in *Oedipus*, but it will come to light in spite of everyone; in spite of the god and in spite of the characters. Or at any rate, it is not so much that the characters will try to bring out the truth—no one takes charge of this work of the truth—as the clash of the different characters' passions in relation to each other, and essentially the clash of Creusa's and Ion's passions, each confronted by the other inasmuch they have not recognized each other and believe themselves to be enemies; it is this clash of passions which will make the truth blaze forth at a given moment, without anyone being in charge, without a will seeking out this truth, without anyone undertaking the inquiry and seeing it through to the end. One of the major differences between *Ion* and *Oedipus the King* is the relationship between *alētheia* and *pathos* (between truth and passion). In the case of *Oedipus*, Oedipus undertakes to seek the truth personally, using his own power. And it is when he has finally found the truth that he falls under the blow of fate and, as a consequence, his whole life appears as *pathos* (suffering, passion). In the case of *Ion*, on the other hand, a number of characters confront each other on the basis of their passions. And it is from the clash, the lightning flash of these passions that, without the characters really willing it, the truth arises between them, as it were, a truth which precisely will bring about complete appeasement of the passions.

So you see now how this alethurgy is brought about. I think we can recognize two major moments. Here again, consider *Oedipus*. You know that in *Oedipus*, when the issue was not the discovery of the crime but the discovery of Oedipus' birth, first of all the servant from Corinth had to tell how Oedipus was not in fact born at Corinth but had been received from someone else from, precisely, Thebes. Then, in the second part, a second part of this second part, we see the old servant from Cithaeron, the old Theban say: Well, yes, I was given Oedipus by Jocasta, and so this really is Oedipus. So, there were two halves. In the same way there are halves in *Ion*. A half concerning the birth will be told by Creusa, who will say: Yes, before marrying Xuthus I had a child; I was seduced by Apollo and had a child who was born on the slopes of the Acropolis. Then a second half will be required to complete the truth, namely that this child, born on the slopes of the Acropolis, was taken by Apollo, or Apollo had Hermes take him, and was brought to Delphi where he became Apollo's servant. And at that moment this will really be Ion. And the two halves of the truth fit together, and we will have the famous two halves of the ceramic token comprising the *sumbolon* involved in *Oedipus the King*.[1]

How, in the first, Creusa half, if you like, is Creusa brought to tell this truth that she dared not tell at the start of the play, when, avoiding the truth, she said: I come on behalf of my sister who had a brief affair and a son that I would really like to find for her? How will she be brought to say: Yes, I had a son? I think this is roughly the point we reached last week. The mechanism which will lead Creusa to recognize her son is the following. You recall that Xuthus, having recognized or believing that he had recognized his son, came to an agreement with Ion that they would return to Athens without telling the whole truth. And so as not to hurt Creusa, they had decided that they would let it be thought that, well, Ion was "just" returning, as a servant, a companion of Xuthus, and then gradually one would say: There you have it, Ion is really the son of Xuthus. And this lie, concocted for the best reasons in the world, was hatched in the presence of the chorus, who had therefore heard the whole conversation and had been warned by Xuthus: Above all, say nothing of this to Creusa, our secret must be closely kept. Now the chorus is made up of Creusa's servants, that is to say, of Athenian women, women of the gynaeceum, and so of women whose status and function is to preserve. Through their status as guardians of the women's place, of births, and also as keepers of their customs, these women are on Creusa's side, on the side of the autochthonous Athenian lineage going back

is exactly the opposite of the truth. It was the god himself who did
this. And who told the dirty little shameful lie that the tutor attributes to Xuthus? Apollo! It was Apollo who, through shame and not
wanting to reveal the child he had fathered with Creusa, thought of
attributing it to someone else. So you see that, in a sense, the tutor is
entirely mistaken, yet in getting it wrong he is fairly close to the truth.
Anyway, with the chorus, Creusa, and the tutor, we are in a world of
half-truths and illusions.

This is the point at which Creusa, in the depths of illusion and
humiliation, bursts out with the truth. But it is important to understand that she does not do so in order to make her own right prevail,
revealing the birth of a glorious son. She bursts out with the truth only
in shame, humiliation, and anger. Creusa does not tell a truth in order
to turn the situation to her advantage, for, in the state she is in and at
the point the plot has reached, she cannot know that the situation will
turn in her favor. But already completely humiliated by all that has
happened, [Creusa] adds a further, supplementary humiliation. Not
only am I sterile, she says, not only do I have no son by Xuthus, and
not only does Xuthus foist a son on me who is not mine, but on top
of that, before marrying Xuthus I committed an offense, and I will
say what it was. And Creusa's confession, anyway the first part of her
confession—for you will see that there are two parts—the first form
of confession is announced by these lines: "Dead, alas, are my hopes
that I thought to see fulfilled by keeping my offense, my tear-drenched
labor, secret.—No, by the starry palace of Zeus, by the goddess who
reigns over my rocks, by the holy shore of the Tritonian Lake, I will
no longer conceal my offense: I want relief from it and to breathe more
freely. Tears spring from my eyes, my soul suffers. All have hurt my
soul, humans and immortals. Ah! I shall convict them of ungrateful
treachery to poor women!"[3] So, a discourse of humiliation, a discourse
of weeping, a discourse in tears, and a discourse of the offense, in which
precisely (we will come back to this shortly) we will have to speak of
the injustice of others. But, once again, if she speaks of the injustice of
others, this is not at all so that she can turn the situation to her advantage. In a way, she does so in order draw to herself, to summon around
herself, all the misfortunes and injustices of which she has been the
victim.

So this is where Creusa's first confession begins. [...]* She speaks
to Apollo and says to him: "Oh you who make the seven string lyre
sing, and the Muse's sonorous hymns vibrate on the rustic animals'
lifeless horns, oh son of Leto, I accuse you in the full light of this day
that shines on me! You came to me, in the radiance of your golden hair,
while I gathered saffron flowers in my robe, reflections of your gold to
weave into garlands. Gripping my pale wrists, you dragged me, crying
out 'mother!' to your bed, deep in a cave, seducer-god, and did without shame what Kypris [Aphrodite; G.B.] wanted! And I bore you a
son, poor soul, who, from fear of my mother, I exposed in your bed, at
the spot where you took—oh wretched embrace!—the pitiful wretch I
am! Woe to me! He is lost, the prey of birds, your son and mine, poor
soul! And you, you play the lyre and do nothing but sing your paeans!
Oh! it is you I call, the son of Leto who dispenses oracles, seated on
your golden throne at the center of the earth. Let this cry reach your
ears! Go on then, cowardly seducer, you, owing nothing to my husband, install a son in his home, while my child, and yours, unworthy
father, has disappeared, taken by the birds of prey, far from his swad-
dling clothes...Delos hates you, and so to the laurel which, with the
fine-haired palm, shelters the cradle where Leto, in noble childbirth,
brought you into the world, son of Zeus."⁴ So I would like to analyze
this passage a little. First of all, I would like us to pause for a moment
on the way in which Creusa addresses Apollo, since Creusa's confession
is made to the one who knows, and who knows better than anyone,
since Apollo himself seduced her and is the father of her child. She
thus turns back against Apollo a truth that he knows full well. How
and why does she turn it against him? Or rather, if we want to know
why, we need to know how—how she addresses him, evokes him, calls
out to him, and names him. There are two passages in the text where
she calls out to Apollo directly. Right at the start: "Oh you who makes
the seven string lyre sing, and the Muse's sonorous hymns vibrate on
the rustic animals' lifeless horns, oh son of Leto, I accuse you in the full
light of this day that shines on me!" And at line 906, at the beginning

* M.F.: This is the one I have photocopied and distributed, so it would be good if you could not
hold on too much individually to the sheets...so it's not like primary school where it's only the
good pupils in the front row who have the right to the truth, so it would be good of you to circulate them a bit. Then, if you like, we will read together the text in which Creusa speaks.

of the final third of this appeal, she says to him: "And you, you play the lyre and do nothing but sing your paeans! Oh! it is you I call, the son of Leto who dispenses oracles, seated on your golden throne at the center of the earth." You see that Apollo is hailed in the same way in these two passages: on the one hand, he is the god who sings, the god of the lyre; second, he is the golden god, the flashing god with golden hair; and finally—this only appears in the second interpellation—he is the god who, at the center of the earth, gives oracles to men and who must speak the truth. Singing god, golden god, god of truth.

I would like to refer here to George Dumézil's work concerning Apollo, in particular in his book *Apollon sonore*.[5] In his second essay, Dumézil studies an ancient hymn, much earlier than Euripides, a Homeric hymn to Apollo, the first part of which is not dedicated to the Apollo of Delphi, but to the Apollo of Delos. Now in this hymn to the Apollo of Delos, this is how Apollo makes his appearance at the moment of his birth. He has just been born and, still a baby, he already speaks and says: " 'Give me my lyre and my curved bow. I shall also reveal in my oracles the infallible designs of Zeus.' At this, he strides off across the world, the archer Phoebus of the pure hair. All the Immortals admired him and all of Delos [Delos: the island, the land where he was born; M.F.] became covered with gold while it contemplated the race of Zeus and Leto, [...] it came into bloom like the summit of a mountain with the blossoming of its forest."[6] In his commentary on this Apollonian hymn, Dumézil notes that three things characterize the god and his status. First, the god calls for his lyre and his bow. Second, he is clearly indicated as the one who reveals the will of Zeus through the oracle: he tells the truth. And third, as soon as he sets foot on Delos it is covered with a mantle of gold and the forest blooms. These three characteristics of the god are related, obviously according to Dumézil, to the three Indo-European functions of the mythology he is studying. First, the gold is to be linked to the function of fertilization, to wealth. The god's bow represents the warrior function. As for the two other elements (the lyre and the oracle), together they represent, or fall within the province of the magical-political function, or as Dumézil says, administration of the sacred. Gold is wealth and fertility; the bow is the warrior function; and the oracle and the lyre are the administration of the sacred. And then Dumézil explains that telling the truth and singing (the coupling of oracle and lyre) are actually two complementary functions, in the sense that the oracle is the form of the voice which tells the truth and through which the god addresses men, while the song is the form of the voice through which men address the gods in order to sing their praises. The oracle and the song are therefore complementary as two senses, two directions in the communication between men and the gods. In this administration of the sacred, in this game of the sacred which takes place between men and the gods, the god tells the truth through the oracle, and men thank the gods through song. Hence the coupling of song and oracle. This is the first element we find in Dumézil's analysis.

Second, in the essay immediately preceding this one—the first essay in the collection[7]—Dumézil traces this genealogy of Apollo, or at any rate of the Apollonian functions, back to a theme found in Vedic literature, and in particular to a hymn of the tenth book of the Veda—I have not read this text myself—which sings of the powers of the voice. In actual fact, what Dumézil wants to show is that, in a way, following the norms or canons of Greek mythology, Apollo is a version of an old divine and abstract entity found in the Veda, and this is the Voice itself. Apollo is the god of the voice, and in this Vedic hymn we see, or hear rather, the Voice which proclaims itself in its three functions: It is through me, says the voice in the Vedic hymn, that man eats food; second, says again the voice, whoever I love, I make strong (magical-political function); third, I tauten the bow so that the arrow kills the enemy of the Brahman, I am the one who fights for men (warrior function).[8]

Finally, the third element, which I am still taking from Dumézil's analyses, is this: of the three functions contained in the old Indo-European structure, which is inflected, as it were, in Apollonian mythology, in the mythology of Phoebus, the third function, of fecundity, is the most fragile, for a number of reasons which Dumézil explains (it is perhaps not worth going into this for the moment). Dumézil shows that this third function of the god who makes the earth flourish and the forest blossom, quickly disappears. The fertility side, aspect, or function no longer appears in and around Apollo, except in the rites of the gift, either in kind or in metal, in gold, brought to the god of Delos or the god of Delphi. This Apollonian function will manifest itself in the exchange or offer of gold, rather than in a natural fertilization of the earth. And Dumézil notes that Apollo is not particularly well-placed to speak with regard to natural fertilization because he is in fact, and this is constant in all the Apollonian myths, much more the god of the love of boys than he is of the love of women. And in fact there are very few children in Apollo's mythological record. Ion is a rare exception, which may explain to some extent the precaution, or reticence rather, that he displays in showing himself to be Ion's father. Moreover, when right at the start of the play Creusa refers to the child that she says her sister had by Apollo, Ion says: With a woman? That would surprise me![9] Apollo is not therefore the god of fertilization, of fertility, and the whole structure revolves around precisely this problem of birth and fertility.

The Apollonian structure that Dumézil talks about in *Apollon sonore* is clearly present. It is present first of all in the form of the first, magical-political function, the function of the administration of the sacred, since Creusa and Xuthus address themselves in fact to the god of the oracle, the god who tells the truth. Second, we find the third function, since it is a question of fertility, of birth, which leads the two consultants to the oracle. If you like, what we find is the confrontation between this oracular function of truth-telling and the function of fertilization, and this constitutes the very heart of the play. The second, warrior function appears in the play only very slightly, discreetly, for a number of reasons. It only appears in this way for political reasons, given that Delphi has a peacemaking function at this time, which is a period of peace, of a truce in the Peloponnesian War, and then it does so because functions 1 and 3 (truth-telling and fertilization) are the main ones in the plot itself. The warrior function appears in some terms, words, and situations (at the start of the play, Ion appears carrying a bow, the bow that is precisely a sign of Apollo's warrior function; and then there are the episodes we will talk about shortly in which Ion pursues the woman he does not know to be his mother, and wants to kill her). But what constitutes, what structures the play are essentially functions 1 and 3: truth-telling and fertilization. Second, still following what Dumézil says, the third function, fertility, is the most problematic. It is, in a strict sense, the function which creates problems. In a way, Apollo's discomfort with regard to his own fertility and paternity is what drives the play. Finally, third, it is clear that the problem of the voice is found throughout the play. The theme of the voice, which according to Dumézil forms the background of Apollonian mythology, is absolutely fundamental throughout the play. Euripides [asks whether] we can trust this voice of the god, which the Vedic hymn said we can trust, or whether men, humans, mortals—in this case, the woman—should not raise her own voice against the silent voice of the god who does not acknowledge his own paternity? It is clear that the tragedy modulates this theme, this structure, which, once again, is easy to recognize and perfectly in line with Apollonian mythology. All I have just been saying to you is in a way the mythical framework. Now we must examine the system of the tragic process, of the tragic development. He we see a tragic modulation of the different mythical themes I have introduced through the grid proposed by Dumézil.

First, the tragic modulation of the theme of the song and the oracle. You recall that a moment ago I told you that in the ancient structures referred to by Dumézil, the oracle is what the gods say to men, the true discourse the gods deliver to men through the intermediary of Apollo. And it is through song, the lyre, that men address the gods, Apollo being the god of the lyre and the song, the god who taught men how to sing and use the lyre. Here you can see that things are not entirely like this and that the distribution between the god's truth-telling and men's song of gratitude does not apply. On the contrary, it is clear that song and oracle are on the same side throughout the play. The god is the god of the oracle, but of a rather reticent oracle. He is also the god of the song, and this song is also modulated, its value and meaning modified: it is not men's song of gratitude with regard to the gods. Men do not sing to the god, the god sings, and he sings for himself, indifferent to men and to their misfortunes which he himself has caused. It is the song of the god's casual unconcern much more than the song of human gratitude. So song and oracle will be grouped together, and their link is understood, since the oracle, aware of his own injustice, dare not go the whole way in what he says but wraps himself up, cloaks himself, as it were, in this song of indifference to human concerns. Since this song-oracle, this song of indifference and reticent oracle is no longer the song that comes from the human side, song having passed over to the side of the gods and into indifference, what is there now on the human side? It is not the song, but the cry: the cry against the oracle which refuses to tell the truth, a voice raised against the god's offhand song of indifference. A voice once again. The voice is still involved, you see, but it is the voice of the woman who raises her cry of pain and remonstration against the joyful song, and makes the stark and public statement of the truth against the oracle's reticence. Against the song, tears; against the reticent oracle, the expression of the truth itself, the undiluted truth. This confrontation, this shift, which means that the song is no longer human, but divine, and that now, on the human side, the cry rises up against the god's song and oracle, can be seen fairly easily in the text. Unfortunately it can be seen more easily in the Greek than in the French text, but, if you like, we will re-read the French text and you will see what happens. "Oh you who make the seven string lyre sing, and the Muse's sonorous hymns vibrate on the rustic animals' lifeless horns." The god is the god of song. "I accuse you in the full light of this day that shines on me!" Here we must refer to the Greek text. We have then the god of song to whom the woman's cries call out. This does not involve the god of the oracle. The god of the oracle does not appear to be involved. Because if you look at the Greek text, it is: "*soi momphan, ō Lathous pai, pros tad' augan audasō.*"[10] *Audasō*: I will proclaim. *Pros tad' augan*: against, facing this light, this brilliance. This is the god's brilliance, the brilliance of the god of the sun, of light, etcetera. Against and facing: *tad' augan*, this brilliance which is yours, and which is here, which is daylight, and which is also the light of the god present in the temple. *Audasō*: I will proclaim. What will I proclaim? The complement is in the previous line. It is *momphan*: the reproach. Now, there is a difference of just one letter between *momphan* and *omphan*, which would be the oracle. "*Soi momphan, ō Lathous pai*": you, to you, o son of Leto, *momphan*, the reproach—but that we can almost hear as the oracle—is what I am going to make against you, that I am going to proclaim facing your light. There is a kind of alliterative play here between reproach and oracle which [indicates] that the woman hurls her reproach against the god of song and against the oracle who avoids speaking and does not want to speak, precisely here where the oracle says nothing, stays silent, and withdraws. Here where there is no *omphē*, the woman cries out her *momphē*.[11] I think this is fairly clearly suggested by this text and this passage.

And this confrontation/substitution of the woman's cry for the silent oracle is found again in the second calling out to the god, the third strophe, the third part if you like, where she says: "And you, you play the lyre and do nothing but sing your paeans! Oh! it is you I call, the son of Leto who dispenses oracles, seated on your golden throne at the center of the earth. Let this shout reach your ears!" There is something here that I am unable to explain, for I have not managed to find someone able to inform me. It is the Greek verb translated into French here as "*distribues les oracles*."[12] You see that we have "*omphan*" (the word "oracle") which was not uttered in the first call and which is like a kind of echo of the *momphan* uttered earlier. Now this oracle is "*distribué* (dispensed)." The Greek verb used here is "*kleroō*," which means "to draw lots." And I really do not know if the verb here should be understood in the strict sense, with a strong meaning of: In reality you dispense your oracles anyhow, as if they were drawn by lot; they do not tell the truth but are, as we would say, random. Or is it a technical term for saying: The oracles come from the god's mouth without us knowing exactly how, which does not prevent them from telling the truth. I will continue to ask the competent people, and if I get an answer I will tell you. Of course, I would like it to be the first solution, that is to say, that the oracle here is, as it were, disqualified, nullified by the alleatory character of his utterance: it does not tell the truth, it is random. In any case, even if we give *klērios* the meaning of dispensing or giving oracles, it remains that the woman opposes her own cry to this oracle. And this reversal, such that although the god should speak to the humans, it is humans who address the divinity, the god, is marked in line 910. "*Eis hous audan karuxō*": I will shout out, I will proclaim, I will address you and shout my complaint in your ears. The god who should be the god who speaks, the god-mouth, becomes the god-ear who is spoken to. The verb "*kēruxō*": *kērux* is the herald, the solemn and ritual proclamation by which one legally summons someone. The god of the oracle finds himself legally summoned by the woman's cry. We had the oracle and the song, the oracle through which the god speaks to humans, and the song through which humans speak to the gods. Now everything is reversed. At any rate, the song moves over to the god's side and becomes the song of indifference; and on the human side, speech [becomes] the speech by which one pressures the oracle.

And at the very moment when he stays silent, when he does not speak, one directs an organized, ritual cry at him: the cry of complaint, of remonstration. This is how I think the first general theme of the voice is modulated in this text.

The second modulation is that of the theme of gold. Apollo, then, is the god of gold, and there is an obsessive presence of gold in the text. At any rate, it returns and is recurrent: "You came to me, in the radiance of your golden hair"; and, a bit further on, at the end of the text: "it is you I call, the son of Leto who dispenses oracles, seated on your golden throne at the center of the earth." So, in the first call we find a very explicit manifestation or expression of the theme of gold, but, as you can see, here again with a modulation. The god appears as the god of gold: the flashing god with golden hair who lights up the world and who, in this light and brilliance, and through this light and brilliance, seduces the young girl. Now look and read what is said concerning the young girl and how Creusa describes herself at the moment of her seduction: "You came to me [she tells the god; M.F.], in the radiance of your golden hair, while I gathered saffron flowers in my robe, reflections of gold to weave into garlands."[13] The young girl also bears the sign of gold, her position is symmetrical to the god's, or rather, there is continuity in the exchange with the god. The god sheds light, but she also bears the sign of gold. She is holding flowers, golden flowers, which she should give, which she wants to give as an offering to the god. Gold here is in fact the medium of the offering I talked about and which Dumézil analyzed. But on this theme of the offering through gold—which is the theme of communication between humans and gods, and which is both the god's generosity in lighting up the world and human offering in the form of the flower—another meaning of the offering and exchange is superimposed: this is the exchange between the seducer god and the young girl who agrees to offer her body and who, she says, offers her "pale wrists"[14] to the god who summons her. An exchange takes place in this light, brilliance, and whiteness, in this gold of the god of flowers and in the whiteness of women's bodies, an exchange which is different from that simply indicated by the theme of gold. This exchange, that of love and sexual union—this appears in the following strophe—is not accomplished in daylight and in the shining light and the sun, but in the darkness of the cave. It was in a cave, she says, that: "you dragged me…to your bed, deep in a cave, seducer-god." Darkness, the dark which conceals the immodesty of the act: "[you] did without shame what Kypris [Aphrodite] wanted! And I bore you a son, poor soul, who, from fear of my mother, I exposed in your bed, at the spot where you took—oh wretched embrace!—the pitiful wretch I am!"[15] So it really is made clear—evidently the chronology and the episodes are not important—that the seduction takes place in a cave; that it is precisely in this cave that Ion is born some time later. And it is there, in this cave, in this night and darkness, that the child will be exposed, taken away, disappear, and consequently, as Creusa believes, die and thus not benefit from that daylight, that shining sun that she had benefited from, or anyway by which she was seduced. And then, from this point, from this passage in the night, in the unjust union, and in this birth followed by disappearance and death, the theme of gold breaks up as it were. In fact, when the theme of gold reappears in the third strophe ("it is you I call, the son of Leto who dispenses oracles, seated on your golden throne at the center of the earth"), gold is no longer the element of communication from the divine to the human, from the god with shining hair to the young girl who offers him golden flowers. Gold is no longer the sign of the god. It is the throne on which he sits and from where he reigns all-powerful, while he—god of the sun, enthroned above the earth, at Delphi, seated always and everywhere on the golden throne—is faced with a somber, accursed, sterile woman who has lost her child and cries out against him. The gold is now the god's gold, and, opposite, there is only this dark little silhouette. Thus the theme of gold is modulated.

The third theme is that of fertility…If you like we will pause for a moment and then take this up after.

1. *Oedipus the King*, 219-221, French pp. 211-212: "I speak as a man who is foreign to the report he has heard, and to the crime itself, the investigation of which will not get far, if he claimed to direct it alone, without having the least clue (*ouk ekhōn ti sumbolon*)"; English p. 19: "Hark to me; what I say to you I say/as one that is a stranger to the story/as stranger to the deed. For I would not/be far upon the track if I alone/were tracing it without a clue." Two joined halves of a broken ceramic object served as a sign of recognition (*sumballein*: bring, put together). The whole of the analysis that Foucault undertakes in his lecture at the Collège de France on 16 January 1980 consists in understanding the dramaturgical structure of Sophocles' tragedy as a regulated adjustment of veridictions. See below, note 11.

2. Euripides, *Ion*, 815-821, French p. 217; English p. 66.

3. Ibid., 866-880, French pp. 218-219; English p. 66: "…no hope left now./I thought, if I hid my ravishing,/If I hid my baby's birth, and all my tears,/I could bring those hopes to fulfilment;/ But I could not. Now by the starry throne of Zeus,/By the Guardian of the Rock of Athens,/By the holy shore of the Tritonian Lake,/I will ease the load from my heart,/Hold my secret no longer./With tears falling from my eyes, my soul tormented/By the scheming cruelty of man and god alike,/Who demand love and give treachery in return—/I will expose them!"

4. Ibid., 881-906, French pp. 219-220; English pp. 67-68: "Listen, Apollo, you who can wake to song/The seven strings of your lifeless lyre/Till they chant immortal music to lonely shepherds—/Here in the white light of heaven I denounce you!/You came to me, with the gleam of gold in your hair,/As I was picking an armful of yellow flowers/Whose petals, pinned on my dress, mirrored the same golden gleam;/You gripped my bloodless wrists,/ Dragged me, shrieking for help, into the cave,/Bore me to the ground—a god without shame or remorse!—/And had your will—for the honour of Aphrodite!/I bore you a son; and, in dread of my mother's eye,/With many tears I laid him/On the same cruel bed where you ravished me./Where is he now, our little child?/Torn and devoured!—and why should you/ Lay down your bragging lyre, or stop your song?/Listen to me, Apollo, seated at the earth's centre,/Dispensing oracles from your golden throne—/I shout it in your ear: vile betrayer!/ My husband never did you service,/Yet you give him a son to inherit his house,/While my child—yes, and yours—like a beast you leave to die,/To be torn by vultures from the crib where his mother laid him./Your very birth-place hates you,/Your sacred laurel and soft palm-tree hate you,/Where Leto laboured in her holy labour/And bore you, the Son of Zeus."

5. G. Dumézil, *Apollon sonore et autres essais. Vingt-cinq esquisses de mythologie* (Paris: Gallimard, 1982).

6. Ibid., pp. 26-27.

7. "Vāc," ibid., pp. 13-24.

8. Ibid., pp. 15-16.

9. Euripides, *Ion*, 339 and 341, French p. 197; English p. 52.

10. Ibid., 885-886, French p. 219; English p. 67.

11. *Ompha* and *mompha* are the Doric forms of *omphē* and *momphē*.

12. "*Omphan klērois*," Euripides, *Ion*, 908, French p. 220; English p. 68: "Dispensing oracles."

13. Ibid., 887-890, French p. 219; English pp. 67-69.

14. Ibid., 891, French p. 219; English p. 69.

15. Ibid., 895-900.

eight

26 JANUARY 1983

Second hour

[*Tragic modulation of the theme of fertility.* ∽ Parrēsia *as impre-cation: public denunciation by the weak of the injustice of the pow-erful.* ∽ *Creusa's second confession (*aveu*): the voice of confession (*confession*).* ∽ *Final episodes: from murder plan to Athena's appearance.*]

SO, IF YOU LIKE, we will continue to study the tragic transformation or modulation of the theme of fertility. I think we should note that throughout the text we have just been reading Apollo is always hailed as Leto's son. There is absolutely nothing strange about this, and is the absolutely ritual invocation. But in this text this invocation serves as a kind of dotted line directing us to the final lines of the text when, still turned against Apollo, Creusa tells him: "Delos hates you, and the laurel hates you, which, with the fine-haired palm, shelters the cradle where Leto, in noble childbirth, brought you into the world, son of Zeus."[1] There is something in this story of impregnation, and in Apollo's reluctance to recognize his son Ion, that Creusa cannot fail to find unjust. In fact you know that according to the legend Apollo is Leto's son. Leto, who was seduced by Zeus, took refuge on the island of Delos to give birth alone, and on this island her two illegitimate children, Apollo and Artemis, were born. So, exactly like Ion, Apollo is an illegitimate son resulting from an affair between a mortal and a god. And, exactly like Ion, Apollo is born alone and abandoned. And, exactly like Apollo's mother, Leto, Creusa gave birth alone, abandoned by everyone. This theme appears in the different references to the son of Leto and finally bursts out in this curse in which the laurel of Delphi and the palm of Delos are brought together in the evocation of Apollo's "noble" birth, which Creusa can easily contrast with Ion's shameful birth. So that this discourse that Creusa directs against the god, that she shouts in the ear of the god who should have spoken, this reproach that she solemnly proclaims like a herald, and in a way drives home, this reproach (*momphē*) where the oracle (*omphē*) has not spoken, this shrill discourse directed against the god and shouted in his ear is the solemn proclamation—hence the reference to the herald (*kērux*)—of an injustice in the strict, juridical and philosophical, sense of the word "injustice," because it is a proportion not maintained, a proportion that has not been observed. The homology of the two births, of Apollo and of Ion, means that Creusa and Leto are basically in symmetrical positions. And the position of Apollo, Ion's father, is symmetrical to Ion's. Both Apollo and Ion are of illegitimate birth. And Creusa, who is in a way Leto's daughter-in-law, her son's mistress in short, is in the same position as Leto herself. So you have a Leto-Creusa analogy (Creusa's relationship with Apollo is similar to the relationship Leto had with Zeus; and Ion was born of their union as Apollo himself was born). It is precisely this homology, this proportion emphasized in the text, that Apollo did not want to respect. For he, born of an affair between a mortal and a god, bastard son become god of light, always benefited from a brilliance which is, as it were, consubstantial with him. It is he who presides over the lives of mortals, makes the earth fruitful with his warmth, and must tell the truth to everyone. Ion, on the other hand, born in exactly the same way, in a position absolutely symmetrical to Apollo's, has been doomed to misfortune, obscurity, and death, the prey of birds (these are Apollo's birds; the bird theme comes in here and again later). So Apollo has abandoned him, left him to die, and he may even have sent his birds to kill him. And worse than this—this is indicated at the end of the text when she says: "you, owing nothing to my husband, install a son in his home, while my child, and yours..."[2]—on top of all this, he has just given an oracle which foists someone else's son on the wretched Creusa. The whole order of proportions is disrupted. And Creusa's confession consists in the protest against and the open proclamation of this perfectly defined injustice, pinpointed in the text by this comparison between the two births, and defined as symmetry not respected, as proportion disrupted and ignored by the god.

Now this speech act, by which someone weak, abandoned, and powerless proclaims an injustice to the powerful person who committed it, this complaint of injustice hurled against the powerful by someone who is weak, is a speech act, a type of spoken intervention which is recorded, or anyway perfectly ritualized in Greek society, as well as in other societies. What can the poor, unfortunate, weak, and powerless do, those who have only their tears—you recall how insistently Creusa, at the start of her confession, says that truly she has only her tears left—when they are the victim of injustice? They can do only one thing: turn against the one with power. So publicly, in front of everyone, in broad daylight, in the light that falls on her, Creusa addresses the one with power and tells him what his injustice was. In this discourse of injustice proclaimed by the weak against the powerful there is at once a way of emphasizing one's own right, and also a way of challenging the all-powerful with the truth of his injustice, of jousting with him as it were. This ritual act, this ritual speech act of the weak person who tells the truth of the injustice of the strong person, this ritual act of the weak who, in the name of his own justice, remonstrates against the strong who committed this injustice, is linked to other, not necessarily verbal rituals. For example, in India there is the ritual of the hunger strike. The hunger strike is the ritual act by which someone powerless emphasizes in front of someone powerful that he who can do nothing has suffered the injustice of he who can do anything. Some forms of Japanese suicide also have this value and meaning. It involves a sort of agonistic discourse. For someone who is both the victim of an injustice and completely weak, the only means of combat is a discourse which is agonistic but constructed around this unequal structure.

Now this discourse of injustice, which in the mouth of the weak emphasizes the injustice of the strong, has a name. Or rather, it will have a name in texts from a bit later. The word is not found [with this meaning] in any of the classical texts, in the texts of this period (Euripides, Plato, etcetera), but it is found in later treatises on rhetoric from the Hellenistic and Roman period. The discourse, through which someone weak, and despite this weakness, takes the risk of reproaching someone powerful for his injustice, is called, precisely, *parrēsia*. In a text cited by Schlier—obviously I did not find this myself, in the bibliography I gave you the other day I forgot to tell you that there is an article devoted to *parrēsia* in Kittel's *Theologische Wörterbuch*, which, like all the articles in the *Theologische Wörterbuch*, is essentially concerned with the Bible, the Old and especially the New Testament—there are some indications on classical Greek or Hellenistic usages of the word.[3] In this article on *parrēsia*, Schlier quotes an Oxyrhynchus papyrus (which therefore gives you some evidence for the possible nature of Greek society, practice, and law in Egypt)[4] in which it is said that in the case of oppression by the leaders, one must find the prefect and speak to him *meta parrēsias*.[5] The weak person, victim of oppression by the strong, must speak with *parrēsia*. In the text called *Rhetorica ad Herennium*, *licentia*, the Latin translation of *parrēsia*, is defined as that which someone addresses to persons he should fear and honor.[6] And, speaking on his own behalf for his right to people he should fear and honor, he reproaches these powerful people for an offense they have committed. So *parrēsia* consists in this: a powerful person has committed an offense; this offense is an injustice for someone weak, powerless, with no means of retaliation, who cannot really fight or take revenge, and who is in a profoundly unequal situation. So, what can he do? He can do one thing: he can speak, at risk and danger to himself he can stand up before the person who committed the injustice and speak. And at this point his speech is called *parrēsia*. A fairly similar definition is given by other rhetors, other theorists of rhetoric.

Once again, we do not find this kind of discourse defined as *parrēsia* in the classical texts. Nevertheless, in Creusa's imprecation to Apollo it is very difficult not to see something exactly of the order of *parrēsia*, since at the beginning of the play, at line 252, Creusa appears for the first time and, after telling Ion, who she has not yet recognized, that she wishes to consult Apollo, she says: "Oh! what wretched souls we women are! Oh! the crimes of the gods! [a phrase which for her obviously refers to what happened to him, but which Ion cannot understand because he still knows nothing of what happened; and Creusa—and this is in a way the sign, the epigraph of the play, which gives its stamp to all the speeches she makes later, and in particular to the great imprecation to Apollo—says: (M.F.)] Where shall we go to demand justice when it is the iniquity of the powerful that destroys us?"[7] Well, what can we do when the iniquity of the powerful destroys us and we must demand justice? We can do precisely what Creusa does throughout the play, and precisely in the passage we are analyzing: we can resort to *parrēsia*. It is this type of discourse, which is not yet, but will later be called *parrēsia*, which answers the question Creusa formulates when she comes on the scene: "Where shall we go to demand justice when it is the iniquity of the powerful that destroys us?"

In this discourse of imprecation I think we have an example of what will later be called *parrēsia*. I have stressed this for several reasons. The first, of course, is that, as you can see, in order to formulate the truth sought from the start of the play, the truth which will finally enable Ion to have the right to speak, to *parrēsia*—in the political sense of the term, if you like, as the right of the stronger to speak and to guide the city reasonably through his discourse—in order for Ion to obtain this right, called *parrēsia* in the text, a whole alethurgy is required, a whole set of procedures and behavior which will bring out the truth. And among these, the one which appears first of all and constitutes the very center of the play is this discourse of the powerless victim of injustice which is turned against the powerful and speaks with what will be called *parrēsia*. The something more than power which Ion needs in order to guide the city properly will not be established by the god, by the god's authority, by oracular truth. What will enable it to appear through the clash of passions will be this discourse of truth, this discourse of *parrēsia* in a different, virtually opposite sense of the discourse addressed by the weaker to the stronger. For the stronger to be able to govern reasonably—at any rate, the play takes up this theme—the weaker will have to speak to the stronger and challenge him with her discourse of truth.

This was my reason for stressing this, because there is a fundamental ambiguity here. Once again, this ambiguity is not in the word *parrēsia*, which is not used here, but concerns two forms of discourse facing each other, [or rather] profoundly linked to each other: the rational discourse enabling one to govern men and the discourse of the weak reproaching the strong for his injustice. This coupling is

very important, because we will find it again as a matrix of political discourse.* Basically, when the problem of government arises in
the Imperial epoch as not only a problem of the government of the
city, but also of the government of the entire Empire, and when this
imperial government is in the hands of a sovereign whose wisdom is
an absolutely fundamental element of political action, then the all-
powerful sovereign will need to have at his disposal a *logos*, a reason,
a rational way of saying and thinking things. But to support and
establish his discourse he will need the discourse of someone else as
guide and guarantee, someone who will inevitably be weaker than
him and who, if necessary will have to take the risk of turning to
him and telling him what injustice he has committed. The discourse
of the weak telling of the injustice of the strong is an indispensable
condition for the strong to be able to govern in accordance with the
discourse of human reason. We can just see this coupling—which will
only structure political discourse much later, in the Empire—taking
shape in this passage, in the game of Creusa's confession which in
this form of imprecation, of recrimination, appears indispensable for
establishing Ion's right.

So much for Creusa's first confession. But in fact—I began to tell
you this last time, but it was a bit rushed and schematic—Creusa is
not satisfied with this recriminatory declaration against the god. She
will recount the same story again immediately after this imprecation.
There is no apparent reason for this in terms of the dramatic organization of the scene and the episodes, because she has just told the god
a truth which everyone can perfectly understand, since she tells him:
You gave me a son; you abandoned us in that place; I exposed him; he is
dead, disappeared; and now you continue to sing and shed the radiance
of your gold, your glory, and your light. Everyone can understand and
no further explanation is needed. Now, immediately after having said
this, Creusa turns to the tutor and begins again. She begins again in a
completely different form which is no longer that of the imprecatory
chant, but that of the system of interrogation. It is no longer the confession (*aveu*) of the weak to the strong in the form of the proclaimed

---

* The manuscript adds: "it is a whole matrix of philosophical discourse: the man deprived of any
power proclaims the nature of injustice in front of the tyrant: the Cynic."

injustice of the latter, but a game of question and answer which I will quickly read to you.

> "*Creusa*: I am ashamed of it, old man, but I will speak [she has just spoken, but it is a new confession which starts, like the previous confession, as the recriminatory confession to the god, in the form of: I am ashamed; so this speech must overcome the barrier of shame; M.F.].
>
> *Old Man*: Speak, I have ample tears for my friends.
>
> *Creusa*: Listen. Do you know those caves called the High Rocks on the north side of Cecropia [the Acropolis; G.B]?
>
> *Old Man*: I know; near Pan's sanctuary and altars.
>
> *Creusa*: There, long ago, I waged a terrible battle.
>
> *Old Man*: Speak: my tears anticipate your words.
>
> *Creusa*: Against my will I was joined with Phoebus, oh! wretchedly...
>
> *Old Man*: My daughter, so that was what I noticed?
>
> *Creusa*: I don't know, I will not deny it if you speak the truth.
>
> *Old Man*: When you were groaning quietly from a secret illness...
>
> *Creusa*: Yes, that was the misfortune I confess to you now.
>
> *Old Man*: How did you hide Apollo's deed?
>
> *Creusa*: I gave birth: force yourself, old man, to listen to me.
>
> *Old Man*: But where? Who helped you? Alone, in your suffering...?
>
> *Creusa*: Yes, alone, in that cave where the god took me...
>
> *Old Man*: Where is the child? At least you are no longer barren!
>
> *Creusa*: Oh! old man, he is dead, the prey of beasts."[8]

Whatever the historical destiny of this form of confession (*aveu*)—which will be lengthy, you can imagine—I will spend much less time on it than on the previous form. I would just like to note that, as you can see, this confession (*confession*) to the old man is accompanied by the old man's tears which are constantly invoked and referred to. Whereas the god against whom one made the great recrimination remains silent and goes on singing, the old man one confides in does not cease to groan and weep: "your look fills me with pity"; "Speak, I have ample tears for my friends"; "Speak: my tears anticipate your words";[9] and Creusa, addressing the old man: "Why, old man, do you cover your head and weep?—Old Man: Alas! Because I am seeing your father and you unhappy!"[10]). Second, you can see that this confession takes a very different form from that of the great recrimination against Apollo's silence. It is a game of questions and answers, line by line. Old man's question, Creusa's answer, with a moment of inflection which is at once important, interesting, and beautiful, and has, as you know, an equivalent in Phaedra's confessions. This is when Creusa, having begun to speak and answer the old man's questions:

> "*Old Man*: Speak: my tears anticipate your words.
> *Creusa*: Against my will I was joined with Phoebus, oh! wretchedly...
> *Old Man*: My daughter, so that was what I noticed?
> *Creusa*: I don't know, I will not deny it if you speak the truth."

We arrive at the crux of the confession (*aveu*). The old man has not understood, or pretends not to understand what she said: "with Phoebus." So she begins again: I went with Phoebus.

> "*Old Man*: My daughter, so that was what I noticed?
> *Creusa*: I don't know, I will not deny it if you speak the truth."[11]

That is to say, at the point of the confession she demands answers from the person who is questioning her, and to whom she must respond. And she, with a nod of the head, or with a word, will say: Yes, that's right, "you are the one who named him."[12] This scenic movement, this inflection in the system of the confession, in which the person to whom confession must be made is the person who must express the central content of the confession, is found in *Hippolytus*,[13] and it is found in *Ion*. The third comment is this. What is at stake throughout the dialogue between the old man and Creusa is not the god's injustice, as in the great imprecation against Apollo. There is absolutely no question of the god's injustice, but, rather, of Creusa's offense. She constantly says: I have committed an offense, I am ashamed, I waged a terrible battle, "that was the misfortune I confess to you now."[14] The confession of the offense is therefore given directly as the offense of the person speaking, and not at all as the injustice of the person being addressed. But, at the same time, confession of the offense is linked to its assertion as misfortune. The offense committed is asserted as being a misfortune. There is no accusation against Apollo in all these lines of Creusa's replies. It is the old man who, from time to time, will say that Apollo is unjust. It is the confidant, not the person who confides, who will call Apollo "*Apollōn ho kakos*" (Apollo the cruel, vicious, bad).[15] Again, it is the old man who says to Creusa: You were guilty, no doubt, but the god even more so.[16] I would have liked to read you Phaedra's confessions in Euripides' *Hippolytus*, to show you the analogy between the two forms—I have forgotten to bring the text, but it doesn't matter, you can look it up.[17] Moreover, Racine's text is almost a line by line translation of Euripides.[18]

Anyway, you can see that we have two ways of confessing the same truth, and in no way is it the role of one to complete the other, since both say exactly the same thing and what was said as imprecation to the gods is just literally repeated. It is clear that what is at stake in this double confession is that, after a mode of truth-telling concerning an injustice one has suffered and against which one protests to the person who inflicted it, it is necessary to bring out another type of confession in which, on the contrary, one takes upon oneself, on one's own shoulders, both one's own offense and the misfortune of that offense. And one does not confide it to someone more powerful than oneself and against whom one makes reproaches, but to someone to whom one confesses, someone who guides and helps us. Discourse of imprecation and discourse of confession: these two forms of *parrēsia* will split apart in future history, and we see, as it were, their matrices here.

As we must move on and leave *Ion*, to conclude I would now like to go quickly over the end of the play. So we now have, with Creusa's double confession—the confession-imprecation and the confession-confidence, the confession-angry chant and the confession-dialogue with the tutor—half of the truth. We have no more than half of the truth, namely, that we now know that Creusa had an illegitimate son by Apollo and that this son has been lost. But we still do not know that this son is Ion. And the end of the play will be devoted to fitting this half-truth, which has just been said by Creusa, to the reality we have in front of us, that Creusa has facing her and that she does not recognize, namely, that this young man called Ion is her son. Creusa has told all her truth, but who will be able to tell the other half of the truth, namely, that this son is not dead, that he was taken to Delphi, and that at Delphi he is a servant of the god. It cannot be Creusa; she does not know it. And there is no one in *Ion* like the herdsman from Cithaeron in *Oedipus* who basically knew everything and who, knowing everything, was so afraid that he took refuge in the forests and hid, but who is able to tell the truth when he is brought on the scene. Here, no subject possesses the whole truth. Or rather, there is one, of course, and that is Apollo. Apollo is, if you like, in a position symmetrical to that of the herdsman from Cithaeron in *Oedipus*. He is the one who knows everything and so the last drop of truth must be extracted from him. It is through Apollo and only through him that the truth uttered twice by Creusa must be fitted together with Ion's presence, and consequently his enthronement as the real son of Creusa and Apollo rather than as the supposed son of Xuthus.

Now although Apollo, and only Apollo, can make this link—no human possessing this truth—you will see that all the same we should not count on the gods too much, nor on the function of truth-telling which belongs to at least one of them, precisely Apollo. Here again it is humans and their passion which will be the source, the mainspring, the force which will push aside this difficulty of telling the truth, which will push aside the shame of humans to tell the truth, and the god's reluctance to utter a clear oracle. And the driving force of this new advance, this final step in the truth will again be passion; once again it will be anger, Creusa's anger, which will be met by Ion's anger. What will Creusa do after having told this truth, or at least the half of it that is all she knows? The situation of this half-truth cannot be connected up with any other episode by itself. It is, as it were, a blocked truth: well, yes, she had a child who has completely disappeared. How could one know that this child is Ion?

And it is here that an episode takes place, again wholly similar to what we find in *Phaedra*, in which the confidant (the equivalent of the detestable Oenone), the somewhat depraved tutor—who had just spread false rumors about Xuthus and to whom we have just seen Creusa confide her secret—says to Creusa: Since you were in fact deceived by the

god who took advantage of you, have had a child, and have allowed it to
die, you must avenge yourself. And without pause he lists the options:
Set fire to Apollo's temple (revenge).[19] To which Creusa gives a one line
retort: Oh! I have too many troubles as it is without any more. Second
advice: Kill your husband then.[20] And she replies: You know we once
loved each other. And because of the kindly feelings and affection we
had in the past, I do not want to kill him, he was good. The tutor's
third suggestion: Well then, kill Ion, you can just slit his throat.[21] To
which she says: I do not like the idea of iron as a means.—So poison
him (a woman's murder method).[22] She agrees and proposes to wait
until he is in Athens to carry out the murder. And the tutor says: But
there is no point waiting until you are in Athens, for everyone would
know that you did it in your own house.[23] It will be better to poison
him straightaway. And she says: Very well, it would be better in fact.
And then she finds in her purse two little drops of poison *[laughter in
the audience]*. I am joking, it's not in very good taste, I know...But it is
necessary to schematize because some very interesting and important
mythical elements are introduced here: the poison she takes from her
purse is made from the blood of the Gorgon, the Gorgon with which
Minerva defended Athens. Here we are deep in Athenian mythology
which it would be important to analyze, but this is not my problem. In
any case, the tutor leaves the scene with this poison and goes to join the
feast that Xuthus, you recall, is offering to celebrate what he believes
to be his son's homecoming. The tutor pours into Ion's cup a drop of
the poison that should kill him. And at this point something happens:
one of the slaves attending those who are feasting does something blas-
phemous. It is not said what this is, but it is something that Ion—who,
being close to Apollo, knows the temple's rules and rituals—interprets
as a bad omen. Consequently, because it is a bad omen, all the wine
poured into the cups for the great ritual libation must be emptied on
the ground: one must not drink the wine and make the libation after
this bad omen. So, if you like, the god does intervene here, but only
minimally: he has merely made sure that some kind of non-ritual act,
an act contrary to the ritual, is performed which will interrupt the ritual and ensure that the wine is thrown away. The wine is emptied on
the ground. Apollo's doves—this is again a small element coming from
the god—arrive to drink and intoxicate themselves with the rejected

wine. All the doves are delighted with it, except, of course, for the one that drinks the poisoned wine from Ion's cup—and this dove dies. The dove dies and, as a result, it is apparent that Ion's cup was poisoned. It is not difficult to see that it is the old man behind Ion who poured the poison. So the old man is discovered.

This, if you like, typically Euripidean episode is interesting for us insofar as you can see the form in which and the system in accordance with which the god intervenes. He does not intervene by telling the truth; it is not even his oracle, but merely this game of quasi-natural signs (a dove's death) which is interpreted by humans and which in fact prevents the murder from being committed. Having discovered that someone wants to poison him, that it was the tutor, and therefore, behind him, Creusa, Ion lays his charge before the Delphi notables, who decide that Creusa must be stoned to death.[24] Then there is a new scene (the poisoning does not take place on stage but is recounted afterwards by a messenger, but this is not important) in which Creusa is pursued by Ion and those who want to exact vengeance on her. And at this point the series of final scenes are put into action. Creusa enters pursued by Ion [...],—the scene is not only the god's temple, but his very altar—and there is only one thing for her to do in order to escape Ion's anger, which is to take refuge at the god's altar, embrace it, and perform the ritual by which even criminals become inaccessible to their enemies. No one can touch her. Creusa's embrace of the god's altar obviously has a series of superimposed meanings. It is the ritual action by which one saves one's life. But, in embracing the god's altar she embraces the altar of he who was her lover, and in this way she reconstructs, resumes, and revives the old embrace that gave birth to Ion. But Ion continues to circle this altar, furious and armed with a sword, wanting to kill her. And once again there is a blocked situation. One is untouchable; the other does not want to touch her. Ion lays siege, as it were, to the altar. Then the god makes a new intervention, but you can see again how economical, how minimal it is. At this point, with the situation completely blocked, the doors of the temple open and we see the Pythia arrive, the one who should have told the truth, whose function is always to tell the truth. And she arrives almost silent, holding a basket in her hand, the basket of Ion's birth. Here you are, look, she says, and nothing more. Ion says to her: But why did you not show me

before now this basket in which I was brought to Delphi?—Because
the god forbade me, the Pythia says. Creusa, leaning over to look at this
basket, has no difficulty in recognizing it as the one in which she had
put Ion. She also recognizes some ritual objects in the basket: the neck-
lace of serpents, which was hung around Athenian children's necks for
protection, and which refers back to the serpents of Erichthonius, that
is to say, to the famous dynasty to which Creusa herself belongs, thus
attesting to that continuity; Athena's green branch; and, third, a piece
of embroidery, that she had started but which remained unfinished. It
is on seeing this object that Creusa says: This is as good as an oracle.[25]
Now here you see that discovery of the truth takes place without the
Pythia speaking. The Pythia is silent; it is just an object, the object of
birth. There are divine signs—the signs of the Erechthean tradition and
Athena's sign—and then there is a specifically human object. There is
strictly no trace of Apollo himself. And of all these signs, two of which
are signs of the gods and the third is simply a piece of woman's work,
it is with regard to the third, this human object, this woman's work
that Creusa says: This is as good as an oracle. Instead of the god's silent
oracle, one must again call on the work, voice, and hands of humans for
the truth to come to light. So, there you are, Ion finally has a mother.
He recognizes her, and that's it, it's all over.

But no, it's not all over. There are some more episodes, and recognizing the unbroken chain of the truth from beginning to end is infinitely
more difficult than one thinks. There are still a whole range of little
doubts which come to light and little gaps to be filled in. Because Ion
now finds that he has a mother. He had received, or thought he had
received a father in Xuthus. Everything should be settled. Moreover,
Ion believes that it is settled and says to Creusa: Very well, you are my
mother. And since Xuthus is my father (see the first part of the play),
there you are, I have a father and mother, let's go. Except, that is not
what happened at all, because Ion is not the son of Xuthus. At this
point, Creusa who wants to tell the truth, for the whole truth must
be known, says to him: Listen, no, it is not like that at all. In actual
fact you are not his son, you are the son of Apollo. And this, she says,
is much better, because it will establish your rights in Athens better
than being the son of a foreigner like Xuthus. Except that Ion is very
dubious about this and says: But even so, when you tell me that a god

gave you a child, isn't it really that you simply got pregnant by a slave in some corner of the house[26]—a suspicion symmetrical to his suspicion about Xuthus—and what is the proof that I really am the son of Apollo? Then there is discussion, and Ion lets himself be more or less convinced, not without [her telling him], which is an essential component in the play: "Listen, my child, to what I think. Loxias [Apollo; G.B.] has introduced you into a noble household for your own good."[27] This is what happened, Creusa says: Phoebus thought it simpler to set you up in a noble household by way of Xuthus. Ion replies: "I am not happy with such a poor account; I will enter the temple to learn from Phoebus whether I am the son of a mortal or of Loxias."[28] So his mother's confessions, what she tells him about his divine birth, are not enough for him. He cannot be satisfied with "such a poor account," he must have the final truth which will assure him that he really is the son of Apollo and Creusa, and not of Creusa and Xuthus, or of Creusa and a slave or anybody else. He must have the truth, and he moves to enter the temple finally to consult this god who has remained silent since the beginning of the play.

And at this moment, when he, Apollo's son, the priest, or anyway the servant of Apollo's temple, who must be enthroned by the gods as master at Athens, when Ion is finally about to set about extracting the truth from the god who it was said, at the beginning of the play, must tell the truth to every Greek, there is an abrupt turn of events. The *mekhanē*[29] descends on the stage, and who do we see appear? Apollo? Not at all, we see Athena, who settles on Apollo's temple in her chariot, superimposing her authority on that of the god who did not want to speak. And it is she who will pronounce the discourse of truth and right, of both the truth of Ion's birth and his right to exercise power now in Athens. And so Athena makes her great discourse, an Athenian-Apollonian discourse, if you like, or anyway a discourse in which the Apollonian prediction will be settled, will be said.[30] Athena says: This is what will happen. You will return to Athens, be king in Athens, and you will found the four tribes, all of which will be Ionian. And then, from Xuthus and Creusa you will have half-brothers, one of whom, Dorus, will found the Dorians, and the other, Achaeus, will found the Achaeans. It is a prophetic discourse, but [inasmuch as it is] made by Athena, goddess both of the city and of reason, it is a discourse which actually founds right in the city. It is the founding goddess of the city, the goddess who thinks and weighs things up, it is no longer the oracle but the goddess of the *logos* who tells the truth that the god was unable to formulate. She tells the truth and the veil covering what happened is lifted. And right will be established? Well no, there is still something else. What is to be done about the problem of the two fathers Ion now finds himself with, the real and divine father, Apollo, and the apparent father, Xuthus? The goddess gives her advice: Say nothing to Xuthus; let him continue to think he is the real father of this son. You will return to Athens with Xuthus convinced that you are his son. He will grant you tyrannical power, since coming to the city as a stranger, the off-spring of Zeus, Xuthus can only exercise a certain kind of power, that of the *turannos*. You will enter Athens and sit on the tyrannical throne, the text says.[31] And then you will found the Athenian tribes, that is to say, democracy, [or rather] the political organization of Athens will be able to spread on the basis of your Erechthean and Apollonian birth, but under the cover of birth from Xuthus, who we will leave under the illusion for a time. And this is how, if you like, the whole play unfolds: from the silence of the oracular truth-telling because of the offense committed by the god; through the clamorous protest of the human truth-telling (the clamor of imprecation or the clamor of confession, of the confidence); up to the third stage, the third moment, which is the enunciation, not by the oracular god, but by the reasonable god, of a truth-telling which leaves truth under the reign of a share of illusion, but which, at the price of this illusion, establishes the order in which the speech which commands can become a speech of truth and justice, a free speech, a *parrēsia*. That's it, so we have finished *Ion*.

1. Euripides, *Ion*, 919-921, French p. 220; English p. 68.

2. Ibid., 913-915.

3. H. Schlier, "Parrêsia, parrêsiazomai," in G. Kittel, ed., *Theologisches Wörterbuch zum Neuen Testament* (Stuttgart: Kohlhammer Verlag, 1949-1979) pp. 869-884.

4. What is called the "Oxyrhynchus papyrus" covers a set of ancient Greek papyri dating from the Hellenistic period and found in the Egyptian town of Oxyrhynchus during excavations begun in 1896. The University of Oxford has already published seventy volumes of them, but there are forty still to be edited.

5. Oxyrhnchus papyrus VIII 11100, 15, quoted by Schlier, "Parrêsia, parrêsiazomai," p. 871.

6. Anonymous, *Rhétorique à Hermennius*, Book IV, §48, trans. G. Archard (Paris: Belles Lettres, no date) p. 191: "There is forthrightness (*franc-parler*) (*licentia*) when, before people we should respect or fear, we formulate—using our right to express ourselves—a deserved reproach directed towards them or those they love, concerning some wrong"; English translation by Harry Caplan, *Cicero, I. Rhetorical Treatises. Rhetorica ad Herennium* (Cambridge, Mass.: Harvard University Press "Loeb Classical Library," 1954) p. 349: "It is Frankness of Speech when, talking before those to whom we owe reverence or fear, we yet exercise our right to speak out, because we seem justified in reprehending them, or persons dear to them, for some fault."

7. *Ion*, 252-254, French p. 193; English p. 48: "Oh! the wrongs of women! the wickedness of gods! When our oppressor is all-powerful, where shall we fly for justice?"

8. Ibid., 934-948, French pp. 220-221; English p. 69:
"CREUSA: I will tell you; though I am ashamed—you have known me so long.
SLAVE: I can sympathize all the better.
CREUSA: Listen, then. You know a cave on the north side of the Acropolis—a place called the Long Rocks?
SLAVE: I know; there is a temple of Pan and an altar.
CREUSA: It was there that I suffered a terrible ordeal.
SLAVE: Suffered? What? There are tears in my eyes already.
CREUSA: Apollo…raped me.
SLAVE: Oh my daughter! Then—that was what I noticed?
CREUSA: What did you notice? If you are right I will tell you.
SLAVE: You were ill and miserable, but you kept it to yourself.
CREUSA: That was what I tell you of now.
SLAVE: But—how did you hide what had happened?
CREUSA: I bore a child.—Why should you have to listen to all this?—but be patient!
SLAVE: Where? Who helped you? Or did you go through that alone?
CREUSA: Alone; in the same cave where—
SLAVE: But where is he now? You need not be childless any longer!
CREUSA: Dead. Given to the beasts."

9. Ibid., 925, 935, and 940. English, 925, p. 68: "My daughter, the look in your eyes makes me grieve for you."

10. Ibid., 967-968, French p. 222; English p. 70:
"CREUSA: Friend, why do you cover your face and weep?
SLAVE: Because you and the royal line are brought low, and I have lived to see it."

11. Ibid., 941-943, French p. 221; English p. 69.

12. See below, notes 17 and 18.

13. See below, note 17.

14. *Ion*, 945, French p. 221; English p. 69: "That was what I tell you of now."

15. Ibid., 952.

16. Ibid., 960.

17. Euripide, *Hippolyte*, 350-352, in *Tragédies*, vol. III, trans. L. Méridier (Paris: Les Belles Lettres, 1927) p. 43: "NURSE: What do you love, my daughter? Is it a man, and which one?—PHAEDRA: The one—man or not—who the Amazon gave birth to.—Nurse: Hippolytus, are you saying?—Phaedra: You are the one who named him"; Euripides, *Hippolytus*, 350-352, in *Three Plays: Alcestis, Hippolytus, Iphigenia in Tauris*, trans. Philip Vellacott (Harmondsworth: Penguin, 1974) p. 94: "NURSE: What are you saying, my daughter? You love a man? What

man?—PHAEDRA: Why, who else should it be? It is he, the Amazon's—NURSE: You mean Hippolytus?—PHAEDRA: You spoke his name, not I."

18. This refers to the third scene of the first act.
   "PHAEDRA: You know that son of the Amazon, That prince oppressed for so long by me? ŒNONE: Hippolytus! Great Gods!
   PHAEDRA: You are the one who named him."
19. *Ion*, 974, French p. 222; English p. 70.
20. Ibid., 976.
21. Ibid., 978.
22. Ibid., 985, French p. 224; English p. 71. In actual fact it is Creusa who has the idea of poisoning.
23. Ibid., 1024.
24. Ibid., 1212-1222, French p. 228; English p. 76. (It should be noted that, line 1222, the punishment is that Creusa should be thrown from a rock.)
25. It is actually Ion who utters these words. Ibid., 1424, French p. 239: "Look, here it is...It is true like an oracle"; English p. 82. [The French translation differs somewhat from the Philip Vellacott's English translation which does not contain the words quoted above. Instead there is the following exchange: "ION: O Zeus! Is Fate tracking me down?—CREUSA: And it has a fringe of snakes, like Athene's aegis.—ION: Look: here is the cloth. It is as you describe it."
26. Ibid., 1472, French p. 244; English p. 84. (Ion is less precise than this, merely evoking his illegitimacy.)
27. Ibid., 1539-1540, French p. 244; English p. 86: "This is how I see it, my son: it is out of kindness that Apollo is establishing you in a royal house."
28. Ibid., 1546-1548; English: "That is mere trifling. I am looking for a better answer. I will go into the temple and ask Apollo himself whose son I am."
29. A "*mekhanē*" in Greek is a piece of theatrical machinery usually used for the appearance of the gods.
30. *Ion*, 1575-1588, French pp. 245-246; English pp. 86-87.
31. Ibid., 1570-1571, French p. 245: "Creusa, go with your son to the land of Cecrops and sit him on the royal throne (*thronous turannikous*)"; English pp. 86-87: "Creusa: take your son home with you to Athens, and give him the place and power of royalty."

nine

2 FEBRUARY 1983

First hour

[*Reminder of the Polybius text.* ∿ *Return to* Ion: *divine and human veridictions.* ∿ *The three forms of* parrēsia: *statutory-political; judicial; moral.* ∿ *Political* parrēsia: *its connection with democracy; its basis in an agonistic structure.* ∿ *Return to the Polybius text: the* isēgoria/parrēsia *relationship.* ∿ Politeia *and* dunasteia: *thinking of politics as experience.* ∿ Parrēsia *in* Euripides: The Phoenician Women; Hippolytus; The Bacchae; Orestes. ∿ *The Trial of Orestes.*]

I WILL START BY taking up some of the things I told you in the previous lectures concerning *Ion* and the notion of *parrēsia*, because several of you have asked me questions and remarked that, in the end, what was brought out in this reading of *Ion*, with regard to the structure and meaning of this term *parrēsia*, was not entirely clear. In actual fact, I have spoken at such length about this text by Euripides so as to answer a question raised by a text by Polybius that I quoted, I believe, right at the start of the lectures, and which is a well-known, famous, and almost statutory text with regard to *parrēsia*. This is the text (in Book II, chapter 38)[1] in which, speaking of the nature and form of Achaean government, he says that among the Greeks the Achaeans are defined by the fact that their constitution involved *isēgoria* (let's say, equality of speech, equal right to speech), *parrēsia*, and in short, *alēthinē dēmokratia* generally. That is to say, you see that Polybius made use of two notions whose meaning we will have to examine, and he related them to democracy in general. This definition or characterization of democracy is interesting. First of all because, as you can see, democracy in general is characterized or specified only by these two elements or notions (*isēgoria* and *parrēsia*); and then we must try to find out, on the one hand, what the relationship is between these two notions and the working of the whole democratic system, and, on the other, what the difference is between *isēgoria* (equality of speech, equal right to speech) and this *parrēsia* that we are trying to study.

We know that in the theoretical texts of Plato, Aristotle, and others it is relatively easy to obtain the, let's say, morphological definition of democracy, at least as opposed to and distinct from monarchy, aristocracy, and oligarchy: it is government by the *dēmos*, that is to say, by the body of citizens. However, you know that if this morphological definition is relatively simple, the characterization of what democracy consists in—its characteristics, the elements indispensable for it to function well, its qualities—is much more uncertain in the Greek texts. And in order to characterize these internal and functional elements of democracy, one generally introduces notions like, for example, that of *eleutheria* (freedom), which refers to national independence, the independence of the city as opposed to its domination by another city; *eleutheria* refers also to internal freedom, that is to say, to the fact that power is not held despotically or tyrannically by a single leader. The citizens are free. This is one characterization. You know that democracy is also characterized by a *nomos*, that is to say, by the fact that the rule of the political game and of the exercise of power operates within the framework of something like law, tradition, a constitution, or basic principle, etcetera. Democracy is also related to *isonomia*, or rather *isonomia* is given as a characteristic of democracy. And Athenian democracy in particular prides itself on, makes itself out to be strong [by practicing] *isonomia*, which is to say, roughly, the equality of all before the law. And then another characteristic invoked is *isēgoria*, which, in the etymological sense of the term, is equality of speech, that is to say, the possibility for any individual, provided, of course, that he is part of the *dēmos*, to have access to speech. Speech is to be understood here in several senses: it may be judicial when one speaks before the tribunals either to attack someone or to defend oneself; it is also the right to give one's opinion by voting for a decision or for the choice of leaders; and finally *isēgoria* is the right to speak, to give one's opinion in a discussion or a debate.

If this is *isēgoria*, what then is *parrēsia*? What is this notion which refers to speaking? And how is it that Polybius, wanting to character-ize democracy in general, true democracy, in the briefest possible way, avails himself of only two characteristics, both of which concern, of course, this problem of speech (*isēgoria* and *parrēsia*), how is it that he uses these two terms which are so close to each other and which seem so difficult to distinguish? What is the difference between the consti-tutional right of each to speak and then this *parrēsia* which is added to this constitutional right and is, according to Polybius, the second major element by which democracy can be characterized? What is the nature of the relationship of these two notions to democracy, and how are they distinguished with regard to the political use of speech? I would like to elucidate something of this today. It will no doubt be a bit plod-ding, but I think that these questions are important enough to warrant spending some time on them.

However literary and theatrical it may be, I think *Ion* can provide us with some elements concerning the theoretical content of the notion of *parrēsia*. In a sense, in its dramatic development, *Ion* says more about this notion than the short and enigmatic formula of Polybius. So, if you like, I will do two things at the same time: on the one hand, I will re-systematize somewhat the path we have followed reading *Ion*; and then, at the same time, I will set out some markers to fix and mark out a little the field of this notion. In [this play] then, which we may think of as the tragedy of truth-telling, we were able to isolate a central core, or let's say an underlying theme. This underlying theme is very simple and I come back to it quickly. This young man, Ion, an unrecog-nized descendant of the old Erechthean dynasty of Attica, of Athens, is born in the caves of the Acropolis, and this descendant of Erechtheus, member of the race of Erechtheus in which the gods, the earth, and humans are already mingled, this unrecognized and exiled native, Ion, will not be able and moreover does not wish to return to Athens to exercise the power linked to his race, except on condition that he pos-sess a certain right. This right and power are linked to a status which depends on his birth. And this right, this power and status comprises, leads to, or opens onto an absolutely important and explicitly named element, *parrēsia*: the freedom to speak and to speak out freely. This is the underlying theme of the play.

Now, given that the dramatic mainspring of the play is how the exiled native, Ion, will be able to return home and obtain the right to speak in the form of free-spokenness, I have tried to show you that this *parrēsia* will not be obtained by the hero as a result of him accomplishing some exploit, undergoing some preliminary test, or winning a victory. He will not be enthroned as the result of a judgment which soothes quarrels and distributes rights. This is not what enables the hero to obtain *parrēsia*. It is, you recall, a series of manifestations of truth, a series of operations and procedures through which the truth is told. And these are generally characterized by the following: the cry of humans was needed to extract from the silent god the discourse which will rightly establish the power to speak.

The development of the drama around this general core is thus organized as the succession of these different rituals of truth, of veridiction, which are necessary for Ion finally to regain his homeland and obtain his right to speak. You recall that in fact these different elements of veridiction do not involve the discovery of the truth through a search and investigation, as in *Oedipus the King*. They are difficult, costly speech acts, painfully extracted in spite of shame, through the intensity of passions, and in conditions such that this truth-telling is always accompanied by its shadowy double: the lies, blindness, and illusions of the characters. Very schematically, we can recognize four major episodes, or let's say four major forms of these veridictions which gradually transfer Ion from anonymous exile at Delphi to Athens, to his speaking homeland as it were. These four elements of veridiction are the following.

First is the veridiction of the god, of the oracular god of Delphi. You recall that this veridiction is blocked, prevented by Apollo's offense, the injustice he has committed, and even by the shame he would feel in having to confess it. The oracle cannot be ashamed. Or rather, because its god is ashamed, the oracle will not speak, it will remain silent, except for, first of all, giving a misleading answer to Xuthus, and then strewing Ion's and Creusa's path, the path of turbulent human passions, with signs which enable the truth to come to light. So, there is the blocked and prevented veridiction of the gods. Second, we have Creusa's first

veridiction in the form of the violent imprecation addressed to the god
and turned against him. This is the imprecation of the weak who has
justice on her side and who reproaches the powerful for their injustice.
And this first veridiction is produced in Creusa's despair, which prevents her from recognizing that Ion is her son. Creusa's first veridiction
is produced in this blindness. Creusa's second veridiction is no longer
the imprecatory veridiction but the veridiction of confession. It is the
confession to a confidant in a relationship of trust, but a relationship
which is itself wrought, distorted, and warped by the fact that the
confidant gradually leads Creusa from her despair to anger, and from
anger to the wish to kill Ion, whom she fails to recognize as her son.
And it is from this monstrous project to kill her son that the truth
gradually emerges. Finally, the fourth veridiction is the final, trium-
phant veridiction, which brings about a consecration. This is the veridiction of the gods, the Atheno-Apollonian veridiction in which, as you
know, the power of prediction is transferred from Apollo to Athena,
and in which the future of Athens comes from Athena's mouth and is
set out as a sort of great process which will go from tyrannical power,
received by Ion from his father, up to the organization of Athens into
four tribes, and finally to a sort of privilege of kinship that the city will
be able to exercise, first over the Ionians, and then over the Achaeans
and Dorians, all, of course, on the basis of the illusion which will continue to make Xuthus and others believe that Ion is not the son of
Apollo, but of Xuthus.

Now, and it may be here that what I said to you last time was not
entirely clear, none of these four veridictions—whether it be of the
gods, of Apollo, of course, and Athena, or the two human veridictions
of Creusa, the imprecation and the confession—is called or designated
in the text as *parrēsia*. The only thing called *parrēsia*, once again, is that
to which Ion devotes his search, or anyway that which is for him a condition of his return to Athens. Only this, the political right to speak
out freely in his city, is called *parrēsia*. All I wanted to point out to you
last week was that Creusa's two veridictions (the veridiction-impre-
cation and the veridiction-confession), which Euripides does not call
parrēsia, will take this name, will be designated by this term later on.
The imprecation of the weak against the strong, the weak calling for
justice against the strong who oppresses him or her, will later be called

parrēsia, as too will that confiding opening of the heart which means that one confesses one's faults to someone who is capable of guiding us. But in this text, the word *parrēsia* is reserved solely for the right which Ion will finally obtain.

So, to summarize, we can, if you like, say this. On the one hand, none of the gods is the bearer of *parrēsia*. Neither the reticent oracle of Apollo, nor Athena's proclamatory declaration at the end of the play fall within the domain of *parrēsia*, and in Greek literature the gods are never endowed with *parrēsia*. *Parrēsia* is a human practice, a human right, and a human risk. Second, *Ion* brings together three practices of truth-telling. One is called *parrēsia* by Euripides in this text. We may call this, let's say, political *parrēsia*, or statutory-political *parrēsia*: it is the well-known statutory privilege, connected to birth, which is a way of exercising power by what is said and by truth-telling. This is political *parrēsia*. Second, we see a second practice, which is connected to a situation of injustice, and which, far from the right exercised by the powerful over his fellow citizens in order to guide them, is instead the cry of the powerless against someone who misuses his own strength. This, which is not [designated as] *parrēsia* in the text, but will be later, is what could be called judicial *parrēsia*. And finally, we see a third practice in the text, a third way of telling the truth which is also not [designated as] *parrēsia* in the text, but will be later. We could call this moral *parrēsia*, which consists in confessing the offense which weighs on one's conscience, and confessing it to someone who can guide us and help us out of our despair or out of feeling at fault. This is moral *parrēsia*. So, in this great ritual of forms of truth-telling which organizes the whole play, I think we see the appearance of, on the one hand, the explicitly named notion of political *parrēsia*, and then, on the other, two schemas, two dotted outlines, if you like, of practices of truth which will later be called *parrēsia*: judicial *parrēsia* and moral *parrēsia*. This may disentangle a little, no doubt too schematically, what there is concerning *parrēsia* in the play. But I would like to come back again to political *parrēsia*, since this, after all, is what is at the heart of the play—the two others (judicial and moral) being present instrumentally and not even named as *parrēsia*. Let us return to the stake, the very heart of the play, the political *parrēsia* Ion needs in order to return to Athens. What does it involve?

First, I think we should keep firmly in mind that this *parrēsia* for which Ion feels such a great need, which is so necessary for Ion's return, is first of all profoundly linked to democracy. And we can say that there is a sort of circular relation between democracy and *parrēsia*, since if Ion wants to return to Athens, or rather, if Ion's destiny means that he must return to Athens, what is it in order for him to do there? Well, it is to carry out the transformation to which his name will be linked, that is to say, the organization of Athens into four tribes, into that constitutional form which will give the different inhabitants of Athens the right to give their opinion on problems concerning the city and in choosing leaders. Ion needs *parrēsia* so that he can return to Athens and found democracy. Consequently *parrēsia*, in the person of Ion, will be the very foundation of democracy, anyway its point of origin, its foundation stone. In order for there to be democracy there must be *parrēsia*. But conversely, as you know—and the text of Polybius I quoted a short while ago also shows this—*parrēsia* is one of the characteristic features of democracy. It is one of the internal dimensions of democracy. That is to say, democracy is necessary for there to be *parrēsia*. For there to be democracy there must be *parrēsia*; for there to be *parrēsia* there must be democracy. There is a fundamental circularity, and I would now like to place myself within the framework of this circularity and try to disentangle the relationships between *parrēsia* and democracy, let's say quite simply: the problem of truth-telling in democracy.

We need to recall the field of notions with which this notion of *parrēsia* is associated (still in this play, *Ion*, which I assure you I will finish with shortly). You recall that Ion ends his great tirade with the following assertion: Be that as it may, I do want to return to Athens, but I do not want to return without knowing who my mother is. I need to know who my mother is, because unless I know I will not have *parrēsia* in Athens. In this great tirade that we analyzed two weeks ago, this necessity, Ion's expressed need for *parrēsia* was linked to certain things. First: Ion's wish to be in the front rank of citizens. He uses the expression "*prōton zugon*," which means the front rank.[2] And once again, being in the "front rank" should not at all be understood as being the first ahead of all the others, but quite precisely as being in the small group of people who form the front line of citizens. I think it is important to keep in mind the image of the front line of soldiers. It is a set of individuals who will be in the front rank. If he wishes to have *parrēsia* it is so as to be in this "front rank."

Second, in this tirade, the wish to have *parrēsia* was connected to a very interesting classification of citizens in terms, not of wealth, as in another play by Euripides,[3] but of the problem of *dunamis* (of strength, power, of power exerted, the exercise of power). And he distinguished three categories of citizens: the *adunatoi* (those without power, those who do not exercise power and are, roughly, ordinary people); second, those who are sufficiently wealthy and well-born to take charge of the city's affairs, but who in fact do not do so; and then, third, those who actually do concern themselves with the town.[4] The first, then, are the powerless. The second are the *sophoi* (the wise). And then the others are those who are powerful and take charge of the town. It is clear that *parrēsia* concerns this third category, since those who lack ability, who are powerless, do not have to speak, and the text says very clearly that those who do not concern themselves with the affairs of the city remain silent. If they remain silent, then they do not use *parrēsia*. So, *parrēsia* concerns those who take charge of the town.

Finally, third, in this same text it was very clear that the use of *parrēsia* presupposed a series of problems, or rather exposed the person who resorts to *parrēsia* to risks and dangers. This was the hatred of the common people, of the *adunatoi* (the powerless). It was the mockery of the *sophoi* (the wise). And finally it was the rivalry and jealousy of those who take charge of the city. So we can say that *parrēsia* characterizes a particular position of some individuals in the city which is not defined just by citizenship or status. I would say that it is much rather characterized by a dynamic, by a *dunamis*, by a certain superiority which is also an ambition and effort to be in a position such that one can direct others. This superiority is not at all identical to that of a tyrant, who exercises power without rivals, as it were, even if he has enemies. The superiority connected to *parrēsia* is a superiority shared with others, but shared in the form of competition, rivalry, conflict, and duel. It is an agonistic structure. Even if it implies a status, I think *parrēsia* is connected much less to status than to a dynamic and a combat, a conflict. So, a dynamic and agonistic structure of *parrēsia*.

Now you see that in this agonistic field, in this dynamic process by which an individual maneuvers around in the city in order to occupy the front rank, in this perpetual joust with his equals, in this process in which the pre-eminence of the first citizens is asserted within an agonistic field, *parrēsia* is always explicitly associated in this text with a type of activity designated as: *polei kai logō khrēstai*.[5] *Polei khrēstai* means to take charge of the city, to take its affairs in hand. *Logō khrēsthai* means to make use of discourse, but of rational discourse, the discourse of truth. Consequently I think we can summarize all this by saying that *parrēsia* is something that characterizes much less a status, a static position, or a classificatory characteristic of certain individuals in the city, than a dynamic, a movement which, beyond pure and simple membership of the body of citizens, puts the individual in a position of superiority in which he will be able to take charge of the city in the form and through the practice of true discourse. What I think is associated with the game of *parrēsia* is speaking the truth in order to direct the city, in a position of superiority in which one is perpetually jousting with others.

Well let us now return to the text by Polybius which characterized democracy by *isēgoria* and *parrēsia*. It seems to me that what I have just spent too long recalling concerning *Ion*, and which the play explicitly says concerning *parrēsia*, enables us to explain the very odd juxtaposition of *isēgoria* and *parrēsia* as fundamental characteristics, for Polybius, of true democracy. What is *isēgoria*? *Isēgoria* is the right to speak, the statutory right to speak. It is the fact that, in terms of the town's constitution (its *politeia*), everyone has the right to give his opinion, whether this be, once again, by defending oneself before a tribunal, by voting, or possibly by voicing one's views. This right of speech is constitutive of citizenship, or again it is one of the elements of the city's constitution. As for *parrēsia*, it is linked both to the *politeia* (the city's constitution) and to *isēgoria*. It is obvious that there cannot be *parrēsia* if citizens do not have this right to speak, give their opinion by voting, or testify in court, etcetera. So, for there to be *parrēsia* there must be this *politeia* which gives each individual the equal right to speak (*isēgoria*). But *parrēsia* is something different. It is not just the constitutional right to speak. It is an element which, within this necessary framework of the democratic *politeia* giving everyone the right to speak, allows a certain ascendancy of some over others. It is what allows some individuals to be among the foremost, and, addressing

and experience." First of all I would like to put *Ion* together with some other texts by Euripides, which I will consider much more quickly, in which there is also a question of *parrēsia*, and in which the use of the word *parrēsia* allows us to confirm some of the things I said about *Ion* and also, at the same time, to bring out other themes and problems. In the surviving texts by Euripides there are four other uses of the word *parrēsia*, four other texts in which the word is employed.

First, the word is employed in *The Phoenician Women*, in which Euripides presents the famous Oedipal dynasty (of Eteocles and Polyneices), and in which, according to the particulars or the plot he adopts, Polyneices broadly represents democracy, the position of the democrat, and Eteocles represents that of the tyrant. And, still according to his plot, Jocasta is still alive. Jocasta is still alive and present after the discovery of the oedipal drama. And she is present between her two sons; the son of democracy and the son of tyranny. According to the plot, Polyneices, who is in exile, driven out of Thebes—while Eteocles has remained in Thebes where he exercises power—meets Jocasta. Jocasta meets her son Polyneices and questions him about what it is like being exiled. "Is it a great sorrow," Jocasta asks, "to be deprived of your homeland?" And Polyneices replies: "Great indeed. Much worse than it sounds." Jocasta: "What is this sorrow, what is the exile's greatest misfortune?" Polyneices: "The biggest drawback": *oukh ekhei parrēsian* (he does not have *parrēsia*; "it removes *franc-parler*" says the [French] translation). Jocasta: "That's being a slave, to silence one's thought (*mē legein ha tis phronei*)." Polyneices: "One has to be able to put up with the foolishness of the master" (when one is in exile and lacks *parrēsia* then). Jocasta adds: "Another suffering, to be mad with the mad!", anyway, to be unable to be wise when one is subject to the power of those who are not wise (*tois mē sophois*).[8] Again, I do not want to dwell too long on this passage, I would just like to point out this: you see that we have here—and this was already quite clear in *Ion*—the designation of a necessary connection between *parrēsia* and an individual's status. When an individual is driven from his town, when he is no longer at home, when therefore he is exiled, clearly he cannot have in exile the rights of a citizen at home, he does not have *parrēsia*. Another thing that is also found in *Ion* is that when one does not have *parrēsia* one is like a slave (*doulos*).[9] But there is also something new with regard to *Ion*, which is this: the text says that when one does not have *parrēsia* one has to put up with the foolishness of the masters. And nothing is harder than being mad with the mad, a fool with the foolish. What is meant and shown by the fact that without *parrēsia* one is in some way subject to the madness of the masters? Well, it shows that the function of *parrēsia* is precisely to be able to limit the power of the masters. What does the parrhesiast, the person who practices *parrēsia*, do when *parrēsia* exists but the master is mad and wishes to impose his madness? Well, precisely, he will stand up, speak, and tell the truth. He will tell the truth against the master's foolishness, madness, and blindness, and thereby limit the master's madness. When *parrēsia* is lacking, men, citizens, all are doomed to the master's madness. And then nothing is more painful than to have to be mad with the mad. *Parrēsia* will thus be the limitation of the master's madness by the truth-telling of the person who must obey but who, faced with the master's madness, is justified in opposing him with the truth.

The second text in which we find the term *parrēsia* is in the tragedy *Hippolytus*, at the end of Phaedra's confessions at the start of the play. Phaedra confesses her offense, or rather her love of Hippolytus. She confesses it, as you know, to her servant, the one who becomes Oenone in Racine's tragedy. And the term appears when, after having confessed, she recognizes and seals, as it were, her awareness of her own fault, and curses all women who dishonor their marriage bed.[10] She justifies this curse in three ways. First argument: women who dishonor their bed in this way give a bad example, and if noble women engage in this shameful practice, others will have all the more reasons for doing so too.[11] Second argument: how can one look the companion one has deceived, one's husband, in the face? Shadows themselves could speak. One should fear the open, public dishonor one inflicts on one's husband.[12] And finally, third, the problem of children. She says: "Ah, may they be able to live in illustrious Athens with the free-spokenness (*parrēsia*) of free men, and with pride in their mother! For although he may have a bold heart, a man is slave when he knows a mother's or a father's misdeeds."[13] What this means is that in a case like this *parrēsia* is a right one may exercise only on condition that one's parents have not committed an offense. What sort of offense? It is absolutely not the kind of offense which could remove someone's status as citizen, which could strike him and his descendants with legal infamy. It is a moral offense. The text says that the mere fact of someone, a son, being aware of his mother's or father's offenses renders him slave. That is to say, once again, according to the principle that a man of noble birth is a slave if he cannot speak freely, then awareness of his mother's or father's offense is enough to make a man slave and deprive him of free-spokenness. Here it is perfectly clear that *parrēsia* is not simply given by status. Although citizen status is necessary to have *parrēsia*, something more is needed: the moral qualities of ancestors, of the family—and so of descendants also—are involved. A personal qualification is necessary in order to be able to benefit from *parrēsia*.

The third text comes from *The Bacchae* [where] the use of the word *parrēsia* is even more marginal than in the previous texts, but which is interesting nevertheless. This time the word is employed by a messenger, that is to say, a servant, who brings some rather unpleasant news that he has to tell Pentheus concerning the excesses of the Bacchae. So the servant arrives before Pentheus and says to him: I would like to know whether I should report this news (concerning the excesses of the Bacchae) quite frankly (*parrēsia*) or whether I must watch my words.[14] For "I fear your angry spirits oh Prince, I fear your swift wrath and the excess of your royal temper!" To which Pentheus replies: "You may speak: you have nothing to fear from me. One should not be angry with he who does his duty."[15] And in fact it is the Bacchae who are punished. So here you have a use of the word *parrēsia* which on this occasion does not refer to the status of the governor, or of the man among the citizens who sticks his neck out, speaks, persuades, and directs others. This is the *parrēsia* of the servant, but precisely of the servant who is in a situation somewhat similar to that [in which] we saw Creusa. He is weak, facing someone more powerful, and to that extent he takes a risk. He takes the risk of arousing the anger of the person he addresses and he, the servant, does not want to say what he has to say unless he is sure that the frankness with which he will say it (his *parrēsia*) will not be punished. To be able to make use of his *parrēsia*, he wants assurance that we will not be punished. And Pentheus replies as a good, wise sovereign: What concerns me is to know the truth and you will not be punished for telling the truth. You can speak; you have nothing to

fear from me: "one should not be angry with one who does his duty."
The servant who tells the truth does his duty. Pentheus himself guarantees that he will not be punished. This is what could be called, if you
like, the parrhesiastic pact: if he wishes to govern properly, the one
with power must accept that those who are weaker tell him the truth,
even the unpleasant truth.

Finally, the fourth text in which the word *parrēsia* is employed, and
which is doubtless more important than the previous three, is the tragedy *Orestes*, at line 866 and after. What is at issue at this point in the
play's development? Orestes, then, has killed Clytemnestra to avenge
the death of Agamemnon. And, after the murder of his mother, Orestes
is seized by the Argives and those who took Clytemnestra's side. He
is brought before the tribunal, that is to say the assembly of the citizens of Argos who have to judge him. They have to judge him, and in
the play this is how this trial is recounted to Electra by a messenger:
"When the assembly of Argives was complete, the herald stood up and
said: 'Who wants to speak, to say whether or not Orestes deserves
death for matricide?' [which is exactly the formula employed before
the Athenian *ekklēsia* when someone was to be judged for such a serious crime. It is a ritual formula then: Who wants to speak? Then four
characters get up in turn; M.F.] Then arose Talthybius, who helped
your father [Agamemnon; M.F.] at the sack of the Phrygians [in
Homer, Talthybius is Agamemnon's herald, the spokesman for those
with power, the one who speaks for them; M.F.]. Always a slave to the
powerful, he used double talk: going into raptures over your father, but
at the same time disapproving of your brother—in a discourse mixing
blame with praise—to define for parents some odious practices; and his
eye always smiling at Aegisthus' friends. For this lot [heralds; M.F.]
are like that: it is to those favored by fortune that heralds always run;
their friend in the city is whoever has power and office. After him
King Diomedes spoke [in Homer, Diomedes is a hero of both courage and good advice; M.F.]. He rejected the death penalty both for
you [Electra; M.F.] and your brother [Orestes; M.F.]; condemnation to
exile seemed to him to satisfy piety. Some applauded him, shouting out
that he was right, but others disapproved of him. Then some character
with an unbridled tongue stood up, forceful in his audacity, an Argive
without really being one, foisted on the city, trusting in the roar of his

voice [you will see: I think this is a small mistranslation; M.F.] and the crudeness of his *parrēsia*, but persuasive enough to plunge the citizens into disaster one day...He proposed that you and Orestes be stoned to death; and it was Tyndareos who suggested to the one who demanded your death that he speak in that way. But another stood up to oppose him [oppose the one with the unbridled tongue; M.F.]. His appearance was not flattering, but he was a brave man [a courageous man: *andreios*; M.F.], with little contact with the town and those of the public square, a cultivator (*autourgos*), one of those who alone are the salvation of the country, of shrewd intelligence moreover, ready for the tussle of oratorical combat, a man of integrity and irreproachable conduct: 'For Orestes, son of Agamemnon' he said, 'I demand a crown: for he wished to avenge his father by killing a guilty and impious woman, since men would not have the glorious desire to arm themselves and campaign far from home if those left at home dishonor the guardians of the hearth by corrupting the wives of the brave.' And the honest people thought he was right."[16] The honest people thought he was right, but you will see that things do not remain there.

We have here, then, the typical image, the faithful representation of a trial with the familiar ritual formulas. We have four orators who speak (*logō khrēstai*: make use of *logos*).[17] First is Talthybius, the herald, that is to say, the official spokesman, the person who conveys messages, who speaks in the name of those who exercise power. Ambassador abroad, spokesman in the city, etcetera. By definition his speech is not free, since his function is precisely to deliver the speech of those who exercise power already. Consequently, he cannot stand up and say, in his own name and on his own behalf: I am going to give you my opinion and here is what I think. His speech is subservient, obedient, the speech of already constituted power. And it is curious that the text does not say what advice he gives to the Assembly. The text simply says that his words are *dikhomutha*:[18] double talk, words which can satisfy the Agamemnon dynasty, Orestes, and Electra, etcetera, because they are still powerful; but Aegisthus must also be pleased. As a result, this counsel, whose content, once again, we do not know, will be a *dikhomuthos* (double talk).

Confronting him we have Diomedes who is also a hero of the *Illiad*, a mythical hero who represents a model of courage and an example of persuasive eloquence. He—and here the contrast with the previous character is very clear and very interesting—will give a moderate view. Whereas the first used double talk, Diomedes will give as it were the middle way, the moderate path between the two extremes. Whereas the first gives as it were the two extremes and superimposes the two views in order to satisfy everyone, Diomedes will take the middle way. Between the supporters of acquittal and the supporters of condemnation to death, he will propose the moderate, wise decision of exile. Unlike the *dikhomutha* of Talthybius, which aims to satisfy everyone, the average and measured speech of Diomedes will split the audience. And the text says that there are those who approve of him and those who rebuke him. One, the flatterer naturally, will get everyone's approval. And then there are those who, taking the middle way, divide the Assembly [between] those who approve and those who rebuke.

These are two Homeric characters, two characters from legend. The next two characters are, on the contrary, taken directly from the history of Athens at the time the play was written. And the play, we will come back to this shortly, was written in 408, that is to say, ten years after *Ion*, ten years [during which] precisely the problem of *parrēsia*, the problem of the *politeia* and *dunasteia*, the problem of the exercise of power within the Athenian constitution will have taken on a new scale, intensity, and dramatic character. Anyway, here we have two characters who are like the civil replicas, the civil repetitions, I was going to say contemporary, bourgeois versions of the two Homeric characters (the hero and the herald, Diomedes and Talthybius). What is their reply?

How is this personage with the unrestrained language, the scholiast—and Greek tradition said that this figure was the reproduction, the caricature of Cleophon, the famous demagogue[19]—characterized? He is characterized by his violence and audacity. He is characterized by the fact that he is Argive/non-Argive and that he was forced on the city. Again we find this problem: the true parrhesiast, the one who uses good *parrēsia*, must be a full citizen, a citizen by origin. As in the dynasty of Erechtheus, he must be native born. Those characters who obtained rights in the city late, who were assimilated afterwards, without their family belonging to the body of citizens, cannot truly exercise *parrēsia* properly and appropriately. The text says that the *parrēsia* of the third character is *amathēs*, that is to say, uneducated, rough, and coarse.[20] It is a *parrēsia* which, if it is *amathēs*, is therefore not indexed to the truth. It is not capable of being formulated in a discourse which is rational and tells the truth. What can it do? Well, the text says that it can persuade (*pithanos*).[21] He may act on his hearers, he may influence them, and he may carry the day, but he does not do so because he tells the truth. Being unable to tell the truth, he wins the day by using flattery, rhetoric, and passion, etcetera. And this is what leads to disaster.

The characterization of the fourth figure, who is also clearly contemporary and is not given a name because he is a typical social character, is quite remarkable. First, he is someone who does not have a flattering appearance. So he will not be able to play on his physical glamour. On the other hand, what does he have in his favor? *Andreios*: he is courageous. This courage refers to two things: on the one hand, as the text shows, it refers to physical courage, the soldier's courage, the courage of someone who is capable of defending his land (this is said in the text); he is also prepared to take part in oratorical battles. That is to say, it refers to a military courage against enemies, and also a civic courage facing rivals, enemies internal to the city, those who are always ready to flatter the rabble. His second characteristic is that he is *akeraios*,[22] that is to say, pure, without stain, and also irreproachable. And this refers both to the integrity of his morals and to his concern for justice. Finally, he is *xunetos*, prudent.[23] We have here, in prudence (intellectual quality), moral quality, and courage, the three traditionally recognized fundamental virtues. But to these three virtues, which give the true and good *parrēsia*, is added an interesting social and political characterization. First, you recall that the text says that this man endowed with all the virtues rarely goes into town and to the *agora*. That is to say, he is not always there in session, wanting all the time to give and impose his views, wasting his time getting lost in endless discussions. Second, he is an *autourgos*: someone who works with his hands. This is not an agricultural worker, or a servant, but a small farmer who puts his hand to the plough on the patch of land which he owns, cultivates, and fights for. And this is what the text refers to when it says: he belongs to that category of people who save their land (*gē*). So there is an opposition here between *agora* and *gē*: the *agora* is the place of often sterile political discussion with its dangerous jousts; *gē* is the land one cultivates, the very wealth of the soil for which one is prepared to fight. That this *autourgos*, this small peasant who is capable of fighting for his land, really is the positive political reference of Euripides—a reference of course to the Peloponnesian War and all the other struggles that had taken place—is confirmed by the basic argument that this *autourgos* gives in favor of Orestes: killing Clytemnestra, Orestes had avenged all the soldiers deceived by their wives while they were away at war. It may be thought that this argument, in comparison with what could be said about Orestes in the tradition of Greek tragedy, and in particular in Aeschylus, is somewhat mundane. It is nevertheless very interesting inasmuch as a category of small landowners is designated who were precisely those to whom a very important political movement in Athens at this time wanted to reserve the effective exercise of power. What Euripides shows, what he clearly points out in this passage, is that *dunasteia*, the real exercise of power in the city, is not to be entrusted to those who hang about in the *agora* all day, or stroll about the town, but that this *dunasteia* should be effectively reserved to the *autourgoi*, to those who work their own fields with their hands and are ready to defend the city. Furthermore, many of the projects of reform at this time which were directed against Athenian democracy or demagogy, and which we call, if you like, reactionary, revolved around this. There was, in particular, the reform project of Theramenes.[24]

Now we should note, and I will stop here for the moment, what happens and how the Assembly decides after this confrontation between the four characters (the two mythical characters on the one hand, and the two, let's say present day characters, the demagogue and the small landowner, on the other). So, the *autourgos* has just spoken. "And the honest people thought he was right. No one else asked to speak."[25] Then Orestes comes forward and presents his own defense. And here now is the outcome and verdict. Orestes "did not persuade the crowd, although he was thought to be right. Victory went to the other, vile orator who, appealing to the mob, called for the death of your brother and yourself."[26] In this way Orestes is condemned to death. Why? Well, because victory went to the bad orator, to the one who used an uneducated *parrēsia*, a *parrēsia* not indexed to the *logos* of reason and truth. And with this victory, in this play which, once again, was written and performed ten years after *Ion*, the somber, dark profile of the bad face of *parrēsia* looms up. Ion had sought this *parrēsia* for a long time and could not return to Athens without it, since it had to found democracy, and this democracy had to make room for *parrēsia* in turn. Well, now this positive circle of *parrēsia* and the city's constitution, the circle which constitutes good democracy, is in the process of coming apart. The bond between *parrēsia* and democracy is problematic, difficult, and dangerous. Democracy is in the process of being overrun by a bad *parrēsia*. So, in a moment I would like to take up the problem raised by this text of the ambiguity of *parrēsia*.

1. Polybe, *Histoires*, Book II, 38, trans. P. Pédech (Paris: Les Belles Lettres, 1970) p. 83: "It would not be possible to find a regime and an ideal of equality, liberty, in a word of democracy, more perfect than that of the Achaeans (*isēgorias kai parrēsias kai katholou dēmokratias alēthinēs sustēma kai proairesin eilikrinesteran ouk an heuroi tis tēs para tois Akaiois huparkhousēs*)"; English translation by W.R. Paton, Polybius, *The Histories*, vol. 1, Books I and II (Cambridge, Mass.: Harvard University Press, "Loeb Classical Library," 1922) p. 337: "One would not find a political system so favourable to equality and freedom of speech, in a word so sincerely democratic, as that of the Achaean league."

2. Euripides, *Ion*, 595, French, p. 208; English, p. 60.

3. Euripide, *Les Suppliantes*, 238-245, in *Tragédies*, t. III, trans. H. Grégoire, p.112; Euripides, *The Suppliant Women*, in *Orestes and Other Plays*, trans. Philip Vellacott, p. 201.

4. *Ion*, 597-602, French p. 208; English p. 60.

5. Ibid., 602-603.

6. We may recall here the project put forward by Foucault in September 1972 of a "dynastics of knowledge" in "De l'archéologie à la dynastique" in *Dits et Écrits*, II, no. 119, p. 406: the study of "the relationship existing between those major types of discourse that we can see in a culture and the historical, economic, and political conditions of their appearance and formation."

7. This distinction is particularly studied by Claude Lefort in, for example, "Permanence du théologico-politique?" (1981) and "La Question de la démocratie" (1983), both reprinted in *Essais sur le politique* (Paris: Le Seuil, 1986).

8. Euripide, *Les Phéniciennes*, 388-394, in *Tragédies*, t. V, trans. H. Grégoire and L. Méridier (Paris: Les Belles Lettres, 1950) p. 170; Euripides, *The Phoenician Women* in *Orestes and Other Plays*, trans. Philip Vellacott, p. 248:
"JOCASTA: What is an exile's life? Is it great misery?
POLYNEICES: The greatest; worse in reality than in report.
JOCASTA: Worse in what way? What chiefly galls an exile's heart?
POLYNEICES: The worst is this: right of free speech does not exist.
JOCASTA: That's a slave's life—to be forbidden to speak one's mind.
POLYNEICES: One has to endure the idiocy of those who rule.
JOCASTA: To join fools in their foolishness—that makes one sick."

9. Ibid., 392, French: "That's being a slave (*doulou tod' eipas*), to silence one's thought"; English: "That's a slave's life—to be forbidden to speak one's mind."

10. Euripide, *Hippolyte*, 407-409, in *Tragédies*, t. II, trans. L. Méridier, p. 45: "Perish with cruel death the first woman who dishonored her bed with strangers!"; English translation by Philip Vellacott, Euripides, *Hippolytus*, in *Three Plays*, p. 95: "Whatever woman first betrayed her marriage-bed / With other men, all deadly curses crowd on her!"

11. Ibid., 409-412: "This evil was born among women of noble households. When dishonor is approved by the great, one thing is certain: the wicked will see it as honorable"; English: "It was from noble houses that this plague first fell / On women; when the high-born choose a shameful course, / The common herd will surely find it right for them."

12. Ibid., 415-418: "How, sovereign Kypris goddess of the sea, can they look in the face their bed companion, without fearing that the complicit shadows and roof may one day speak?"; English p. 96: "Oh, sovereign, sea-born Aphrodite! How can they / Look in their husbands' eyes, without a shudder felt / Lest sheltering darkness and their guilty walls should speak?"

13. Ibid., 421-423; English: "I want my two sons to go back and live / In glorious Athens, hold their heads high there, and speak / Their mind like free men, honoured for their mother's name. / One thing can make the most bold-spirited man a slave: / To know the secret of a parent's shameful act."

14. Euripide, *Les Bacchantes*, 668, in *Tragédies*, t. VI, trans. H. Grégoire (Paris: Les Belles Lettres, 1968) p. 269; English translation by Philip Vellacott, *The Bacchae*, in Euripides, *The Bacchae and Other Plays*, p. 215.

15. Ibid., 669-673; English:
"HERDSMAN:
   …I fear your hastiness,
   My lord, your anger, your too potent royalty.

PENTHEUS:
>From me fear nothing. Say all that you have to say;
>Anger should not grow hot against the innocent."

16. Euripide, *Oreste*, 884-930, in *Œuvres complètes*, t. VI, trans. F. Chapouthier and L. Méridier (Paris: Les Belles Lettres, 1973) pp. 67-69; English translation by Philip Vellacott, *Orestes*, in Euripides, *Orestes and Other Plays*, pp. 332-333:

>"When the full roll of citizens was present, a herald
>Stood up and said, 'Who wishes to address the court,
>To say whether or not Orestes ought to die
>For matricide?' At this Talthybius rose, who was
>Your father's colleague in the victory over Troy.
>Always subservient to those in power, he made
>An ambiguous speech, with fulsome praise of Agamemnon
>And cold words for your brother, twisting eulogy
>And censure both together—laying down a law
>Useless to parents; and with every sentence gave
>Ingratiating glances towards Aegisthus' friends.
>Heralds are like that—their whole race have learnt to jump
>To the winning side; their friend is anyone who has power
>Or a government office. Prince Diomedes spoke up next.
>He urged them not to sentence either you or your brother
>To death, but satisfy piety by banishing you.
>Some shouted in approval; others disagreed.
>   Next there stood up a man with a mouth like a running spring,
>A giant in impudence, an enrolled citizen, yet
>No Argive; a mere cat's-paw; putting his confidence
>In bluster and ignorant outspokenness, and still
>Persuasive enough to lead his hearers into trouble.
>...
>He said you and Orestes should be killed with stones;
>Yet, as he argued for your death, the words he used
>Were not his own, but all prompted by Tyndareos.
>   Another arose, and spoke against him—one endowed
>With little beauty, but a courageous man; the sort
>Not often found mixing in street or market-place,
>A manual labourer—the sole backbone of the land;
>Shrewd, when he chose, to come to grips in argument;
>A man of blameless principle and integrity.
>He said, Orestes son of Agamemnon should be
>Honoured with crowns for daring to avenge his father
>By taking a depraved and godless woman's life—
>One who corrupted custom; since no man would leave
>His home, and arm himself, and march to war, if wives
>Left there in trust could be seduced by stay-at-homes,
>And brave men cuckolded. His words seemed sensible
>To honest judges."

17. Ibid., 885, French p. 67: "the herald stood up and said: 'Who wants to speak (*tis khrēzai legein*)?'"; English, p. 332: "...a herald / Stood up and said, 'Who wishes to address the court /...?'"

18. Ibid., 889-890, French p. 68: "Always a slave to the powerful, he used double talk (*dikhomutha*)"; English, p. 332: "Always subservient to those in power, he made / An ambiguous speech...."

19. On this character, "clever rhetor, of Thracian origin on his mother's side, and, according to Aeschines, fraudulently inscribed on the roll of citizens," see the "Notice" to *Orestes*, p. 8.

20. Euripides, *Orestes*, 905, French p. 68: "trusting in the roar of his voice and the crudeness of his free-spokenness (*kamathai parrēsia*)"; English, p. 332: "...putting his confidence / In bluster and ignorant outspokenness...."

21. Ibid., 906, French: "persuasive (*pithanos*) enough to plunge the citizens into some disaster one day"; English: "Persuasive enough to lead his hearers into trouble."

22. Ibid., 922, French: "a man of integrity (*akeraios*) and irreproachable conduct"; English, p. 333: "A man of blameless principle and integrity."

23. Ibid., 921, French: "of shrewd intelligence (*xunetos de*) moreover"; English, "Shrewd."

24. An Athenian politician, Theramenes was one of the leaders of the conservative party hostile to Pericles. After the coup d'État of 411 he took part in the drafting of the new constitution.

25. *Orestes*, 931, French, p. 69; English, p. 333: "His words seemed sensible / To honest judges; and there were no more speeches."

26. Ibid., 943-945, French p. 70; English, p. 333:
    "Yet he did not convince the assembly, though his words
    Seemed plausible. That wretch who held the people's ear,
    Demanding your death and your brother's, won the day."

ten

2 FEBRUARY 1983

Second hour

[*The rectangle of* parrēsia: *formal condition, de facto condition, truth condition, and moral condition.* ∽ *Example of the correct functioning of democratic* parrēsia *in Thucydides: three discourses of Pericles.* ∽ *Bad* parrēsia *in Isocrates.*]

I WOULD NOW LIKE quickly to touch on the problem of what could be called the deterioration of *parrēsia*, or the deterioration of the relations between *parrēsia* and democracy. To present things a bit schematically and to understand this process, we could speak, if you like, of a sort of constitutive rectangle of *parrēsia*.

At one corner of the rectangle we could put democracy, understood as the equality accorded to all citizens, and consequently the freedom of each to speak, be in favor or against, and thus to take part in decision making. There will be no *parrēsia* without this democracy. The second corner of the rectangle is what could be called the game of ascendancy or superiority, that is to say, the problem of those who, speaking in front of and above others, get them to listen, persuade them, direct them, and exercise command over them. So: a pole of democracy and a pole of ascendancy. The third corner of *parrēsia*: truth-telling. For there to be *parrēsia*, a good *parrēsia*, there needs to be not just democracy (formal condition) and ascendancy, which is, if you like, the de facto condition. In addition, ascendancy and speaking must be exercised with reference to a certain truth-telling. The *logos*, which exercises its power and ascendancy and is delivered by those who exercise ascendancy over the city, must be a discourse of truth. This is the third corner. Finally, the fourth corner: since this exercise of the right to speak in which one tries to persuade through a discourse of truth takes place precisely in a democracy (first corner), it will therefore take the form of a joust, of rivalry, and confrontation, with the consequence that those who want to deliver a discourse of truth must demonstrate courage (this will be the moral corner). Formal condition: democracy. De facto condition: the ascendancy and superiority of some. Truth condition: the need for a rational *logos*. And finally, moral condition: courage, courage in the struggle. I think this rectangle—with a constitutional corner, the corner of the political game, the corner of truth, and the corner of courage—is what constitutes *parrēsia*.

[...] How is the possibility of a good *parrēsia* and the conditions under which there can be a correct relationship between *politeia* and *parrēsia*, between democracy and *parrēsia*, reflected upon and analyzed in the period we are now considering—that is to say, at the end of the Peloponnesian War, with external disasters on the one hand, and, on the other, internal struggles, with the confrontation in Athens between supporters of a radical democracy and supporters of a moderate democracy, or of an aristocratic return, an aristocratic reaction? And how can one explain the fact that things are not working and that the relationship between *parrēsia* and democracy can produce the ugly effects we have noted and which are denounced in 408 by Euripides in *Orestes*?

First, the good functioning of *parrēsia*. How does *parrēsia* function, in what does it consist, and how can we describe the good relationships between democracy and *parrēsia*? I think we have a very explicit model, a very exact description in the texts of Thucydides devoted to Pericles and Periclean democracy, although the word *parrēsia* is not used in this series of passages. I think that Periclean democracy was represented as a model of the good adjustment between a democratic *politeia* and a whole political game permeated by a *parrēsia* indexed to the *logos* of truth. Anyway, [with] this good adjustment of the democratic constitution to truth-telling through the game of *parrēsia* involves the problem, which you know is not a minor problem: how can democracy withstand the truth? Well, the three discourses (of war, of the dead, and of the plague) that Thucydides puts in the mouth of Pericles in Books One and Two of *History of the Peloponnesian War*—obviously leaving aside the problem of how far this is the discourse of Pericles or of Thucydides, which is not very important for what I want to say, since my problem is the representation of this interplay between democracy and *parrēsia* at the end of the fifth century—seem to me to give an example of what Thucydides imagined this good adjustment to be.

First the discourse of war. You find it in chapter 139 and the following chapters of Book One of *History of the Peloponnesian War*. You remember that the situation is this: Spartan ambassadors have come to Athens and have asked the Athenians not only to limit but to give up some of their imperial conquests over Greece. It is a sort of ultimatum. An assembly is called and this is how Thucydides describes it: "The Athenians called the assembly (*ekklēsian*) and were able to express their views. Many of those present spoke out and opinions were divided: some thought that war was inevitable, others that the decree should not be an obstacle to peace."[1] We have here, if you like, the representation, or the indication of what I called the *politeia* corner in the game of *parrēsia*. Athens functions as a democracy, with an assembly bringing together the people and at which each of those present is free to have their say. This passage points precisely to the *politeia*, to *isēgoria*. Then, each having expressed his opinion and opinion being divided, "Pericles, the son of Xanthippus, stood up to speak. At that time he was the most influential man of Athens, the most skillful in speech and in action. This is the advice he gave the Athenians."[2] Here then you have the second corner of the rectangle I was just talking about, that of ascendancy. In the democratic game set up by the *politeia*, which gives everyone the right to speak, someone comes on the scene to exercise his ascendancy, which is the ascendancy he exercises in speech and in action. You will no doubt say that in this case it is not exactly a matter of the game I pointed out a moment ago, since I insisted on the fact that the power exercised in *parrēsia* must never be the power of just one person. For there to be *parrēsia*, there must be a joust between different persons, it must not be monarchical or tyrannical power but there must be people who are the most influential, those in the front rank. In actual fact—we will come to this shortly and Thucydides says it—it is precisely both the paradox and genius of Pericles to have been at the same time the single most influential man and yet not to have exercised his power through *parrēsia* in a tyrannical or monarchical way, but in a truly democratic manner. So that Pericles, all alone as he may be, being the most influential and not just one among a group of the most influential, is the model of this good functioning, of this good adjustment of *politeia/parrēsia*. So, with the arrival of Pericles we have the corner or angle of ascendancy in the game of *parrēsia*. And this is the discourse of Pericles, or at least how it begins: "My opinion remains, Athenians, that we should not yield to the Peloponnesians. I am well aware however that one is less eager when it comes to action than when one is decreeing war, and that human opinions change according to circumstances. Yet I see that the advice I must give you is always exactly the same."[3] Pericles says: I give you my opinion, it really is my opinion that we should not yield to the Peloponnesians. The advice I must give you is always exactly the same. That is to say, the discourse he will deliver before the Athenians is not only the discourse of political rationality, the true discourse, but a discourse that he lays claim to as his own, so to speak, a discourse with which he identifies himself. Or rather, he delivers a discourse in which he characterizes himself as the person who, in his own name, really is delivering, and has always delivered throughout his life, this discourse of truth. He really is, throughout his political career, the subject who speaks this truth. And we have here the third corner, that of the discourse of truth. The introduction to the discourse continues in this way: "I like to think that, in the event of failure, those I manage to persuade will stick to our common resolutions, unless they are prepared to renounce any claim to merit in the event of success. For public affairs, as well as individual plans, often disappoint our expectations. Thus, we usually blame fortune when our calculations turn out to be defective."[4] What is at issue in this end to the introduction of Pericles' discourse? Well, it is a question, precisely, of risk. When a man stands up, speaks, tells the truth, says this is my opinion, and carries the decision of the Assembly and the city, then, as events unfold, things may not turn out as expected. What then should happen? Should the citizens turn against the person who brought about this failure? I am happy, Pericles says, for you to turn against me in the event of failure, on condition that, if we succeed, you do not claim any merit for the victory. In other words: If you want us to stick together when we are victorious, we must also stick together when we meet with failure, and consequently you will not punish me individually for a decision that we will take together if I persuade you with my discourse of truth. You see the problem of risk appearing here, the problem of courage, and the problem of what will take place between the person who won the decision and the people who followed him. It is this game of risk, danger, and courage which is indicated here, with, if you like, this parrhesiastic pact which corresponds somewhat to the pact we mentioned a short while ago in the play by Euripides. It is a parrhesiastic pact: I tell you the truth; if you so wish, you will go along with it; but if you go along with it, bear in mind that you will show solidarity whatever the consequences may be, and that I will not be the sole person responsible for them.

In this discourse—or rather, in the preliminaries of this discourse, the way in which Thucydides introduces it, and in the introduction of the text itself—I think we have the four elements which form what I have called the rectangle of *parrēsia*. We could say that the introduction of this text represents the scene of the good and great *parrēsia* in which, in the framework of the *politeia*—that is to say, of a democracy which is respected, where everyone can speak—*dunasteia*, the ascendancy of those who govern, is exercised in a discourse of truth which is their own discourse and with which they identify themselves, even if this entails risks that both the person who persuades and those who are persuaded agree to share together. Such is the good *parrēsia*, such is the good adjustment of democracy and truth-telling. So much for the discourse of war.

Then comes the discourse of the dead when, after a year of war, Athens buries its dead and gives a ceremony for them. This discourse is perhaps less interesting for the problem of *parrēsia*. It is found at the beginning of Book Two, starting at chapter 35. Athens, then, is burying its dead, and it has called on Pericles to deliver the eulogy for the dead. Praising the dead, or rather, in order to praise the dead, Pericles begins by praising the city itself. And in this praise of the city, Pericles recalls first of all that "with regard to private disagreements, the law guarantees the equality of all [this is the principle of *isonomia*: the laws are equal for all; M.F.], but with regard to participation in public life, each is considered according to his merit, and the class to which he belongs matters less than his personal value."[5] This is precisely the game of *isēgoria* and *parrēsia* I was talking to you about, *isēgoria* ensuring that the right to speak is not dependent merely on birth, wealth, and money. Everyone will be able to speak, but nevertheless, for participation in public affairs and in this game of participation in public affairs, it is personal merit which ensures the ascendancy of some, an ascendancy which it is good that they exercise, since this is what will guarantee the survival of democracy. It is worth noting that Pericles, just before this passage moreover, said that Athens well deserves the title of democracy. Why does Athens really deserve this name? Because, he says, the city is administered in the general interest, and not in the interest of a minority.[6] You see that it is noteworthy that Pericles does not define democracy by the fact that power is shared out equally between everyone. He does not define democracy by the fact that each can speak and give his opinion, but by the fact that the city is administered in the general interest. That is to say, Pericles refers, if you like, to the great circuit, the great trajectory of *parrēsia* I have been talking about, in which, on the basis of a democratic structure, a legitimate ascendancy exercised through a true discourse, and by someone with the courage to assert this true discourse, actually ensures that the city will take the best decisions for all. This then is what one will be able to call democracy. All in all, democracy is this game based on a democratic constitution, in the strict sense of the term, which defines an equal status for everyone. The circuit of *parrēsia*: ascendancy, true discourse, courage, and, as a result, formulation and acceptance of a general interest. This is the great circuit of democracy, the *politeia/parrēsia* connection.

Finally, the third discourse of Pericles in Thucydides is the dramatic discourse of the plague. The plague is ravaging Athens and military failures and reverses are multiplying. We are at the fourth corner: risk. The parrhesiastic pact Pericles offered the Athenians in the introduction of the first discourse, the discourse of war, is being broken. The Athenians blame Pericles and are angry with him. They send ambassadors directly to the Lacedaemonians to make peace behind his back, and it is at this point that Pericles, who is still the military commander, calls the Assembly. His discourse begins at chapter 60 of Book Two of *History of the Peloponnesian War*, and he says: "I was expecting this display of your anger against me [this was the risk taken and stated, although he wanted to avoid it at the beginning of the discourse of war; M.F.]; I know the reasons for it. I have called this assembly in order to appeal to your memory [the memory of the discourse delivered, but also the memory of the history of Athens and of the good functioning of democracy; M.F.] and to reproach you if your irritation with me is groundless and if you lose courage in the face of adversity."[7] This passage is interesting because we can see here precisely how, when people turn against him, the politician, the one who proposed the parrhesiastic pact in the first discourse, instead of flattering the citizens or shifting responsibility for what has happened on to something or someone else, turns round against his citizens and reproaches them. You reproach me, but I reproach you. You reproach me for the decisions which were taken and the misfortunes of war, well I now turn to you and, without flattery, I address my reproaches to you. This courageous turnaround of the man who tells the truth when others break the parrhesiastic pact he has made with them is typical of the person who truly has the sense of *parrēsia* in democracy.

A bit further on, Pericles will portray himself to the Athenians. He tells them (still in this passage of reproaches): "You are angry with me, with one who is inferior to no one [a classical formula and understatement for saying: I am superior—referring to an ascendancy; M.F.] in identifying the public interest and expressing what they think in speech, one who is devoted to the city and impervious to corruption."[8] In this phrase you can see a reference to some of the qualities of someone who is a politician, democrat, and parrhesiast: he knows how to identify the public interest, he knows how to express his thought in speech. He is the parrhesiast inasmuch as he delivers the true discourse and uses it to direct the city. And he enlarges upon the qualities he has just listed and attributed to himself: "To perceive the public interest" he says "but fail to make one's fellow citizens see it clearly is exactly as if one had not thought about it." He means: it is all very well for a politician to be able to identify the good, but it is still necessary for him to say it, and to get his fellow citizens to see it clearly, that is to say, to have the courage to say it, even if it displeases, and to have the ability to set it out in a *logos*, in a discourse that is sufficiently persuasive to get citizens to obey it and come round to it. "To perceive the public interest but fail to make one's fellow citizens see it clearly is exactly as if one had not thought about it. To have these two talents [perceiving the public interest and then setting it out properly; M.F.] and yet be ill-intentioned towards one's country is to be condemned to not giving any useful advice to the State [seeing the good, knowing how to say it, and, third condition, having the courage to say it, not being ill-intentioned towards his country, being devoted, consequently, to the general interest; M.F.]. Someone may love his country but be open to corruption, and such a person is capable of selling everything for money."[9] So one needs not simply these three conditions (seeing the truth, being capable of telling it, being devoted to the general interest), but also one must be morally reliable, honest, and incorruptible. It is by having these four qualities that the politician will be able to exercise through his *parrēsia* the ascendancy necessary for the democratic city to be governed—in spite of or through democracy. If, Pericles says, "you admitted that I possessed these different qualities [knowing, being capable of saying, being devoted to the general interest, not being corrupted; M.F.], be it only slightly more than others [once again, claim to ascendancy; M.F.], and if as a result of this you followed my advice for the war, then you would be wrong to accuse me of a crime now."[10] This is how Pericles, in this dramatic situation in which he is threatened by the Athenians, theorizes the proper adjustment between democracy and the exercise of *parrēsia* and truth-telling, an exercise which, once again, necessarily entails the ascendancy of some over others. So this is the image of good *parrēsia* given by Thucydides.*

Only there is also the image of the bad *parrēsia*, the *parrēsia* which does not work in a democracy and does not remain true to its own principles. This image of bad *parrēsia* will be an obsession after the death of Pericles, who was always referred to as the man of the good

---

* The manuscript clarifies:

"The risks and dangers of *parrēsia*: a good democracy (*alēthinē dēmokratia*) must be such that if the right to speak is given to each, the game must be open in such a way that some can stand out and assume an ascendancy. Now of course this game is not tolerated by a tyranny (cf. Eteocles/Polyneices). But there are also democracies that do not allow it: the man who wants to oppose what the majority think is exiled or punished. We may note however that the transfer of the problem of the ascendancy of the courageous parrhesiast of democracy to autocracy (this involving exercising the necessary ascendancy over the Prince's soul, the discourse of truth that he must be got to listen to by educating and persuading him, and the risk the advisor takes by opposing the prince and getting him to take a decision which may turn out badly) has to a great extent been carried out by the philosopher. Also the problem of *parrēsia* developed as art of government which, with Raison d'État in the sixteenth and seventeenth centuries, acquired autonomy in relation to morality and the Prince's education."

adjustment of *parrēsia* and democracy. After the death of Pericles, Athens will represent itself as a city in which the game of democracy and the game of *parrēsia*, of democracy and of truth-telling, do not manage to combine and suitably adjust to each other in a way which will enable this democracy to survive. This representation, this image of the bad adjustment of democracy and truth, of democracy and truth-telling, is found in a number of texts, two of which seem to me to be particularly revealing and clear. One is in Isocrates, the beginning of *Peri tēs eirēnēs*, *On the Peace*, and the other in Demosthenes, the beginning of the *Third Philippic*, but we could find many others. I would like to read you some passages from the beginning of the discourse *On the Peace* by Isocrates in which he shows how and why things are not going well. You will see how close this is to the representation of bad *parrēsia* that I read earlier from Euripides' tragedy *Orestes*.

Right at the beginning of this treatise in which a possible peace offered to the Athenians must be discussed, Isocrates, who is a supporter of the peace, says: "I see that you [he is addressing the Assembly; M.F.] do not give an equal hearing to the speakers, that you pay attention to some, while you cannot stand even the voice of others. Moreover, it is not at all surprising that you act in this way, for your custom is always to throw out speakers who do not agree with your desires."[11] So, there is bad *parrēsia* when measures are taken against orators, or orators are threatened with such measures, like expulsion—but these measures may go as far as exile, or ostracism, and also, in some cases (and Athens had experienced this and will do so again in the future) death. There is no good *parrēsia*, and consequently no good adjustment between democracy and truth-telling, when this threat of death hangs over stating the truth. A bit further on, in paragraph 14 of *On the Peace*, Isocrates says: "For my part, I am well aware that it is tough opposing your state of mind, and that in the heart of democracy there is no free speech except for the most unreasonable people here in this place, who have no concern for you, and for comic writers in the theater. And the most dangerous thing of all is that to those who portray the faults of the State to other Greeks [that is to say, authors of comedies, those who parade the State's faults before the eyes of the Greeks; M.F.] you give grateful acknowledgement that you do not accord even to those who do you good, and you are as bad tempered with those who reprimand you and correct you as you are with those who do harm to the State."[12] In other words, the question raised here is, if you like, the place of criticism. Isocrates reproaches the Athenians for accepting a representation of their own faults, defects, and errors provided that this is in the theater in the form of comedy. The Athenians accept this criticism, whereas in fact it holds them up to ridicule in the eyes of all Greeks. On the other hand, within the framework of politics, the Athenians cannot stand any criticism in the form of a reproach addressed directly to the Assembly by an orator. They get rid of orators or politicians who play this game. This is the first reason why *parrēsia* and democracy no longer get on well together and no longer call on or imply each other, as was the dream, or as was found on the horizon of the tragedy *Ion*.

But besides this negative side, this negative reason, we should add some positive reasons: if there is no longer this good understanding between *parrēsia* and democracy, it is not just because of the refusal of truth-telling, it is because truth-telling gives way to something which imitates it, to false truth-telling. And those who deliver this discourse of false truth-telling are precisely the flatterers. What is the discourse of flattery, demagogic discourse? Here again we can turn to the discourse of Isocrates which evokes the flatterers: "You have managed to get professional orators to exercise and devote their skill, not to what will be useful to the State, but to the means of giving speeches agreeable to you. And right now this is the direction in which most of them are rushing. Everyone could see that it would please you more to hear those who exhort you to war than those who counsel peace."[13] I am passing briefly over these and other elements given in this text. [But, to summarize,] what does this bad *parrēsia* consist of, which, like bad money, drives out and takes the place of the good?

First, it is characterized by the fact that just anybody can speak. What qualifies someone to speak and gives him ascendancy [is no longer] those old ancestral rights of birth and especially of belonging to the soil—of the nobility, but also, as we saw earlier, of the small peasants—it is no longer belonging to the soil and to a tradition, any more than it is qualities like those of Pericles (personal qualities, moral qualities of integrity, intelligence, devotion, and so forth). Henceforth, anybody can speak, which is a constitutional right. But just anybody will in fact speak and will in fact exercise ascendancy by speaking.

Even those who have recently become citizens, as was the case with Cleophon, may exercise ascendancy in this way. It will be the worst therefore, and not the best. In this way ascendancy is perverted. Second, this bad parrhesiast who arrives from anywhere does not say what he does because it represents his opinion, or because he thinks that his opinion is true, or because he is intelligent enough for his opinion to correspond in fact to the truth and what is best for the city. He speaks only because and to the extent that what he says represents the prevailing opinion, which is that of the majority. In other words, instead of ascendancy being exercised through the specific difference of true discourse, the bad ascendancy of anybody is achieved through conformity to what anybody may say and think. Finally, the third characteristic of this bad *parrēsia* is that the armature of this false true discourse is not the singular courage of the person who, like Pericles, is able to turn against the people and reproach them in turn. Instead of this courage, we find individuals who seek only one thing: to ensure their own safety and their own success by pleasing their listeners, by flattering their feelings and opinions. The bad *parrēsia* which drives out the good is then, if you like, "everybody," "anybody," saying anything, provided it is well received by anybody, that is to say, everybody. Such is the mechanism of bad *parrēsia*, which is basically the elimination of the distinctive difference of truth-telling in the game of democracy.

What I wanted to tell you today can therefore by summarized in this way. I think that the new problem of the bad *parrēsia* at the turn of the fifth and fourth centuries at Athens, [and more generally] the problem of *parrēsia*, good or bad, is basically the problem of the indispensable, but always fragile difference introduced by the exercise of true discourse in the structure of democracy. On the one hand in fact, there can only be true discourse, the free play of true discourse, and access to true discourse for everybody where there is democracy. However, and this is where the relationship between true discourse and democracy becomes difficult and problematic, it has to be understood that true discourse is not and cannot be distributed equally in a democracy according to the form of *isēgoria*. Not everybody can tell the truth just because everybody may speak. True discourse introduces a difference or rather is linked, both in its conditions and in its effects, to a difference: only a few can tell the truth. And once only a few can tell the truth, once this truth-telling has emerged into the field of democracy, a difference is produced which is that of the ascendancy exercised by some over others. True discourse and the emergence of true discourse underpins the process of governmentality. If democracy can be governed, it is because there is a true discourse.

And then you see a new paradox now appears. The first paradox was: there can only be true discourse through democracy, but true discourse introduces something completely different and irreducible to the egalitarian structure of democracy. But, to the extent that it really is true discourse, that it is good *parrēsia*, this true discourse is what will enable democracy to exist, and to continue to exist. True discourse must have its place for democracy actually to be able to take its course and be maintained through misadventures, events, jousts, and wars. So democracy can continue to exist only through true discourse. But on the other hand, inasmuch as true discourse in democracy only comes to light in the joust, in conflict, confrontation, and rivalry, it is always threatened by democracy. And this is the second paradox: there is no democracy without true discourse, for without true discourse it would perish; but the death of true discourse, the possibility of its death or of its reduction to silence is inscribed in democracy. No true discourse without democracy, but true discourse introduces differences into democracy. No democracy without true discourse, but democracy threatens the very existence of true discourse. These are, I think, the two great paradoxes at the center of the relations between democracy and true discourse, at the center of the relations between *parrēsia* and *politeia*: a *dunasteia* indexed to true discourse and a *politeia* indexed to the exact and equal distribution of power. Well, in a time like ours, when we are so fond of posing the problems of democracy in terms of the distribution of power, of the autonomy of each in the exercise of power, in terms of transparency and opacity, and of the relation between civil society and the State, I think it may be a good idea to recall this old question, which was contemporary with the functioning of Athenian democracy and its crises, namely the question of true discourse and the necessary, indispensable, and fragile caesura that true discourse cannot fail to introduce into a democracy which both makes this discourse possible and constantly threatens it. That's it, thank you.

1. Thucydide, *Histoire de la guerre du Péloponnèse*, t. I, ch. 139, trans. J. Voilquin (Paris: Garnier Frères, 1948) p. 90; English translation by Rex Warner, Thucydides, *History of the Peloponnesian War* (London: Penguin Books, 1972) Book One, 139, p. 118: "The Athenians then held an assembly in order to debate the matter, and decided to look into the whole question once and for all and then to give Sparta her answer. Many speakers came forward and opinions were expressed on both sides, some maintaining that war was necessary and others saying that the Megarian decree should be revoked and should not be allowed to stand in the way of peace."

2. Ibid.; English: "Among the speakers was Pericles, the son of Xanthippus, the leading man of his time among the Athenians and the most powerful both in action and in debate. His advice was as follows."

3. Ibid., ch. 140; English: "'Athenians,' he said, 'my views are the same as ever: I am against making any concessions to the Peloponnesians, even though I am aware that the enthusiastic state of mind in which people are persuaded to enter upon a war is not retained when it comes to action, and that people's minds are altered by the course of events. Nevertheless I see that on this occasion I must give you exactly the same advice as I have given in the past'."

4. Ibid., French pp. 140-141; English pp. 118-119: "...and I call upon those of you who are persuaded by my words to give your full support to these resolutions which we are making all together, and to abide by them even if in some respect or other we find ourselves in difficulty; for, unless you do so, you will be able to claim no credit for intelligence when things go well with us. There is often no more logic in the course of events than there is in the plans of men, and this is why we usually blame our luck when things happen in ways that we did not expect."

5. Ibid., Book Two, ch. 37, French p. 120; English p. 145: "When it is a question of settling private disputes, everyone is equal before the law; when it is a question of putting one person before another in positions of public responsibility, what counts is not membership of a particular class, but the actual ability which the man possesses."

6. Ibid., French: "Because the State is administered in the interest of the mass and not of a minority, our regime has taken the name of democracy": English: "Our constitution is called a democracy because power is in the hands not of a minority but of the whole people."

7. Ibid., ch. 60, French pp. 133-134; English p. 158: "I expected this outbreak of anger on your part against me, since I understand the reasons for it; and I have called an assembly with this object in view, to remind you of your previous resolutions and to put forward my own case against you, if we find that there is anything unreasonable in your anger against me and in your giving way to your misfortunes."

8. Ibid., French p. 134; English p. 159: "So far as I am concerned, if you are angry with me you are angry with one who has, I think, at least as much ability as anyone else to see what ought to be done and to explain what he sees, one who loves his city and one who is above being influenced by money."

9. Ibid.; English: "A man who has the knowledge but lacks the power clearly to express it is no better off than if he never had any ideas at all. A man who has both these qualities, but lacks patriotism, could scarcely speak for his own people as he should. And even if he is patriotic as well, but not able to resist a bribe, then this one fault will expose everything to the risk of being bought and sold."

10. Ibid.; English: "So that if at the time when you took my advice and went to war you considered that my record with regard to these qualities was even slightly better than that of others, then now surely it is quite unreasonable for me to be accused of having done wrong."

11. Isocrate, *Discours*, t. III, "Sur la paix", 3, trans. G. Mathieu (Paris: Les Belles Lettres, 1942) p. 12; English translation by George Norlin, "On the Peace" in *Isocrates*, Vol. 2 (Cambridge and London: Harvard and Heinemann, "Loeb Classical Library," 1968) §3, pp. 7-9: "I observe...that you do not hear with equal favor the speakers who address you, but that, while you give your attention to some, in the case of others you do not even suffer their voice to be heard. And it is not surprising that you do this; for in the past you have formed the habit of driving all the orators from the platform except those who support your desires."

12. Ibid., §14, French p. 15; English p. 15: "But I know that it is hazardous to oppose your views and that, although this is a free government, there exists no 'freedom of speech' except that which is enjoyed in this Assembly by the most reckless orators, who care nothing for your welfare, and in the theatre by the comic poets. And, what is most outrageous of all, you show greater favour to those who publish the failings of Athens to the rest of the Hellenes than you show even to those who benefit the city, while you are as ill-disposed to those who rebuke and admonish you as you are to men who work injury to the state."

13. Ibid., §5, French p. 13; English p. 9: "Indeed, you have caused the orators to practise and study, not what will be advantageous to the state, but how they may discourse in a manner pleasing to you. And it is to this kind of discourse that the majority of them have resorted also at the present time, since it has become plain to all that you will be better pleased with those who summon you to war than with those who counsel peace."

eleven

9 February 1983

First hour

[
Parrēsia: *everyday usage; political usage.* ∼ *Reminder of three exemplary scenes: Thucydides; Isocrates; Plutarch.* ∼ *Lines of evolution of* parrēsia. ∼ *The four great problems of ancient political philosophy: the ideal city; the respective merits of democracy and autocracy; addressing the Prince's soul; the philosophy/rhetoric relationship.* ∼ *Study of three texts by Plato.*
]

SINCE IT IS THE vacation and I have just received in my letter box an auditor's objection, I would like to take advantage of this to clarify maybe one or two things that may not have been clear. The objection is interesting in fact. The auditor tells me that he is not very satisfied with what I have said about *parrēsia*, and he refers me to a definition of *parrēsia* which could be said to be canonical, which, he says, signifies generally any form of free speech; and second, within the framework of the democratic city and in the political sense of the term, *parrēsia* is this freedom of speech given to every citizen, and only to citizens of course, but to all of them, even if they are poor. So, I would like to recall the following with regard to these two aspects of the definition of *parrēsia*.

First, it is of course understood that the term *parrēsia* has an everyday sense which means free speech. Joined to this notion of free speech, in which one says whatever one likes, is the notion of frankness. That is to say, in *parrēsia* one not only speaks freely and says whatever one likes, but there is also the idea that one says what one really thinks, what one actually believes to be true. In this sense *parrēsia* is frankness, and we could say it is the profession of truth. So, I would correct this everyday definition of the word *parrēsia* by saying that it is not just freedom of speech; it is frankness, the profession of truth. Having said that, it is obvious that this notion or term *parrēsia* is sometimes and even often employed in a completely everyday sense outside of any technical or political context or framework. And in the Greek texts you frequently find someone saying: Listen, to speak to you frankly (*"parrēsia"*: with *parrēsia*), a bit as we say: to speak to you quite freely. When we say "speaking freely," this is of course an everyday, ready made expression which does not have a strong meaning. Nevertheless, it remains the case that free speech is a political problem; freedom of speech is a political problem, a technical problem, and also a historical problem. I would say the same is true of *parrēsia*: it has an everyday, current, familiar, and obvious meaning, and then this precise and technical meaning.

Second, with reference to this precise and technical meaning, I do not think that we can simply sum up the meanings and especially the problems raised by the notion of *parrēsia* by saying that it is the freedom of speech granted to every citizen, rich or poor, in a democracy. Why don't I think this is sufficient? First because, once again—and here I refer you to what I was telling you last week—in the definition of democracy we find these two notions, *isēgoria* and *parrēsia* (I refer you to the text by Polybius, but there are others). *Isēgoria* is in actual fact the constitutional, institutional, juridical right accorded to every citizen to speak, to have one's say in all the forms that this may take in a democracy: political, judicial, interpellation, and so on. So what is the difference between *isēgoria*, by which someone can speak and say whatever he thinks, and *parrēsia*? I think it is that *parrēsia*, which is of course underpinned by *isēgoria*, refers to something a bit different, which is actual political practice. If in fact it is part of the democratic game, part of the internal law of democracy, that anybody can have his say, then this raises a technical, political problem: who in fact will speak and actually be able to bring his influence to bear on the decisions of others, who will be capable of persuading, and who, proffering what he judges to be the truth, will be able to serve as a guide for the others? To that extent I do not think that the problems raised by *parrēsia* are simply a matter of the equal distribution of the right to speak to all citizens, rich or poor, in the city. It is in this respect that this definition of *parrēsia* seems to me to be insufficient. Second—and this is what I will try to begin to analyze today—we absolutely should not think that this question of *parrēsia*—in the political sense of who will speak, tell the truth, assume ascendancy over the others, persuade, and, consequently, govern in the name of the truth and on the basis of the truth?—arises only in the field of democracy. On the contrary, we will see that *parrēsia* poses technical, political problems even in the autocratic game of power. These problems will be: How is one to address the Prince; how is one to tell him the truth? How, on what basis, and through what training should one act on his soul? What is the Prince's counselor? So I would say that the notion of *parrēsia* should be a bit more strictly defined than just *isēgoria* in the field of democracy. It raises supplementary problems and calls for supplementary definitions in relation to the notion of *isēgoria*, that is to say, of the equal distribution of the right to speak. And in another, broader sense, it is not just a question of the game of truth or of the game of the right to speak in democracy, but of the game of the right to speak and of the game of truth in any, even an autocratic form of government.

I reply to this objection, first because I am very pleased that it is put to me. It's good. Given the difficulties of circulation in this kind of audience, well, some have to write and others to reply orally. And, second, this objection no doubt actually corresponded to some inaccuracies in my account, at any rate, I think these objections could have been made by others, so I am happy to have been able to reply to them in this way. [...]*

I would like now to start again with the three texts or scenes we came across in the previous accounts. These three texts refer to three scenes of Greek political life, three real scenes moreover, but what matters for me is obviously the way in which these scenes are reflected in the texts which set them out.

---

* M.F. adds:
> I don't know... If the auditor in question, who I do not know personally, is not entirely satisfied with what I have just said, well, he can write to me again [*a voice is heard in the audience*: I am satisfied]. Anyway, in one of the sessions after the vacation, as we did previously, we will be able to continue the discussion. But, it's OK more or less? Finally, I think that this practice of written question and oral response is, once again, a possible form of exchange in an institution which, to my regret, is evidently not really meant for dialogue and shared work.

The first scene, or rather the first text, you remember, is that of Thucydides, recounting in a more or less creative, symbolic, or in any case reorganized way, the famous debate that took place in Athens after the Spartans had sent the Athenians an ambassador with a sort of ultimatum and the question was whether to accept or reject it, that is to say, whether to go to war or make peace. So it is the famous decision which was so crucial for the history of Athens and the whole of Greece; the decision which unleashes the Peloponnesian War. Thucydides' description, you remember, refers to some important elements. First, the fact that, of course, the Assembly of the people was called in a completely regular way, that each had been able to express his opinion (*isēgoria*), and that these different opinions had divided the Assembly into different tendencies. It was at this point that Pericles—who Thucydides recalls was the most influential Athenian—stood up, came forward, and, after having let everyone express themselves, said what he had to say. And he carefully emphasized that he not only considered what he had to say to be true, but that it was something that was his opinion. It was what he thought, what he thought at that moment, but also basically what he had always thought. So it was not just a statement of prudence or conjunctural political wisdom. He really professed to be telling the truth in this order of things, and he identified himself with this profession of truth. Finally, you recall the last aspect of this scene. From the start of his discourse he envisaged the possibility of the war not necessarily having a favorable outcome. And he says clearly that if in actual fact the enterprise is not crowned with success, and if in actual fact the people voted for war, then those who backed him in this way should not turn against him. If the people are ready to share possible success with him, then they really should share defeat and failure with him as well, if this should occur. This is the aspect of risk and danger in political truth-telling. I would like to start again from this first scene.

Then I would like to remind you of a second scene which we have come across and which is less historically real, although it refers to elements that it is perfectly possible to place: this is the discourse of Isocrates I referred to at the end of the last lecture, *On the Peace*, which was written sixty or seventy years later, around 355-356, and in which Isocrates has to speak either in favor of or against a peace proposal.

This discourse, like all of Isocrates' discourses, was not in fact delivered to the Assembly. It is much more a sort of...not pamphlet but, let's say, manifesto in the form of a possible discourse to the Assembly in favor of peace. And in the exordium of this discourse Isocrates recalls that the question of war and peace is, of course, extremely important. War and peace, he says, are things which have the greatest weight in the life of men and with regard to which it is essential to make a good decision (*orthōs bouleuesthai*: decide well).[1] Continuing his exordium, Isocrates says that in actual fact the Assembly does not treat all those who speak for or against peace in the same way. Some are received well, others are expelled. Why are they expelled? Well, because they do not speak in line with the desires of the Assembly. And because they do not speak as the Assembly would have them speak, they are driven out. Now, he says, there is something in this which is absolutely unjust and which disrupts the game of democracy and truth-telling. For why would those who fall in line with the Assembly's desires go to the trouble of finding and formulating rational arguments? They need only repeat what others say. They need only reproduce the babble of opinion. Those, however, who think differently from what the Assembly in general desires, he says, really must look for rational and true arguments in order to persuade the Assembly and get it to change its opinion. Consequently, an assembly would do much better listening to those who speak to it against its opinion, than to those who merely repeat what it thinks.

Finally, the third scene I would like to mention, the third text, is a text and a scene I talked about at the start of the lectures, in the second week I think. It is that famous scene in which Plato, with Dion at the Sicilian court of Dionysius the Younger, is confronted by the tyrant.[2] Actually this scene is reported by Plutarch long after the period I am considering for the moment, but it recounts a scene which took place precisely in this period, that is to say in the first half of the fourth century. What do we see in this scene? Well, we see two characters: Dion, the uncle of Dionysius the Younger, and the philosopher Plato, who has come at Dion's request to form the soul of Dionysius the Younger. Both are confronted by the tyrant, and both make use of *parrēsia* (truth-telling, frankness). Doing so, they obviously run the risk of angering the tyrant. And we see the two outcomes: on the one hand, Plato, effectively driven out by Dionysius, is not only threatened with death, but

Dionysius plots to kill him; Dion, however, continues to retain ascendancy over Dionysius, and in the latter's court and entourage, only Dion can still influence him.

I have spent some time recalling these three scenes for the following reason. It seems to me that by collating them we can see the emergence of the definition, the outline of a political, historical, and philosophical problem. What is found in these three scenes? In the first place there are some common fundamental elements. First, *parrēsia* is played out and unfolds in a constituted political space. Second, *parrēsia* consists in a particular kind of speech which claims to tell the truth and in which the person who tells the truth also proclaims that he is telling the truth and clearly identifies himself as the enunciator of this true proposition or these true propositions. Third, what is in question, what is played out in these three scenes is the ascendancy which will or will not be assured by the person who speaks and tells the truth. In any case, one tells the truth in order to exercise ascendancy, whether over the Assembly or the Prince is not important, which will really influence the way in which decisions are taken, the way in which the city or the State is governed. And finally, the fourth common element in these scenes is the risk taken, that is to say, the fact that the leader, the person responsible, the person who has spoken may be rewarded or punished by the people or by the Prince according to the success of the undertaking, the result to which his truth-telling has led, or just simply according to the humor of the Assembly or Prince. We have here these same elements.

But at the same time you can see that these three scenes differ from each other. The first scene from Thucydides—Pericles coming forward before the Assembly of the people and speaking out—represents good *parrēsia*, *parrēsia* as it should operate. Among all the citizens who have the right to speak and who actually have been able to give their opinion, and who moreover will give their opinion with their vote, there is one who exercises a form of ascendancy, a good ascendancy, and who takes these risks, explaining exactly what they are. This is good *parrēsia*. The other two—that evoked by Isocrates at the beginning of *Peri tēs eirēnēs*, [and] that evoked by Plutarch's account of Dion's life—are bad *parrēsiai*, or anyway *parrēsiai* which do not succeed as they should, since, in the case evoked by Isocrates, the person who tells the truth is not listened to. And his not being listened to is to the advantage of those who flatter and who, instead of telling the truth, only repeat the opinion of the Assembly. In the case of Dionysius we see a tyrant who, after the philosopher has spoken, can't wait to expel him and plots to have him put to death. It seems to me that through these three scenes with their common and different elements we can see the emergence of what will be both the new problematic of *parrēsia* and an entire field of political thought which will be an enduring feature of Antiquity at least until the end of the second century, or anyway until the great crisis of imperial government in the middle of the third century C.E. I think that to some extent we can look at these five, six, or seven centuries of ancient philosophical thought through the problem of *parrēsia*. What I mean more precisely is this.

First, *parrēsia*, which was presented in Euripides' *Ion* as a privilege or a right to which it was legitimate to aspire on condition that one was a citizen in a city, and which was so strongly desired by Ion, now appears in these three scenes as an ambiguous practice. *Parrēsia* is necessary in democracy, it is also necessary around the Prince: *parrēsia* is a necessary practice. And at the same time it is dangerous, or rather, it risks being both powerless and dangerous. It risks being powerless because there is no guarantee that it will actually function as it should, that it will not lead to a result which is the opposite of that intended. And, on the other hand, it may involve the person who practices it risking his life. So the problematization of this *parrēsia*, an ambiguity about its value, is the first transformation we see through the collation of these three scenes.

Second, a further transformation concerns, as it were, the actual place of *parrēsia*. In Euripides, it was clear and explicitly said that *parrēsia* and democracy formed one body by virtue of a circularity, which you recall we referred to, since, on the one hand, Ion really had to have *parrēsia* for Athenian democracy to be founded and, on the other, it was within this democracy that *parrēsia* could function. *Parrēsia* and democracy formed a single body. Now you see that in the last scene I referred to (the scene from Plutarch involving Plato, Dion, and Dionysius), *parrēsia* no longer forms a single body with democracy. *Parrēsia* has a positive, determinant role to play in another, autocratic type of power. There is, then, a shift of *parrēsia* from the democratic structure, to which it had been linked, to a non-democratic form of government.

Third, through the last scene recounted by Plutarch we see a sort of splitting in two of *parrēsia*. On the one hand, *parrēsia* appears as something that is certainly necessary in the political field strictly speaking. *Parrēsia* is a directly political act which is exercised either before the Assembly, or before the leader, governor, sovereign, tyrant, and so on. It is a political act. But, on the other hand, and this is clear in Plutarch, it is also an act, a way of speaking which is addressed to an individual, to his soul, and it concerns the way in which this soul is to be formed. The development of the Prince's soul, and the role of those around the Prince in relation to this rather than directly in the political sphere, inasmuch it is the Prince who will have to play the political role, shows that *parrēsia* is uncoupled, as it were, from its strictly political function, and that added to political *parrēsia* there is what could be called a psychagogic *parrēsia*, since it involves leading and guiding an individual's soul. So there is a splitting of *parrēsia*.

Finally, fourth—and obviously this will be the essential thing—still [in] the scene recounted by Plutarch, [with] the question of *parrēsia* we see the appearance of a new character. What have we been dealing with in the game of *parrēsia* until now? We have been dealing with the city, citizens, and the question of which citizens could and should be the most influential. We have been dealing with the leader and ultimately with the despotic and tyrannical sovereign. Only now, in the scene recounted by Plutarch—which, again, is also placed at the beginning of the fourth century—Plato, that is to say the philosopher makes his appearance, insofar as the philosopher now has an essential role in this scene of *parrēsia*. For sure, this is not the first time that the philosopher, as philosopher, plays an essential role in the city. There was already a strong ancient tradition, perfectly attested in the fifth century, that the philosopher was, could be, and had to be a lawgiver (a *nomothetēs*) in the city, or else a peacemaker, the one who succeeded in adjusting the balance of the city in such a way as to put an end to dissensions, internecine struggles, and civil wars. The philosopher was in fact a lawgiver, a peacemaker for the city. But in the scene of Plato and Dion confronted by Dionysius, the philosopher makes his appearance as a parrhesiast, as the person who, in a particular political conjuncture, tells the truth on the political stage in order to guide either the city's policy or the soul of the person who directs the city's policy.

In short, through the juxtaposition and collation of these three scenes (that of Thucydides [from] the second half of the fifth century, and the two others, one recounted by Plutarch and the other evoked by Isocrates, both from the first half of the fourth century) we can say that we see the practice of *parrēsia*, first, problematized; second, become a general problem in all political regimes (in all *politeiai*, democratic or not); third, split into a specifically political problem and a problem of psychagogical technique, although both problems are directly connected to each other; and finally, fourth, become the object and theme of a specifically philosophical practice. I think that we can see taking shape here what could be called the four great problems of ancient political thought, which we find already formulated in Plato.

First, is there a regime, an organization, a *politeia* of the city which is such that the indexation of this regime to the truth can do without this always dangerous game of *parrēsia*? Or again: can all the problems of the relations between truth and the organization of the city be settled once and for all? Is it possible for the city to have, once and for all, a clear, definite, fundamental, and as it were immobile relationship to the truth? This is, roughly speaking, the problem of the ideal city. I think the ideal city, of the kind that Plato and others after him will try to design, is one in which the problem of *parrēsia* is resolved in advance, as it were, since the founders of the city founded it in a relationship to the truth that it will not be possible to break apart or dissolve in the future, and all the perils, ambiguities, and dangers peculiar to the game of *parrēsia* will thereby be resolved. This is the first problem, the first theme.

Second, in ancient political thought another theme appears which is also, I think, connected to the first. Which is better? For the life of the city to be indexed properly to the truth, is it better that all those who can, want to, or think they are able speak, be permitted to do so in a democracy? Or is it better to rely on the wisdom of a Prince enlightened by a good advisor? I think that there is a crucial feature here on which we should focus, namely that the great political debate in ancient thought between democracy and monarchy is not just a debate between democracy and autocratic power. It is a confrontation between two couples: the couple of a democracy and certain people who stand up to tell the truth (consequently, if you like: democracy and orator, democracy and the citizen who exercises his right to speak), and the other couple of the Prince and his advisor. The confrontation between these two couples, their comparison, is, I believe, at the heart of one of the great problematics of political thought in Antiquity.

Third, you see the appearance of the problem of the formation and conduct of souls, which is indispensable to politics. The problem appears clearly, of course, when it is a matter of the Prince: how should one act on the Prince's soul, how should one advise him? But even before the advisor, how should one form the Prince's soul so that it may be open to the true discourse that must be delivered to him constantly while he is exercising power? The same question arises with regard to democracy: how will it be possible to form those citizens who will have to take responsibility for speaking and for guiding the others? This, then, is the question of pedagogy.

And finally, the fourth great problem is this: who is capable of taking up this *parrēsia*, this indispensable game of truth in political life—which we may imagine in the very foundation of the city, in an ideal constitution, as well as in the game of democracy with orators, or of the Prince with his advisor, with their comparable respective merits—who is capable of taking up this truth-telling necessary for conducting citizens' souls or the Prince's soul? Who is capable of being the artisan of *parrēsia*? What mode of knowledge, or what *tekhnē*, what theory or practice, what body of knowledge, but also what exercise, what *mathēsis* and *askēsis* will make it possible to take up this *parrēsia*? Is it rhetoric or philosophy? And I think this rhetoric/philosophy question will also run through the field of political thought. It seems to me that this is how we can understand some of the developments fundamental to this form of thought, starting from the fate, the evolution of this practice and problematic of *parrēsia*.

These are the problems that I will take up in the following lectures: the problem of philosophy compared with rhetoric, the problem of psychagogy and education in terms of politics, the question of the respective merits of democracy and autocracy, and the question of the ideal city. But before taking up these different questions, in this session I would like to go back to what could be called the Platonic crossroads, that is to say, to the moment when these different problems are specified and connected up with each other.*

Obviously, it could be said that, in a sense, the whole of Plato's philosophy is present in this problem and that it is difficult to talk about "truth and politics" with regard to Plato without making another general exposition, another general re-reading of his work. I would just like to make a survey and refer to four or five major passages in the Platonic oeuvre where the word *parrēsia* is actually used in this technical, politico-philosophical sense. The term can be found in many other places, precisely in its everyday sense of speaking frankly, speaking freely, etcetera. But there are some texts in which the term *parrēsia* is inserted in an identifiable theoretical context which throws light on the problems posed.

I will not refer to these texts in chronological order, or rather the first three are in chronological order, but, for reasons you will quickly understand, I will leave until last a passage from the *Gorgias*, which was written earlier. The first text I would like to recall is found in Book VIII of the *Republic* from 557a-b. As you know, this is the description of the transition from oligarchy to democracy, and the constitution, the genesis of the democratic city and the democratic man. I will briefly recall the context. The question is that of the genesis of democracy. In the *Republic* Plato says that democracy arises from an oligarchy, that is to say, from a situation in which only some have power and wealth, those famous people having *dunasteia* (that is to say, political influence in the city) through their status, wealth, and the exercise of political power that they reserve for themselves. How does oligarchy become democracy? You remember the genesis:[3] it is basically economic, since those with power and wealth in an oligarchy have no interest in preventing and no desire to prevent the impoverishment of others around them; quite the contrary. The fewer wealthy people there are, the

---

* The manuscript claries here:

"To go back to the Platonic crossroads where we see the criticism of bad *parrēsia*, that of democracy and the orators, of rhetoric, shifting towards the problematic of good *parrēsia*, that of the wise advisor, of the philosopher; in fact many of Plato's texts could be re-read in this perspective; all of Platonic philosophy could be seen from the perspective of the problem of truth-telling in the field of political structures and in terms of the philosophy/rhetoric alternative. Since what is at issue here is the genealogy of the art of governing and the formation of the theme of the prince's advisor, I will go through Plato quickly picking out some texts where we come across the actual use of the word *parrēsia*."

fewer there will be of those in a position to share power with them or likely to want to share power with them. The impoverishment of others is therefore the necessary law, or anyway the natural objective of every oligarchy. To enable others, as it were, to become increasingly impoverished, the oligarchs are careful not to make laws against luxury: the more people lose in mad and vain expenditure on luxury and pleasure, the better things are. Nor do oligarchs make laws to protect debtors against creditors. Instead they allow creditors to pursue debtors in such a way as to increasingly impoverish them, so that we arrive at that well known juxtaposition, described as you know in a famous text, of the very rich and the very poor.[4] When the citizens of an oligarchic city come together in religious liturgies, military gatherings, and civic assemblies there are the very rich and the very poor. Jealousies are aroused and thus begin the internecine wars in which the poorest and most numerous struggle against the others, call on foreign allies, and end up seizing power and overturning the oligarchy. Democracy, Plato says, "is established when the poor, defeating their enemies, massacre some, banish others, and share government and public offices equally with those remaining."[5] This involves what he calls the "*ex isou metadōsi politeias kai arkhōn*": the equal sharing out of the *politeia* (of the constitution, of citizenship and its related rights) and then of the *arkhōn* (of public offices). You have right here the definition of that famous democratic equality which the texts in favor of democracy always said was the very foundation of the democratic city: the characteristic *isonomia* and *isēgoria* of democracy. However, whereas the positive definitions of democracy present this equality as a sort of fundamental structure conferred on the city by a lawgiver, by a legislator, or anyway by legislation which establishes peace in the city, here democratic equality is not only obtained through war, but it continues to carry the trace and mark of this war and conflict within itself, since, after their victory and having exiled the oligarchs, those who remain share out the spoils, so to speak, that is to say, government and public offices. Equality, consequently, rests on this war and relation of forces. Anyway, *isonomia* is established under bad conditions, but it is established nevertheless. What is the result of this *isonomia*? Implicit in Plato's text we find the constitutive elements of democracy. The first consequence of this democracy is *eleutheria* (freedom). And Plato immediately describes this freedom with its two classical components. First, *parrēsia*: freedom of speech. But it is also freedom to do as one likes, not only to give one's opinion, but actually to choose the decisions one wants, license to do as one likes.[6] This structure, this game of freedom in democracy constituted in this way, should be understood in three ways.

First, it really is a matter of the freedom to do and say what one likes in the sense [just defined]. But it is also a matter of a freedom understood in the strictly political sense of the term, each in this democracy being, as it were, his own political unit. *Parrēsia* and the freedom to do as one likes are far from being the condition for the emergence of a common opinion; in the *parrēsia* and *eleutheria* that characterize democracy constituted in this way, each has, so to speak, his own little State: he says what he likes and does as he likes for himself. Not being forced to command in this State, although one is able to do so, not being forced to obey either, if one does not want to, not being forced to wage war when others are doing so, and, if one does not want peace, not being forced to keep the peace when others are doing so; and, on the other hand, commanding and judging if the fancy takes you, despite the law that denies you any political or judicial office; such practices are therefore connected to democracy constituted in this way. Are not such practices, asks the speaker ironically, "divine and delicious at the time?"[7] So, in democracy operating in this way, *parrēsia* is not the element in which a common opinion is formed; it is the guarantee that each will have his own autonomy, his own identity, his own political singularity.

Another consequence of freedom thus understood is that freedom of speech will allow anyone to get up and flatter the crowd. "This indulgence, this extreme broad-mindedness, this contempt for the maxims that we set out with such respect when planning our city, when we said that, except he be endowed with an extraordinary nature, no one can become a good man unless his play since childhood has been with fine things and he applies himself to the study of fine things, with what pride it tramples such maxims underfoot, without bothering about the studies with which a politician has prepared himself for the administration of the State, but if he calls himself a friend of the people this is enough for him to be covered with honors!"[8] So, each has his own political unity. And, on the other hand, he can the address himself to the crowd and get what he wants by flattering it. This is the double negative aspect of *parrēsia* in democracy thus founded: each has his own identity and each can lead the crowd where he wants. Whereas the game of the good *parrēsia* is precisely to introduce the differentiation of true discourse which will make possible the proper direction of the city through the exercise of ascendancy, here, on the contrary, there is a structure of non-differentiation which leads to the worst possible guidance of the city.

Corresponding to this description of the genesis of the bad democratic city, Plato's text describes the soul of the democratic man, which is, as you know, in the image of the democratic city. What is this image of political democracy in man's soul? Well, it is the same as what takes place with desires and pleasures. That is to say, Plato refers to a classical distinction, not unique to him, between necessary and superfluous desires. A properly formed soul is perfectly capable of distinguishing a necessary from a superfluous desire. On the other hand, a democratic soul is precisely one which does not know how to distinguish between each sort of desire, a soul [in which] superfluous desires can enter freely [and] clash with necessary desires.[9] And since there are infinitely more superfluous than necessary desires, it is the former which prevail. So in this game of desires, we have, in fact, the image, the *analogon* of what took place in the revolution that installed democracy. But it must be understood that in this text it is not just a matter of a relationship of resemblance or analogy. In fact the same flaw which produces political anarchy in the democratic city produces anarchy of desire in the soul. If there is anarchy in the city this is quite simply because *parrēsia* does not function properly. *Parrēsia* here is no more than the freedom to say anything, rather than that by which the caesura of true discourse will be produced and that through which the ascendancy of rational men over others will be brought about. What is lacking in a democratic soul, in which the anarchy of desire reigns, what is it that ensures that the anarchy of desires has become so dominant? It is, Plato says, because the *logos alēthēs* (the discourse of truth) has been pushed outside the soul and is denied entry into the citadel.[10] It is this absence of true discourse which will constitute the fundamental characteristic of the democratic soul, just as the bad game of *parrēsia* in the city produces that anarchy peculiar to bad democracy.

The text goes even further than this. There is not just this general analogy between democratic State and democratic soul, there is not just this identity in the lack, the absence of true discourse. In addition there is an even more direct entanglement of the democratic soul and the democratic State. Because the democratic man, his soul lacking *logos alēthēs*, lacking true discourse, is precisely someone who will enter into the political life of democracy where he will have his effect and exercise his power. What will the democratic man lacking *logos alēthees* do? In the anarchy of his desires he will want always to satisfy greater desires. He will seek to exercise power over others, power which is desirable in itself and which will give him access to the satisfaction of all his desires. "Rushing to the tribune, he says and does whatever comes into his head [description of bad *parrēsia*; M.F.]. One day he envies military people and goes over to their side; another day it is the business men, and he throws himself into commerce. In short, he knows neither order nor restraint,"[11] and he drags the rest of the city along with him. In this text, in which the notion of *parrēsia* plays an essential role, you see that in this double description of the democratic man and the democratic city the essence of the evil is the lack of the rightful ascendancy of true discourse. The lack of *alēthēs logos* means that anyone will be able to speak and exert his influence in the democratic city. This lack also means that in the democratic soul all desires will be able to confront, oppose, and struggle with each other, leaving victory to the worst desires. So this puts us on the track of the splitting of the two forms of *parrēsia* (that which is necessary to the life of the city and that which is indispensable to man's soul). Civic or political *parrēsia* is connected to a different *parrēsia*, although each calls for the other. It is this other *parrēsia* that must be able to introduce *alēthēs logos* into the individual's soul. What I think appears quite clearly in this text is a double layering of *parrēsia*.

The second text I would like to talk about is found in the *Laws*, in Book III, 694a. It is a very interesting text because it offers us a completely different image and context of *parrēsia* than the one we have just looked at. In this text we find a description of the kingdom of Cyrus which Plato says represents the "middle course" between servitude and freedom.[12] You know that in some circles, those, moreover, to which both Xenophon and Plato belonged, the Persian monarchy

of Cyrus represented the model of the good and just political constitution. Xenophon's *Cyropedia* is devoted to this theme, and we find
here, in the *Laws*, as well as in some of Plato's late texts, very positive
references to the Persian Empire, or at least to that phase or episode—
fairly mythical for the Greeks—of the reign of Cyrus over the Persian
Empire—the reign of Cyrus was an important political myth at this
time and in this current of opinion. How then does Plato describe the
empire of Cyrus in the *Laws*? First, he says, when Cyrus had carried
off the great victories which put him at the head of his empire, he was
very careful not to allow the victors to exercise unlimited power over
the vanquished. Instead of acting like the bad sovereigns who establish
the despotic rule of their family or friends over the vanquished, Cyrus
appealed to the natural, pre-existing leaders of the defeated populations. First, these leaders became friends of Cyrus and his representa-
tives in the defeated populations. An empire in which the victors put
the vanquished chiefs in the same rank as themselves is an empire
which is properly directed and governed. Second, he tells us that the
empire of Cyrus was a good empire inasmuch as the army was formed
in such a way that the soldiers were the friends of their commanders and, as such, they were prepared to expose themselves to danger
when ordered to do so. Finally, the third characteristic of the empire of
Cyrus was that if there was someone among the sovereign's entourage
who was intelligent and capable of giving good advice, then the king,
being free of any jealousy, gave him full freedom of speech (*parrēsia*).
And not only did he give him full freedom of speech, but he rewarded
and honored anyone who showed that they were capable of advising
him properly. Thereby, through the freedom thus given to his most
intelligent advisors to speak as they wished, he provided the means for
bringing his advisor's capabilities to light, in the interests of everyone.
Henceforth, the text concludes, the Persians prospered in everything
thanks to freedom (*eleutheria*), friendship (*philia*), and community of
views, collaboration (*koinōnia*: the community).[13]

I think this text is very interesting because we see here both the
maintenance of certain values, of a certain theme peculiar to *parrēsia*,
and, at the same time, a shift and transformation of this theme which
enables it to adapt to the completely different political context of autocratic power. In democratic *parrēsia* each had the right to speak. It was

also necessary that those who spoke were the most able. And this was one of the problems peculiar to the operation of democracy. Here there is the same problem, the same theme: some of the Prince's counselors are more competent than others. And the Prince's task, his function, will be precisely to distinguish who is the most fit, intelligent, and able among his counselors.

Second, in democratic *parrēsia*, there was the risk for the person who spoke that his undertakings would not turn out as he thought; this was the danger intrinsic to this *parrēsia*. There was also the more serious or more immediate and even more dangerous risk of displeasing the Assembly and being expelled, possibly being exiled from the city, driven out, and losing one's rights as a citizen, etcetera. There is the same danger in the field of autocratic power, and the Prince's task—which is actually what Cyrus does—is precisely to ensure that the person speaking in front of and facing him is not threatened by his own freedom of speech. Cyrus gave "full freedom of speech and honors to whoever was capable of advising him."[14] We have here the idea of what could be called the parrhesiastic pact. The sovereign must act so that he opens up the space within which his counselor's truth-telling can be formulated and can appear, and in opening up this freedom he undertakes not to punish his counselor and deal ruthlessly with him.

Finally, the third important element to recall is that the peculiar characteristic of democratic *parrēsia* was that it could only really function on condition that some citizens were distinguished from the others and, assuming ascendancy over the Assembly of the people, guided it in the right direction. In democratic equality *parrēsia* was a principle of differentiation, a caesura. Now in the good empire of Cyrus you can see that *parrēsia* is the most manifest form of an entire process which, according to Plato, guarantees the good functioning of the empire, namely that the hierarchical differences that may exist between the sovereign and the others, between his entourage and the rest of the citizens, between officers and soldiers, and between victors and vanquished, are in a way attenuated or compensated for by the formation of relationships which are designated throughout the text as relationships of friendship. *Philia* will unite victors and vanquished, *philia* unites soldiers and their officers, with *philia*, friendship, the sovereign will listen to the counselor who tells him the truth, and the same *philia* will also mean that the counselor will necessarily be called for, anyway will be inclined to speak and to tell the Prince the truth [...]. In this way, the text says, the entire empire will be able to function and work according to the principles of "*eleutheria*" (a freedom), not in the constitutional form of shared political rights, but in the form of freedom of speech. This freedom of speech will give rise to *philia* (friendship). And this friendship will ensure *koinōnia* throughout the empire, between victors and vanquished, soldiers and officers, courtiers and other inhabitants of the empire, and between sovereign and entourage.[15] This freedom of speech, this *parrēsia* is therefore the concrete form of freedom in autocracy. It is a freedom which founds friendship—friendship between different hierarchical levels of the State—and collaboration—the *koinōnia* which ensures the unity of the entire empire.

Finally, the third text is also found in the *Laws* in Book VIII, from 835. It is a rather curious text. You recall that the problem dealt with in Book VIII is, roughly speaking: what assures the moral, religious, and civic order of the city? The whole of the first part of Book VIII is devoted to the organization of religious festivals, of choirs and choral singing, military exercises, and then to the legislation and regimen of pleasures and, very precisely, sexual life. The passage on *parrēsia* is at the heart of this series of considerations, between things concerning religious festivals and military exercises on the one hand, and the sexual regimen on the other. A passage right at the start of the book indicates that these practices (religious festivals, choral singing, military exercises, etcetera) are absolutely indispensable to the city and that where they are lacking the *politeiai* (the cities) are not real organizations but sets of individuals mixed together who fight in the form of "faction."[16] So, for the city to constitute a coherent organization there must be these different elements: religious festivals, choral singing, military exercise, and sexual life, good order in sexual life. What then is needed to establish this unity, this unitary and solid social organization? There must be an authority, he says, which is willingly exercised over people who willingly accept it, an authority of a kind that the citizens can obey and actually want to obey. Consequently, citizens must be personally persuaded of the validity of the law which is imposed on them and which they take up as it were on their own account. And it is at this point that the need for *parrēsia* appears. *Parrēsia* is the true discourse that someone must deliver in the city in order to convince the citizens of the need to obey, at least to obey in that aspect of the city's order which is the most difficult to obtain, which is precisely the citizen's individual life and the life of their soul, or rather the life of their body, that is to say, of their desires and pleasures. And this is how Plato writes when he tackles the analysis of sexual legislation: Here now is "a subject of no small importance where it is difficult to get people to listen, where it would be for God to act, if it were possible that the required prescriptions might come from him. In fact, it seems that a man is needed, a bold man, who, putting frankness (*parrēsia*) above all else, proclaims what he thinks is best for the city and its citizens, prescribes against corrupt souls what is entailed and called for by our whole constitution, says 'no' to all our most powerful passions, and alone, without support from anyone, follows the voice of reason."[17] This text is curious because, once again, we are dealing with the description of an ideal city in which one might think that the very organization of the city, the laws foreseen, the hierarchy of public offices, and the way in which offices are defined, all constitute, as it were, the fundamental link between the organization of the city and the truth. The truth was present in the legislator's mind and what need is there for someone else to tell the truth once he has formulated his system of laws? Now this is precisely what we see in the text. We have a system of laws, everything is settled, public offices are as they should be, and then, when we come to tackle this problem of individual life, of the life of individuals' bodies and desires, we need someone else. Possibly a god is needed, but if the god is not there, then you will need a man. And what will this man have to do? Well, possibly all alone, with no help from anyone else, and speaking in the name of reason, he will address individuals and frankly tell them the truth, a truth which must persuade them to conduct themselves as they ought. I think we have here the idea of a kind of supplement of *parrēsia* that the organization of the city, the order of laws, however rational it may be, will never be able to ensure. Even in an ideal city with perfect order and the best trained magistrates whose functions are exercised exactly as they should be, if citizens are to conduct themselves properly in the order of the city and actually form that coherent organization the city needs in order to survive, then they will still need a supplementary discourse of truth, and someone will be needed to address them in complete frankness, using the language of reason and truth to persuade them. What we see designated in this text is this supplementary parrhesiast as the moral guide of individuals, as the moral guide of individuals in their totality, a kind of high moral functionary of the city. And here again you see *parrēsia* in its complexity or its double articulation: *parrēsia* is in actual fact what the city needs in order to be governed, but it is also what must act on citizens' souls so that they are the citizens they should be, even in the well governed city.

Obviously there is then the text of the *Gorgias*,[18] which I would have liked to explain to you this morning, but we will return to it anyway when we talk about this problem of the guidance of individual souls. It is a text in which *parrēsia* is now completely dissociated from the political problem, where it is simply a matter of *parrēsia* as the test of one soul against another, as the means by which the truth can be passed from one soul into another. In any case, in the three texts of Plato I have talked about, and possibly adding to these that of the *Gorgias*, what I have tried to show you is the disconnection of the problem of *parrēsia*, or rather the range of the problem opening out. The problem of civic, political *parrēsia*, linked to democracy and the problem of the ascendancy of some over others, takes on new aspects in the texts of Plato. It is, on the one hand, the problem of *parrēsia* in a different context than the democratic context; it is the problem of *parrēsia* as action to be exerted, not only on the body of the entire city, but on the individual's soul, whether this be the Prince's soul or the citizen's soul; and finally we see the problem of *parrēsia* appearing as the problem of philosophical action strictly speaking.

This is quite clearly developed in another set of Plato's texts which I would like to talk about in the second hour: the letters, which are Platonic texts that clearly show how it is as a philosopher and on the basis of philosophy that *parrēsia* can be deployed. I will try to analyze this in a few minutes' time.

1. Isocrate, "Sur la paix," 2, p. 12: "We are here in order to deliberate on war or peace, things which have the greatest weight in the life of men and in which it is necessarily the authors of the most rational decisions (*orthōs bouleuomenous*) who get the best results"; English, Isocrates, "On the Peace," §2, p. 7: "For we are assembled here to deliberate about War and Peace, which exercise the greatest power over the life of man, and regarding which those who are correctly advised must of necessity fare better than the rest of the world."

2. See above, lecture of 12 January, first hour, pp. 48-57.

3. Plato, *La République*, livre VIII, 555b-557a, trans. E. Chambry (Paris: Les Belles Lettres, 1934) pp. 23-25; English translation by Paul Shorey, *Republic* in *Plato: The Collected Dialogues*, ed. Edith Hamilton and Huntington Cairns (Princeton: Bollingen Series LXXI, Princeton University Press, 1963) pp. 784-785.

4. Ibid., 556c-d, French pp. 24-25; English p. 785.

5. Ibid., 557a, French p. 25; English p. 785: "And a democracy, I suppose, comes into being when the poor, winning the victory, put to death some of the other party, drive out others, and grant the rest of the citizens an equal share in both citizenship and offices...."

6. Ibid., 557b, French p. 26: "Is it not true that first of all one is free in such a State, and that freedom (*eleutheria*) and free-spokenness (*parrēsia*) reign everywhere, the license to do as one likes?"; English p. 785: "To begin with, are they not free? And is not the city chock-full of liberty and freedom of speech? And has not every man license to do as he likes?"

7. Ibid., 558a, French p. 27; English p. 786: "is not all that a heavenly and delicious entertainment for the time being?"

8. Ibid, 558b; English: "And the tolerance of democracy, its superiority to all our meticulous requirements, its disdain for our solemn pronouncements made when we were founding our city, that except in the case of transcendent natural gifts no one could ever become a good man unless from childhood his play and all his pursuits were concerned with things fair and good—how superbly it tramples underfoot all such ideals, caring nothing from what practices and way of life a man turns to politics, but honoring him if only he says that he loves the people!"

9. Ibid., 558d-561b, French pp. 28-32; English pp. 787-789.

10. Ibid., 561b, French p. 32: "As for reason and truth (*logon alēthē*), I continued, he dismisses them and does not allow them entry into the garrison"; English p. 789: "And he does not accept or admit into the guardhouse the words of truth...."

11. Ibid., 561d, French p. 33; English p. 790: "And frequently he...bounces up and says and does whatever enters his head. And if military men excite his emulation, thither he rushes, and if moneyed men, to that he turns, and there is no order or compulsion in his existence."

12. Plato, *Laws*, Book III, 694a. Plato uses here (see the next note) the translation by L. Robin, *Les Lois*, in Platon, *Œuvres complètes*, t. II (Paris: Gallimard, "La Pléiade") p. 732; English translation A.E. Taylor, *The Laws* in *Plato: The Collected Dialogues*, p. 1288.

13. Ibid., 694a-b, French: "It is a fact that the Persians, when, under Cyrus, they kept to the middle course between servitude and freedom, began by being freed then to become the masters of a great many peoples: leaders who gave to those they lead the gift of freedom and raised them to a level equal to their own; soldiers, who were rather friends to their generals; bold moreover in offering to face danger. And if among them there was someone more intelligent and capable of giving good advice, the king, being free of all jealousy, giving rather a full freedom of speech (*didontos de parrēsian*) and honors to whoever was capable of advising him, offered him the means of bringing his intellectual capabilities into the light, in the interests of everyone. Subsequently, everything progressed at this time among the Persians, thanks to freedom (*eleutherian*), friendship, and collaboration (*philian kai nou koinōnian*)"; English p. 1288: "While the Persians steered a middle course between subjection and liberty, in the time of Cyrus, they began by winning their own freedom and went on to make themselves masters of numerous peoples. As a government they gave these subjects their share of liberty and placed them on equal terms with themselves; their soldiers thus grew attached to their commanders and showed themselves forward in danger. Again, if a subject was a man of wisdom and a capable advisor, the king showed no jealousy of him, but permitted him free speech and bestowed distinctions on such competent counselors, so that the gift of wisdom was freely placed at the disposal of the public service. Hence the

combination of liberty with amity and generally diffused intelligence led, for the time, to all-round progress."

14. Ibid.

15. See above, note 13.

16. Platon, *Les Lois*, livre VIII, 832c, trans. E. des Places (Paris: Les Belles Lettres, 1965) p. 71; Plato, *Laws*, p. 1398: "party."

17. Ibid., 835b-c, French pp. 74-75; English pp. 1400-1401: "But there is a matter of vast moment, as to which it is truly hard to inspire conviction. The task, indeed, is one for God himself, were it actually possible to receive orders from him. As things are, it will probably need a bold man, a man who puts plain speaking before everything, to declare his real belief about the true interest of state and citizens, and make the regulations the whole social system requires and demands in a corrupt age—a man who will oppose the passions at their strongest, and stand alone in his loyalty to the voice of truth without one creature on earth to second him."

18. See below, pp. 364-373, the analysis of the text in the lecture of 9 March, second hour.

twelve

9 February 1983

Second hour

[
Plato's Letters: *the context.* ∼ *Study of Letter V: the* phōnē *of constitutions; reasons for non-involvement.* ∼ *Study of Letter VII.* ∼ *Dion's history.* ∼ *Plato's political autobiography.* ∼ *The journey to Sicily.* ∼ *Why Plato accepts:* kairos; philia; ergon.
]

[...]* I WOULD NOW LIKE to talk to you about several texts from Plato's letters, or letters attributed to Plato. They are interesting because they are documents which attest, if not to the real role of philosophers of the Platonic school in Greek political life, at least to the way in which they thought about this possible intervention, and of how they wanted to be recognized as playing the role of those who state the truth in the field of Greek politics. You know that Plato's letters are extremely controversial texts which were brought together fairly late in Antiquity, at a time when collections of fictional or real

---

* The lecture begins as follows:
    —I would like to respond, not to a theoretical objection, but to a practical question. Someone said to me last week: these two hours really are very long, and stopping for five minutes and starting again breaks everything up. What do you think? I myself rather prefer this arrangement.
    —Your way is good, it's better to have a bit of a rest.
    —You are in favor of two hours with a short break? It would be possible to do an hour and a half without a break...No, you prefer? Note that it is in any case tiring for the victim! *[he laughs]* So we will continue like this. I am not very happy, by the way, with everything I am telling you this morning. It's true that it is textual analyses which require rather a private session. Talking about texts that you don't have before you, which we cannot discuss, is a bit...

letters was an important genre. For some time, almost throughout the
nineteenth century, harsh criticism denied the authenticity of these
letters. It is now generally accepted that letter VI, the great letter VII,
and also letter VIII are genuine letters, or at any rate come from circles
very close to Plato himself, whereas others are certainly much later and
were not written by Plato or his immediate circle. The set of letters is
interesting nevertheless, inasmuch as all of them are texts which come
from Platonist circles and they show how the Academy—either while
Plato was alive or after his death—thought that philosophical activity
could be a source not merely of reflection on politics but, I would say,
of political reflection and intervention. Plutarch attests to this and in
his anti-Epicurean *Reply to Colotes*[1] he recalls that while the Epicureans
always scorned politics, the merit of philosophers like Plato and his
disciples was that they were much more concerned to get involved in
political life and to give advice to their contemporaries. He recalls the
different disciples sent by Plato while he was alive to advise different sovereigns. So let us take these texts as evidence, independently
of any problem of authenticity, of this political intervention, while
emphasizing that the political context of these Platonic and especially
post-Platonic political interventions is of course that of the decline of
the Greek city-states and democracies. It is the time of the formation
of the great Hellenistic monarchies in which political problems will be
completely displaced from the operation of the *agora* to [that of] the
ekklēsia. Although municipal democracy may still function, the main
political problems will be shifted from the *agora*, which is, so to speak,
municipalized, to the sovereign's court. The stake will now be the role
of philosophy in the sovereign's court. The scene is now the sovereign,
the court, and the sovereign's entourage. The major political stage will
now, and no doubt for centuries, be here. I would like to pick out two
or three of these letters.

To my mind, the first, letter V, which is not attributed to Plato but
which is very old, is extremely interesting. This is not a letter by Plato,
and it is obviously not a real letter, which does not mean that it was
not written by Platonists. This letter, as no doubt letter VII also, which
is attributed to Plato, is a fictional letter, that is to say, it was intended
to circulate as a manifesto, a small treatise, as a sort of public letter, if
you like, by which the public, or at any rate the cultivated public, was

called upon as witness. Letter V is interesting for this reason: it was written to Perdiccas, who was the brother of Philip and who had ruled for a time over Macedonia. The letter assumes that Plato had sent him his disciple Euphraeus. I say "assumes." Actually Plato really had sent his disciple Euphraeus, but it is very likely, even certain, that the letter was not actually sent to Perdiccas at the time Plato sent his disciple. It is a text from later justifying Plato's real action of sending his disciple to Perdiccas. The letter raises two questions concerning the role of philosophy and the role of the philosopher as political [advisor]. The first question: What does it mean to give political advice to constitutions or governments which are very different from each other? Is it not rather the advisor's role to say what the best *politeia* (the best constitution) is? The question is not raised like that, directly and brutally in the text, but it is clear that the text is responding to this objection. Is it right to give advice to any type of government, even monarchical, autocratic ones? Is it not philosophy's task to say what the best government is? To reply to this implicit question running through the text—which is fairly short moreover, just three pages—Plato says the following: Every constitution (every *politeia*) should be likened to a living being. And like every living being, every *politeia* has its own voice (*phōnē*). It has its own voice, and when a *politeia* speaks with its own voice, the voice naturally suited to it, the voice nature intended it to have, when it speaks with its own *phōnē* to address men or the gods, then the *politeia* prospers and preserves itself. It is saved. On the other hand, a *politeia* is lost when it imitates the *phōnē* (the voice) of another *politeia*.[2]

This passage is interesting first of all for the comparison that should be made with another passage in the *Republic* in which the question is also that of the *phōnē* and the *politeia*, or anyway of the *phōnē* and how one should understand what is expressed as voice in the political body. The text is in Book VI of the *Republic*, from 493a. In this text the body of citizens (the *plēthos*, the mass) is said to be like an animal, and those who wish to guide this mass of citizens have to learn, as it were, the voice of this animal formed by the mass of citizens. One must understand its growls, anger, and desires, and then one can guide it.[3] However, in this text from the *Republic*, the analysis of the government's role with regard to this *phōnē* takes the form of a critical description. It is critical in the sense that, first, it is not exactly concerned with the *politeia*, with the constitution strictly speaking. It is concerned with the mass, with the *plēthos*, with precisely that amorphous, or rather poly-morphous, motley mass of the citizens' assembly, of the mass of citizens when they come together. And what is the voice that this mass makes heard? It is, the text says, the voice of anger and of appetites, that is to say, of all that is not rational. And the bad leader is precisely the one who, learning how to understand this vocabulary of desire, will echo it and guide the mass in the same direction as it desires to go.

You can see that this is very different from the text in letter V, despite the comparison with the crowd. For we can see that letter V is not concerned with the "*plēthos*," but with the "*politeia*," that is to say, the constitution insofar as it has a structure in the form of a democracy, or an aristocracy or oligarchy, or a monarchy. It is concerned with the *politeia* in its structure. This *politeia* has a *phōnē* which must conform to the essence of the *politeia*. And things go wrong, the city or State is lost precisely when, instead of conforming to the very essence of the *politeia*, the *phōnē* models itself on or lets itself be led astray by the image or model of another constitution, in other words when someone in the city gets up and speaks the language of another constitution. On the other hand, the city works properly if the *phōnē* is always in line with the *politeia*. We may wonder why Plato gives this exposition in this fairly short letter which informs, or is supposed to inform Perdiccas of the sending of his advisor. The text needs to be understood at dif-ferent levels. Of course, in the manifest text, which is not designed for Perdiccas but for the listener, it is a matter of saying: Yes, I can send a counselor to a monarchical or autocratic government, and I find it entirely logical and normal to do so, for the problem is not so much one of defining the best constitution, but rather of seeing to it that each *politeia* functions in accordance with its own essence. So we see absolutely clearly here the theme I was just referring to: *parrēsia* is not restricted to operating only within the framework of democracy; a par-rhesiastic problem, if you like, a problem of *parrēsia* arises under any form of government.

Second, you see that sending the advisor, the philosopher, Plato's disciple is connected to the question of the voice. Question of the voice: that is to say, what function will the advisor he sends to Perdiccas per-form? Although this is not said explicitly in the text, the existence, the presence of this exposition concerning the *phōnē* clearly shows that the role of the dispatched philosopher will be to see to it that the *phōnē* thus articulated in the *politeia*, in the constitution, is in keeping with this constitution. And this is what philosophers do: formulate, articulate what is said in a State in such a way that what is said really is in keeping with the State's nature. Only the philosopher can do this, since only he knows in what each State's nature consists. But as a counselor his role is not so much that of saying which State is the best, although he may well have posed this question elsewhere. As a counselor he has to leave to one side the question of which State is the best and keep his eye on the nature and essence of each *politeia*, and—this is his *parrēsia*, his truth-telling—he has to see to it that the voice expressed in discussions and debates, in the opinions formed, and in the decisions taken, really is in keeping with the *politeia*. He is the guardian of the voice of each constitution. The truth-telling of the philosopher and counselor is to see to it that this voice conforms to the essence of the constitution. He does not tell the truth about the nature of States, he tells the truth so that what is said in a State is in line with the truth of the State.

Still in this same letter, a second question is raised, another objection which clearly was made to Plato or to the Platonists and to which it was the letter's task to reply. How can a philosopher be sent to advise an autocrat? You have had the answer. The second question is: Why have you not given advice to Athens itself? You (Plato or the people of the Academy) keep quiet in Athens, so why do you address yourself to a king to give him advice? The answer which the redactor of the text attributes to Plato is: the population of Athens has acquired such bad customs over such a long time that it is no longer possible to reform it. If Plato were to give advice to an Athenian population which is now so far from all truth, he would endanger himself pointlessly.[4] Here then we have the image of, the reference to the nature of bad *parrēsia* in a democratic city. In the democratic city of Athens things have come to such a pass that one can no longer speak, one can no longer see to it that the *phōnē* is in accordance with the very essence of democracy. Things have come to such a pass that if anyone were to try to make the voice of true democracy heard in this democracy which is now lost, he would run the risk of all parrhesiasts, but it would be a risk which is no longer worth running since action is no longer possible, change is no longer possible. One would put oneself in danger for nothing, and Plato refuses to do this. This is why he keeps quiet at Athens, where *parrēsia* is no longer possible. But he sends, or is supposed to send his disciple to Perdiccas, for there he does hope to be able to make the *phōnē* of the true monarchy heard by a monarch who is prepared to listen to the philosopher's discourse. This is what we find in letter V.

I would now like to move on to letter VII, clearly the great letter in which Plato both recounts what his real career as political advisor has been and gives the theory of what a philosopher's political advice to a tyrant can and should be. Forgive me, I am going to recall very briefly the historical context; it is somewhat muddled and I will try not to get too bogged down in it. You know that it involves relations between Plato and Dionysius of Syracuse, Dionysius the Younger. You remember the situation. There is, then, this tyrant, Dionysius the Elder, who had exercised despotic, tyrannical power over Syracuse, and what is more had come to dominate all or a part of Sicily. In his old age, Dionysius the Elder had married a young woman whose very young brother was Dion. So we have two characters: Dionysius the Elder and Dion, his young brother-in-law.

Dionysius dies, is gone, and Dion, who Plato had already met during a visit to Sicily, asks Plato to return to Sicily to serve as political counselor and teacher to Dionysius the Younger, the son of Dionysius the Elder and the heir to power. This is Plato's second journey. I am skipping the details. In the episode I referred to earlier, Plutarch recounts how it turned out very badly in fact. Dion is exiled, Plato sets off for Greece again, and after some time Dionysius the Younger makes a new appeal to Plato, saying: Yes agreed, it is true, I exiled Dion, but I will recall him. But I will only recall him on condition that you return. So Plato comes to Sicily for the third time, for the second time as counselor to Dionysius, and for what will be his last stay in Sicily. Once again things go very badly. Plato leaves again without the agreement made with Dionysius ever being honored, without Dion returning to Syracuse or having his rights restored to him. So Plato leaves for the third time, after this third visit. The struggle between Dionysius and Dion continues. Finally, Dionysius is driven out and Dion takes power. A new episode: Dion is killed during the internecine struggles which develop in Syracuse at this time. And Dion's family and friends write

to Plato again, or anyway make contact with Plato to ask him to intervene, and to intervene as counselor, as it were, for the fourth time. First
he had been Dion's teacher. Then he came twice to advise Dionysius.
And now, after Dion's death, his entourage asks Plato [to come].

The letter is situated at this point. It therefore comes right at the
end of all of Plato's Sicilian episodes and is a kind of balance sheet.
Plato recounts what has taken place since his youth, his whole political career, and why he came to do what he did. At the same time he
will give the theory of the political advisor. And I think that if reading
the *Republic* and *Laws* is, of course, absolutely indispensable in the history of philosophy and political thought, I think that reading Plato's
Letters, and the seventh letter in particular, is very interesting, because
it makes apparent to us that other side of political thought, the genealogy of which I would like to make a bit of a start on here, which is
political thought as advice for political action, political thought as the
rationalization of political action, much more than as the foundation
of right or as the foundation of the organization of the city. Political
thought not from the side of the basic contract, but political thought
from the side of the rationalization of political action, philosophy as
advice. Well, if we were to undertake this history, I think that Plato's
seventh letter would clearly be important.

So, I will summarize something of what is found in this seventh
letter. First there is the aspect of Plato's political autobiography. He
recalls what could be called his double disappointment, when, as a
young Athenian belonging to the high aristocracy on the one hand,
and a student of Socrates on the other, he sees certain events taking
place around him, and specifically two major episodes which are like
the exemplification of two forms of government: first, the regime of the
Thirty; second, the return to democracy. As his first political experience—when he must have been very young—he recalls the fact that
Athenian democracy, compromised by the resounding defeats of the
Peloponnesian War, was overturned by a group of aristocrats including Critias and Charmides, that is to say his relatives—Charmides was
certainly a relative, and Critias[5]—I no longer remember—anyway, students of Socrates, people close to his circle. So these people take power.
Plato explains how he is seduced, or at any rate interested, by this new
form of political life at Athens, but then is immediately disappointed.

He is immediately disappointed by the violence unleashed by this government, and in particular by the arbitrary arrests. And it is in order to [get him] to participate in such an arbitrary arrest that the tyrants ask Socrates to take part in an illegal judicial action, and Socrates refuses. Socrates refuses, and in doing so he gives, as a philosopher, an example of philosophical resistance to political power, an example of *parrēsia* which will remain for a long time a model of the philosophical attitude towards power: the philosopher's individual resistance. After the overthrow of the regime of the Thirty there is a return to democracy. And again Plato recalls how sympathetic he had been towards this democracy in its early stages. But then there was the second, negative episode, symmetrical to the first, and again revolving around Socrates: this time it is not Socrates refusing to obey the government, giving an example of resistance, it is rather Socrates prosecuted by the democratic government on the grounds of his supposed relations with the previous government. And despite the resistance he had shown, Socrates was arrested and executed. Two experiences—oligarchy, democracy—both negative.

In his letter, Plato draws a very interesting conclusion from these two experiences. This is that, after these two experiences, he says, he realized that political action is no longer possible. It is no longer possible because two elements are lacking. First, friends (*philoi, hetairoi*) are lacking, that is to say, in a badly governed city the personal relationships of friendship, the bonds which can join men together and form them into pressure groups, so to speak, thanks to which and through which one could win power and guide the city, are no longer possible.[6] Second, he says, the opportunities (*kairoi*) are lacking. The opportunity is the good moment, which is defined by the existence at a given moment of something like a slight improvement, an upturn, a favorable moment for seizing power. Now, Plato says, things are going from bad to worse and there is never an opportunity.[7] Consequently, without friends, without that free community of individuals, and without that opportunity defined by the circumstances, there is no question of seeking to act in the political realm. What to do then? Well, he says, having understood that without friends and opportunity it is not possible to act within the order of the city, then one must draw this conclusion, which he formulates and which is, almost to the word, the

well known text in Book V of the *Republic*, 473d, namely, that philosophers must now come to power (*eis arkhas*: this is a technical word
which designates the actual exercise of public office; the *arkhai* are the
public offices, political responsibilities). So philosophers must occupy
the positions of political responsibility and the leaders, those with *dunasteia* (*dunasteuontes* the text says) must begin to practice philosophy.[8]
Henceforth, only the perfect equivalence of the exercise and practice of
philosophy and the exercise and practice of power will make possible
what both oligarchy and democracy made impossible.

One thing that I think should be understood is that the resort to
philosophy in this text, the desired coincidence between the practice
of philosophy and the exercise of power, is presented by Plato—and
some importance should be attached to this—as the consequence of an
impossibility, that is to say, of the fact that the previously customary
political game of *parrēsia* (of truth-telling) is no longer possible in the
field of democracy or in the Athenian city. The place of truth-telling is
no longer solely the field of politics, which means that henceforth the
parrēsia that we saw formulated fairly clearly in Euripides, for example, or afterwards in Isocrates, the *parrēsia* that should characterize
the action of some citizens in relation to other citizens, is no longer to
be given by citizenship and is no longer the exercise of moral or social
ascendancy of some over others. *Parrēsia* [...], truth-telling in the political realm can only be founded on philosophy. It is not just that this
parrēsia, this truth-telling must refer to an external philosophical discourse, but truth-telling in the field of politics can well and truly only
be philosophical truth-telling. Philosophical truth-telling and political truth-telling must be the same, inasmuch as none of the ways of
conducting politics witnessed by Plato can assure the true functioning
of this *parrēsia*. This dangerous and perilous game I have been talking
about is no longer possible. I think the absolute right of philosophy
over political discourse is clearly central in this conception of Plato.

After this autobiographical account of his youth, of his political
experiences, and the conclusion he draws regarding the relationship
between power and philosophy, Plato recalls [his] first two visits to
Sicily. He describes the first journey he made privately, so to speak,
when he met Dion who, still young and under the rule of Dionysius
the Elder, became interested in philosophy. And he recalls, on the one

hand, how struck he was by the state of debauchery, luxury, and moral laxity of Syracuse and the entourage of Dionysius, and, on the other hand, how he was impressed by Dion's virtue and qualities.[9] Then Plato recalls how Dion approached him when Dionysius the Younger had taken power after the death of Dionysius the Elder. So Dion turns to Plato and, Plato recalls, tells him first of all that Dionysius the Younger (the tyrant, despot, or anyway the new monarch of Syracuse) and his entourage are ready to listen to the lessons of philosophy.[10] And, Plato says, quoting or anyway referring in indirect style to what Dion said to him: Thanks to Dionysius the Younger and his entourage, circumstances have never been so favorable for realizing "the union in the same men of philosophy and the conduct of great cities."[11] We have here therefore precisely the definition of the *kairos* that was lacking in the experiences of democracy or oligarchy in Athens. We have a *kairos*[12] in which, a young monarch having come to power and being ready to listen to philosophy, one will be able to realize that union of the practice of philosophy and the exercise of power that Plato now regards as the only way that truth-telling can be got to function in the political realm. To explain his visit, which is his second to Sicily but his first political visit, Plato adds two considerations to that of the favorable conjuncture. One concerns his friendship for Dion. He says that if in fact he, Plato, had refused Dion's invitation, if he refused to come to indoctrinate Dionysius, then Dionysius, not having been educated as he should have been, could have turned against Dion and harmed him, and through him the whole city. So Plato had to come and attempt to educate Dionysius.[13] Second, Plato says, a further consideration led me to accept Dion's invitation. This consideration is interesting. It is that Plato did not want to appear to be merely *logos*, to be only discourse. Plato does not want to be merely *logos* and be thought of as such. He wants to show that he is also capable of taking part and putting his hand to *ergon* (to action).[14] For sure, there is an opposition between *logos* and *ergon* in this text which is very classical and constant in Greek vocabulary. You have this opposition *logō* and *ergō*: in word and in reality, in discourse and in action, etcetera. But we should remember that here it is precisely a question of philosophy, and of philosophy in the field of politics. For Plato, it is clear that to be no more than the philosopher who is the author of the *Republic*, that is to say, who says what the ideal city should be, is to be no more than *logos*. Now the philosopher cannot be merely *logos* with regard to politics. To be more than just "hollow words," he must take part in and put his hand directly to action (*ergon*).

I think we have here an injunction that is absolutely important and which corresponds somewhat—you will see it moreover in the text, it becomes clear—to what is found in the first texts, the first Platonic dialogues, concerning philosophy having to be not merely *mathēsis* but also *askēsis*. If it is true that philosophy is not merely the apprenticeship of a knowledge but should also be a mode of life, a way of being, a practical relationship to oneself through which one elaborates oneself and works on oneself, if it is true that philosophy therefore should be *askēsis* (ascesis), then when the philosopher has to tackle not only the problem of himself but also that of the city, he cannot be satisfied with being merely *logos*, with being merely the person who tells the truth, but must be the person who takes part, who puts his hand to *ergon*. And what is it to put one's hand to *ergon*? It is to be the real counselor of a real politician in the field of the political decisions he really has to take. And I think that if the *logos* is in fact related to the construction of the ideal city, then the *ergon*, which must complete the philosopher's task with regard to politics, is actually the task of the political counselor and of the elaboration, through the Prince's soul, of the rationality of the real conduct of the city. It is by taking part directly, through *parrēsia*, in the formation, maintenance, and exercise of an art of governing that the philosopher will be not merely *logos* in the political realm, but really *logos* and *ergon*, in accordance with the ideal of Greek rationality. In reality, *logos* is complete only if it can lead to *ergon* and organize it according to the necessary principles of rationality. This, Plato says, is why he met with Dion. I will finish this letter VII next week and we will move on to other problems raised by the history of *parrēsia* and its practices.

1. Plutarque, "Contre l'Épicurien Colotès," in *Les Œuvres morales & meslées*, trans. J Amyot (Paris: 1575); English translation by Benedict Einarson, Philip H. De Lacy, "Reply to Colotes in Defence of the Other Philosophers" in Plutarch, *Moralia, Vol. IV* (Cambridge, Mass., and London: Harvard University Press, "Loeb Classical Library," 1967).

2. Platon, lettre V, 321d-e in *Œuvres complètes*, t. XIII-1: *Lettres*, trans. J. Souilhé (Paris: Belles Lettres, 1960) p. 23: "Each government has its tongue, as if they were living beings (*estin gar dē tis phōnē tōn politeiōn hekastēs kathaperei tinōn zōōn*). One is that of democracy, another that of oligarchy, and another that of monarchy [...]. Every State which speaks its own language towards the gods and men and acts in conformity with this language, always prospers and preserves itself, but if it imitates another it perishes": English translation by L.A. Post, *Letters*, "Letter V" in *Plato: The Collected Dialogues*, ed. Edith Hamilton and Huntington Cairns, p. 1605: "Each form of government has a sort of voice as if it were a kind of animal. There is one of democracy, another of oligarchy, and a third of monarchy... Any form of government that utters its own voice to god and man and duly acts in harmony with its voice, is always flourishing and endures. When it copies another it perishes."

3. Platon, *La République*, Book VI, 493a-b, p. 114: "One would say a man who, having to nourish a great strong animal, after having carefully observed its instinctive movements and appetites, how one should approach it and touch it, when and why it is most aggressive or more gentle, in relation to what it is accustomed to let forth this or that cry (*phōnas*), and what tones of voice calm or irritate it, yes, I say, after having learned all this by living with it for a long time, would give his experience the name of science." Plato here is criticizing Sophists who call their technique of manipulating the masses science. English translation by Paul Shorey, *Republic*, in *Plato: The Collected Dialogues*, ed. Edith Hamilton and Huntington Cairns, p. 729: "It is as if a man were acquiring the knowledge of the humors and desires of a great strong beast which he had in his keeping, how it is to be approached and touched, and when and by what things it is made most savage or gentle, yes, and the several sounds it is wont to utter on the occasion of each, and again what sounds uttered by another make it tame or fierce, and after mastering this knowledge by living with the creature and by lapse of time should call it wisdom...."

4. Platon, lettre V, 322a-b, in *Lettres*, p. 24: "Hearing what I say, perhaps it will be said: 'Plato, it appears, claims to know what is good for democracy, and yet while it was possible for him to speak to the people and give it excellent advice, he has never come forward to make his voice heard.'—To this, reply: Plato was born late in his country, he found the people already too old and formed by their ancestors in all kinds of habits of life opposed to his counsels. For sure he would have been only too happy to advise them, as he might a father, if he had not thought that this would endanger him pointlessly, with no chance of success"; English, *Letters*, p. 1605: "If anyone, when he hears this, says, 'Plato apparently pretends to know what is for the advantage of a democracy, yet, though he has the right to address the assembly and give them the best advice, he has never taken the floor to utter a word'—say in reply that Plato was born late in his country's history, and the people, when he came to them, were already rather well on in years and had acquired from his predecessors the habit of doing many things at variance with his advice. 'For he would have been altogether delighted,' you must explain, 'to advise the people as he might have counseled a father, if he had not supposed he would be risking his life in vain without any hope of accomplishing anything.'"

5. Charmides was Plato's maternal uncle (one of the Ten responsible for the political supervision of Piraeus) and Critias was his mother's cousin (one of the undisputed leaders of the extremist branch of the Thirty). Both died in 403 during a battle in which the democrats tried to recapture Piraeus.

6. Plato, Letter VII, 325d, *Letters*, French p. 29: "Seeing this and seeing the men who led politics, the more I considered the laws and mores, and also the older I became, the more difficult it seemed to administer the affairs of the State well. On the one hand, without friends and faithful collaborators (*aneu philōn andrōn kai hetairōn pistōn*) this did not seem possible to me"; English p. 1575: "Now as I considered these matters, as well as the sort of men who were active in politics, and the laws and the customs, the more I examined them and the more I advanced in years, the harder it appeared to me to administer the government correctly. For one thing, nothing could be done without friends and loyal companions."

7. Ibid., 325d-326a, French p. 30: "I did not cease looking out for possible signs of an improvement in these events and especially in the political regime, but I was always waiting for the good moment to act (*tou de prattein au permenein aei kairous*)"; English p. 1575: "while I did not cease to consider means for improving this particular situation and indeed of reforming the whole constitution, yet, in regard to action, I kept waiting for favorable moments."

8. Ibid., 326a-b, French p. 30: "So, the evils will not cease for human beings until the race of pure and genuine philosophers come to power (*eis arkhas elthē tas politikas*) or the city's leaders (*tōn dunasteuontōn*), through divine grace, truly begin to philosophize"; English p. 1576: "the human race will not see better days until either the stock of those who rightly and genuinely follow philosophy acquire political authority, or else the class who have political control be led by some dispensation of providence to become real philosophers."

9. Ibid., 327a-b, French p. 31; English p. 1576.

10. Ibid., 327c; English p. 1577.

11. Ibid., 328a; English: "the same man both philosopher and ruler of a great city."

12. Ibid., 327e, French p. 32: "What better opportunity (*tinas gar kairous*) can we expect, he said?"; English p. 1577: "'What combination of circumstances,' said he, 'more promising...are we to wait for?'"

13. Ibid., 328b and 328d-e, French p. 32 and p. 33; English p. 1577 and p. 1578.

14. Ibid., 328b-c, French pp. 32-33: "As I reflected and hesitantly asked myself whether or not I should take to the road and cede to the appeals, what tipped the balance was the thought that if ever one could undertake the realization (*apotelein egkheiresoi*) of my legislative and political plans, this was the time to attempt it: it was only necessary to persuade one man sufficiently and all would be won. In this state of mind I ventured forth. I was certainly not driven by the motives that some people imagine, but I blushed to see myself as hollow words (*mē doxaimi pote emautō pantapasi logon monon atekhnōs einai*) who never puts his hand to work (*ergou de oudenos an pote hekōn anapsasthai*)"; English pp. 1577-1578: "Hence as I considered and debated whether I should hearken and go, or what I should do, the view nevertheless prevailed that I ought to go, and that if anyone were ever to attempt to realize my ideals in regard to laws and government, now was the time for the trial. If I were to convince but one man, that in itself would ensure complete success. Such were the considerations that inspired and emboldened me to leave home on this journey. I was not guided by the motives that some men attributed to me, but chiefly by a concern for my own self-respect. I feared to see myself at last altogether nothing but words, so to speak—a man who would never willingly lay hand to any concrete task."

thirteen

16 FEBRUARY 1983

First hour

[
Philosophical ergon. ∽ *Comparison with the* Alcibiades. ∽ *The reality of philosophy: the courageous address to power.* ∽ *First condition of reality: listening, the first circle.* ∽ *The philosophical oeuvre: a choice; a way; an application.* ∽ *The reality of philosophy as work of self on self (second circle).*
]

LAST WEEK WE GOT to the analysis of the Letter VII by Plato, or attributed to Plato, a text anyway which dates at best from Plato's old age, and at worst from his very first followers. You know this is a text which presents itself as a letter supposedly addressed to Plato's Sicilian friends, that is to say, to Dion's circle, since it was written after the latter's death, and which is in fact a sort of political manifesto, a sort of public letter in which the author presents in all three sets of reflections. First, to justify his conduct in Sicily and towards Dionysius, he recounts the series of events which took place: the invitation, journey, stay, the injustices suffered at the hands of Dionysius, the false promises made to Plato and Dion, and so on. The second set of considerations, apart from those dealing with these events, form a sort of political autobiography in which Plato goes back over his career since his youth, and in particular since his two great disappointments at Athens, first, under the aristocratic regime of the Thirty, and then with the return to democracy, which was sanctioned by Socrates being put to death. Finally, the third set of considerations comprises those in which Plato explains, in the most general terms, what for him it means to give advice to a Prince, what it means to enter into the field of political activity and play this role, this character of *sumboulos*, of counselor in political matters to those who exercise power. And so we reached the point where Plato explains how and why he was led to leave for Sicily and undertake what was chronologically his second journey to Sicily, but his first political visit. During the first journey, you recall, he had only met with Dion. He had been seduced by his intelligence, had taught him philosophy, and then returned to Athens. And he was in Greece when he received an appeal from Dion to return to Sicily a second time, but now with a relatively well defined political role, or at any rate with a political task or mission, since it involved serving as a political counselor, or more exactly as a teacher of Dionysius the Younger who had just inherited power in Syracuse. In the passage of the letter I would now like to analyze, the question Plato wants to answer is this: why did he agree to come to Syracuse, why did he agree to the request and to the political game proposed to him, why did he agree to be close to the person in Syracuse who was heir to a despotism to which Plato was in principle hostile?

To explain this, Plato emphasized two sets of considerations. The first relates, if you like, to the conjuncture, to what he calls precisely the *kairos* (the opportune moment). You may recall that the reason he gave for having renounced participation in any political activity at Athens was that he had not found any slight improvement, any break in the bad situation of Athens. At no time had he thought that there was something like a *kairos*, an opportunity. Now here, in Sicily, something like an opportunity arises. This is the accession to power of a new monarch, Dionysius, who is young, and who Dion portrays as someone who really wants to devote himself to philosophy. What is more, he is someone whose circle, led by Dion, is entirely favorable both to philosophy and to Plato. And finally, the last important argument— because we will come across it frequently in the theory of advice to the Prince, of the Prince's counselor—is the fact that, unlike in a democracy where one has to convince many, to persuade the mass (the *plēthos*), in a monarchy it is enough to persuade just one man. Everything will be achieved by persuading one and only one man.[1] This is in Plato's text. And this is the principle, the motive which means that if the Prince really does give some encouraging signs, one may think that one has a *kairos*: a single character to convince, and one who seems to want to be convinced. This is the *kairos* aspect. Now with regard to Plato himself, why did he want to seize the opportunity that presented itself in this way? It is here, you recall, that Plato formulates two reasons. One of these is *philia*, his friendship for Dion. And then the other reason—it was exactly here that we stopped—is the fact that if he, Plato, refused the mission proposed to him by Dion, if he refused to confront the task presented to him in this way, then he would feel that he, Plato, was only *logos*, pure and simple discourse, whereas it is necessary for him, he wants to try his hand at, to put his hand to the *ergon* (that is to say, to the task, the work).

So this is where we got to last week, and I think there is an important point here. It is important because it poses a question that is at once very familiar, obvious, and transparent, and at the same time not at all well known, and on the other hand because it seems to me that this text poses this question of the philosophical *ergon* (task) throughout the letter in terms which are, I think, surprising if we compare them to other texts by Plato, or at any rate to an image and interpretation which is usually given of Plato and late Platonism.

To analyze this problem of the philosophical *ergon* (of the philosophical task) in relation to politics, and to map it out a little, I would like to go back for a moment to a text I spoke about last year, which is a rather enigmatic text moreover, since there are many uncertainties about its date and because its outline of the nature of the philosophical task is very different from the one that we come across here. This text is, you recall, the *Alcibiades*, a dialogue which, in some respects, appears to be an early text—with the same scenario, the same scenography, the same episodes, the same kind of characters—but which in other aspects includes many elements which refer to Plato's late philosophy. No matter, you maybe remember the situation represented by this dialogue. Here too it was a question of the philosopher's intervention on the political scene.[2] What was the opportunity, the *kairos*, which led to Plato getting involved, so to speak, with the political question in this dialogue? The situation, the opportunity was this: thanks to his birth, his ancestors, his wealth, and his status generally, the very young Alcibiades was naturally one of the foremost citizens of the city. But he pointed out, or rather let Socrates point out that in fact Alcibiades had no intention of spending all his life (*katabiōnai*)[3] as one among the foremost, but that he wanted to be absolutely and exclusively *the* foremost, to be himself alone the foremost not only in his city, which he wanted to persuade and take control of, but also in relation to all other sovereigns, since he wanted to prevail over the enemies of Athens, like Sparta or the king of Persia, which he represented as his rivals, his personal rivals. This was the project in which Socrates intervened and which posed very precisely the problem of *parrēsia* in a democratic situation. I said "this is the very problem of *parrēsia* in a democratic context," since this is precisely what is involved: each having the right to speak, some, the foremost, have the task, function, or role of asserting their ascendancy over the others. And the problem in this agonistic game of the foremost in relation to the others, and of the foremost among themselves, is whether it is possible, legitimate, and desirable for there to be—as Pericles had been—just one who prevails over all the others.

This was the problem of *parrēsia*. This is that famous crisis, that famous problematic of *parrēsia* which very clearly marks the operation of democracy and, generally, the operation of some of the political institutions in Greece at this time. In this sense, you see that, despite the different context, the situation is somewhat analogous to that of Plato having to advise Dionysius. Here, it is not a tyrant, despot, or monarch that Socrates has to advise, but a young man who wants to be the foremost. Plato, on the other hand, will have to deal with someone who is the foremost by status and inheritance, and by virtue of the very structure of the *politeia*. But both cases involve addressing them, speaking to them, telling them the truth, convincing them of the truth, and thereby governing their souls, the souls of those who have to govern others. The situations then are analogous, despite the different political contexts. However—and this will be one of the main themes I would like to pursue today—it seems to me that between *Alcibiades* (the role of Socrates in relation to Alcibiades) and Plato (in his role in relation to Dionysius) there is a series of absolutely major differences which mark out a kind of division in Platonic philosophy.

Anyway, a first difference immediately leaps to the eyes. This is that in the case of Alcibiades and Socrates, Socrates himself also had to answer the question: why are you interceding with Alcibiades? And this is the question to which all the first part of the dialogue replied. Socrates explained: I held back when Alcibiades was desired and pursued by so many others, but now I am interested in him. I have stayed in the background until now, but now he is getting a little older and the lovers who pursued him are fewer and fewer and will soon turn away from him, I on the contrary come forward. Why do I come forward? Well, precisely because Alcibiades wants to place himself at the head of the city, to advance to the front rank, and to exercise power alone. This is the *kairos*. And if I seize this *kairos*, it is out of love of Alcibiades. It is the *erōs* I had for Alcibiades, and which on the god's instructions I have held back until now, that now leads me to seize this *kairos* (opportunity) of Alcibiades' wish to move to the forefront of the city and become its leader. So, if we compare this Socratic situation and justification with regard to Alcibiades and Plato's situation with regard to Dionysius, then you can see of course the striking difference of the latter. Plato also seizes the *kairos*, but why does he do so? It is not because of a relationship in the realm of *erōs*, but is due to a sort of internal obligation, which is not so much planted as a desire in the philosopher's soul, but is the very task of philosophy, which is to be not just *logos*, but also *ergon*. Or, more precisely, the philosopher himself should not be just *logos* (discourse, only discourse, bare discourse). He must also be *ergon*. This obligation, and no longer *erōs*, will be the philosopher's reason for seizing the *kairos* (the opportunity). That the reason for intervening in the realm of politics is not the philosopher's desire for the person he addresses, but the internal obligation of philosophy to be *ergon* as well as *logos*, is clearly not a minor shift. This is the first remark I wanted to make.

The second is this. In worrying about the idea that he could be no more than discourse (*logos*), the philosopher (Plato) seems to me to pose a problem which is precisely, as I was just saying, both familiar and not well known. When he worries about being only *logos*, when, instead of being merely *logos*, he wants to try his hand at the task itself (at the *ergon*), it seems to me that Plato raises a question that could be called the question of philosophy's reality. What is the reality of philosophy? Where is the reality of philosophy to be found? And straightaway we see that the way in which Plato answers the question, or rather, the way in which he poses the question proves that for him, at this moment at least, the reality of philosophy is not, is no longer, anyway, is not merely *logos*.

We should define this question a bit: what is the reality of philosophy? I think this question about philosophy's reality is not a question of what reality is for philosophy. It does not consist in asking what the reality is to which philosophy is related, or with which it must be compared. It does not consist in asking what philosophy can be measured against to assess whether or not it tells the truth. To question oneself about the reality of philosophy, as I think this seventh letter does, is to question oneself about what the will to tell the truth is in its very reality, what this activity of telling the truth is, what this completely particular and singular act of veridiction called philosophy is (an act of veridiction which may perfectly well be mistaken and say the false moreover). It seems to me that this question is: How, in what way, in what form is philosophical truth-telling, the particular form of veridiction that is philosophy, inserted in reality? Schematically, it seems to me that the question we see being formulated, emerging, coming to light in a very fleeting but nevertheless quite decisive way in this worry about philosophy having to be not merely *logos* but also *ergon*, is not: What is the reality that enables one to say whether what philosophy says is true or untrue? It is: What is the reality of this philosophical truth-telling, what makes it more than just a futile discourse that tells the truth or says something untrue?

It is the reality of philosophical discourse that is involved in this question. And the answer given, or rather sketched out in the simple phrase that I recalled last week and with which I am now starting again—namely that philosophy wishes to be not just *logos*, but wants to try its hand at the *ergon*—the answer that we must now try to develop appears in all its simplicity: the reality, the test by which philosophy will demonstrate its reality is not the *logos* itself, it is not the game intrinsic to the *logos* itself. The reality, the test by which and through which philosophical veridiction will demonstrate its reality is the fact that it addresses itself, can address itself, and has the courage to address itself to whoever it is who exercises power. There should be no misunderstanding here. I do not mean in any way that this text by Plato defines a function of philosophy which is to tell the truth about politics, laws, and the constitution, and to give useful and effective advice on the decisions to be taken. On the contrary, we will see in this same text, for example, how Plato dismisses for the philosopher the fact of being able to propose laws, or at least situates it in a very particular and by no means central place. It is not telling the truth about politics, it is not even dictating imperiously what the constitution, politics, or government of cities must be that gives philosophy, philosophical discourse its own reality. It seems to me that in this text, for Plato, philosophy demonstrates its reality as soon as it enters the political field in forms which may be quite diverse: lawgiving, advising a Prince, persuading a crowd, etcetera. It enters the political field in diverse ways, none of which is essential, but always marking its specific difference in relation to other discourses. And it is precisely this that distinguishes it from rhetoric. From the point of view of philosophy, rhetoric—and we will have to come back to this at much greater length—is no more than the instrument by which the person who wants to exercise power can only repeat exactly what the crowd, leaders, or Prince wants. Rhetoric is a means of persuading people of what they are already persuaded. The test of philosophy, on the contrary, the test of philosophy's reality, is not its political effectiveness; it is the fact that it enters the political field in its specific difference and has its own particular game in relation to politics. It is this specific game in relation to politics, this test of philosophy's reality in relation to politics that I would like now to analyze a little, while keeping in mind—because I think it is really quite important in the history of philosophical discourse—just this: this short passage from Letter VII, in which the philosopher does not want to be just *logos* but also to intervene in and affect reality, seems to me to mark one of the fundamental features of what is and will be philosophical practice in the West. It is true that for a long time some have thought, and some still think today, that philosophy's reality is sustained by the fact that it can tell the truth, and that it can tell the truth about science in particular. For a long time it was thought, and it is still thought, that basically the reality of philosophy is being able to tell the truth about truth, the truth of truth. But it seems to me that, and anyway this is what is indicated in Plato's text, there is a completely different way of marking or defining what philosophy's reality may be, the reality of philosophical veridiction, whether what this veridiction says be true or false. This reality is marked by the fact that philosophy is the activity which consists in speaking the truth, in practicing veridiction in relation to power. And it seems to me that this has definitely been one of the permanent principles of its reality for at least two and a half millennia. Anyway, what I would like to show you and tell you today is how this Letter VII and its different developments can be seen as a reflection on philosophy's reality, manifested through the veridiction practiced in the political game.

I will not follow all the twists and turns and details of this very complex letter, but to schematize a little, I would like to group its contents under two broad questions. First, it seems to me that in several passages, some of which are successive and others scattered here and there in the exposition, the letter answers this question: under what conditions can philosophical discourse be sure that it will not be just *logos*, but will be well and truly *ergon* in the field of politics? In other words: under what conditions can philosophical discourse find its reality, attest to its reality for itself and for others? Second set of questions: what really will philosophy have to say in this function of reality that it will exercise in the political realm, in this assumption of its own specific reality in the political realm? This second set of questions is actually so bound up with the first, it derives from it so directly that I think we will be able to summarize it fairly quickly. On the other hand, I think we have three or four passages which may enlighten us on the first series of questions (that is to say: on what conditions will a *logos*, which philosophical discourse claims to be and means to be, really be able, as the text says, to accomplish its own task, put its hand to its own work; on what conditions will it be able to pass the test of reality successfully?).

The first I would like to talk about [...]* is at 330c-331d. For philosophical discourse really to be able to find its reality, to be real as philosophical veridiction and not just empty verbiage, the first condition—which may seem paradoxical—concerns those to whom it is addressed. For philosophy not to be pure and simple discourse but actual reality, it should not be addressed to all and sundry but only to those who wish to listen to it. This is what the text says, beginning

---

* M.F. adds: this is not the one I have distributed, I will try to comment on that one shortly.

in this way: "Is not the first duty of someone advising a sick man who is following a bad regime to get that man to change his way of life? If the sick man wishes to obey, he will give him new prescriptions. If he refuses, I hold that an upright man and real physician should not agree to further consultations."¹ And a bit further on, at 331d, the paragraph ends in this way: "In the case where it does not seem to him to be well governed [that is to say: in the case where the State seems to the counselor, to the philosopher, not to be well governed; M.F.], let him speak [let him, the philosopher speak, in the case of the State not being well governed; M.F.], but only if he does not have to speak pointlessly or if he is not risking his life [for the philosopher to speak he must be sure that his discourse will at any rate not be rejected; M.F.], but he must not use violence to overthrow the constitution of his country. When one can achieve good only at the cost of banishments and massacres, he must stay calm and beg the gods for good for him and the city."⁵ Being listened to and meeting with the listener's willingness to follow the advice given is the first condition of the exercise of philosophical discourse as task, work, *ergon*, reality. One must give advice only to those who agree to follow it. If they do not, one must act like the physicians who leave when clients and patients are unwilling to take heed of their prescriptions. You will tell me that this is pretty banal, but I think we may clarify this text a little by following up this comparison with medicine, a comparison which is a commonplace frequently found in a number of texts in Plato which relate or liken political advice to the practice of medicine. In particular, there is the passage of Book IV of the *Republic* at 425e,⁶ and Book IV also of the *Laws* from 720a.⁷

But what does this reference to medicine signify more precisely? To start with, medicine is generally characterized in three ways, not only in Platonic texts but more generally in Greek texts of the fourth century and even later. First, medicine is an art of the conjuncture, of the opportune moment, and also of conjecture, since, through the signs one is given, one must recognize the illness, foresee its evolution, and thus choose the appropriate therapy. It is an art of conjuncture and an art of conjecture which depends, of course, on a science, on a theory, on knowledge, but which must at every instant take into account particular conditions and bring a practice of decipherment into play. Second, as well as being characterized as a both theoretical and general

knowledge of conjecture and conjuncture, medicine is also always characterized as an art, and an art of persuasion. The good physician is also
someone who is able to persuade his patient. I refer you, for example, to the famous distinction between two kinds of medicine in the
Laws, Book IV, 720a-e.[8] The medicine for slaves and practiced by slaves,
whether through a pharmacy or by visiting their patients is not important, is a medicine which is content to give prescriptions, to say what
is to be done (medicine, medication, scarification, incisions, amulets,
etcetera). Then there is the free medicine for free people practiced by
physicians who are themselves free men. And this medicine is characterized by the fact that physician and patient speak with one another.
The patient tells the physician about his ailments, his regime, how he
has lived, and so on. In return, the physician explains to the patient
why his regime was not a good one, why he has become ill, and what he
must now do to get better, until he is really persuaded of what he must
do to take care of himself. Good medicine, the great, free medicine is
therefore an art of dialogue and persuasion. Finally, the third characteristic that generally defines medicine is the fact that good medicine
is not concerned with just this or that illness to be treated, but is an
activity, an art which takes into account and takes in hand the patient's
whole life. It is true that prescriptions have to be given to get rid of the
illness, but one must establish a whole regime of life. And it is precisely
with regard to this regime of life that the task of persuasion, specific to
medicine and the physician, becomes more important and decisive. For
the patient really to be cured, and for him to be able to avoid further
illness in the future, he must agree to change everything, his drink, his
food, his sexual relations, his exercise, his whole way of life. Medicine
is concerned with the regime just as much as with the illness.

If we take these three characteristics which are frequently evoked
in Platonic texts to characterize medicine, if we take these different
expressions and relate them to the task of the political counselor who,
according to the text of the Letter VII, must conduct himself like a
doctor, then we see that the role of the political counselor will not be
to exercise the office of a ruler who has to take decisions on a normal day to day basis. As a political counselor, the philosopher has to
intervene only when things are going wrong, when there is illness [...].
And in that case he will have to diagnose the city's illness, seize the

opportunity of intervention, and restore the order of things. The philosopher has, if you like, a critical role in the sense of a role performed in the realm of crisis, or at any rate of trouble and illness, and of the patient's, in this case the city's and citizens' awareness that something is wrong. Second, the role of philosophy and the philosopher will not be like that of slave physicians who are satisfied with saying: Do this, don't do that, take this, and don't take that. The philosopher's role must be like that of free physicians who address themselves to people who are free, that is to say, who persuade at the same time as they prescribe. Of course, he has to say what is to be done, but he must explain why it has to be done, and precisely to that extent the philosopher will not be just a legislator who points out to a city how it should be governed and what laws it should obey. The philosopher's role will actually be to persuade both those who govern and those who are governed. Finally, third, the philosopher will not simply have to give advice and opinions regarding this or that trouble affecting the city. He will also have to rethink entirely the city's regime, he will have to be like those physicians who think not just to cure present ills but wish to take the whole of the patient's life into account and in hand. So, the object of the philosopher's intervention must be the entire regime of the city, its *politeia*.*

In a sense, we may wonder whether there is something of a contradiction between this definition of the philosophical counselor's task—who has to intervene in the ills of the city, therefore, in a persuasive form and in such a way as to question the whole *politeia*—and the passage I quoted from Letter V[9] in which Plato says: There are a number of different *politeiai*; there is the democratic constitution, the aristocratic constitution, and that which restricts power to a single person. And in a letter which was to accompany the arrival of a counselor to the king of Macedonia (Perdiccas), he said: Basically it does not matter what the *politeia* is, the problem is to hear, understand, and know the nature of the voice peculiar to each *politeia*, its *phōnē*, what is evil for the city generally being the fact that its *phōnē* (voice) does not correspond to

---

* The manuscript clarifies here:
  "What Letter VII says is very close to the *Republic* [Book IV] 426a-427a. It is only worth undertaking to take care of the city if it is possible to change the *politeia* and the way in which it is *politeuomenē*."

its constitution. Here it seems that the problem the counselor has to resolve is not simply adjusting the city's voice to its *politeia*, but well and truly rethinking the *politeia*. So we may think, suppose, or suspect that there is a contradiction between what is said in Letter VII and what is said in Letter V—obviously with the rider that, as Letter V is quite clearly apocryphal and anyway later than Letter VII, this contradiction should not raise too many problems. On the other hand, it does seem that Plato's injunction to take the whole of the city's *politeia* in hand is also somewhat in contradiction with other parts of the same letter, and in particular with the enigmatic passage in which Plato says: Anyway, there is absolutely no question of the philosopher becoming the lawgiver or legislator, the person who lays down the laws of a city. Actually, it seems to me that when Plato speaks here of the need for the good counselor to take into account the whole *politeia* (as a good physician takes into account the whole regime of a life), he does not mean the *politeia* in the, as it were, strict and institutional sense of the legal framework within which the city must live. What I think he understands by *politeia* really is the city's actual regime, that is to say, the ensemble formed by the laws themselves, but also by the conviction of both those who govern and those who are governed, the foremost and the least, that one must follow those laws that are good, and finally by the way in which these laws are in actual fact followed in the city. To the *politeia* in the strict sense, which is the institutional framework of the city, must be added this conviction, this persuasion of rulers and citizens, and how this persuasion is translated into action. All this constitutes the *politeia* in the broad sense.

It seems to me that when Plato likens the philosophical counselor's function to that of the physician, and when consequently he makes it seem that the counselor must take the whole *politeia* into account, it is actually a question of the *politeia* in this broad sense. To what, basically, must the counselor address himself? It seems to me that the counselor, as Plato defines him by likening him to the physician, is essentially someone who, once again, does not speak in order to lay down fundamental laws—as the city's point of departure or institutional framework—but basically someone who must address himself to the political will. He has to inform that will, whether it is the will of the monarchy, of oligarchic or aristocratic leaders, or of citizens. But if the philosopher addresses himself to the political will that gives life to the *politeia*, that lets itself be persuaded by the laws, that accepts them, recognizes them as good, and really wants to apply them, if this is the political will directing and giving life to the *politeia* that the philosopher addresses, then it must also be understood that he can only do so if this will is, as it were, a good will, that is to say, if the Prince, leaders, or citizens really want to listen to the philosopher. If they do not want to listen to him, that is to say, as the end of the text clarifies, if what the philosopher says is seen as no more than hot air, or even worse, if he is put to death, then in both cases the philosopher is rejected and philosophy cannot find its reality. The philosopher who speaks without being listened to, or again who speaks under the threat of death, basically only speaks hot air and pointlessly. If he wants his discourse to be a real discourse, a discourse of reality, if he wants his philosophical veridiction really to belong to the realm of reality, his philosopher's discourse must be listened to, understood, and accepted by those to whom it is addressed. Philosophy does not exist in reality solely by virtue of there being a philosopher to formulate it. Philosophy exists in reality, finds its reality, only if, corresponding to the philosopher who delivers his discourse, there is an expectation and listening of the person who wants to be persuaded by philosophy. And I think that here we come across what could be called the first circle (we will find others in the text). This is the circle of listening: philosophy can only address itself to those who want to listen. A discourse which only protested, challenged, shouted, and raged against power and tyranny would not be philosophy. No more would a violent discourse, which forces its way into the city and spreads threats and death around it, find its philosophical reality. If the philosopher is not listened to, and to such an extent that he is threatened with death, or again if the philosopher is violent, and to such an extent that his discourse brings death to others, then in both cases philosophy cannot find its reality; it fails the test of reality. The first test of reality of philosophical discourse will be the listening it meets with.

A whole series of consequences clearly follow from this, which we can rapidly run through: philosophy always presupposes philosophy; philosophy cannot talk to itself alone; philosophy cannot put itself forward as violence; philosophy cannot appear as the table of laws; and philosophy cannot be written and cannot circulate as a kind of writing which falls into any and every hand. The reality of philosophy—and this is its first characteristic—is that it addresses itself to the philosophical will. And, the last conclusion, you see how philosophy is completely different from rhetoric (obviously we will have to take this up again later). Rhetoric is precisely that which can both be deployed and be effective quite independently of the will of those who listen. The game of rhetoric is to seize hold of the listener's will in spite of itself, as it were, and to do what it wants with it. Philosophy, however, is not rhetoric, and it can only be the, as you like, modest or imperious opposite of rhetoric, because it can only exist by being listened to. This listening, philosophy's wait to be listened to in its own way is part of its reality. I think this is the first point we can get from the first explanation given by Plato concerning the counselor's role. If he went to Sicily, it was because he was promised a sympathetic ear. If his discourse in Sicily remained an empty *logos*, it is precisely because this listening did not take place and the promise made to him was dashed by the very person who ought to have listened to him. That is the first theme we come across.

The second, which is immediately linked to this, is this question: if it is true that philosophy gets its reality only when it can be listened to, how can you recognize those who will listen to you? How is it that the philosopher will be able to accept the test of reality on the basis of the certainty that he will be listened to? This is an important problem, and also, you recall, Socrates' problem. Socrates also had to ask himself if it was worth attempting to persuade this or that young man. And you know that Socrates demanded and saw, or thought he saw the certainty that he could be listened to in a boy's beauty, or anyway in what could be read in a boy's face and look. Here, obviously, is a completely different criterion involving something else entirely. The test which will enable one to decide whether or not one may be listened to is explained by Plato in paragraph 340b [...],* which I would now like to analyze. This passage is actually some way from the one I have just been reading, although it is clear enough that it is

---

* M.F. adds: and this is the text I have made some photocopies of and distributed. I am sorry for never having enough, but one never knows how many of you there are...

close to it logically. It involves an explanation which does not focus on the first political visit to Sicily (that is to say, the second chronologically), but on the second political visit (the third chronologically). But if you like, for convenience of exposition, I put them together, for I think that this passage (on how to recognize the person who can listen, on how the person one addresses should be tested) is directly connected to the question I was just touching on: one cannot speak, and philosophy cannot be a real discourse, cannot really be a veridiction if it is not addressed to someone who wants to listen to it. So the question is: How can we recognize those who can listen and want to listen? So, if you like, let us quickly read this text: "On my arrival, I thought I should first of all assure myself that Dionysius really was burning with enthusiasm for philosophy or whether everything that had been reported at Athens was without foundation."[10] You see, this is very directly the problem of listening: how can we know he will listen? "Now there is an elegant method for this test. It is well suited to tyrants, especially if they are full of badly understood philosophical expressions, which I soon realized was very much the case with Dionysius: one must show them what philosophical work is [we will come back shortly to the Greek words here, in short on how this translation should perhaps be tightened up a bit; let us just read it; M.F.] in its full extent, its peculiar character, its difficulties, and the hard work it demands. Is the listener a true philosopher, suited to this science and worthy of it because he is endowed with a divine nature? The path one teaches appears marvelous to him; he must set off on it at once, or else he would not be able to live. Then, redoubling with his own efforts those of his guide, he does not leave off until he has fully achieved the goal or gained enough strength to conduct himself without his instructor. It is in such a state of mind that this man lives: no doubt he engages in his usual actions, but in all things and at all times he sticks to philosophy, to that way of life that gives him, with a sober mind, a ready intelligence, a tenacious memory, and skill in reasoning. Any other conduct is always detested by him [and the text ends, I am skipping some lines; M.F.]. [...] Here is a clear and infallible experiment when it is a question of people devoted to pleasure who are incapable of effort; they should blame themselves, not their teachers, for their inability to practice what is necessary to philosophy."[11]

The first element to note in this text is the very explicitly and solemnly experimental and methodical character Plato gives to this criterion. It is not just, as in the case of Socrates, a perception or intuition which leads him to discern the quality of a boy's soul through his beauty. Here, it is a matter of a method, of a clear method, and of a method which must be completely determining and give indubitable results. What is this method? "It is well suited to tyrants," the text says, "especially if they are full of badly understood philosophical expressions." One must show tyrants (here I am following the translation) "what philosophical work is in its full extent, its peculiar character, its difficulties, and the hard work it demands." Translating the Greek text in a very rough, crude, and word for word way gives us this: one must show such people, these tyrants, what *to pragma*[12] is (what this thing, the thing itself is—I will come back to this); through what activities, what practices (*di'hosōn pragmatōn*) [it is practiced]; and what effort it involves and presupposes (*kai hoson ponon ekhei*).

You see that the word *pragma* appears twice. Now the word *pragma* has two meanings in Greek. In terms of grammar or logic *pragma* is the referent of a term or proposition. And here Plato says very clearly that one must show these tyrants what *to pragma* is (what the referent is), what philosophy is in its reality. They claim to know what it is, they know some of its words, they have heard some trivialities, and they think this is philosophy. One must show them *pan to pragma*: the reality of philosophy in its entirety, all the reality of philosophy, all that philosophy is, as referent of the notion of philosophy. And in what does this *pragma*, this reality of philosophy consist? One must show it *"hoion te kai hosōn pragmatōn kai hoson ponon ekhei."* What is this *pragma*? It is the *pragmata*. And what are *pragmata*? They are the concerns, activities, difficulties, exercises, and all the forms of practices in which one must train oneself, to which one must apply oneself, for which one must take great pains, and which really give one a lot of trouble. And here we have the second meaning of the word *pragma*, which is no longer the referent of a term or proposition. *Pragmata* are activities, everything with which one is occupied and to which one applies oneself. And you know that *pragmata* is opposed in this sense to *skholē*, which is leisure or free time. To tell the truth, philosophical *skholē*, philosophical leisure consists precisely in occupying oneself with certain things which are the *pragmata* of philosophy.

In any case, there is a double meaning of the word *pragma* in this text, which is this: Tyrants, or those who think they know philosophy, the text says, must be shown what the reality of philosophy is, what the word "philosophy" refers to, what it means to philosophize. And one shows them this by showing them what? That "philosophizing" is precisely a whole set of activities and *pragmata* which constitute philosophical practices. The text says no more or less than this, which is fundamental nevertheless, that the reality of philosophy, the reality of philosophizing, that to which the word philosophy refers, is a set of *pragmata* (practices). The reality of philosophy is the practices of philosophy. And what are these practices? Well, this is precisely what the text develops from this sentence, and I think we can find three sets of indications.

The practices of philosophy are represented as a path to go down, a path which the person one wishes to test and put to the proof must recognize straightaway and demonstrate that it is the path he has chosen, the path he will follow, the path whose end he wishes to reach, and that he cannot live otherwise. "*Ou bioton allōn*": it is not possible for him to live differently. This philosophical choice, this choice of the philosophical way is one of the first conditions. Second, on the basis of having made this philosophical choice, the candidate, the person tested, must hasten down this path with all his strength and directed by a guide who takes his hand and shows him the way. The candidate, the person put to the test, must hasten with all his strength and he must hasten and urge on his guide as well in order to arrive as quickly as possible at the goal. He must not relax his efforts in these activities (these *pragmata* of philosophy), and must always work and toil right through to the end of the path. And—this is again an indication found in the text—he must not abandon the direction of his guide until he has gained enough strength to conduct himself without his instructor and be guided by himself. This is a first set of indications.

The second set of important indications are those that come immediately after: "This is the state of mind in which such a man lives: no doubt he engages in his usual actions, but in all things and at all times he sticks to philosophy, to that way of life that gives him, with a sober mind, a ready intelligence, a tenacious memory, and skill in reasoning."[13] So this text is important because, you can see, it indicates

that the choice of philosophy must be made once and for all, maintained to the end, and not broken off until completion. But on the
other hand, and this is what appears here in this part of the exposition,
the choice of philosophy is not only not incompatible with everyday
actions, but consists in using philosophy, in bringing it into play even
in everyday life and during the actions one has to perform from day to
day. One is a philosopher even in one's everyday actions, and the practice of philosophy is translated into three abilities, three forms of attitude and aptitude: one is *eumathēs*, which is to say one can learn easily;
one is *mnēmōn*, which is to say one has a good memory and permanently
retains everything one has learned in a lively, present, and active way,
since one was *eumathēs*. So, one is *eumathēs*, one is *mnēmōn* (one retains
what one has learned), and finally one is *logizesthai dunatos* (one can reason, that is to say, in a given situation and conjecture* one knows how
to use reasoning and apply it to make the right decision). So you see,
there is a first set of indications marking what the philosophical choice
consists in, in its principle, permanence, and uninterrupted effort, and,
on the other hand, a set of indications showing how this philosophical
choice links up with and immediately and continually engages with
everyday activity.

Now if we compare this with the text from the *Alcibiades* I was just
talking about, and on which we commented last year, you see that there
is a very different definition of the relationship between philosophy
and, let's say, political activity. You remember that Alcibiades was
consumed with the desire to exercise power, and to exercise sole and
exclusive power in the city. This is the point at which Socrates took
hold of him, took him by the sleeve and said: But do you know how to
exercise this power? And then a very long dialogue took place in which
it turned out that, not even knowing what justice was, or the good
order or harmony that he wanted to install in the city, Alcibiades had
everything to learn. But he could not learn all this without first and
foremost taking care of himself. Taking care of himself involved knowing himself. Now knowing himself entailed the conversion of his gaze,
turning his eyes towards his own soul, and in the contemplation of his
own soul, or in the perception of the divine element of his own soul, he

---

* [This appears to be a slip and should perhaps read "conjuncture": G.B.]

would be able to perceive the foundations of justice in its essence, and as a result he would be able to know what the foundations and principles of a just government were. So we had the image, or the definition rather of a philosophical progression which in actual fact, as here, is indispensable for political action. But you see that in the *Alcibiades* this philosophical progression had the form of this turning back of self on self: contemplation of the soul by itself, and contemplation of the realities which can found a politically just action.[14]

Here the philosophical choice, philosophical activity, the indispensable philosophical *pragmata* which constitute the *pragma* (the reality) of philosophy, the philosophical practices which are the reality of philosophy, are quite different. In no way does it involve looking; it involves a way. It is absolutely not a question of conversion, but rather of following a path with an origin and an end. And a lengthy and arduous labor must be maintained along this way. Finally, attachment in this text is not attachment to eternal realities; it is the practice of daily life, that kind of day by day activity within which the subject will have to show that he is *eumathēs* (able to learn), *mnēmōn* (able to remember), and *logizesthai dunatos* (able to reason). In the case of the great conversion defined in the *Alcibiades*, the problem was knowing how the subject, when he had risen to the point where he was able to contemplate reality, could come back down again and effectively apply what he had seen to everyday life. You remember moreover, in the *Republic* as well, how difficult it was to send back down into the cave those who had once contemplated the reality outside. Here something quite different is involved. It is a choice which has to be made at the start, once and for all, and then developed, unfolded, and practically converted into the assiduous work of daily life. It is a quite different type of conversion. In the *Alcibiades* it is a conversion of the gaze towards something else. Here it is a conversion defined by an initial choice, a way, and an application. It is not a conversion of the gaze, but of the decision. It is not a conversion which aims at contemplation, the contemplation of oneself, but one which, directed by a guide along a lengthy and arduous way, should make possible at the same time learning, memory, and sound reasoning in everyday activity.

Clearly some conclusions can be drawn from this. The first, you have seen, is that it seems to me that we have the definition of another circle in this text. Earlier, based on the previous passage, I referred to the circle of listening, which consists in philosophical truth-telling, philosophical veridiction presupposing the other's willingness to listen. Here we have another, completely different circle, which is no longer the circle of the other, but the circle of oneself. In fact it is a matter of the reality of philosophy being found, recognized, and effectuated only in the practice of philosophy. The reality of philosophy is its practice. More exactly, and this is the second conclusion to be drawn, the reality of philosophy is not its practice as the practice of *logos*. That is to say, the reality of philosophy will not be its practice as discourse, or even as dialogue. It will be the practice of philosophy as "practices," in the plural; the practice of philosophy in its practices, its exercises. And the third, obviously essential conclusion concerns what these exercises are directed towards, what is at stake in them. Well, quite simply, it is the subject itself. That is to say, it is in the relation to self, in the work of self on self, in the work on oneself, in this mode of activity of self on self that philosophy's reality will actually be demonstrated and attested. Philosophy finds its reality in the practice of philosophy understood as the set of practices through which the subject has a relationship to itself, elaborates itself, and works on itself. The reality of philosophy is this work of self on self.

That is the second passage in the seventh letter I wanted to comment on. There is a third passage which I will comment on in a moment, and I think this will bring us to a third circle and a third definition, a third approach of this reality of philosophy.

1. Platon, lettre VII, 328b, in *Œuvres complètes*, t. XIII-1: *Lettres*, p. 33: "it was only necessary to persuade one man sufficiently and all would be won"; English, "Letter VII" in *Plato: The Collected Dialogues*, p. 1577: "If I were to convince but one man, that in itself would ensure complete success."

2. On this point, see the lectures of January 1982 in *The Hermeneutics of the Subject*.

3. Platon, *Alcibiade*, 104e-105a, trans. M. Croiset (Paris: Les Belles Lettres, 1970) pp. 61-62: "If you had seemed to me to be satisfied with the advantages I have just listed and decided on enjoying them for all your life (*en toutois katabiōnai*), I would have ceased loving you a long time ago"; English translation by W.R.M. Lamb, *Alcibiades I*, in *Plato XII* (Cambridge, Mass., and London: Harvard University/William Heinemann, "Loeb Classical Library," 1927) p. 103: "For if I saw you, Alcibiades, content with the things I set forth just now, and minded to pass your life in enjoying them, I should long ago have put away my love."

4. Plato, letter VII, 330c-d, French p. 36; English p. 1579: "One who advises a sick man, living in a way to injure his health, must first effect a reform in his way of living, must he not? And if the patient consents to such a reform, then he may admonish him on other points? If, however, the patient refuses, in my opinion it would be the act of a real man and a good physician to keep clear of advising such a man."

5. Ibid., 331d, French p. 37; English p. 1580: "If he thinks that the constitution of his city is imperfect, he should say so, unless such action will either be useless or will lead to his own death, but he must not apply force to his fatherland by revolutionary methods. When it is impossible to make the constitution perfect except by sentencing men to exile and death, he must refrain from action and pray for the best for himself and for his city."

6. Platon, *La République*, 425e-426a, pp. 14-15; *Republic*, pp. 667-668.

7. See below, note 8.

8. Platon, *Les Lois*, livre IV, pp. 71-72; Plato, *Laws*, Book IV, pp. 1310-1311.

9. See above pp. 210-213.

10. Letter VII, 340b, French p. 49; English pp. 1587-1588: "When I had arrived, I thought I ought first to put it to the proof whether Dionysius was really all on fire with philosophy or whether the frequent reports that had come to Athens to that effect amounted to nothing."

11. Ibid., 340b-341a, French pp. 49-50; English p. 1588: "Now there is an experimental method for determining the truth in such cases that, far from being vulgar, is truly appropriate to despots, especially those stuffed with secondhand opinions, which I perceived, as soon as I arrived, was very much the case with Dionysius. One must point out to such men that the whole plan is possible and explain what preliminary steps and how much hard work it will require, for the hearer, if he is genuinely devoted to philosophy and is a man of God with a natural affinity and fitness for the work, sees in the course marked out a path of enchantment, which he must at once strain every nerve to follow, or die in the attempt. Thereupon he braces himself and his guide to the task and does not relax his efforts until he either crowns them with final accomplishment or acquires the faculty of tracing his own way no longer accompanied by the pathfinder. When this conviction has taken possession of him, such a man passes all his life in whatever occupations he may engage in, but through it all never ceases to practice philosophy and such habits of daily life as will be most effective in making him an intelligent and retentive student, able to reason soberly by himself. Other practices than these he shuns to the end... This test then proves to be the surest and safest in dealing with those who are self-indulgent and incapable of continued hard work, since they throw the blame not on their guide but on their own inability to follow out in detail the course of training subsidiary to the project."

12. See a first analysis of this concept with reference to spiritual exercises and more precisely to philosophical listening in *L'Herméneutique du sujet*, p. 332; *The Hermeneutics of the Subject*, p. 349. See also the article by P. Hadot on this notion in P. Aubenque, ed., *Concepts et Catégories dans la pensée antique* (Paris: Vrin, 1980).

13. Letter VII, 340b, French p. 49; English p. 1588 (see above, note 11).

14. On this point, see the lectures of January 1982 in *The Hermeneutics of the Subject*.

fourteen

16 FEBRUARY 1983

Second hour

[
The failure of Dionysius. ∽ *The Platonic rejection of writing.* ∽
Mathēmata *versus* sunousia. ∽ *Philosophy as practice of the
soul.* ∽ *The philosophical digression of Letter VII: the five elements
of knowledge.* ∽ *The third circle: the circle of knowledge.* ∽ *The
philosopher and the legislator.* ∽ *Final remarks on contemporary
interpretations of Plato.*
]

[…]* THE FIRST QUESTION IN this set of texts I am analyzing for you
was that of listening: philosophy will be a discourse, will be real, only if
it is listened to. Second, philosophical discourse will be real only if it is
accompanied, sustained, and exercised as a practice and through a set of
practices. This was the second thing. Now, the third set of texts comprises
those which refer to the test to which Plato actually put Dionysius, or
rather to how Dionysius failed to respond positively to this test. The text
I distributed earlier, you recall, showed that what was involved was a
systematic test which Plato presented as a sure and certain means. And, in
the lines and pages that follow, Plato shows how Dionysius failed the test.
In fact, this long exposition can be broken up in the following way. First,
the failure of Dionysius: how and why, through what defect regarding philosophy did Dionysius fail? And second, the positive side of this critique,
of the failure of Dionysius, namely: a particular theory of knowledge.

---

* M.F.: So, shall we continue? One is tired at this time of the year.

First, the negative side: how did Dionysius fail the test of philosophy, the test of the *pragma* of philosophy, of the reality of philosophy which must be in the *pragmata*, the practices of philosophy? Plato shows this failure in two ways, or gives two signs of it. The first, entirely negative sign is this: Dionysius refused precisely to choose the lengthy path of philosophy pointed out to him. Rather he did not listen to the first lesson of philosophy, thinking that he already knew the most important things (*ta megista*) and already knew enough philosophy to have no need of further development.[1] This is simple. But there is something else, for beyond his inability to follow the long way of philosophy, that is to say, to take the hard path of exercises and practices, Dionysius made, as it were, a direct and immediate error, he positively made an error. And this error is very interesting and very important: he actually wrote a treatise of philosophy.[2] And Plato takes the fact that he had written this treatise as the sign that Dionysius was unable to find the reality of philosophy. The text written by Dionysius was in fact written after Plato's visit, and Plato refers to it merely as a sort of sign *a posteriori* that in actual fact his visit could not succeed, since Dionysius was likely to be one of those who, a bit later, in order to attest to his own philosophical worth and to show that the faults were really on Plato's side, writes a treatise on the most important questions of philosophy. In this, Plato says, he made two errors.

First, he wanted to be seen [as] the author of texts which were really no more than transcriptions of lessons [he had received]. But this is not the most important or decisive thing in the reproach. Wanting to write on questions of philosophy, and on the most important questions of philosophy, is to show that one understands nothing of philosophy. So this text, which is obviously of the utmost importance, can be compared with another, which is known and frequently cited as the proof, demonstration, and final expression of Plato's great refusal of writing. This text of the great refusal of writing is, as you know, in Letter II, right at the end, where Plato says: "Think about this therefore and take care not to have to repent one day of what today you shamefully allow to be divulged. The greatest safeguard (*megistē phulakē*) will be not to write, but to learn by heart, for it is impossible for writings not to end up in the public domain. Also, I myself have never ever written on these questions. There is no work by Plato and never will be. What is presently called such is by Socrates in the time of his fine youth. Farewell and obey me. As soon as you have read and re-read this letter, burn it."[3] We should remember however that Letter II is clearly later than Letter VII, which I am analyzing, and is, to some extent, a summary or, I should say, a Neo-Platonist version of it. If we take the older text of Letter VII, it seems to me that we see the refusal of writing formulated in a quite different way, in a quite different, well, relatively different mode. Here, in the later text of Letter II I have just read, it is quite clear that—we should look more closely—the general theme is that of esotericism. Some knowledge should not be divulged; to divulge this knowledge exposes one to dangers. Any work said to be "by Plato" may not and should not be considered to be Plato's. Even the letters he writes must be burned. This is a precaution of esotericism in which there is undoubtedly a Pythagorean influence. This is not at all how the rejection of writing is presented in the text of Letter VII, which I would now like to analyze for you.

So, Dionysius has published some texts which he wanted to pretend he wrote and which are texts on the most fundamental questions of philosophy. Now, Plato says, one cannot speak of the essential things in philosophy; philosophical discourse cannot find its reality, its *ergon*, if it takes the form of *mathēmata*.[4] Here, the word *mathēmata* should be understood in its double meaning. *Mathēmata* are, of course, particular items of knowledge, but they are also the formulae of knowledge. The word means both knowledge in the sense of its content and the way in which this knowledge is given in mathemes (*mathèmes*), that is to say, in the formulae which may fall within *mathēsis*, that is to say, the learning of a formula which is given by the teacher, heard by the disciple, and learned by heart, thus becoming the disciple's knowledge.

This development of *mathēmata*, giving knowledge the form of taught, learned, and known formulae, is not, the text says, the path actually taken by philosophy. That is not how things are, and philosophy is not passed on through *mathēmata*. How is it passed on? Well, he says, one acquires philosophy through "*sunousia peri to pragma*."[5] And a bit later he employs the verb *suzēn*.[6] *Sunousia* is being with, meeting, conjunction. In everyday Greek vocabulary the word *sunousia* frequently has the sense of sexual union. This connotation is absolutely not present here, and I do not think we should over-interpret by saying that there is something like the relationship of sexual union between someone who philosophizes and philosophy. But someone who has to subject himself to the test of philosophy must "live with" or, let's use the word, "cohabit" with it—here too with, as you are well aware, the possible meanings of cohabiting. That the person who philosophizes has to cohabit with philosophy is what constitutes the practice of philosophy and its reality. *Sunousia*: cohabitation. *Suzēn*: living with. What does Plato say will take place by dint of this *sunousia*, through this *suzēn*? Well, that the light will come on in the soul, a bit as a light ("*phōs*") flares (the [French] translation says "a flash"[7]), that is to say, as a lamp flares when one brings a flame to it. Being close to philosophy as when one is close to fire, until the lamp in the soul is lit, or the lamp is lit as a soul, is the way in which philosophy will in fact find its reality. And when the lamp is lit it will have to feed itself from its own oil, that is to say, philosophy, lit in the soul, will have to be fed by the soul itself. This is the way in which philosophy lives, in this form of cohabitation, of the light which is passed on and lit, of the light which feeds on the soul itself. You see that this is exactly the opposite of what happens in the case of *mathēmata*. There is no *sunousia*, no necessary *suzēn* in the *mathēmata*. Mathemes, knowledge contents, had to be given shape. They must be passed on and kept in the mind until possibly being erased by forgetfulness. Here, on the contrary, there is no formula, but coexistence. There is no learning of a formula, but an abrupt and sudden coming on of the light within the soul. And there is no inscription and depositing of ready made formulae in the soul, but the perpetual feeding of philosophy by the secret oil of the soul.

To that extent we cannot really think that philosophy can be taught by something like written material which precisely gives knowledge the form of *mathēmata* which are then passed on by any teacher to any disciples who have to do no more than learn them by heart. In any case, the fact that philosophy cannot be passed on as *mathēmata*, Plato says, is the reason why he himself never agreed to write any book on philosophy, although he would have been in the best position to have done so.[8] Of course, he adds, if this could be done, and if in fact philosophy could be written in the form of mathemes and passed on as such, this would of course be the most useful thing in the world. Imagine how fine it would be, he says, if we could bring *tēn phusin* (nature) into the light for everyone.[9] But in fact this would be either pointless or dangerous. It would be dangerous, because those who do not know that philosophy has no other reality than its own practices would think that they do know philosophy, and they would become self-important, vain, and contemptuous of others. As for the others, those who know perfectly well that the reality of philosophy resides in its practice and practices, it would be completely pointless teaching it and passing it on through writing. Those who know what the reality of philosophy really is and who practice this reality have no need of this explicit teaching in the form of *mathēmata*. For them an *endeixis*,[10] an indication, is sufficient. The teaching of philosophy will be able to be practiced through these structures of indication. All of this is in the letter, 341b-342a.[11]

That then is the negative side of the test of Dionysius, which culminates in this false practice, which is the practice of writing. Now this rejection of writing is explained and justified in a paragraph immediately following the one I have just analyzed, and which is, in a way, like its positive side, and which should, I think, give the true meaning of this rejection and refusal. Actually, after having explained how philosophy cannot be taught—after having said: For some it is useless since they need only an indication, and the others "we would fill with an unjust contempt or a vain self-importance"[12]—Plato writes: "Moreover, I intend to dwell at some length on this question: maybe some of the points I deal with will become clearer when I have explained myself. There is a serious reason, in fact, against trying to write anything on such matters, a reason I have often put forward before, but which I think I have to repeat again."[13] So, it is perfectly clear that Plato introduces this passage, called a bit further on a "digression" moreover,[14] in the clearest way and without the least ambiguity as the explanation of his refusal of writing. What then is this explanation? The explanation apparently starts off far from writing. It presents itself as a theory of knowledge and science (*epistemē*): "In all beings we distinguish three elements which enable us to acquire the science of them."[15]

This text is very difficult and I would like here merely to bring out some aspects which are relevant for our problem. We can say that Plato distinguishes five things, five elements regarding what it is that makes it possible to have knowledge of things. The first three are: the name (*onoma*); the definition (*logos*, understood in the strict sense, that is to say, the definition which, Plato himself says, includes names and verbs); and the image (the *eidōlon*). And then there are two other levels, two other means of knowing: the fourth is what he calls the science (the *epistemē*, which, he says, is also right opinion—*orthē doxa*—and *noūs*), and finally there is a fifth element. To schematize this text, I think we could say this: the first three modes of knowledge (by the name, definition, and image) are modes of knowledge such that they make the thing known through that which is heterogeneous, or even, Plato says, contrary to the thing itself. Take the example of the circle, Plato says, and it is clear that the arbitrary name (*kuklos*) we use to designate the circle is entirely unlike, at any rate extraneous to the circle itself. Likewise, the definition we give of the circle, made only of names and verbs, is equally extraneous to the circle itself. Third, the image we trace of the circle in the sand is itself extraneous to the circle. It is made up of elements, he says, which are only short straight lines, which are obviously contrary to the actual nature of the circle. Therefore all of this (name, definition, image) is foreign to the actual nature of the circle. As for the fourth means of knowing, the *epistemē*, which is both *orthē doxa* (right opinion) and *noūs*, unlike the others, this fourth level or form of knowledge does not reside in the outside world. Words are sounds, drawn shapes are material things. This fourth element, *epistemē*, resides only in the soul. Of what does it give knowledge? Not of things extraneous or external to the thing itself; it gives knowledge of the qualities of the thing. But it does not give knowledge of the very being of the thing: *to on*, that in which the very essence of the thing consists.

The fifth form of knowledge is that which enables us to know the thing itself in its own being (*to on*). What is this fifth form of knowledge, in what does it consist? And here there is something important. What is it that effectuates this fifth form of knowledge? What is the agent of this knowledge? What is it that gives us access to the reality of the thing in its very being? It is *noūs*, which is said to be actually present in the preceding, fourth mode of knowledge, with *epistemē* and *orthē doxa*. Second, how can we form the knowledge which Plato says we acquire in this way, and which enables us to grasp the very being of the thing? We can acquire it through the coming and going, the ascent and descent through the four other degrees of knowledge and through the instruments that characterize these other forms of knowledge. In this way, by rising from the name to the definition, from the definition to the image, and from the image to the *epistemē* (to the knowledge), and then going back down, and then rising again, we will gradually succeed in grasping the fifth form of knowledge of the very being (the *to on*) of the circle and of the things we wish to know. But for this work of ascent and descent through the other degrees of knowledge really to be able to lead us to the fifth degree, it is also necessary that the soul be of good quality. It must have an affinity with, must be *suggenēs* with the thing itself, with precisely *to pragma*.[16]

When the good quality soul undertakes this slow, lengthy, arduous work of going up and down through the other forms of knowledge, when he has practiced what Plato calls *tribē*—in the strict sense: rubbing or friction—knowledge of reality in its very being thereby becomes possible.[17] This word *tribē* is important. Materially it is rubbing, friction (*frottement*). There is an echo and reminder here of that image of the fire which must be lit in the soul as in a lamp.* In a more general and abstract sense, *tribē* is also everything which is exercise, training. It is everything through which one gets used to something, practices something. Consequently, you see that the fifth kind of knowledge is absolutely different from the four other degrees of knowledge. But this final knowledge is arrived at and acquired only through a constant, perpetual practice of rubbing or friction between the other modes of knowledge.

Obviously, I am schematizing, for the formulations of this text give rise to a great many difficulties concerning the Platonic theory of knowledge, the meaning to be given to words like *doxa* and *epistemē*, and the whole problem of the conception of the *noūs*, etcetera. What I would like to emphasize, and the angle from which I would like to consider this text is that it quite precisely and appropriately gives meaning to everything we have said until now on the reality of philosophy. You see that it is lodged quite precisely in the problem which appears to me to dominate the whole of this Letter VII, or at any rate its central and theoretical theme, namely: what is philosophy when rather than as merely *logos*, one wants to think of it as *ergon*? Well, it seems to me

---

* [One strikes a match (*frotte une allumette*) by rubbing it along a rough friction strip (*frottoir*); G.B.]

that we can make out here what could be called a third circle. We have
had the circle of listening: for philosophy really to be real, for it to find
its reality, it must be a discourse which is listened to. Second, for philosophy to find its reality it must be practice (both in the singular and
plural, a practice and practices); the reality of philosophy is found in its
practices. And now finally, we have what could be called the circle of
knowledge, namely, that philosophical knowledge, specifically philosophical knowledge, is in fact completely different from the four other
forms of knowledge. But nevertheless, the reality of this knowledge can
be arrived at only through the unremitting and continuous practice of
the other modes of knowledge.

Anyway, Plato draws some conclusions, expressed in the same text,
from this theory of knowledge, this analysis, which, once again, he
explicitly presents as the explanation of the reason for the refusal of
writing. Plato says: If it is true that knowledge is this, that there are
five degrees of knowledge and that knowledge of reality in its very
being can be produced only through the *tribē* (the friction) produced
between these modes of knowledge, then, he says, a serious man (*spou-
daios*) cannot deal with these things in writing.[18] He cannot deal with
these things in writing for reasons which are not given in the text but
which emerge quite clearly, since precisely by giving what is known and
to be known the [form*] of the matheme, of the *mathēma*, of *mathēmata*,
which in a way are the instrument by which ready made knowledge is
conveyed to someone who has to know it, writing, which is therefore
bound up with the form of *mathēmata*, cannot in any way correspond to
the reality of philosophical knowledge: the constant friction between
the different modes of knowledge.

The first conclusion Plato draws from the principle that no serious
man can deal with the things of philosophy in writing is, of course,
that Dionysius has understood nothing about the nature of philosophy.
And he draws this further conclusion, which is more important for us,
and, what is more, paradoxical in relation to Plato: if in actual fact philosophy cannot be practiced and learned in the form of *mathēmata*, then
a philosopher's role will never be that of a lawgiver, it will never be to
present a system of laws to which citizens must submit for the city to be

---

* M.F.: the formula (this is the translation of *mathēma* in the Budé edition).

governed properly. He says quite explicitly, at the end of this passage, at 344c: "From this we should draw this simple conclusion: when we see a written work, whether by a legislator on the laws [*en nomois*, and this is a matter of a *"nomethetēs"*; M.F.], or by anyone else on no matter what subject, we can say that if the author is himself someone serious, he has not really been serious about this, and that his thought remains locked away in the most precious part of the writer. If he really put his thoughts about things of great importance in [written; M.F.] characters, 'then surely' it was not the gods, but mortals who 'made him lose his mind'."[19] So we have here a text which completely challenges the activity of proposing laws for a city, that is to say, which, apparently at least, denies the legitimacy of a text like the *Republic*, and especially the *Laws*, which is quite precisely devoted to writing on laws from the lawgiver's point of view. It is said that such a text cannot be serious.

I put to you a pure and simple hypothesis: just as Plato says that *muthos* (myth) should not be taken literally and, in a way, is not serious, or that one should put all one's seriousness into interpreting it seriously, could we not say the same thing about those well known texts of the *Laws* and the *Republic* which are often interpreted as the ideal form Plato gives to the city that he would like to be real? Should not the activity of the lawgiver in Plato's thought, the legislative and constitutional schema put forward by the *Republic* and the *Laws*, basically be handled as cautiously as a myth? May it not be that what is serious in philosophy is found elsewhere? Is not the activity of lawgiver that Plato seems to be taking on in the *Laws* and the *Republic* a game? Is it not a game like myth is a game, although obviously in a different way. So what philosophy has to say will certainly be said through this nomothetic game, as it is through the mythical game, but in order to say something else. If the reality of philosophy, the reality of philosophy in politics, is understood to be something completely different from giving men laws and proposing the constraining form of the ideal city, then I think we could make some remarks starting from this reading of these texts from the seventh letter.

Two, let's say, critical remarks, and one on the very meaning of the question posed and of the answer given in this letter. First, you see that if in fact the refusal of writing should be given the meaning I am suggesting, then in no way should we see in this Platonic refusal of writing something like the advent of a logocentrism in Western philosophy.[20] You can see that it is more complicated than that. For the refusal of writing here, throughout this text from Letter VII, is not at all presented in terms of an opposition between writing and the meaning and valorization of *logos*. On the contrary, what this letter takes up is precisely the theme of the insufficiency of *logos*. And the refusal of writing is set out as a refusal of a knowledge arrived at through *onoma* (the word), *logos* (the definition, the interplay of substantives and verbs, etcetera). It is all of this, writing and *logos* together, which is well and truly rejected in this letter. Writing is not rejected because it is opposed to *logos*. On the contrary, it is because they are on the same side, and because writing is, in its way, like a derivative and secondary form of *logos*. And on the other hand, this refusal of writing, of writing and of the *logos* associated with it, or of the *logos* to which writing is subordinated, is not therefore made in the name of *logos* itself (rejected like writing and even before writing), but in the name something positive, in the name of *tribē*, of exercise, effort, work, in the name of a certain painstaking mode of relationship of self to self. What we should decipher in this refusal of writing is not at all the advent of a logocentrism, but the advent of something else entirely. It is the advent of philosophy, of a philosophy whose very reality would be the practice of self on self. It is in fact something like the Western subject which is at stake in this simultaneous and conjoint refusal of writing and of *logos*.

The second conclusion and critical remark is that any reading of Plato which finds in texts like the *Republic* and the *Laws* something like the foundation, origin, or major form of, let's say, to hurry, because time is passing, "totalitarian" political thought, must undoubtedly be completely revised. And the somewhat fanciful interpretations of the good Karl Popper[21] do not, of course, take account of the actual details and Plato's complex game with regard to this problem of lawgiving, of formulating and laying down laws. In this letter Plato challenges, he removes, as it were, the ground on which he undoubtedly set the *Republic*, the *Laws*, and that nomothetical activity which now appears as a non-serious activity.

As a result, the relationship of philosophy to politics, the test of philosophy's reality with regard to politics, will not take the form of an imperative discourse in which men and the city will be given constraining forms to which they must submit for the city to survive. But, having played this game of the ideal city, it should be recalled that philosophy's seriousness is elsewhere. The seriousness of philosophy does not consist in giving men laws and telling them what the ideal city is in which they must live, but in constantly reminding them (those at least who wish to listen, since philosophy's reality comes only from it being listened to), that the reality of philosophy is to be found in its practices, which are the practices of self on self and, at the same time, those practices of knowledge by which all the modes of knowledge, through which one rises and descends and which one rubs against each other, finally bring one face to face with the reality of Being itself.

And so you see that what we come to—and at any rate this will be the positive and provisional conclusion at which I would like to stop—is that it appears from this Letter VII that, if it is true that the test of philosophy's reality is in the approach which Plato illustrated when, at Dion's request, he met with someone who exercises political power, if the test of philosophy's reality is there, if that is where and how philosophy escapes the danger of being no more than *logos*, if that is how it handles the *ergon*, then the test of philosophy in politics directs us to this: the reality of philosophy is found in the relationship of self to self. And it is indeed in setting out the problem of the government of self and the government of others that philosophy, here, in this text, formulates its *ergon*, at once its task and its reality.* That's it, thank you.

---

* The manuscript ends:

"What can we conclude from all this? For the question I wanted to raise: the history or genealogy of truth-telling in the political field, we see then the existence of a double obligation: the person who wants to govern needs to philosophize; but the person who philosophizes has the task of confronting reality. This double bond formulated in this way is linked to a certain redefinition of philosophy as *pragma*, that is to say, as a lengthy work comprising: a relationship to a guide; a permanent practice of knowledge; a form of conduct of life, including everyday life. And in this way two complementary figures are avoided: that of the philosopher who turns his gaze towards another reality and is detached from this world; that of the philosopher who arrives with the table of the law already written."

1. Platon, lettre VII, 341b, in *Lettres*, French p. 50; Plato, Letter VII, 341b, in *Letters*, p. 1588.
2. Ibid.
3. Letter II, 314b-c, French pp. 10-11; English p. 1567: "Consider these facts and take care lest you sometime come to repent of having now unwisely published your views. It is a very great safeguard to learn by heart instead of writing. It is impossible for what is written not to be disclosed. That is the reason why I have never written anything about these things, and why there is not and will not be any written work of Plato's own. What are now called his are the work of a Socrates embellished and modernized. Farewell and believe. Read this letter now at once many times and burn it."
4. Letter VII, 341c, French p. 50: "There is no way, in fact, of putting them [= philosophical problems] in formulae (*mathēmata*)"; English p. 1589: "...for there is no way of putting it in words."
5. Ibid.
6. Ibid., 341c-d, French: "When one has accompanied these problems (*ek pollēs sunousias*), lived with them (*suzēn*), the truth suddenly lights up in the soul, like light flashing from a spark"; English: "Acquaintance with it must come rather after a long period of attendance on instruction in the subject itself and of close companionship, when, suddenly, like a blaze kindled by a leaping spark, it is generated in the soul."
7. In fact the [French] translation speaks of a "spark (*etincelle*)." See the previous note.
8. Letter VII, 341d, French p. 50: "There is no doubt, I know full well, that if it were necessary to set them out in writing or speech, I would do it best"; English p. 1589: "Besides, this at any rate I know, that if there were to be a treatise or a lecture on this subject, I could do it best."
9. Ibid., French: "...bring to light for all the true light of things"; English: "to bring the nature of things to light for all men."
10. Ibid., 341e, French: "...except for an elite, for whom some indications suffice (*dia smikras endeixeōs*)"; English: "...except in the case of some few who are capable of discovering the truth for themselves with a little guidance."
11. Ibid., 341b-d, French p. 50: "In any case, this is what I can affirm regarding all those who have written or will write and claim knowledge of the matters which are the object of my concerns, whether through having been taught by me or others, or through having discovered it for themselves: in my view it is impossible that they have understood anything about the matter. By me, at least, there is no work and certainly never will be any work on such subjects. There is no way, in fact, of putting them in formulae (*mathēmata*) as one does for the other sciences, but it is when one has accompanied these problems, lived with them (*suzēn*), the truth suddenly lights up in the soul, like light flashing from a spark, and then grows by itself (*rhēton gar oudamōs estin hōs alla mathēmata, all'ek pollēs sunousias gignomenēs peri to pragma auto kai tou suzēn exaiphnēs, hoion apo puros pēdēsanto exaphten phōs, en tē psukhē genomenon auto heauto ēdē trephei*)"; English pp. 1588-1589: "One statement at any rate I can make in regard to all who have written or who may write with a claim to knowledge of the subjects to which I devote myself—no matter how they pretend to have acquired it, whether from my instruction or from others or by their own discovery. Such writers can in my opinion have no real acquaintance with the subject. I certainly have composed no work in regard to it, nor shall I ever do so in future, for there is no way of putting it in words like other studies. Acquaintance with it must come rather after a long period of attendance on instruction in the subject itself and of close companionship, when, suddenly, like a blaze kindled by a leaping spark, it is generated in the soul and at once becomes self-sustaining."
12. Ibid., 341e, French p. 51; English p. 1589: "to do so would excite in some an unjustified contempt in a thoroughly offensive fashion, in others certain lofty and vain hopes, as if they had acquired some awesome lore."
13. Ibid., 341e-342a; English: "It has occurred to me to speak on the subject at greater length, for possibly the matter I am discussing would be clearer if I were to do so. There is a true doctrine, which I have often stated before, that stands in the way of the man who would dare to write even the least thing on such matters, and which it seems I am now called upon to repeat."
14. Ibid., 344d, French p. 54; English p. 1591: "deviations."

15. Ibid., 342a, French p. 51; English p. 1589: "For everything that exists there are three classes of objects through which knowledge about it must come."

16. Ibid., 343e-344a, French pp. 53-54: "But by dint of handling all of them, ascending and descending from one to another, we only just manage to create the science, when both the object and the mind are both of good quality. If, on the contrary, natural aptitudes are not good—and for most of the time this is indeed the state of the soul with regard to knowledge or what we call morals—if they have been spoiled, not even Lynceus would be able to give sight to such people. In a word, the person who has no affinity with the object (*ton mē suggenē tou pragmatos*) will not obtain the vision either through his mental aptitude or through his memory"; English p. 1591: "Consideration of all of the four in turn—moving up and down from one to another—barely begets knowledge of a naturally flawless object in a naturally flawless man. If a man is naturally defective—and this is the natural state of most people's minds with regard to intelligence and to what are called morals—while the objects he inspects are tainted with imperfection, not even Lynceus could make such a one see. To sum it all up in one word, natural intelligence and a good memory are equally powerless to aid the man who has not an inborn affinity with the subject."

17. Ibid., 344b-c, French p. 54: "It is only just when one has rubbed (*mogis de tribomena*) the names, definitions, and visual perceptions and sense impressions against each other, when one has examined them in benevolent discussions through questions nor answers not dictated by envy, that the light of wisdom and intelligence shines (*exelampse phronēsis peri hekaston kai noūs*) on the object studied with all the intensity that human strength can bear"; English p. 1591: "Hardly after practicing detailed comparisons of names and definitions and visual and other sense perceptions, after scrutinizing them in benevolent disputation by the use of question and answer without jealousy, at last in a flash understanding of each blazes up, and the mind, as it exerts all its powers to the limit of human capacity, is flooded with light."

18. Ibid., 344c, French: "That is why any serious man will take good care not to deal in writing with serious questions"; English: "For this reason no serious man will ever think of writing about serious realities."

19. Ibid., 344c-d; English: "In a word, it is an inevitable conclusion from this that when anyone sees anywhere the written work of anyone, whether that of a lawgiver in his laws or whatever it may be in some other form, the subject treated cannot have been his most serious concern—that is, if he is himself a serious man. His most serious interests have their abode somewhere in the noblest region of the field of his activity. If, however, he really was seriously concerned with these matters and put them in writing, 'then surely' not the gods, but mortals 'have utterly blasted his wits'." [Quotation from Homer, *The Illiad*, 7.360, 12.234.]

20. This is a clear reference to the theses defended by Jacques Derrida in "La Pharmacie de Platon" in his *La Dissémination* (Paris: Le Seuil, 1972); English translation by Barbara Johnson, *Dissemination* (London: Athlone, 1981).

21. K. Popper, *The Open Society and its Enemies. Volume One: The Spell of Plato* (London: Routledge, 1945).

fifteen

23 FEBRUARY 1983

First hour

[
The enigmatic blandness of Plato's political advice. ∿ *The advice
to Dionysius.* ∿ *The diagnosis, practice of persuasion, proposal of
a regime.* ∿ *Advice to Dion's friends.* ∿ *Study of Letter VIII.* ∿
Parrēsia *underpins political advice.*
]

[...]* TODAY I WOULD LIKE to continue and end what I began to
tell you about Letter VII. You recall that we picked out two sets of
elements in Letter VII. [In the first place,] there are considerations
concerning the activity which consists in a philosopher undertaking to
give advice to a Prince, to someone who practices politics. These bore
on the circumstances in which it was opportune to give advice, the
reasons precisely why it was necessary to give advice. And through this
question concerning the status of advice and the advisor, we were able
to see a much more fundamental question being formulated involving
nothing less than what could be called the reality of philosophy. Under
what conditions can philosophy be other than *logos*, than pure and simple discourse? When and under what conditions can it affect reality?
How can it become a real activity in reality? Well, on condition that
it maintains a certain relationship with politics which is defined by

---

* M.F.: To start with I ask you to forgive me, because I've got a bit of the flu today. It would
have been rude of me to let you come and then not come myself, so I am going to try to give the
lecture. There's a risk of being a bit washed out, but I will try to hold on until the end of the
two hours.

the *sumboulē* (the advice). So what we saw last week was this relation-ship to politics as the test of reality for philosophy, for philosophical discourse.

Now there is clearly another group of elements in this letter which I would like to study today. And these, of course, concern the advice itself. This letter—which is addressed to Dion's friends, no doubt fic-titiously, [or rather] which is basically a public letter in which Plato, whether or not he really is addressing Dion's friends, explains to his readers why and how he advised Dion first of all, then Dionysius, and then Dion's friends—contained considerations on the principle of advice. And then there was the advice itself. In fact he gives examples, summaries at least, of the successive pieces of advice he gave to dif-ferent Syracusans who asked for his views. This is what we must now study in its form, content, nature, and what it says, etcetera.

Around the question of the content of this advice we see another problem emerge, which is no longer the problem of philosophy's real-ity, or of what can and must be the test by which philosophy is able to define its reality. It seems to me that what we see appearing in the actual content of this political advice is nothing more or less than the sovereign's mode of being insofar as he has to be a philosopher. Only we must not anticipate things because, however important this prob-lem may be, the advice Plato gives risks being rather disappointing when we look at it. When we actually examine the political advice that Plato prides himself on having given Dion, Dionysius, and then Dion's friends, it would appear to be little more than a set of views which are more philosophical than political, more moral than really political: some general themes on justice and injustice, on the interest anyway in practicing justice rather than injustice, some advice of moderation, advice also for reconciling conflicting parties, advice to sovereigns to practice friendship with subject peoples instead of violently subjecting them, and so on. In truth, at first sight there is nothing which appears to be very interesting.

I will give you an example. [Plato] explains that he and Dion exhorted Dionysius "to concern himself first of all with winning friends among his relatives and companions of his age who are in harmony with each other in striving towards virtue, and especially to make this harmony reign in himself, for he had great need of it. We did not speak [Dion

and Plato, to Dionysius; M.F.] so openly—it would have been dangerous—but did so in veiled terms, and we laid stress on the fact that this
was the means for any man to look after himself and those he governed,
and that to act otherwise would produce absolutely opposite results. If,
proceeding down the path we pointed out to him, becoming thoughtful
and prudent, he [Dionysius; M.F.] were to restore the devastated towns
of Sicily, bind them together with laws and constitutions which would
strengthen their mutual unity and agreement with him for defense
against the barbarians, he would not only double the size of his father's
kingdom, but would in truth multiply it."[1] You can see that this kind
of advice is a long way from what one day will be arts of government,
or even from the political reflections of someone who has had to practice politics and think about it. We are a long way from the *Mémorial de
Sainte-Hélène,*[2] from Richelieu's *Testament,*[3] and from Machiavelli. We are
even far from the discourse, reported by Dio Cassius, that Maecenas
was supposed to have delivered to Augustus.[4] And if we want to stick to
references closer in time to Plato's text, we can refer to the advice to the
Athenians that Thucydides put in Pericles' mouth some years before.
You recall the famous speech in which Pericles gives the Athenians his
views on the opportunity for waging war against Sparta, just after the
Spartan ambassadors had given the Athenians an ultimatum.[5] Should
we or should we not wage war? Well, Pericles gives both diplomatic
and strategic advice. And you know the kind of argument he makes,
its density, and the richness of his reflections on the relations between
the geography, resources, social structures, and type of government of
a country, on the one hand, and then, on the other, the political behavior one can expect from this country, the type of decision it may take,
its capacity to resist military offensives, and how, with what kind of
political will, if you like, a country like Sparta is likely to be able to
oppose Athens given these geographical, social, and economic facts. It
is clear that this is a far richer and more interesting type of political
analysis than the few, in inverted commas, "bland platitudes" I have
just read to you from Letter VII.

Only, is this the problem exactly? Should we say that Plato is, after
all, just a somewhat more moralizing and therefore naive counselor? As
a philosopher, does Plato give the politician advice that is less intelligent, informed, and structured than that of Pericles, or than the advice

Thucydides attributes to Pericles? Or does he actually give a different type of advice? Are Plato's opinions and the advice he gives to Dion, Dionysius, and Dion's friends simply of a lesser quality and more crudely worked out politically than the advice Pericles may have given, or is it a different kind of advice? In short, the question I would like to pose—and you see straightaway how I would like to resolve it—is this: when Plato gives advice, when the philosopher tests the reality of his discourse, is his role, function, and objective to say what should be done in the realm of political decision making, or is it to say something else? In other words, must philosophy's need to confront politics, must philosophy's need to seek its reality in the confrontation with politics consist in formulating a philosophical discourse which is at the same time a discourse that prescribes political action, or is something else involved? And if something else is involved, what is it? This is the question I would like to try to sort out a bit today. And to do this I would like to study three passages: two are from Letter VII, and a third is in Letter VIII. These three passages are no longer reflections on the need and opportunity to give political advice; they are political advice.

The first passage in Letter VII—you remember that the letter was written after the dramatic events which lead to Dion's exile and then death, and also to Plato's departure from Sicily—is the one in which Plato recalls the advice he gave to Dionysius when he was at Dionysius' court and the latter was pretending to be interested in philosophy. So we have a first passage in which he recalls this advice. Then there is a second passage, which I will study afterwards, in which, speaking in the present in which the letter is being written, he says: Given the present situation, given the failure of my first advice to Dionysius, Dion's exile and then his death, and now that only you remain, what advice can I give you? So this is advice to Dion's friends after Dion's death, and after the exile of Dionysius himself moreover, driven out sometime previously by Dion. Finally, I will add to this passage a [text] from Letter VIII.

Letter VIII is shorter than Letter VII, contains fewer philosophical reflections, and is more political if you like, responding more immediately to a dramatic situation which developed at Syracuse in the months following the context of Letter VII. That is to say, after the exile of

Dionysius, driven out by Dion, and then the death of Dion himself, assassinated at Syracuse, there is civil war and confrontation between the parties of Dionysius and Dion. This is the context in which Plato writes Letter VIII. In the letter he gives emergency advice, as it were, at the time of this civil war, to show how to get out of this situation. I will put this passage from Letter VIII together with the analysis of the two texts from Letter VII because of its interest, and because the advice is in direct continuity with these two other passages, and then, you will see, for another reason which concerns the status of *parrēsia* and so takes us back to the heart of our problem.

The first passage in Letter VII begins at 331d: "This is how I would advise you, therefore, just as, in agreement with Dion, I urged Dionysius, first of all, to live each day...."[6] So the advice he recalls having given Dionysius refers to a quite precise historical, factual context. At this time Dionysius is quite young. He has just inherited power in Syracuse from his father, Dionysius the Elder, a monarchical, tyrannical, autocratic power, which he now has to manage. And it is quite remarkable that here, you will see, Plato is very careful not to advise changing the structure of power and institutional organization of the city. He does not give advice concerning what *politeia* to adopt. Basically he does only what will be said in Letter V: listen to the *phōnē* of the existing *politeia* at Syracuse. Given that we are dealing with this autocratic power, what is the best way to manage it?

Second, this passage comes immediately after the considerations we talked about last week, in which Plato analyses the nature of the counselor's role. And he explains precisely just what a counselor's role as a doctor in the political realm must be. You recall that this role was characterized by three things. First, a good doctor is, of course, someone who acts when there is an illness and so his role is to restore health by treating diseases. He must know these diseases. So the doctor has to undertake a work of observation, of diagnosis, and he has to enter into a dialogue with his patient to try to identify the nature of the illness. Second, the good doctor is not like the slave doctor who runs after clients and is then content to hand out prescriptions and instructions. The good doctor persuades, that is to say, he speaks to his patient and convinces him that he is suffering from a disease and what the means are to cure it. Finally, third, the good doctor is not just someone who diagnoses by reflecting, someone who persuades by talking. He is also someone who through his persuasion succeeds in convincing his patient that it is not enough to take medication, but [that he must] completely change his way of life, his regimen, his diet. I think these are the three medical functions brought into play in the first pieces of advice Plato recalls giving Dionysius. I think we can find these three functions in these two pages from Plato. First, Plato tries to diagnose the disease from which Syracuse is suffering, at a time, however, when the crisis has not yet come into the open since Dionysius had exercised power, established strong authority at Syracuse, and organized in addition a sort of empire around Syracuse almost on the scale of the whole of Sicily, or anyway a part of Sicily, and his heir has just received this power. Apparently there is no crisis, and yet there is a disease. And in the advice found in the argument starting at 331d Plato will try to reveal this disease, this illness.

What then is the disease from which Syracuse is suffering despite its apparent good health? Plato says this: Dionysius the Elder, from whom Dionysius the Younger had just inherited power, established an empire. How did he do this? By reestablishing, by restoring the Sicilian towns destroyed during the wars against the barbarians (this is obviously the wars against the Carthaginians). He reestablished the towns that had been destroyed in the process of being won back from, freed from the Carthaginians. However—and this is where a first symptom of the disease comes in—the text says that Dionysius was not able to establish *politeiai pistai* in these towns (dependable, sound constitutions or regimes able to generate trust).[7] He says that these regimes have not been able to create trust either when Dionysius entrusted them to foreigners, or when he entrusted them to his brothers. Then, at this point, we realize what is meant by *politeiai pistai* (these dependable constitutions, regimes). Dependable, here, does not mean that they would be sound, stable regimes with citizens who trust their governors, or governors who trust those they govern. In reality it is a relationship of loyalty and trust between these towns—thus restored and, after restoration, maintained under the domination of Syracuse—and between them and the metropolis, Syracuse itself. Dionysius entrusted the management, the administration, the government of these towns either to foreigners or to his own brothers, whom he had made into rich and powerful individuals. But neither these strangers nor his brothers, neither the administration of the former nor that of the latter could establish a relationship of trust between Syracuse and these different *politeiai*. And Plato develops this idea, adding that, generally speaking, Dionysius was not able to establish what he calls *koinōnia arkhōn*.[8] *Koinōnia arkhōn* is the community of power, the sharing out of power, if you like, what we could call the distribution of power. He never managed to get his subordinates, those to whom he had entrusted this or that responsibility, or the populations over whom Syracuse had to exercise domination, to take part in power. He was unable to realize that community of power by either persuasion, or teaching, or benefits, or kinship. Finally, Plato's diagnosis is expressed in these terms: Dionysius had indeed held on to his power at Syracuse and the power of Syracuse over the other cities. He had held on to it, but only with difficulty. Why? Because, he says, he wanted to make Sicily *mia polis* (one and the same city). And he lacked friends and trustworthy people (*philoi* and *pistoi*).[9]

I think this very short description of the government of Dionysius and the disease from which Sicily suffers is interesting. It is interesting because you can see that in this diagnosis there is no question of criticizing a monarchical, autocratic, or tyrannical government. Or at any rate, if there is an implicit criticism of tyrannical, monarchical, or autocratic power, it is not of what it is in itself, in its structure or institutional system. [Plato condemns] two defects of Dionysius' government, namely: wanting to have made Sicily into a single city, that is to say, basically not having been able to establish an empire in a plural form, not having thought out properly, if you like, the dimensions and form of this new political unit which would be a sort of empire. The framework of the *polis*, which was the framework in which relations of power could develop, be established, institutionalized, and function properly, was unable to deal with what the powers are bound to be on the scale of something like Sicily, which for the time was a large political unit in comparison with the Greek city. The error was in wanting to apply the module of the Greek city to something relatively large and complex—absolutely large and complex for the Greeks and for the Greek city, namely: a set of cities on the scale of Sicily. And the second mistake, which is the other side of the first moreover and also its cause, is that he was unable to establish relations of friendship and trust. Relations of friendship and trust with other leaders, those governing the other cities—instead of wanting to apply the module of the single, unitary city—would have allowed each city to maintain its independence. And each city having retained its independence, there could have been relations of friendship and trust between the leaders of these subordinate, federated, colonized cities, and between them and the leader of Syracuse himself. The error of Dionysius, and this is what constitutes the disease, was enforced unification (in the form of *mia polis*, of the single, unitary city) and the absence of a bond and friendship permitting the just distribution of powers guaranteed and sealed by friendship and trust. This is Plato's diagnosis of Sicily's disease. You can see that this is, after all, rather interesting, because it touches on a set of political-historical problems which were highly significant at the end of the first half of the fourth century, that is to say, precisely just before the point at which the *polis*, the Greek city as a political unit, will break up under the impact of the meteoric development of the great kingdoms, and in particular of the Macedonian Kingdom and the empire of Alexander.

After this medical diagnosis, the second level of Plato's advice, the second function of the medical counselor, of the philosopher counselor, is to persuade. The good doctor diagnoses. Secondly, he persuades. In performing this persuasive function, to carry out this work of persuasion in the advice he recalls giving Dion, Plato gives some examples. According to the principles of rhetoric and the work of truth in a Greek discourse, the example serves to persuade. He gives two examples: Persia and Athens. First of all, the example of Persia. It is interesting that he gives this example, because for a long time, and throughout the fifth century in particular, Persia was for Greek thought the, as it were, repellent, negative example: the autocratic, violent regime, the large empire which subjugates others, etcetera. [Now] however, in the fourth century, Persia is becoming a positive example, at least for some of those who are opposed to the traditional democracy. Anyway, Plato gives the example of Persia at several points in his late texts. In the *Laws*, in Book III in particular, Plato refers to the Persian regime, and precisely to the way in which Cyrus governs. You recall—I quoted this passage—Plato explains how Cyrus came to give room for *parrēsia* in his entourage, in his court, when he allowed the wisest members of his entourage to give him the frank advice he might need.[10] The positive example of Persia is also found in the dialogue I have talked about, the *Alcibiades*, which, once again, we do not know whether it is a late or early dialogue. In the *Alcibiades* there is a positive reference to the way in which the Persian sovereigns, princes are brought up, and according to some commentators this reference would indicate that it is a late dialogue.[11] No matter, the theme of Persia is present anyway in Plato's texts, in the later texts at least. You know that it is also crucial in Xenophon's work, since Xenophon wrote a *Cyropaedia*,[12] and I will return to elements of this shortly. Why is the Persian example interesting? Well, precisely because Plato sees in Persia the example of an imperial system which works, and which works positively. In fact, he explains in this text, the Persians have established an empire on the basis of a number of successful wars and conquests, over the Medians in particular. But Persia always did this, and Cyrus always did this, Plato says, with the help of allies who remained friends throughout. That is to say, Plato refers here to a Persian system, or anyway to a system he attributes to them, in which conquest does not simply take the form of a uniform subjugation of everyone to a single Persian authority, but through a system of federation and alliance which manages to establish a complex system of relations between subordinates, federates, allies, and so on. Second, still with regard to the Persians, Plato says that, having achieved their conquest, Cyrus took care to divide his kingdom into seven parts in which he found dependable collaborators (it seems that Plato was mistaken historically regarding this seven, or at any rate that he refers to a division which is not attested to elsewhere, but it's not important). Anyway, Plato refers here to the possibility of an imperial type of government which rests on the cooperation and collaboration of a number of governors who transmit authority locally and on the spot.

After the Persian example, and still concerning the work of persuasion that a good doctor must accomplish, Plato gives the Athenian example. And it is very interesting to see that, in this work of persuasion, Plato gives the example of Persia first, and then that of Athens. That is to say, he refers to two completely different political regimes— one an autocratic monarchy, the other a democracy—clearly showing by this that in this type of advice the problem is not so much one of choosing between democracy and autocracy as of knowing how both of them can be got to work properly. Now, he says, the example of Athens points in exactly the same direction as that of Persia. In fact the Athenians, he says, have not sought at all to create what we would now call colonial settlements. That is to say, they did not seek to establish towns which would in some way be parts of the city, of Athens itself, but not on Athenian territory. They took already populated towns which were under barbarian domination, and he refers to the Ionian federation that the Athenians wished to and actually did construct in the second half of the fifth century, they left the existing population in place, and they left power in the hands of those who were or should have been exercising it naturally (those who in our terms we would call, if you like, the "local elites"). In this way, Plato says, the Athenians were able to find and keep *andras philous* (friends and trustworthy men) on whom they based their authority in all the towns they freed from the barbarian yoke and integrated into their empire.[13]

These are the elements with which Plato, after diagnosing the disease from which Syracuse vaguely suffered under the reign of Dionysius, tries to persuade Dionysius the Younger that he should change his way of governing. And then, at this point in Plato's text, there is the positive advice given directly to Dionysius—which would correspond, if you like, to the function of giving a regimen in medical work, in the medical role. What regimen does Plato propose for Dionysius? Well, he says, instead of making Sicily a single city, he should, first of all, give each city in Sicily its own *politeia* (its own constitution, institutions, political regime) and *nomoi* (laws). Second, he should bind the cities together with Syracuse and with the person who reigns in Syracuse, and he should do this also through *nomoi* and *politeiai*. That is to say there should be both local laws and regimes. Also, between each of these different cities and the city around which they are federated, the city which serves as their metropolis, between each of the cities organized in this way, and between them and Syracuse, there should be a set of relationships ordered by something like a *politeia* existing between the different *poleis*, the different cities, a sort of political network or institution over and above each city, thus linking them together and attaching them to the metropolis. And finally, he says, this kind of

plural and differentiated unit, with institutions for each city and institutions which regulate the relations between them, will be even stronger, since one will call on it to struggle against a common enemy, that is
to say, the barbarians, and in the event the Carthaginians. And unity,
with its elements of plurality, will be preserved through this frontal
struggle with the barbarians. And in this way, he says, Dionysius the
Younger will be able not only to double, but even multiply the size of
Dionysius the Elder's empire.

But Plato adds further advice to that concerning the organization
of the cities, of the relations between them, and of their relation to
Syracuse. And this advice concerns Dionysius himself as an individual,
and as an individual who has to rule and exercise power. Dionysius, he
says, must work on himself. And he uses the expression *apergazein* (that
is to say: develop, work on, improve). What must he improve, develop,
and work on? Himself, so as to make himself *emphrōn* and *sumphōnos*
(that is to say: thoughtful and wise, moderate).[14] He must ensure that
he is in harmony, in symphony, in *sumphōnos* with himself,[15] just as the
cities he has to govern must be in symphony with Syracuse and with
each other. You see that in this theme of *sumphōnous*, of *sumphōnia*, we
find again the idea in Letter V that each constitution has its *phōnē*, its
voice.[16] And, once again, the problem of good government is not that of
changing a constitution into a supposedly better one in an authoritarian manner according to a formula given in advance. Good government
involves understanding the nature of the *phōnē*, the voice of each *politeia*,
and then governing in harmony with this *phōnē*. Now you see that here,
the idea of *sumphōnia* is developed in the sense of *phōnē* being understood as a voice that each city should have. In the great federation that
[Dionysius] organizes around Syracuse, each city should have its own
voice, but all these voices should work together to form a harmony and
symphony. But, as the guarantor of this symphony of the different cities, the leader must also be *sumphōnos* with himself, that is to say in harmony with himself. And this harmony with himself is formulated from
the start of Plato's advice, when he recalls that he urged Dionysius first
of all to live each day in such a way as to become increasingly master of
himself (*egkratēs autos hautou*).[17] This expression—*egkratēs autos hautou*—is
interesting, because the most general sense of *egkratēs* is precisely to be
in control, to be in control of oneself. Commonly, *egkratēs* designates

self-control, the control of one's desires and appetites, and more especially temperance with regard to food, wine, and sexual pleasure.[18]
Now the strengthening of the expression here—*egkratēs autos hautou*—
indicates that it must be given a more general sense, although the particular sense is still present. The leader, the person who commands, the
sovereign really must be master of himself, in the sense that he must
be temperate, able to keep his desires within appropriate limits, to
moderate them, thus avoiding the discord which prevents symphony.
But this temperance is explained as a relation of power of the individual over himself. *Egkratēs autos hautou*: control of himself with regard to
himself, if you like. This reduplication with regard to the usual sense
of *egkratēs* shows that what is designated here is not the quality or virtue of temperance as this is generally defined, but a certain relation of
power of himself to himself. And this is what will seal, as it were, the
good government that Dionysius should be able to maintain at Syracuse
and over her allies. This is what can be found in the first set, the first
wave of advice that Plato gives in Letter VII.

The second set of advice is, if you like, current advice—Plato simply
recalls the advice I have just been talking about, he recalls the advice
he gave when, as the young tyrant of Syracuse, Dionysius gave signs, as
it turned out false signs, that he wished to practice philosophy. Now,
a bit further on in the letter, Plato says: In the present situation, after
all the misfortunes which have taken place—Dion's exile, civil war, the
confrontation between the rival supporters of Dion and Dionysius, the
exile of Dionysius, Dion's return, and then his death—what advice can
I give you friends of Dion, now that he is dead? This passage begins
with the following instruction, which we should note: Be under no
illusion, the advice I am now going to give you in this new situation is
exactly the same (*hē autē sumboulē*), and I am going to give it to you most
solemnly, as if it were a third libation.[19] Plato here is actually alluding
to two things. First, he is alluding to the fact that at Syracuse he thinks
he has given advice to Dion, [then] to Dionysius (those we have just
been talking about), and is now going to give advice a third time to
Dion's friends. Second, he is alluding to the ritual which requires the
third libation at a banquet to be the most solemn. It is the most solemn
because it is the libation addressed to Zeus, or more exactly to Zeus
the savior, to Zeus insofar as he saves. So, this advice, repeated as in a

third libation, is intended to save Syracuse. It is the same advice, and yet we may note that between the advice given to Dion's friends and the advice he recalls having given Dionysius there is something like a different emphasis. There is a different emphasis first of all because little is said about, let's say, the imperial system and the problem of the relationship between Syracuse and the other cities. He contents himself with saying merely that each city should have its laws. On the other hand, since the situation at the time he is speaking is one of imminent civil war at Syracuse, with the two sides confronting each other (Dionysius, in exile but trying to return; Dion's friends, deprived of Dion but in the city), the most important element, the most important stake in the advice to be given is obviously the problem of the *politeia* of the city itself, the *politeia* of Syracuse.

And it is here that Plato outlines some measures to be taken which do in fact concern the institutions and organization of the city. He says that one should find some wise men, men whose wisdom will be recognized through some clear and obvious signs. To recognize the wise men a city needs, they must of course have "wives and children." Second, they must come "from good stock," from a good family. And finally they must possess "sufficient" wealth.[20] Roughly, he says, out of a thousand people you should find about fifty persons of this kind. These wise men will be asked to propose the laws. You see that Plato does not put himself forward as a lawgiver. The advice he gives does not amount to saying: Here are the laws that the city ought to observe. He confines himself to saying to the inhabitants of the city: You ought to entrust the task of lawgiver to these people, to these wise men who have wives and children, are of good descent, and who possess sufficient wealth. Second, he says, when your conflicts have calmed down and the two groups currently confronting each other (the supporters of the exiled Dionysius and the supporters of the assassinated Dion) are reconciled, there should be no differences between the victors and the vanquished. The victors must not lay down the law to the vanquished; you should establish *koinois nomos* (a common law).[21] Even better, he says, you should go further than this. Not only should the law be common, but the victors, those who consequently have most influence in the city, should show that they are even more obedient to the laws than the vanquished themselves. And this leads us to the most important

part of this passage, which is the problem of the moral training of individuals. How will the victors be able to demonstrate that they are more
obedient to the laws than those they have defeated?

Two things are needed: a theoretical training and a moral training. The theoretical training first of all. The text is interesting because
you remember, I referred to this last week, how much Plato was irritated by the theoretical and speculative pretensions of Dionysius who
wanted to show how well versed he was in philosophy by writing texts
which demonstrated both that, since he wrote, he did not understand
the very meaning of philosophy, and that the philosophical knowledge
he displayed was no more than the copy of what Plato himself had said.
So [Plato] showed that he was extremely mistrustful of what could be
called the theoretical knowledge of the man who has to exercise political power. Now what type of theoretical training does Plato demand
Dion's supporters introduce so that, if they are the victors, they will
be able to show that they submit to the laws more than the defeated
do? Well, the theoretical teaching he gives is very simple. It is nothing other than a sort of variation on a theme that we found in the
Gorgias and other texts by Plato, namely: it is always better to be just,
even when one is unfortunate, than unjust, even when one is fortunate. And he takes for his example precisely Dion and Dionysius. Of
course, Dionysius is not exactly fortunate, since he has been exiled
by the revolt against him, but he is living after all. Dion, on the other
hand, may be considered unfortunate since, although having driven out
Dionysius, he ended up assassinated in Syracuse. However, between
the dead but just Dion, and the living but unjust Dionysius, we should
prefer Dion's fate, we should prefer his way of life. Injustice is always
to be shunned, even if it is happy. Justice is always to be preferred,
even if it is unhappy. On what does Plato base this banal theme in
Letter VII, a theme which, once again, runs through so many of his
dialogues? He bases it on theoretical considerations in fact. What are
these theoretical considerations? First of all, he says, is the fact that, as
we know, the soul and the body are two distinct things, that the body
is mortal and the soul is immortal; and after [the] death [of the body]
this immortal soul will be judged according to its actions during life,
and if it has committed injustices in its life it will suffer terrible pun-
ishments and long peregrinations underground. This, to say the least,

simple theoretical teaching is what Plato proposes should serve Dion's friends as the basis of their political attitude and their extreme diligence with regard to obedience to the laws. We should note that in this text Plato does not in any way present this teaching as a philosophical doctrine, which would be his own philosophical doctrine and form the very heart, as it were, of his teaching. In the text in question he says that if political men, the victors are to conduct themselves properly, if they are to be more obedient to the laws than the vanquished, then they must know this doctrine: "We must truly believe in the ancient and holy traditions which reveal immortality to us."[22] The text calls these ancient and holy traditions "*tois palaiois te kai hierois logois*" (these discourses which are both ancient and sacred). That is to say, what is represented here is not at all the philosophical thought of Plato himself. What gives them their authority, and the reasons why those who have to command others must submit to them, is the fact that they are ancient, already known discourses. They get their authority from their age and at the same time from the sacred, religious components which mark them. It is these non-philosophical discourses, these discourses of religious beliefs and sacred traditions that must form the theoretical basis to which the politician refers. As for his practical training, it is barely sketched by Plato in this text. He confines himself to saying that politicians should live how the ancestors lived, in the Dorian manner. So this passage, like the preceding one, is not very rich in either its political or its specifically philosophical elaboration. But I think the most general and doubtless most interesting theme of this advice is the way in which Plato shows through this advice how the moral training of those who govern is indispensable for good government of the city.

There is a passage worth noting in which he says that one will be able to govern properly precisely when one knows these ancient and holy traditions and how to respect them, when one has really applied and put to work this Dorian way of life, this indispensable way of life in the manner of the ancestors. Governing properly will mean that one is able to govern by utilizing two resources.[23] First *phobos* (fear). Those who govern must make fear reign over those who are governed, and they will do this by demonstrating their strength (*bia*, the text says).[24] This material strength must be effectively present and visible, and this fear will ensure good government. But at the same time, and this will be the second means of governing, the governors must show *aidōs* (that is to say, a sense of decency and respect). This *aidōs* is not directly the respect that the governed owe to those who govern them, but this *aidōs* (respect) must be, as it were, an internal relationship of the governors to themselves, their respect for their obligations, for the city, and for the laws of the city. *Aidōs* will mean that one is able to submit to the laws like a slave (he uses the term *douleuein*).[25] Being a slave of the law, wanting to constitute oneself as a slave of the law will characterize the *aidōs* (respect) of the governors with regard to themselves, the city, and its laws. And this respect will then bring about the respect that others—the governed—may have for them. So "*aidōs*" should be understood as a virtue which characterizes the relationship of the governed to the governors, but which also and especially characterizes the attitude of the governors towards themselves.

Finally, the third text I would like to talk about is in Letter VIII, which was therefore written a little after Letter VII and the threatening civil war has broken out in Syracuse. The text is interesting for two reasons. The first, of course, is that Plato advances, so to speak, into that region or domain with regard to which he had previously shown great reserve and discretion, that is to say, the actual organization of the city. And secondly, the text is interesting because his advice is introduced and underpinned by a general reflection on *parrēsia*, and so here we come back again to our problem. Very quickly, what advice will Plato give the Syracusans now that they are tearing themselves apart in civil war? First, there is reference to a familiar theme in Plato. It is a theme developed in *Gorgias*, from 477b,[26] where, as you know, Plato says that it is necessary to distinguish between things that concern the soul, things that concern the body, and things that concern wealth. Matters of the soul are obviously the concern of the governors; those of the body are the concern of the warriors; and those to do with wealth obviously concern the activity of merchants and artisans. And he says that the *politeia*, the organization of a city, must respect this hierarchy and not give more importance to wealth than to the body and the soul. On this general theme, then, Plato proposes an organization, a *politeia* in the strict sense, and once again let us not forget that it is [because of] the civil war that he proposes a *politeia* (a [constitution]) in his intervention. That is to say, the actual organization of the State has broken down, so he proposes an organizational system for the city. This can be represented schematically in the following way. First of all, a monarchy, but in the Spartan manner, that is to say, one in which in actual fact the monarchs have no real power. Their power is to be above all religious, and the text proposes that, for a number of reasons, there will be three of these monarchs, rather than two as in Sparta. He wants, and says that he wants, to integrate the descendants of Dionysius the Younger, another descendant of Dionysius the Elder, and Dion's son. Because of this there will be three kings, but their function will basically be religious. Apart from these three kings, a system will have to be organized to ensure both the existence and maintenance of the laws. Hence he proposes the organization, the institution of a body of what he calls the guardians of the laws. He proposes thirty five guardians,[27] which will be the formula we find again in the *Laws*, apart from the fact that in the *Laws* it is not thirty five but thirty seven[28]—according to the commentators, this little detail proves the authenticity of the letter and enables us to date it; it proves its authenticity because if it was an apocryphal letter written after Plato's death and making use of material from the *Laws*, it is clear that the apocryphal author would have copied the real figure of thirty seven and not have given thirty five; consequently it is reasonable to think that in this letter Plato sketched out what will be developed in the *Laws*, with some modifications and in particular the change from thirty five to thirty seven guardians of the laws— and a series of courts, in which again we find in a few lines what is developed at length in the *Laws*. So, in this advice, we have for the first time what we could call nomothetical advice, but which once again we should remember is called for not so much by the philosopher's general function with regard to the city as by the actual situation of the city. When civil war has broken out and is raging it is natural that the philosopher's role be not, of course, to advise the reigning prince, or to help him establish an empire, but well and truly to reconstruct the city itself.

What I want to emphasize is that the advice in Letter VIII is introduced by a passage, which is purely and simply a transitional passage if you like, but which does indicate that Plato regards this advice as part of his office as a parrhesiast. It really is an exercise of *parrēsia* to which he is committed. The passage is found in Letter VIII at 354a where he says the following: "I will now try to give you my own view quite frankly (*egō peirasomai pasē parrēsia*) with just and impartial reasoning. I am speaking, as it were, as an arbitrator addressing two parties [...], and to each as if he were alone [in particular; M.F.] I give my old advice (*sumboulēn*)."[29] So we are in the realm of political *sumboulē* which is at the same time a manifestation and practice of *parrēsia*. Now if we take this passage and follow some of the elements in the advice I have just summarized, I think we see that actually *parrēsia* is indeed involved here and that Plato really is engaging in a parrhesiastic activity. What are the characteristics of this discourse of advice and what makes it a case of *parrēsia*?

First, from the first lines that I have just read to you, but also throughout the text, Plato of course emphasizes the fact that he is speaking personally in his own name. It is his opinion, what he thinks, what he believes, what he says himself. And there are a whole series of expressions which actually refer to this absolutely personal character of the enunciation. This is not the voice of the city or of the laws, the voice for example that spoke to Socrates and persuaded him that he had to accept his trial and condemnation.[30] No, it is Plato himself giving his views: "*ho de moi phainetai*" (what I myself think); I will try for my part to convince you, I am telling you what is *emē sumboulē* (my advice)[31]...At 354c you find: "This then is what my present discourse recommends to everyone."[32] It really is his discourse. Now, at a given moment, this personal character of the discourse appears to break down, or get distorted by the fact that, after speaking in his own name in this way, Plato says: It would be simpler if I were to make Dion speak rather than myself, or rather if I were to tell you what Dion, who was assassinated and has been dead for some time now, would have told you. And I am quoting what Dion would have told you, I am reconstructing what Dion would tell you in the present circumstances, because basically we share the same view. And it is here, I think, that we can see that the contribution of this dead character, Dion, following a rhetorical procedure absolutely familiar to Greek eloquence (bringing in someone who is dead to validate what one is saying), is not Plato's way of releasing himself from his office as parrhesiast, since he emphasizes that what Dion says is what he himself thinks and that they share the same opinion (*koinos*: it is a *koinos logos* to Plato and Dion[33]—he recalls moreover that Dion was trained by him; it is therefore his own, Plato's opinion). Apart from the rhetorical convention permitting one to introduce a dead person into one's speech in order to lend it greater authority, if Plato brings in Dion we should not forget that Dion is precisely someone who paid with his life for the truth-telling that he employed against Dionysius and tried to promote in Syracuse. Plato brings Dion in on his side as a parrhesiast who was prepared to risk his life and who ultimately paid with his life for his truth-telling.

Second, we should note that in the *parrēsia* deployed by Plato there is a sort of tension between the entirely particular, conjunctural character of the advice he gives [and its reference to general principles]. Throughout the text Plato constantly recalls that he is giving advice in terms of the current situation, that it is what appears to him now (he uses the expression *ta nun*: at the moment),[34] and that it is also advice that he relates to the struggle, to the civil war taking place, and he recalls certain conjunctures in the history of Sicily. But this *parrēsia*, which is thus a discourse of circumstance and conjuncture, is a discourse which refers at the same time to general and constant principles. He recalls that this has always been his view. His *sumboulē* has remained the same and he uses some principles or general rules. He recalls, for example, that excessive servitude and freedom are great evils. He employs the following kind of formulae: slavery (*douleia*), submission to God, corresponds to the happy medium, but *douleia* to man is always excessive.[35] So, if you like, you have a discourse of *parrēsia* which stretches between reference to general principles and reference to particular circumstances.

Third, this *parrēsia* is a discourse addressed to everyone, to both parties in the Syracusan confrontation. It is, he says, a *logos koinos*. "This is what my discourse recommends to everyone" he says at 354c. At 355a he says: I pray that Dion's friends communicate my advice to all Syracusans. And right at the end of the text, at 357b, he says: That is what I advise everyone (*pasin sumbouleuō*) to decide and carry out in common (*koinē*); I call on everyone (*parakalō pantas*) to carry out these actions. But while appealing to everyone, while addressing everyone, the discourse of *parrēsia* is also addressed to each, and to each of the two parties. This is what he says right at the start of the text in the passage I have quoted: I am speaking to everyone and at the same time to each as if he were alone.[36] That is to say, it is not just this general discourse which is addressed to the city in order to impose prescriptions and laws; it is actually a discourse of persuasion which is addressed to each in order to elicit a certain kind of behavior, a certain conduct, a certain way of doing things.

The fourth characteristic of this *parrēsia* is that Plato says that when he speaks in this way and addresses the two contending parties in Sicily, he does so as *diaitētēs*. *Diaitētēs* is a legal term which designates, and which designated in Athenian law, the arbitrator to whom one resorted to settle a dispute out of court. The *diaitētēs* is therefore the arbitrator one can consult outside of court proceedings. An indication of the nature and functions of the *diaitētēs* can be found in Aristotle's *Politics*, Book Two, chapter 8, from 1268b.[37] So being a *diaitētēs* is an extra-judicial function but with a defined place in Athenian institutions. We should not forget that the *diaitētēs*, as the etymology shows, is the person who gives the diet, the regimen. And the two senses of the word *diaitētēs* are attested to in classical Greek. *Diaita* is arbitration, and it is also medical regimen. The *diaitē tēs* is an arbitrator, but he is equally someone who gives a regimen to those who need it. And the communication between the two senses (arbitration and diet)—moreover, the word's etymology is connected to the same root as *zēn*: to live—is evident, inasmuch as the diet is precisely the set of rules by which one can arbitrate between opposing qualities, between hot and cold, dry and humid, and between the different humors which make up the body. It is this arbitration that constitutes the diet, the medical regimen. Consequently, when Plato, as parrhesiast, says that he is *diaitētēs*, he is at once the arbitrator between the different parties and someone who gives the regime (the medical regimen of the city) and will thus make possible arbitration between these different forces.

Finally, the fourth characteristic of this *parrēsia* is that it has to confront reality. At several points Plato not only accepts, but takes up and demands this challenge of confrontation with reality. He accepts and even demands that reality demonstrate whether his discourse and advice are true or false. If you put my present assertions to the test, you will really experience the effect of the truth of my advice to you. *Ergō gnōsesthe*: you will know it in reality. For, he says, this is the best touchstone (*basanos*) for everything.[38] Reality, the test of reality, must constitute the touchstone of his discourse. And the very end of his advice to the Syracusans is this. Right at the end of the letter (357c) he says: "Offer homage to the gods with your prayers as well as to all those who it is right to praise along with the gods; invite [in actual fact the verb used is *peithomai*, persuade; M.F.], urge friends and enemies in a friendly way and insistently until all our words [the words which have just been spoken, the advice Plato has just given [...]; M.F.], like a divine dream coming to you while you are awake, are clearly and happily realized through you."[39] The philosopher therefore, is opportune in his enterprise of *parrēsia*, saying what he says somewhat like a divine dream coming to men, but to men who are awake. The divine dream, telling men what will happen and what they must do is for sleeping men what the philosopher's discourse will be for men awake. The philosopher is indeed a god who comes to men, but he speaks to them when they are awake. But the truth of this divine dream will hold up, the dream will have passed its test of truth only on one condition: When you have worked out in reality (the text says *exergasēsthe*), when you have worked until these things are really accomplished and they at that point clearly meet with good fortune (are *eutukhē*).[40] The good fortune, that which will constitute the real happiness of the Syracusans, will be precisely their working out in reality of this divine dream that the philosopher communicated to them while they were awake.

Plato therefore recognizes and lays claim to *parrēsia* as the activity that underpins his activity as counselor. As a counselor he is that *parrēsia*, that is to say he employs *parrēsia* with all the characteristics we have recognized: he commits himself, it is his own discourse, it is his own opinion, it takes account both of general principles and a particular conjuncture; it is addressed to people as a general principle, but it persuades them individually. All of this gives a discourse whose truth must hold to and be proven by the fact that it will become reality. Philosophical discourse will get from political reality the guarantee that it is not just *logos*, not just words given in a dream, but that it really has to do with the *ergon*, with what constitutes reality. We have here a set of elements which match up with what I tried to tell you concerning the parrhesiast's function. So now, if you like, in the second part of the lecture I will try to take up these elements. I am sorry, once again, this Platonic advice has a rather banal appearance which makes its analysis somewhat tedious, but I think that by re-reading them at a certain level it is possible to see some problems or themes appear which are very important for the destiny of the relations between philosophy and politics in Western thought. I will try to explain this to you shortly.

1. Plato, Letter VII, 332d-e, French pp. 38-39; English p. 1581: "After that, in the second place, he must win to friendship with himself and to moral harmony others from among his kinsmen and companions, but especially must he become such a one himself, for in this quality he had shown himself remarkably deficient. We did not put it so plainly—that was not safe—but we veiled our meaning and constantly argued that anyone who takes this course will be prosperous himself and will cause the people whom he rules to prosper, and that on the other hand any other course will have just the opposite result. When he had progressed in the way we mapped out, and had developed in himself an intelligent and constant character, he might recolonize the deserted cities of Sicily and so unite them by laws and institutions that they would be a resource to him and to each other for meeting the attacks of the barbarians. Thus he would not merely double the size of the empire he had inherited, but would really multiply it many times."

2. E. de Las Cases, *Le Mémorial de Sainte-Hélène* (Paris: Le Seuil, [1842] 1999).

3. Richelieu, *Testament politique* (1667) ed., F. Hildesheimer (Paris: Champion/Société de l'Histoire de France, 1995); English translation (selections) by Henry Bertram Hill, *The Political Testament of Cardinal Richelieu* (Madison: University of Wisconsin Press, 1965).

4. Dion Cassius, *Histoire romaine*, Book LII, ch. 14-40, trans. E. Gros (Paris: Librairie Firmin & Didot Frères, 1845); English translation by Earnest Cary, *Dio's Roman History*, vol. 6 (London: William Heinemann, and Cambridge, Mass.: Harvard University Press, 1960 [1917]).

5. Thucydides, *History of the Peloponnesian War*, Book One, ch. 139-146, pp. 118-143.

6. Letter VII, 331d, French p. 37; English p. 1580: "In this same fashion I will advise you, just as Dion and I used to advise Dionysius. We advised him, in the first place, to lead the sort of life day by day...."

7. Ibid., 331e-332a, French: "After having rebuilt them, he could not constitute sound governments in the hands of friends chosen by him (*oukh hoios t'ēn katoikisas politeias en hekastais katastēsasthai pistas hetairōn andrōn*)"; English: "he...was unable to resettle them and set up in each a trustworthy government composed of his friends."

8. Ibid., 332a, French p. 38: "None of them, despite his efforts, could he form as a partner of his power (*toutōn koinōnon tēs arkhēs oudena hoios t'ēn*"; English p. 1581: "None of them was he able to develop by the influence of his eloquence or instruction or benefactions or kinship, so that he could trust him as a partner in the government."

9. Ibid., 332c, French: "But Dionysius, who had brought together Sicily into a single city (*eis mian polin*), in his wisdom trusting no one, held on with difficulty, for he was short of friends and loyal people (*andrōn philōn kai pistōn*)"; English: "Dionysius, however, who brought together Sicily into one city because in his wisdom he trusted no one, all but met with disaster. He was in want of tried and trusted friends...."

10. Plato, *Laws*, Book III, 694a-b. See the analysis of this passage in the lecture of 9 February, first hour, above pp. 201-204.

11. See the analysis of the positive reference to Persian education so as to highlight the deficiencies of Alcibiades in *L'Herméneutique du sujet*, pp. 35-36; *The Hermeneutics of the Subject*, p. 34.

12. Xénophon, *Cyropédie*, trans. M. Bizos (Paris: Belles Lettres, 1972); English translation be Walter Miller, in two volumes: *Cyropaedia*, Books I-IV, in *Xenophon V* (Cambridge, Mass.: Harvard University Press, "Loeb Classical Library," 1914) and *Cyropaedia*, Books V-VIII in *Xenophon VI* (Cambridge, Mass.: Harvard University Press, "Loeb Classical Library," 1914).

13. Plato, *Letter VII*, 332b-c, French p. 38: "Look again at the Athenians. They themselves did not colonize the many Greek towns invaded by the barbarians, but took them already inhabited. Nevertheless, they held power for seventy years, because in every town they had supporters (Fr., *partisans*; Gk., *andras philous*)"; English p. 1581: "Take again the Athenians, who though they were not themselves the founders, took over many Greek cities that had been invaded by the barbarians but were still inhabited. Nevertheless they maintained their empire for seventy years, because they possessed in the various cities men who were their friends."

14. Ibid., 332e, French p. 39: "If, proceeding down the path we pointed out to him, becoming thoughtful and prudent (*heauton emphrona te kai sōphrona apergasamenos*)"; English

p. 1581: "When he had progressed in the way we mapped out, and had developed in himself an intelligent and constant character."

15. Ibid., 332d, French: "We exhorted him to concern himself first of all with gaining, from among his relatives and companions of his age, other friends who are in harmony with each other (*sumphōnous*) in striving towards virtue, and especially to make this harmony reign in himself (*auton hautō*)"; English: "he must win to friendship with himself and to moral harmony others from among his kinsmen and companions, but especially must he become such a one himself."

16. Letter V, 321d-e, French p. 23: "Each government has its tongue, as if they were living beings (*estin gar dē tis phōnē tōn politeiōn hekastēs kathaperei tinōn zōōn*). One is that of democracy, another that of oligarchy, and another that of monarchy [...]. Every State which speaks its own language towards the gods and men and acts in conformity with this language, always prospers and preserves itself, but if it imitates another it perishes"; English, p. 1605: "Each form of government has a sort of voice as if it were a kind of animal. There is one of democracy, another of oligarchy, and a third of monarchy...Any form of government that utters its own voice to god and man and duly acts in harmony with its voice, is always flourishing and endures. When it copies another it perishes."

17. Letter VII, 331d, French p. 37: "It is in this way therefore that I could advise you, just as, with Dion, I urged Dionysius, first of all, to live each day in such a way as to make himself increasingly master of himself (*egkratēs hautou autos*)"; English p. 1580: "In this same fashion I will advise you, just as Dion and I used to advise Dionysius. We advised him, in the first place, to lead the sort of life day by day that would be most conducive to self-control."

18. See M. Foucault, *Histoire de la sxualité*, t. II, *L'Usage des plaisirs* (Paris: Gallimard, 1984), ch. "Enkrateia," pp. 74-90; English translation by Robert Hurley, *The History of Sexuality, Volume Two: The Use of Pleasure* (New York: Pantheon, 1985) Part One, ch. 3, "*Enkrateia*," pp. 63-77.

19. Plato, Letter VI, 334c, French p. 41: "I repeat moreover for the third time the same advice (*tēn autēn sumboulēn*) for you"; English p. 1583: "I give the same counsel and the same discourse now the third time to you my third audience."

20. Ibid., 337b-c, French p. 45; English p. 1585: "who possess wives and children...can reckon the most and the best and the most famous ancestors, and who own...sufficient property."

21. Ibid., 336a-337a, French p. 44; English pp. 1584-1585.

22. Ibid., 335a, French pp. 41-42; English p. 1583: "We must at all times give our unfeigned assent to the ancient and holy doctrines which warn us that our souls are immortal."

23. Ibid., 337a, French p. 44: "They must exercise sufficient self-control, rather, in order to establish common laws as favorable to the defeated as to themselves and to demand their observation by two means of constraint: respect and fear"; English: "Rather, exercising self-control and drawing up equitable laws, that are designed to favor them no more than the defeated party, they must make their opponents observe the laws by bringing to bear two motives, shame and fear."

24. Ibid., French: "They will succeed in producing fear by displaying the superiority of their material strength (*to kreittous autōn einai deiknuntes tēn bian*)"; English: "They will inspire fear because they show that they have the stronger forces."

25. Ibid., 337a-b, French p. 44: "Respect, by showing that they are men who, knowing how to control their desires, prefer to and are able to serve the laws (*mallon ethelontes te kai dunamenoi douleuein*)"; English p. 1585: "shame because they are evidently stronger in resisting their inclinations and in their willingness and ability to be subject to the laws."

26. Platon, *Gorgias*, 477b-c, trans. L. Bodin (Paris: Les Belles Lettres, 1968) p. 153: "Thus, for these three things, wealth, the body, and the soul, you recognize three sorts of imperfection, poverty, disease, and injustice"; Plato, *Gorgias*, trans. W.D. Woodhead in Edith Hamilton and Huntington Cairns, eds., *The Collected Dialogues of Plato*, p. 260: "Then for these three, material fortune, body, and soul, you have named three evils, poverty, disease, and injustice?"

27. Letter VIII, 356d, French p. 73; English p. 1602.

28. Plato, *Laws*, Book VI, 754d, French p. 113; English p. 1335.

29. Letter VIII, 354a, French p. 69; English pp. 1599-1600: "My own view at the moment I will try to make clear with all frankness on a basis of impartial justice. In fact I do speak as

a sort of arbitrator between two parties […], while with respect to each singly I am giving my old advice."

30. This is the well known "Prosopopeia of the Laws" found in the *Crito* at 50d-54d.

31. Letter VIII, 355a, French p. 71; English p. 1600.

32. Ibid., 354c, French p. 70; English p. 1600: "It is my advice to everyone to take this same course now."

33. Ibid., 355a, French pp. 70-71: "Since this is how things are, I pray that Dion's friends communicate my advice to all Syracusans as being our common view (*koinēn sumboulēn*)"; English p. 1600: "Since the law of nature in regard to these things is as I have stated it, I exhort the friends of Dion to publish my words of advice to all the Syracusans as the joint counsel of Dion and myself."

34. Ibid., 354a, French p. 69: "My own view now (*ho de moi phainetai pē ta nun*)"; English pp. 1599-1600: "My own view at the moment."

35. Ibid., 354e, French p. 70: "Submission (*douleia*) to God is according to measure (*selon la mesure*); it goes too far if addressed to man"; English p. 1600: "The due measure of servitude is to serve God. The extreme of servitude is to serve man."

36. Ibid., 354a, French p. 69: "I am speaking, so to speak, as an arbitrator (*legō gar dē diaitētou*) addressing the two parties, the one who exercised tyranny and the one who suffered it, and to each as if he were alone I give my advice"; English p. 1600: "In fact I do speak as a sort of arbitrator between two parties, that of the former tyrant and that of his subjects, while with respect to each singly I am giving my old advice."

37. Aristotle, *Politics*, trans. B. Jowett (revised by Jonathan Barnes) in *The Complete Works of Aristotle, The Revised Oxford Translation*, Volume Two, ed. Jonathan Barnes (Princeton: Princeton University Press, 1984) p. 2013: "Neither is the law to be commended which says that the judges, when a simple issue is laid before them, should make a distinction in their judgment; for the judge is thus converted into an arbitrator (*diaitētēn*). Now, in an arbitration, although the arbitrators are many, they confer with one another about the decision, and, indeed, most legislators take pains to prevent the judges from holding any communication with one another."

38. Letter VIII, 355c, French p. 71: "What I advise you is the truth and if you put my present assertions about laws to the test, you will experience their effect (*ergō gnōsesthe*), for experience is the best touchstone (*basanos*) in everything"; English p. 1601: "That these words of exhortation from me are true you will know by experience if you put to the test what I have just said about laws. Experience seems to be the surest touchstone for everything."

39. Ibid., 357c-d, French p. 74; English pp. 1602-1603: "Now give honor with prayer to all the gods, and to all the others whose due it is along with the gods, and do not desist from urging and calling upon friends and opponents gently and by every means, until the ideal that I have just described, like a heavenly vision presented to your waking sight, become through your efforts a visible reality, complete and successful."

40. Ibid. "Offer homage to the gods with your prayers as well as to all those who it is right to praise along with the gods; invite, urge friends and enemies in a friendly way and insistently until all our words, like a divine dream coming to you while you are awake, are clearly and happily realized through you (*enargē te exergasēsthe telesthenta kai eutukhē*)." For English translation see previous note.

sixteen

23 FEBRUARY 1983

Second hour

[
Philosophy and politics: necessary relationship but impossible coinci-
dence. ⌒ *Cynical and Platonic game with regard to politics.* ⌒
The new historical conjuncture: thinking a new political unit beyond
the city-state. ⌒ *From the public square to the Prince's soul.* ⌒
The Platonic theme of the philosopher-king.
]

I WILL TRY TO be brief. I think that Plato's advice, which, once again, is disappointing to anyone reading it from the point of view of political reflection and analysis in the Greeks, and especially disappointing if you compare it to what can be found in Thucydides, nevertheless, when read in a certain way, enables three important things to be brought out. First, a fundamental and constant feature in the relations between philosophy and politics. Second, a particular historical conjuncture, but one whose historical consequence is sufficiently far reaching practically to determine the fate of the relations between philosophy and politics until the end of Antiquity. Finally, third, and it is this that I would especially like to emphasize, I think this advice shows the point where philosophy and politics, philosophizing and activity meet up, the point, precisely, where politics can serve as philosophy's test of reality.

First, the fundamental and recurrent feature of the relations between philosophy and politics which emerges regarding these texts is basically very simple, [although it] does need to be understood. The, if you like, feeble, banal, and general character of Plato's advice to his correspondents—I do not think I have exaggerated in showing you how these texts did not say very much either from the political or the philosophical point of view—does not demonstrate that Plato was naive as regards politics. It shows that the relations between philosophy and politics are not to be sought in the possible ability of philosophy to tell the truth about the best ways to exercise power. After all, it is for politics itself to know and define the best ways of exercising power. It is not for philosophy to tell the truth about this. But philosophy has to tell the truth—we will leave it there for the moment, if you like, and we will try to specify later—not about power, but in relation to power, in contact with, in a sort of vis-à-vis or intersection with power. It is not for philosophy to tell power what to do, but it has to exist as truth-telling in a certain relation to political action; nothing more, nothing less. Of course, this does not mean that this relation cannot be specified. But it can be specified in different ways, and this relation of philosophical truth-telling to political practice, or to sound political practice, may take many forms.

Precisely in Plato's time, and among Socrates' successors, one of whom was Plato, we find other ways of defining the relation to politics, the necessary, indispensable, resistant, and stubborn relation of philosophical discourse or the philosophical life to political practice. Look at that other side of Socratism, the side which could not be more opposed to Platonism, that is to say, the Cynics. In Cynicism there is also a connection, and a very marked, very emphatic connection between philosophical truth-telling and political practice, but in a completely different way. And, as you know, this mode of connection is one of confrontation, and derision, of mockery and the assertion of a necessary exteriority. We should remember that opposite Plato, who advises the tyrant Dionysius, there was Diogenes. Diogenes, taken as prisoner by Philip after the battle of Chaeronea, was confronted by the monarch, the [Macedonian] sovereign. The [Macedonian] sovereign asks him: Who are you? And Diogenes replies: "I am the spy on your greed."[1] Or again, there is the famous dialogue between Diogenes and Philip's son, Alexander. There is the same question again: "Who are you?" But this time it is Diogenes who puts the question to Alexander, who replies: I am the great king Alexander. And at this point Diogenes replies: I will tell you who I am, I am Diogenes the dog.[2] In this way the absolute exteriority of the philosophical and the royal personages is asserted, which is exactly the opposite of what Plato proposes. What could be further removed from the philosopher king, the philosopher who is king, than this typically, exactly, word for word anti-Platonic reply? I am the great king Alexander. I am Diogenes the dog. Diogenes Laertius does not make it clear whether the explanation was given to Alexander or just generally, but he reports anyway that Diogenes the Cynic explained his aphorism "I am a dog" by saying: I am a dog "because I fawn on those who give me something, I bark at those who don't, and I bite those who are wicked."[3] So you can see the interesting interplay between philosophical assertion (philosophical *parrēsia*) and political power. The philosophical *parrēsia* of Diogenes basically consists in showing himself in his natural nakedness, outside all the conventions and laws artificially imposed by the city. His *parrēsia* is therefore in his very way of life, it is also apparent in this discourse of insult and denunciation with regard to power (Philip's greed, etcetera). Faced with political power, this *parrēsia* appears in a complex relationship since, on the one hand, in saying that he is a dog he says that he "fawns on those who give me something." Consequently, in fawning on those who give him presents he accepts a certain form of political power, integrates himself within it, and recognizes it. But at the same time he barks against those who give him nothing and bites those who are wicked. That is to say, with regard to the power that on one side he accepts, he feels free to say frankly and violently what he is, what he wants, what he needs, what is true and false, what is just and unjust. You have here a game of philosophical *parrēsia*, of philosophical truth-telling, a game of philosophical being-true facing the exercise of political power and the identification of an individual with his power (I am the king Alexander), a game which is clearly very far removed from, and even opposed to Plato's game. Let's say, again very schematically, that in the case of the Cynics we have a mode of connection of philosophical truth-telling to political action which takes place in the form of exteriority, challenge, and derision, whereas in Plato we have a connection of philosophical truth-telling to [political] practice which is rather one of intersection, pedagogy, and the identification of the philosophizing subject and the subject exercising power. We still need to know how this takes place, but in any case it is not necessarily or inevitably as the statement of what political action must be, it is not, if you like, as political program, as intrinsic political rationality that philosophy in its truth-telling has a role to play in politics.

Or again: philosophical discourse in its truth, in the game it necessarily plays with politics in order to find its truth, does not have to plan what political action should be. It does not tell the truth of political action, it does not tell the truth for political action, it tells the truth in relation to political action, in relation to the practice of politics, in relation to the political personage. And this is what I call a recurrent, permanent, and fundamental feature of the relationship of philosophy to politics. It seems to me that this is already very noticeable at the time we are concerned with, and that it remains true and always risks not being true throughout the history of the relations between philosophy and politics. But if we really want to understand these relations, we must keep in mind that, once again, philosophy has to tell the truth in relation to politics, it does not say what politics truly has to do. And the same can be said about some of the major forms of philosophical truth-telling in relation to politics in the modern or contemporary period. The philosophical theory of sovereignty, the philosophy of basic rights, philosophy envisaged as social critique, all these forms of philosophy, of philosophical veridiction, in no way have to say how to govern, what decisions to take, what laws to adopt, or what institutions to develop. But on the other hand, for a philosophy to put itself to the test of its reality, it is as indispensable now as in Plato's time that it be able to tell the truth in relation to [political] action, that it tell the truth in the name of a critical analysis, or in the name of a philosophy, of a conception of rights, or in the name of a conception of sovereignty, etcetera. It is essential for all philosophy to be able to tell the truth in relation to politics, it is important for all political practice to be in a permanent relationship with this truth-telling, but it being understood that the truth-telling of philosophy does not coincide with what a political rationality can and must be. Philosophical truth-telling is not political rationality, but it is essential for a political rationality to be in a certain relationship, which remains to be determined, with philosophical truth-telling, just as it is important for a philosophical truth-telling to test its reality in relation to a political practice.

But I think that this necessary, fundamental relation, which is no doubt constituent of philosophy and political practice in the West, is a phenomenon which is absolutely peculiar to our culture. The coexistence and correlation of political practice and philosophical truth-telling should never be conceived as an established coincidence or as a coincidence to be established. I think that the misfortune and ambiguities of the relations between philosophy and politics stem from and are no doubt due to the fact that philosophical veridiction has sometimes wanted to think of itself in terms of, or has even been set demands formulated in terms of a coincidence with the contents of a political rationality, and conversely that the contents of a political rationality have sought justification in the fact that they were formed as or on the basis of a philosophical doctrine. [...] Philosophy and politics must exist in a relation, in a correlation; they must never coincide.* This, if you like, is the general theme that we can extract from Plato's text. Once again, [this advice] is incommensurable with the forms of political rationality developed by Thucydides, but for a very simple reason, which is that for Plato, and it seems to me for Western philosophy generally, telling politicians what to do has never really been the objective. The objective has always been the existence of philosophical discourse, as philosophical veridiction, facing politicians, political practice, politics. That is the first theme.

The second theme we can draw from the Platonic texts I read in the first hour is this: in these texts we see a very particular historical conjuncture emerging. To be sure, it is a singular conjuncture, but it will be dominant for a long time, and as I was saying to you, it will be dominant practically until the end of Antiquity. Actually, and I have already pointed this out to you, in this advice—and especially in the first advice Plato gives to Dionysius—the place reserved for the actual organization of the city, the place accorded to the constitution, laws, and courts is fairly limited and does not seem to be the most important. On the other hand, [what] does appear important, dominant, in Plato's advice to Dionysius, and then to Dion's friends, is a problem concerning alliances, relations between victors and vanquished, relations between different federated cities, between the metropolis and

---

* Foucault began the sentence saying: Philosophy and politics must coincide.

its colonies, the way of governing subject cities, the question of the delegation of power, and the types of relation to be established between those who command and the others in the city-metropolis. That is to say, most of the problems raised are problems of empire and monarchy. These are undoubtedly problems which concern Sicily, that is to say, a world still very close to the classical Hellenic world organized around small units, cities, with their rivalries, alliances, federation, and system of colonization. But at the time Plato was writing I think they are also problems which, in an obscure way and with things not yet entirely settled or delineated, will become the real political problems of the Hellenistic world, and a fortiori of the Roman world. That is to say, you can see that with the formation of the large Hellenistic monarchies, and of course the organization of an imperial Roman world over the whole of the Mediterranean region, the concrete and precise political problem will be what type of political unit is to be organized when the city, the form or formula of the city clearly can no longer correspond to a type of exercise of power which geographically, in terms of both space and population, must extend beyond these limits. How will one be able to conceive of a political unit? The body of the city is no longer the formula-model, and the political unit can no longer be thought of as the very body of the city or of the citizens. What kind of political unit is conceivable?

Second, a further problem immediately linked to this is how will power, which in its units was only conceived of in the form of a kind of monarchy, which is, in a sense, held by the monarch, how will it be possible to distribute, divide up, and organize this power into a hierarchy covering the entire surface of this large political unit? What is the mode of being of these newly emergent political units, what is the mode of division, distribution, and differentiation of power within them? These are the political problems which come to the surface through the texts of Plato I have just read to you and which begin to be posed at the time, and which can be seen through the Syracusan situation, but which will dominate all political thought up to the Roman Empire. The type of political reflection found in the discourse of Maecenas to Augustus as told by Dio Cassius,[4] and also in Dio Chrysostom on the monarch,[5] and in Plutarch, all the political thought of the first and second centuries C.E. will basically revolve around the problem: What is

the mode of being of these new political units being constructed above
the cities and which, without completely destroying these cities, are
of a different order? And second: What type of power must the monarch exercise here? This is, if you like, the political scene that is taking shape for the Greco-Roman world. In no way do I want to oppose
the fine, articulated, dense, and rich political rationality of Thucydides
concerning small Greek cities, to a Platonic thought which is much
more uncertain but addressed to a new, emergent historical reality.
I do not think this is the interesting contrast, but through this Platonic
discourse in which what is at issue is the relationship between philosophy and politics I think we can see the outline of new political realities
which will last, will continue, for eight centuries until the end of the
Roman Empire. These new political realities are, on the one hand, the
Empire, and on the other, the Prince, the monarch.

The third point I would like to emphasize—the first was the recurrent principle of the non-coincident correlation between political
practice and philosophy throughout Western thought, and the second
was the new historical and political conjuncture which is emerging
at the time Plato was writing—is that it seems to me that by getting
these two things to work together (if you like: the permanent structure of the relations between philosophy and politics, and then this
new conjuncture), we see precisely what Plato means when he insists
that the philosopher speak to the sovereign, [or even] better that the
sovereign must himself be a philosopher. If, as I was saying, there
should be a relationship between philosophical discourse and political
practice, but not a relationship of coincidence, what then, for Plato,
is this relationship and where will it be established? Or again: where
will the test take place through which, as I said last week, philosophy
must make sure of its reality so as not to be just *logos*? Where is the
vis-à-vis of philosophy and politics, which entails both their necessary
relationship and their non-coincidence, to be inscribed? Well, I think
we have a major problem here. I mentioned a moment ago the Cynics'
solution, which basically put the relationship between philosophical
truth-telling and the exercise of political power in the public arena.
The Cynics are men of the street, of the *agora*. They are public men,
and also men of opinion. The site of the relation between philosophical
truth-telling and the exercise of political power, which is now in the

hands of this new personage, this new political reality of the time, the monarch, thus took the form of the confrontation of challenge-derision which Diogenes exemplified in relation to Alexander. Where will the site of this necessary and non-coincident relation between philosophical truth-telling and political practice be for Plato? It is not the public arena. If you like, the Cynics are, in this sense, still men of the city and they will perpetuate these traditions of the city and the public arena in the Roman Empire. For Plato, the site of this non-coincident relation is not the public arena; it is the Prince's soul.

We touch here on something quite important in the history of political thought, philosophy, and the relations between politics and philosophy in the West. It seems to me that the Cynicism-Platonism polarity very quickly became an important, perceptible, explicit, and also durable feature of these relations. Plato and Diogenes confront each other, and Diogenes Laertius gives an account of this. One day, Plato would have seen Diogenes the Cynic washing his salad. Plato sees him washing his salad and, recalling that Dionysius had appealed to Diogenes and that Diogenes had rejected his appeal, he says to him: If you had been more polite to Dionysius you would not have to wash your salad. To which Dionysius replies: If you had acquired the habit of washing your salad "you would not have been the slave of Dionysius."[6] I think this anecdote from Diogenes Laertius is very important and very serious. It indicates the two poles in terms of which, and very quickly, from the fourth century, the problem of the meeting point between philosophical truth-telling and political practice found two points of insertion: the public arena or the Prince's soul. And we will find these two polarities throughout the history of Western thought. Should philosophical discourse be the discourse addressed to the Prince's soul in order to form it? Or should the true discourse of philosophy be delivered in the public arena as challenge, confrontation, derision, and criticism with regard to the Prince's action and to political action? You recall in fact what we saw in the text on the *Aufklärung* with which I began this year's lectures. In his theory of the *Aufklärung*, Kant tried to maintain both things at the same time. He tried to analyze how philosophical truth-telling has two sites simultaneously which are not only compatible, but call on each other: on the one hand, philosophical truth-telling has its place in the public; it also has its place in the

Prince's soul, if he is an enlightened Prince. If you like, there is a sort of Kantian eclecticism which tries to hold together what traditionally, since the story of the salad involving Plato and Diogenes, was the major problem of the relation between philosophy and politics in the West: will this relation be established in the public arena, or will it be in the Prince's soul?

So let's return to Plato, since he's the one we are talking about. It is clear that, for Plato, the philosophy/politics relationship must be established in the Prince's soul, but we still need to know exactly how it is established. Is it not in the form of coincidence? Does saying that the Prince must be a philosopher mean that the Prince must take political decisions and act as a political actor only on the basis of philosophical knowledge that tells him what he must do. So, let's take the texts in which Plato, in Letter VII on the one hand, and in *The Republic* on the other, speaks of this coincidence between political action and philosophy in the Prince's soul. In Letter VII he says the following. I have already quoted this passage, it is at 326b: "So, evils will not cease for human beings until the race of pure and genuine philosophers [the Greek text says very precisely: before the race (*to genos*) of those who pursue philosophy rightly and truly; so it can be translated as "pure and true philosophers," but I prefer that we stay closer to the formulation: the race of those who pursue philosophy correctly and truly; M.F.] come to power or the race of the leaders of those who exercise power truly begin to philosophize."[7] That is what is said in Letter VII, 326b.

You know that this text is no more than the reproduction, the echo, with a few variations, but the faithful echo of what is found in the famous, basic text in Book V of *The Republic* at 473c when Plato wrote (*The Republic* is earlier than *The Letters*): There will be no respite from the evils of States or even of cities (so the same theme: in the letter, evils will not cease for human beings, and here, evils will not cease for States) "until philosophers become kings in the States" or "those we presently call kings and sovereigns (this is the Budé translation; *dunastai* in truth is: those who exercise power) "become true and serious philosophers" (here again the [Greek] text says: start to pursue philosophy in a genuine and *hikanōs*, competent, way) and "we see *dunamas politikē* [political power; M.F.] *kai philosophia* [and philosophy; M.F.]

joined in the same subject."[8] It would appear that we have here the definition of an exact coincidence. Philosophers must become kings or kings must become philosophers—what can this mean but that the philosopher part of the sovereign will tell him what to do as sovereign, and that the sovereign part will do no more than carry out what philosophical discourse tells him in his government's action? But in actual fact, when you look at the text—and that is why I have insisted on the most faithful translation possible—what is at issue is not a perfect fit between philosophical discourse, between philosophical knowledge and political practice. The coincidence involved here is coincidence between those who practice philosophy, who truly and competently engage in philosophy, and those who exercise power.

What is important and pointed out by these two texts, what they indicate, is the fact that someone who practices philosophy is also someone who exercises power. However, from the fact that the person who practices philosophy also exercises power, and the person who exercises power is also someone who practices philosophy, we cannot at all infer that his knowledge of philosophy will be the law of his action and political decisions. What matters, what is required, is that the subject of political power also be the subject of a philosophical activity. But you will say: What is the difference, and what does this identity between the subject of political power and the subject of philosophical practice mean? Why demand of someone who exercises power that he also practice philosophy if philosophy cannot tell the person who exercises power what he should do? Well, I think the answer to this question lies in this: you can see that what is at issue here is philosophy insofar as it is a *philosophein*. The text says it: Those who govern should also be those who philosophize, who practice philosophy. What, for Plato, is this practice of philosophy? Before all else, essentially and fundamentally, this practice of philosophy is a way for the individual to constitute himself as a subject on a certain mode of being. The mode of being of the philosophizing subject should constitute the mode of being of the subject exercising power.

So it is not a question of a coincidence between a philosophical knowledge and a political rationality, but one of identity between the mode of being of the philosophizing subject and the mode of being of the subject practicing politics. If kings must be philosophers it is not so they will be able to ask their philosophical knowledge what they should do in a given set of circumstances. It means that to be able to govern properly one has to have a definite connection with the practice of philosophy; the point of intersection between "governing properly" and "practicing philosophy" being occupied by one and the same subject. One and the same subject must, on the one hand, govern properly and, on the other, have a connection with philosophy. You can see that there is no coincidence of content, no isomorphism of rationalities, no identity of philosophical and political discourse, but rather an identity of the philosophizing subject with the governing subject, which obviously leaves open the fork, the perpendicular, if you like, between the axis on which one practices philosophy and the axis on which one practices [politics]. All in all this amounts to saying that the Prince's soul must be able to govern itself truly according to true philosophy for the Prince to be able to govern others according to a just politics.

Let's say, and I will stop there for today, that, as we saw last week, philosophical truth-telling must find its reality through, on the basis of, and in relation to politics. What I wanted to show you today, still with regard to Letter VII, the reading of which we are now ending, is that this practice of philosophy, which thus finds its reality in its relation to politics,* must not define for politics what it has to do. [It] has to define for the governor, the politician, what he has to be. What is at stake is the politician's being, his mode of being. And philosophy will derive its reality from its relation to politics by [being able] to define—effectively or not, this will be the test—the politician's mode of being. So the question raised is the following: What is the mode of being of the person who exercises power in his coincidence with the philosophizing subject? It seems to me this is a problem which has been absolutely crucial throughout the history of the relations between philosophy and politics in Antiquity. You only have to read Marcus Aurelius, for example, to see that this was the problem he posed, and which he was perfectly aware of having posed.[9] Six or five and a half centuries after Plato, Marcus Aurelius was supposed to be, he was the philosopher sovereign, the philosopher emperor. He is exactly what

---

* [The French text has "*philosophie*," but this must be a slip, either by Foucault or by the French editors; G.B.]

Plato was thinking of five and a half centuries earlier: a man who has to exercise power in a political unit which extends way beyond the unit of the city. So, at the heart of the Empire, at its center, there is the problem of the monarch who not only has to be master of the Empire, but master of himself. Marcus Aurelius was this ideal sovereign and there is nothing in his writing that shows he ever took from philosophy the rationality for dictating what his political conduct had to be with regard to this or that particular problem or situation. On the other hand, he constantly demanded from philosophy that it tell him what it was to be sovereign. That is to say, what in actual fact he asked from philosophy was his mode of being as sovereign. In short, through these texts by Plato we see the Prince's soul appearing as the site of the fundamental relations between philosophy and politics—relations which, once again, are relations of intersection and not coincidence. It is this problem, and problems linked to the question of the Prince's soul, that I will try to analyze for you next week.

1. Diogène Laërce [Diogenes Laertius], *Vie, doctrines et sentences des philosophes illustres*, ed. R. Genaille, vol. 2 (Paris: Garnier-Flammarion, 1933) p. 22; English translation by R.D. Hicks, "Diogenes" in *Diogenes Laertius II. Lives of Eminent Philosophers*, Book VI, §43 (Cambridge Mass. and London: Harvard University Press/William Heinemann Ltd., 1925) pp. 44-45: "on being asked who he was, replied, 'A spy upon your insatiable greed'."

2. Ibid., §60, French p. 22: "Meeting him one day, Alexander said to him: 'I am the great king Alexander'. Diogenes then presented himself: 'and I am Diogenes the dog'"; English p. 63: "Alexander once came and stood opposite him and said, 'I am Alexander the great king.' 'And I,' said he, 'am Diogenes the Cynic.'"* (*Editor's note, p. 62: "Literally 'Diogenes the Hound'.")

3. Ibid., English: "I fawn on those who give me anything, I yelp at those who refuse, and I set my teeth in rascals."

4. Dion Cassius, *Histoire Romaine*, Book LII, ch. 14-40; Dio Cassius, *Dio's Roman History*.

5. Dio Chrysostom, "On Kingship" in *Discourses*, I, trans. J.W. Cohoon (London: William Heinemann, and Cambridge, Mass.: Harvard University Press, 1932).

6. Diogenes Laertius, §58, French p. 28; English pp. 59-61: "Plato saw him washing lettuces, came up to him and quietly said to him, 'Had you paid court to Dionysius, you wouldn't now be washing lettuces,' and…he with equal calmness made answer, 'If you had washed lettuces, you wouldn't have paid court to Dionysius.'"

7. Plato, *Letter VII*, 326b, French p. 30; English p. 1576: "the human race will not see better days until either the stock of those who rightly and genuinely follow philosophy acquire political authority, or else the class who have political control be led by some dispensation of providence to become real philosophers." [See above, lecture of February 9, Second hour, note 8, p. 221. Foucault's quotation differs slightly from that given in the note by the editor; G.B.]

8. Plato, *The Republic*, Book V, 473c-d, French p. 88: "Unless, I resumed, philosophers become kings in the States, or those we presently call kings and sovereigns become true and serious philosophers (*philosophēsousi gnēsios te kai hikanōs*), and we see political power and philosophy (*dunamis te politikē kai philosophia*) joined in the same subject […] there will be, my dear Glaucon, no respite from the evils that afflict States, nor even, I believe, from those that afflict the human race"; English pp. 712-713: "Unless, said I, either philosophers become kings in our states or those whom we now call our kings and rulers take to the pursuit of philosophy seriously and adequately, and there is a conjunction of these two things, political power and philosophical intelligence…there can be no cessation of troubles, dear Glaucon, for our states, nor, I fancy, for the human race either."

9. On this point, see the lecture of 3 February 1982, second hour, in *L'Herméneutique du suject*, pp. 191-194; *The Hermeneutics of the Subject*, pp. 198-202.

seventeen

2 MARCH 1983

First hour

[*Reminders about political* parrēsia. ∿ *Points in the evolution of political* parrēsia. ∿ *The major questions of ancient philosophy.* ∿ *Study of a text by Lucian.* ∿ *Ontology of discourses of veridiction.* ∿ *Socratic speech in the* Apology. ∿ *The paradox of the political non-involvement of Socrates.*]

TO BEGIN TODAY I would like to mark some stages of the path [...*]. The underlying theme I chose for this year's lectures was this complex notion of *parrēsia*, which etymologically, or at any rate in its everyday use, seems to refer to two principles: on the one hand, the principle of everyone being free to speak and, on the other hand, the rather different principle of the frankness with which one says everything. All in all, would not *parrēsia* be the principle that anyone can say anything? In a sense, this is what the word suggests. Actually, you remember, we saw that things were a bit more complicated. In the first place, because *parrēsia* is not freedom of speech, the freedom to speak granted to anyone. In fact, *parrēsia* appears to be linked to an, if not exactly legislative organization, at least to an instituted, customary organization of the right to speak and of the privileges of the right to speak. Second, it appeared

---

* M.F.: You remember that we chose...I have the impression that the sound is even more dreadful than usual...We will try to do something...Like that, is it better? Yes? It is still vibrating? Wait...And like that? Perfect? La Callas!

that *parrēsia* was not just the license to say anything but an obligation to tell the truth on the one hand, and an obligation accompanied by the danger that telling the truth involves on the other. For the analysis of these different dimensions of *parrēsia* I referred to two texts. [The first] was the play by Euripides, *Ion*, which I studied at greater length, and [the second] was the text in which Thucydides shows how Pericles employs his *parrēsia* towards the Athenian people in his intervention on war and peace with Sparta. Then, through these texts, it appeared, first, that *parrēsia* was linked to the working of democracy. You recall that Ion needed *parrēsia* for him to be able to return to Athens and establish the fundamental Athenian political right. On the other hand, Pericles employed his *parrēsia*—Thucydides emphasized this—within the general working rules of democracy. *Parrēsia* founds democracy and democracy is the site of *parrēsia*. First of all then, there is this circular bond of *parrēsia*/democracy, each belonging to the other.

Second, I tried to show you how this *parrēsia* presupposed then a precise institutional structure, that of *isēgoria*, that is to say, the right to speak actually given to all citizens by the law, by the constitution, by the very form of the *politeia*. You recall that Ion did not want to return to Athens as a bastard, since he would not have had the right, the equal right—of citizens only, but of every citizen—to speak. And Pericles only speaks after all the other citizens, or anyway all those who wished to speak, had actually exercised their rights. So Pericles' right exists within this game of *isēgoria*. This was the second point.

The third point is that, even if *parrēsia* functions within this egalitarian field of *isēgoria*, it presupposes, it implies a form of political ascendancy exercised by some over others. If Ion wanted to have *parrēsia*, it was not just so he could be a citizen like others; it was so he could figure in the *prōton* (the front rank) of citizens. And if Pericles spoke, and if this speech had the effects that it had, Thucydides reminds us that this is because Pericles was the foremost citizen of Athens. This is the third characteristic of *parrēsia*.

Finally, you recall that *parrēsia* took place within an agonistic field where it constantly met with the danger involved in practicing true speech in the political field. Ion referred to the people's envy, the envy of the majority, of the most numerous towards those who exercise their ascendancy. He also referred to the jealousy of rivals who cannot tolerate one of them advancing and assuming ascendancy over the others. And Pericles, at the start of his great speech to the Athenians, evoked the possible failure of Athens, demanding that they stand by him in failure as much as they would in victory.

These are, I think, the four points, the four characteristics of *parrēsia* as it appeared in these two texts, the tragedian's and the historian's. Starting from this analysis, I think we were able to see some shifts, some transformations carried out around this notion of *parrēsia*, and this was in texts from the first half of the fourth century, that is to say, later than those of Euripides, or which anyway relate to a situation later than that referred to by Thucydides. Thucydides referred to the situation of Athens at the end of the fifth century. Euripides was also writing at that time. With Plato, Xenophon, and Isocrates we are dealing with people who are writing in the first half of the fourth century and who refer to their contemporary situation. So what do we see? With regard to these four points, we saw that there were some quite remarkable modifications of this notion of *parrēsia*.

First, there is a generalization of the notion in the sense that *parrēsia*, the obligation and risk of telling the truth in the political field, no longer appeared to be linked merely and solely to the working of democracy. *Parrēsia* finds its place, or rather has to make room for itself in different regimes, which may be democratic, autocratic, oligarchic, or monarchical regimes. Sovereigns, like the people, need *parrēsia*. And good sovereigns (Cyrus in Xenophon and Plato, Nicocles in Isocrates) must make room for the truth-telling of their advisors, just as wise peoples listen properly to those who employ *parrēsia* before them. So there is a generalization of the political field of *parrēsia*, or let's say even more schematically that *parrēsia*, truth-telling, appears as a necessary and universal function in the field of politics, whatever the *politeia*. Politics, in whatever way it is practiced, by the people, by some, or by one, needs this *parrēsia*. This is the first shift.

The second shift is, if you like, the development of a certain ambivalence, a certain ambiguity concerning the value of *parrēsia*, as if the immediate and uniformly positive value of the notion in Euripides, or in the portrayal of Pericles by Thucydides, starts to become blurred. The functioning of *parrēsia* appears, in fact, to be accompanied by difficulties, and this is true for both democratic and autocratic governments. In the first place, by allowing anyone who wants to speak to do so, *parrēsia* makes it possible for the worst as well as the best to speak. Second, if telling the truth in *parrēsia* is a risk, if there really is danger in speaking the truth before the people or the sovereign, if the people and the sovereign are unable to moderate themselves sufficiently not to frighten those who wish to tell the truth, if they are too threatening to those who claim to tell the truth, if they become excessively angry* and are incapable of moderation towards parrhesiasts who appear before them, then everyone will keep quiet because everyone will be afraid. This will be the law of silence, silence before the people or before the sovereign. Or rather, this silence will be filled by a discourse, but a distorted discourse, the *mimēsis* (imitation), the bad *mimēsis* of *parrēsia*. That is to say, there will be the pretence of telling the sovereign or the people the truth, but the person speaking will know full well that what he is saying is not true. He knows simply that what he says conforms exactly to what the people or the sovereign thinks, or to what the people or the sovereign would like to hear.

The practice of repeating the already formed opinion of the people or the sovereign, and presenting this as the truth is, so to speak, *parrēsia*'s shadow, its bad and dubious imitation. It is what is called flattery. This contrast between flattery (of the people, of the sovereign) and *parrēsia* may appear to be ultimately rather moralizing and of no great value. Actually, it seems to me that *parrēsia* and flattery are certainly two major categories of political thought throughout Antiquity. Whether you take the theory of flattery that is so important in Socrates and Plato,[1] or the technical texts in Plutarch devoted to the very important problem of how to distinguish a flatterer from a parrhesiast,[2] or finally the descriptions by historians of the emperors, their counselors, and their courts, etcetera, you see that for practically eight centuries the problem of flattery as opposed to *parrēsia* was a political, a theoretical, and a practical problem, one which ultimately was undoubtedly as important during these eight centuries as the both theoretical and technical problem of freedom of the press or freedom of opinion has been in our societies. An entire political history could be written of

---

* M.F. says: if they are too threatening to those who claim to tell the truth, if they do not become excessively angry.

the notion of flattery and all the technical problems which revolved around it in Antiquity. That is the second transformation of the notion of *parrēsia*: the change of register to one of ambivalence, with its bad double, flattery.

The third transformation we saw emerging in these texts from the beginning of the fourth century is, roughly, the splitting of *parrēsia*, its unevenness, inasmuch as the *parrēsia* that Ion wanted to exercise on his return to Athens, and that Pericles employed before the people of Athens, was a way of freely giving one's views on questions concerning the city's organization, its government, the choice between war and peace, etcetera. *Parrēsia* was therefore practiced with regard to the city in its entirety and in a directly political field. Now through the texts of Xenophon, Isocrates, and especially Plato, we see *parrēsia* take on a double task in that it has to address individuals at least as much as it does the whole body of citizens, the *polis*, etcetera. The task of *parrēsia* now involves showing individuals how in both cases, [whether] as citizens who have to give their opinion or as a sovereign who has to impose his decisions, they must govern themselves in order to govern the city properly. Instead of being just a view which is given to the city in order that it govern itself properly, *parrēsia* now appears as an activity which consists in addressing the souls of those who have to govern so that they govern themselves properly and so that in this way the city too is governed properly. I think this splitting or, if you like, this shift of the target, of the objective of *parrēsia*—from the government of the city, which it addressed directly, to the government of self in order to govern others—marks an important shift in the history of this notion of *parrēsia*. And it will make *parrēsia* both a political notion—raising the problem of how to make room for this truth-telling within a government, be it democratic or monarchical—and at the same time a philosophical-moral problem. The second problem is philosophical-moral: what means and techniques are to be employed so that those who have to govern can, through the *parrēsia* of their advisors, govern themselves properly? This is the third transformation of this notion of *parrēsia*, its splitting or, if you like, the shift of its target.

Finally, the fourth important modification in the problematization of *parrēsia* is the following. What were Ion or Pericles when they appeared as parrhesiasts in relation to the city? They were citizens, and they were the leading citizens. Now that *parrēsia* has to be exercised in any regime, whatever it may be, and inasmuch as it has to be practiced in a dangerous, tangled relationship with its double (flattery), consequently raising the problem of distinguishing what is true from what is illusory, when, in short, *parrēsia* does not just involve giving advice to the people on what decision to take but means having to guide the souls of those who govern, who then will be capable of *parrēsia*? Who will possess the ability of *parrēsia*, who possibly will have the monopoly of *parrēsia*? And it is at this point, precisely at the turn of the fourth and fifth centuries, that the great division in Greek culture, or anyway Athenian culture, between rhetoric and philosophy begins to be marked out, a division whose effects will continue to be seen for eight centuries.

Rhetoric as the art of speaking—an art of speaking which can be taught, which can be employed to persuade others, and which can be fully effectuated, realized, and accomplished only if the orator is at the same time *vir bonus* (a good man)—puts itself forward as the very art of truth-telling, of speaking properly and under technical conditions such that this truth-telling is persuasive. As an art possessed by a good man who, knowing the truth, is able to persuade others of this truth with [this] specific art, rhetoric may appear to be in fact the technique peculiar to *parrēsia*, to truth-telling. However, on the other hand of course, philosophy will make itself out to be the only practice of language which can meet the new requirements of *parrēsia*. For, unlike rhetoric, which by definition addresses several, a great many people, which addresses assemblies and operates within an institutional field, philosophical *parrēsia* will also be able to address individuals. It will be able to give particular advice to the Prince and individual advice to citizens.

Second, philosophy, in contrast with rhetoric, will claim that it alone is able to distinguish between the true and the false. For if *parrēsia* really must distinguish truth-telling from flattery, if *parrēsia* must constantly drive out its shadowy double which appears as flattery, what else but precisely philosophy can make this division, this distinction? Because the objective of rhetoric is to be able to persuade the listener of what is false as well as of the truth, of the unjust as well as of the just, of evil as well as of good, whereas the function of philosophy is precisely to say what is true and to drive out the false. Finally, philosophy will present itself as having the monopoly of *parrēsia* inasmuch as it presents itself as operating on souls, as a psychagogy. Rather than being a power of persuasion which would convince souls of anything and everything, philosophy presents itself as an operation which will enable souls to distinguish properly between true and false, and which, through the philosophical *paideia*, will provide the instruments needed to carry out this distinction.

I think this gives us a bit of a perspective, if you like, on the major problems of philosophical thought, of political thought in Antiquity. I have sketched out this excessively brief and repetitive summary of what I have said to you in the previous lectures basically for two reasons. The first is that I think it provides us with a sort of overview on some of the principal aspects of ancient thought up to the development of Christianity. We could—forgive the survey, the schematic character—pick out some of these essential problems. I am not saying that every aspect and all the fundamental problems of ancient thought are here, but I think that on the basis of this problem of *parrēsia* we could pick out some of them which might possibly serve as themes to be studied.

First question: What is the site of truth-telling? Where can truth-telling find its place, on what conditions can and must room be made for it? This amounts to saying, if you like: what is the most favorable political regime for this truth-telling? Democracy or monarchy, of course? But also an autocratic imperial regime, an imperial regime balanced or compensated for by the influence, the role of the Senate? Look at Tacitus, *A Dialogue on Oratory*, for example.[3] In a sense, this is a reflection on the place and conditions of *parrēsia*. Where can this right, or possibility, or risky obligation to tell the truth be accommodated in a given regime? This is also the problem of the Prince's education, of where the person who tells the truth should be placed; in order to educate the Prince, should he be in his antechamber? Should the person who tells the truth be in an assembly like the Senate? Should he be a member of a circle, in a political circle or a philosophical school? Or should he live in the street like the Cynics, stopping and interrogating passers by, thus reviving the Socratic gesture? This whole problem of the place of political truth-telling in the political, the social-political field, appears to me to [be linked to] a whole series of questions found in ancient thought, in philosophers, in moralists, in historians...

Second, I think that starting from this question of *parrēsia* we can also see emerging the question of, broadly speaking, the relations between truth and courage, or between truth and ethics, which is also a fundamental question in Antiquity. Who is capable of giving a true discourse? How can we distinguish true discourse from that of the flatterer? And, from the ethical point of view, from the point of view of his courage, what kind of person must the one who undertakes to make this division between true and false be? Who is capable of the courage of the truth? And what education is necessary? A technical problem: where, then, should the stress be laid in education?

Another series of problems that we see arising on the basis of this question of *parrēsia* concern the government of the soul, psychagogy. What truths does one need in order to conduct oneself and others, and to be able to conduct others well by conducting oneself well.* What practices and techniques are needed? What knowledge is needed, what exercises, etcetera? And finally you see that we are led back to the question I mentioned a moment ago: To whom and to what must one turn for this training in *parrēsia*, and also for the definition of the place of *parrēsia*, of the moral conditions for being able to tell the truth, and of the way of guiding souls? Should one turn to the rhetorician or to the philosopher, to rhetoric or to philosophy? And you know that here I think we finally have what will be the great division within ancient culture for more or less eight centuries.

I would like to end this first outline with a text written by Lucian at the end of the second century [C.E.] which amusingly evokes these relations between philosophy and rhetoric. As you know, Lucian belongs to the movement called the Second Sophistic, which represents the more or less artificial and false revival at the end of the second century [C.E.]

---

* [Foucault drew attention to the meanings of the French *conduire/conduite* in his lecture of 1 March 1978: "...the word 'conduct' refers to two things. Conduct is the activity of conducting (*conduire*), of conduction (*la conduction*) if you like, but it is equally the way in which one conducts oneself (*se conduit*), lets oneself be conducted (*se laisse conduire*), is conducted (*est conduit*), and finally, in which one behaves (*se comporter*) as an effect of a form of conduct (*une conduite*) as the action of conducting or of conduction (*conduction*)." *Security, Territory, Population*, p. 193 and my footnote. As with those lectures, and despite some resulting awkwardness in the English, I have again used the English "conduct"; G.B.]

of some of the basic themes of classical Greek culture. Lucian, as a neo-Sophist, as a Second Sophist, or at any rate belonging to that movement, should be placed more on the side of rhetoric. Anyway, he has a constant mistrust of philosophy, philosophical practice, and philosophers. But then again, to tell the truth, things are a bit more complicated than this, and it would be unfair and insufficient to say that, broadly speaking, in the great division between rhetoric and philosophy Lucian was on the side of rhetoric and an opponent of philosophy. Maybe you know Lucian's text; it was translated some years ago, badly moreover, and with an inappropriate title (*Les Philosophes à l'encan* [Philosophers for auction]) which, if you want to translate it exactly, is called *The Lives Fair, The Lives Market*.[4] It deserves to be republished suitably. So, Lucian wrote this text, *The Lives Fair*, which was a parody, a satire of those philosophers who on the public square offer a choice of different ways of life, for a fee of course. In this text each philosopher peddles the life he offers to potential buyers. After writing this text, which evidently aroused not a little irritation, Lucian wrote a further text called *The Fisherman* in which he imagines the philosophers putting the author of *Philosophes à l'encan* on trial. And Lucian names the author put on trial *Parrēsiade* (the man of *parrēsia*). So Lucian, in the guise of this Parrēsiade, presents himself as someone who tells the truth. And in these proceedings against Parrēsiade brought by the philosophers irritated by his previous text, who is to judge between the two sides? It is Philosophy. Philosophy, called upon to judge between the philosophers and Parrēsiade, will call to her side some associate judges: *Aretē* (virtue), *Dikaiōsunē* (justice), *Sophrōsunē* (wisdom or temperance), and *Paideia* (culture, education, training). And then philosophy's fifth associate judge is *Alētheia* (truth). Called as a judge at the tribunal presided over by philosophy to say whether Parrēsiade really was guilty of wickedly attacking the philosophers, Truth (*Alētheia*) says that she really wants to come to the tribunal to judge Parrēsiade, accused by the philosophers, but she wants two of her companions to accompany her: *Eleutheria* and *Parrēsia*. *Eleutheria* is freedom in general. *Parrēsia* is the freedom to speak with the risk it involves. And what is interesting is that *Eleutheria* (freedom) agrees to come. Not only does she agree to come, but she wants to come without her other companions who are, in particular, *Elegkos* (argument, discussion) and *Epideixis* (praise). At this point *Parrēsia* intervenes to say that she wants to accompany *Eleutheria*, but that she must have some assistants with her. And given that the philosophers who must be fought—or rather the philosophers who attack Parrēsiade and against whom Parrēsiade tries to defend himself—are pretentious, argumentative people who are hard to refute, one needs *Elegkos* (argument) and *Epideixis* (praise).

At this point the trial of Parrēsiade against the philosophers takes place, under the arbitration of Philosophy and her set of judges. Parrēsiade is actually interrogated as in a trial: he is asked his name and origin. And he says that he is Parrēsiade *alēthinos* (Parrēsiade, man of truth), and he declares himself *philalēthēs* (friend of the truth), *philokalos* (friend of beauty), and *philaploikos* (friend of simplicity). And then he sets out his defense in which he explains how and why he came to attack the philosophers. He explains that, like every good young man, he began by learning rhetoric. But, he says, as soon as I saw some of the ugly qualities an orator has to acquire (namely, lying, impudence, and shouting) I wanted to join with philosophy out of the storms and to live thus in a quiet harbor under her protection.[5] You see that in this definition of philosophy—out of the storms, a quiet harbor, etcetera—you again find a theme shared by the Epicureans and the Stoics, and we can say, generally, by all the moral philosophy of the first or second century C.E. It is an extremely frequent metaphor.[6] But you see too that this recourse to philosophy is not primary. It comes after a disappointment arising from rhetoric and its essential defects, defects consubstantial with rhetorical practice and orators. So Lucian does not choose rhetoric because he was disappointed by philosophy; he turns to philosophy because he was disappointed by rhetoric. But in turning to philosophy he becomes aware of another defect, symmetrical, as it were, to those of the orators. The defects of the orators, then, are lying, impudence, and shouting. Well, the philosophers, no doubt employ a completely honorable language, but when one sees how they actually live, one sees only disputes, ambition, and avarice, etcetera. Consequently, one has to turn away from philosophy as one turns away from rhetoric. I have simply brought this text to your attention because, just before the spread of Christianity and the start of the great upheaval of ancient culture, it is one of the clearest and most amusing expressions, if you like, of the great problem which, in Lucian's time, already had six centuries behind it: the problem of the relation of philosophy to rhetoric.

So, in the remaining lectures I would like to take up some of these problems I have spoken about: the problem of the conduction* of souls, the problem of the distinction between flattery and *parrēsia*, and the problem of the technical, but more than technical opposition between philosophy and rhetoric. Before beginning to talk about "philosophy and rhetoric" I would like to emphasize [the following]. Certainly, there are some technical questions in [this problem of] "philosophy and rhetoric," and we will come across them, but it seems to me also— anyway, this is what I would like to show you—that they are not just two techniques or two ways of speaking confronting each other, [but] truly two modes of being of discourse which claim to tell the truth and which claim to implement the truth in the form of persuasion in the souls of others. It is a question of the mode of being of discourse which claims to tell the truth, and you know full well that if I dwell on this question of the mode of being of discourse which tells the truth it is because basically this has always been the question that I have wanted to raise.

What seems to me to deserve an historical and not a just formal analysis—historical analyses in this area seem to me to have been relatively weak, if not discreet—is the problem of what could be called the ontology or ontologies of the discourse of truth. By this I mean the following. A discourse which claims to tell the truth should not be assessed merely by measuring it against a history of knowledge which would permit us to determine whether or not it tells the truth. These discourses of truth deserve to be analyzed differently than according to the measure and from the point of view of a history of ideologies which would ask them why they speak falsely, failing to telling the truth. I think a history of the ontologies of true discourse or of discourses of truth, a history of the ontologies of veridiction would be a history in which one would pose at least three questions. First: What is the mode of being peculiar to this or that discourse, as distinct from others, when it introduces a certain specific game of truth into reality? Second question: What is the mode of being that this discourse of veridiction confers on the reality it talks about, through the game of truth it practices? Third question: What is the mode of being that this discourse

---

* See above, footnote p. 306.

of veridiction imposes on the subject who employs it, such that this subject can play this specific game of truth properly? An ontological history of discourses of truth, a history of ontologies of veridiction would therefore have to pose these three questions to any discourse which claims to be a discourse of truth and to assert its truth as a norm. This implies that every discourse, and particularly every discourse of truth, every veridiction, be considered essentially as a practice. Second, it implies that all truth be understood in terms of a game of veridiction. And it implies that every ontology, lastly, be analyzed as a fiction. Which means again: the history of thought must always be the history of singular inventions. Or again: if we want to distinguish the history of thought from a history of knowledge undertaken in terms of an index of truth, and if we want to distinguish it from a history of ideologies undertaken by reference to a criterion of reality, then this history of thought—this anyway is what I would like to do—should be conceived of as a history of ontologies which would refer to a principle of freedom in which freedom is not defined as a right to be free, but as a capacity for free action.

Now let's move on to the fourth century texts, that is to say, basically Plato's texts, and this confrontation between rhetorical discourse and philosophical discourse, again understood not just as discourses which conform to conflicting laws, principles, and technical rules, but also as modes of being of discourses of truth, of truth-telling. To study this question, to see it emerging in Platonic thought, I will look at two texts. One is the, as it were, practical text par excellence of *parrēsia*. Anyway, it is the text which is supposed to represent Socrates' *parrēsia*. The text refers to the situation in which it was both most necessary and most dangerous for Socrates to practice *parrēsia*, in which philosophical *parrēsia* is at the point of its most acute, life and death conflict with traditional political-judicial eloquence. The text is, of course, the *Apology*. The second text I would like to refer to in order to locate this mode of being of philosophical discourse in contrast with the mode of being of rhetorical discourse is very different from the *Apology*. In a sense, it is one of the most theoretical texts, and in any case one of the most ornate, free, and also complex texts. It does not present itself as the game Socrates plays with his own life before the political-judicial eloquence that wants to kill him. It is a text in which the critical reflection on rhetoric does not center on life or death but revolves round the game of *erōs* [and poses] the problem of the praise of love and [of the] different ways in which rhetoric and philosophy approach the praise of love, the ways in which they reflect on love.

So the first text, the *Apology*, is, in a sense, the simplest, the easiest, but again the most urgent, since it concerns Socrates' death. In this [passage] from *Socrates' Apology*—I don't intend to analyze the whole text—we can pick out what [appears] relevant for an analysis of philosophical truth-telling in its opposition to the rhetorical utterance, to the rhetorical way of speaking. I think we can find this opposition between philosophical truth-telling and rhetorical discourse in three sets of texts. A first set concerns the discourse itself, the way in which Socrates, faced with his accusers' discourse, presents his own discourse (these are the first lines of the text). In another set of texts, Socrates raises the question of his political role and tries to answer the objection: But why have you, who claim to speak the truth, never spoken in an assembly? And lastly, a third set of texts concern his actual role in the city with regard to the citizens, and which, without being directly a political role, is nonetheless precious and even essential for the city.

So, the first set of texts, in which Socrates presents his own discourse in answer to that of his accusers, is right at the start of the *Apology* (the first lines, 17a-18a). Actually, straightaway, Socrates describes his adversaries as people who have only ever spoken falsely. And yet these people, who have never uttered a single true word, nevertheless have a talent. They have an ability to speak such that, to start with, they can persuade those who hear them, and then, Socrates says with a smile, he too is even close to having been convinced, since it turns out that he no longer knows who he is. In what does this persuasive lie with which these people, who have never spoken the truth, have managed to convince their listeners and almost convinced Socrates himself, actually consist? Well, it consists in making people think that Socrates had the ability to speak and was clever in the art of speaking, that he possessed the art of speaking.

How does Socrates present himself against this image [forged by] his adversaries, who are themselves artists in the art of language, who never say anything truthful, but who manage to persuade everyone and almost persuade Socrates himself? He presents himself precisely as someone who speaks the truth, who always speaks the truth, and who does so precisely outside this art and technique of speaking which enables one to persuade others. Socrates presents himself as the man of truth-telling without any *tekhnē*. What are the characteristics of this truth-telling without any *tekhnē*, his truth-telling? First, he says, he is seventy years old. He has never appeared before a court. He has never been either accused or accuser. On the one hand, this should be taken as alluding to the fact that Socrates has never been part of any of the political factions which contended for and followed each other in power in Athens after the period of the Thirty, of the abolition and then return of democracy. [...] But [when] he says that he has never appeared before any court this also means that the speech he is going to give does not conform to any of the usual forms of oratory, or even to the conventional forms of oratory before assemblies and courts. He employs an interesting metaphor. He says: Since I am completely unaccustomed to this kind of eloquence, since I have never spoken in the political and judicial space of assemblies and courts, I appear before you as a stranger (*xenos*).[7] He is a stranger to this political field. I think we should be careful here. On the one hand—this is a frequent theme in the judicial literature of the time, you find it in Nicias, and in Isocrates I think, anyway in a large number of texts [...]—the person who appears before the courts generally begins by saying: You know, I have never been summoned before the courts of law, I have never accused anyone, I am completely incapable of speaking and you must forgive me, I feel like a stranger before you. This was a theme of judicial literature by which the defendant emphasized that he was someone without great power, with few friends and enemies, and not part of any clan. It was also quite simply a way of hiding the truth itself of this judicial eloquence, namely that the person who spoke generally only read his speech, even if he had not delegated someone else to read it for him. That is to say, the speech was written by someone else, a logographer, and consequently the convention was that this speech, written by a logographer, began with: You know, I don't know how to speak, I appear before you, I am all alone, I have no friends and I speak as I can.

Socrates takes up this theme, makes use of it and produces a pastiche of it, with this difference: in the case of Socrates it is true, it is his own speech, or anyway Plato claims that what he reads really is his own speech, and that the strangeness of the speech Socrates will deliver in this political-judicial institutional field is that it is a speech which is foreign to this domain. In what way is it foreign? Socrates tells us in a passage at 17c-d: The language I use is *xenos* (foreign), why? For three reasons. First it is the language I use every day in the public square, the market, and elsewhere. So the first difference from the language of rhetoric is that there is no discontinuity of vocabulary, form, or construction between Socrates' language and the everyday use of language. Second, at 17c Socrates points out that his language is no more than the series of words and phrases which occur to him. I shall speak, he says at 17c, "as best I can, as the expressions occur to me."[8] This theme of a language which does no more than immediately translate the very movement of thought, without reconstruction and without architectural artifice, is frequently found in Plato or Socrates. In *The Symposium*, at 199a-b, Socrates says practically the same thing and practically in the same words.[9] Obliged to take his turn in praising love, he says that it really is very difficult to give the kind of praise in which one is supposed to attribute all the finest things to the object of one's praise. He does not feel he can do that. He will speak with words (*onomata*) and an arrangement of phrases (the construction of the phrase: *thesis*)[10] as they come (*hopoia dan tis tukhē epelthousa*: as it happens, as they come).[11] Finally, the third characteristic of Socrates' non-rhetorical language (the first was the language of every day, [the second] language as it comes) is that it is a language in which he says exactly what he thinks, a language in which there is an act of trust at the heart, at the very basis of the statement, a sort of pact between himself and what he says (*pisteuō dikaia einai ha legō*: I trust, I have faith in the fact that what I say is right).[12]

There are three characteristics then: everyday language; language as it appears; language of trust, faithfulness, and credence (of *pistis*). I think it is important to note that these three characteristics of non-rhetorical discourse, of philosophical discourse as *parrēsia*, as truth-telling are very strongly linked by Plato or Socrates. For Socrates, speaking everyday language, saying what comes to mind, and affirming what one thinks right absolutely go together. And at 17c he says it very clearly...I am not finding it again in the text, but I have copied the quotation—I would have preferred to quote from the Budé translation rather than the one I have taken from the Pléiade edition, from Robin,[13] it is a bit more contorted—: "without embellishment of words and style," "things said in the terms which occur to me: because I trust in the justice of what I have said." You see that Socrates groups the three things—"without embellishment of words," "things said in the terms which occur to me," "trust in the justice"—as forming a unity, which is the unity characteristic of *parrēsia*. Now we can obviously raise the following question. A speech without embellishment, a speech which employs the words, expressions, and phrases which come to mind, and a speech that the person who utters it believes to be true, would describe, for us at any rate, a sincere speech, but not necessarily a true speech, so how is it that, for Socrates or Plato, saying things without embellishment, as they come to mind, and while believing them to be true, is a criterion of truth? And why will philosophical discourse, inasmuch as it conforms to these three criteria, be a discourse of truth?

This is the question that is raised, and I think at this point we should refer to the conception of *logos etumos*,[14] which is found in Plato but goes way beyond the framework of Platonic philosophy and is a sort of general form of the Greek conception of language. This *logos etumos*, this authentic *logos* refers to the idea that language, that words and phrases in their very reality have an original relationship with truth. Language, words, and phrases bring with them what is essential (*ousia*), the truth of the reality to which they refer. If the false enters the mind, if illusion gets round or masks the truth, this is not due to an effect peculiar to language as such, but is rather the result of some addition, transformation, trick, or shift in relation to the distinctive, original form of language. *Etumos* language, I was going to say etymological language, language which is without embellishment, apparatus, construction or reconstruction, language in the naked state, is the language closest to truth and the language in which the truth is expressed. And I think this is one of the most fundamental features of philosophical language or, if you like, of the mode of being of philosophical discourse as opposed to rhetorical [discourse]. Rhetorical language is a language chosen, fashioned, and constructed in such a way as to produce its effect on the other person. The mode of being of philosophical language is to be *etumos*, that is to say, so bare and simple, so in keeping with the very movement of thought that, just as it is without embellishment, in its truth, it will be appropriate to what it refers to. It will be appropriate to what it refers to and it will also be true to what the person who uses it thinks and believes. The philosophical mode of being of language is characterized by the *logos etumos* as the meeting point between the *alētheia* which is expressed in it and the *pistis* (the faith, belief) of the person who states it. Whereas the mode of being of rhetorical language is to be constructed according to rules and techniques (according to a *tekhnē*) and addressed to the other's soul, philosophical language will be without these devices, without these *tekhnai*. It will be *etumos* and as such it will tell the truth of reality and at the same time express the soul of the person who utters it, what his soul thinks. What defines the mode of being of this philosophical language, as opposed to rhetorical language, is the relationship to the speaking subject and not the relationship to the individual being addressed. This is a first set of indications, of reflections on philosophical truth-telling in *Socrates' Apology*.

The second set of reflections, as I said, concern Socrates' political role. The texts are found from 31c to 32a. Socrates has to answer a question concerning his actual political role. He supposes that his adversaries ask him the following question: Fine, you claim to be someone who tells the truth, but how can you lay claim to this role of truth-telling, this role as parrhesiast (the word does not appear, but you will see shortly that it really is this function that is intended)? How can you say that you are the man who tells the truth when you have never wanted to give advice to the people or before the Assembly? You say that you speak the truth, but you have never performed the function of advisor, you have never played the role of the individual who comes before the Assembly, mounts the tribune, and gives his advice. Socrates immediately gives the answer: Why have I never played the role of [public] advisor, why have I never been the political parrhesiast? Well, he says, if "I had engaged in politics, my ruin would have been complete long ago, and I would not have been able to be of use to either you or myself."[15] In actual fact, Socrates continues, if one strongly opposes you one risks one's life. If one wishes to safeguard one's life, one must lead "the life of a private individual."[16] You see here, once again without the word being uttered, one of the most fundamental and common themes concerning *parrēsia* at this time, that is to say, that Athenian democracy does not function or hardly functions as it should inasmuch as the lives of those who could or should feel obliged to play the role of parrhesiast feel their lives so threatened that they prefer to abandon it. Socrates is referring to the bad functioning of *parrēsia* in Athenian democracy, a classical theme at the time: you are punished if you oppose the majority. You remember that we found exactly the same thing in a text by Isocrates. Now what is interesting is that Socrates has no desire to incur the danger associated with *parrēsia* in bad democracy. In his eyes it is not worth taking the risk. *Parrēsia* is not an obligation in such a situation. Consequently, Socrates has never appeared at the Assembly to advise his fellow citizens and give them his views in the political realm. [To explain] this non-participation, this breach of the game of *parrēsia*, this abandonment at any rate of the parrhesiastic function which should or normally could be the function of someone who claims to tell his fellow citizens the truth, Socrates says quite explicitly that he has not performed this parrhesiastic [role] because he has been ordered not to. And he has been ordered not to perform this parrhesiastic function, this truth-telling in politics, by his *daimōn*, the *daimōn* who, as you know, Socrates says, in this text as well as others, never gives him a positive order, never tells him what to do, but simply tells him when he should not do something.[17] And precisely his *daimōn* has told him that he should not try to tell the truth directly, as it were, immediately in the field of politics. This is one of the first aspects of what Socrates says concerning his political role.

But there is another aspect, because he immediately adds that he had been a bouleutes in the name of his tribe, the Antiochides, and had even exercised the office of prytanis. These are not offices which you apply for or demand; they fall to you as a result of the drawing of lots or the rotation of offices between the different tribes. Here, then, he is obliged to exercise a particular office. Within this framework he had to demonstrate something, the nature of which we will see shortly. Second, after the temporary abolition of democracy, during the fleeting period of the dictatorship of the Thirty, he was also given the task of arresting someone. Now in both cases, when he was a bouleutes, and even a prytanis, and then when he was given a task by the Thirty, he refused to do what, in the first case, the majority wanted, and, in the second, what the dictators tried to get him to do. Whereas, when Socrates was a prytanis, the majority of the Council wanted a collective trial of the generals who, following the battle of the Arginuses, failed to retrieve the bodies of those who had fallen, Socrates did not want to accept this illegality—because Athenian law did not recognize this kind of collective responsibility—and he opposed the majority of the Council. [Then], when the Thirty demanded that he go to Salamis to arrest someone (Leon of Salamis), those charged with making the arrest with him [went ahead], but Socrates preferred simply to return home rather than carry out this order which was also illegal.

What is interesting in these two stories is, on the one hand of course, their contrast with what had just been said (that his *daimōn* told him "don't get involved in politics"), and then also that the issue, the problem in these two stories—what took place under democracy and what took place under tyranny—is basically the same. Be it democracy or tyranny—the regime, if you like, of parties and factions, or the regime of an oligarchy—Socrates anyway found himself in a situation that all in all amounted to the same thing. Whatever the regime (democracy or tyranny, the difference is not essential) the parrhesiastic function and role appeared to be of the same type. It should be stressed as well that in both cases Socrates clearly shows that he was risking death. In the case in which he was a prytanis and it was a matter of trying the generals of the Arginuses, he says: "I had to face danger on the side of the Law and justice, rather than put myself on your side out of fear of prison and death"[18] And when it was a matter of the order given by the tyrants: "This time again, indisputably, I made it very clear, not by words but by action, that, with all due respect, death did not matter at all to me."[19] So it is the same thing in the case of democracy and of tyranny: he was prepared to risk his life.

But then we may wonder where is the difference, since a moment before he explained that he did not want to give his views to the people or give them advice, since he would have risked his life doing so, and now he refers to two situations (in democracy and in tyranny) in which he was in actual fact prepared to risk his life. Why must he risk his life in one case but not in another? I think the difference is easy to see if we look at the texts and see what the situation was to which the two things refer. In one case—when he says: I did not want to give advice to the Assembly because it is too dangerous to oppose the majority—it is a matter of a *parrēsia* which is practiced as a direct political power, as an ascendancy exercised over others. It is a matter of political activity as the intervention of a citizen who, to take up Ion's expression in Euripides again, puts himself in the *prōton zugon* (the front rank).[20] This voluntary political intervention, in which the man, the parrhesiast tries to exercise an ascendancy over others in order to speak the truth, belongs to politics, not philosophy. The philosopher, as such, precisely does not have to put himself in the position of wanting to exercise ascendancy over the others by giving political advice to political actors within the political field.

And here we come back to the theme which will be developed by Plato a little later in Letter VII, you know, where we saw that Plato did not give political advice to be applied in politics by the politician. We saw that Plato's philosophical discourse was not a discourse which had to model, as it were, the political field, as if philosophy possessed the truth about politics. Philosophy has to play a certain role in relation to politics; it does not have to play any role in politics. And Plato refuses to give any advice in the field of politics, before the Assembly, to those who will have to take decisions. Philosophical *parrēsia* will not be this type therefore. It does not tell the truth to politics in politics.

Nevertheless, and this is the second attitude, it remains that with regard to politics the philosopher has to play a role of parrhesiast at the cost of his life. In actual fact, in the [first] situation, it was not a matter of a direct and immediate action by which the philosopher would have told politicians what to do. But he was caught up within a system, within a game of the *politeia*. The constitution of Athens, its social and political structure, meant that at a certain moment he was given a particular post, as bouleutes, as prytanis. Or again, under a tyranny—ultimately it amounts to the same—he was appointed to do something. And then, when he is called upon to do something as part of a definite social and political field, when therefore he has to engage in an activity defined by the post assigned to him, *parrēsia* is possible. Even better, it is necessary. It is necessary, because what would happen if he did not make use of this *parrēsia*? He himself would commit an injustice. Out of care for himself, through being concerned about himself and taking care of what he is himself, he refuses to commit this injustice. And in doing so he brings out a truth at the same time. In the first case, the philosopher, as a philosopher, does not have to prevent the city from folly or injustice. On the other hand, when he has to do something as someone who is part of the city—either as a citizen in a democracy or as a citizen who is subject to a tyrannical or despotic power—then inasmuch as the injustice would be one that he himself would commit, either in his role as citizen or his role as subject, the philosopher must say no. The philosopher must say no and he must invoke his principle of refusal, which is at the same time a manifestation of truth.

You see that, in the first case, in the form of, I would say, direct political activity, Socratic *parrēsia* is negative and personal. It involves renouncing any political ascendancy and power over others. On the other hand, in the political field not constituted by one's ascendancy over others but by one belonging to a political field, then the philosopher has to be parrhesiast inasmuch as it is the formulation and emergence of this truth which will keep him from what would be the thing for him to avoid above all else: being the agent of injustice. You see that here—and we can find its repercussions in what I said to you last week regarding the governing subject and the philosophizing subject—what is really at issue is always this question of the subject, of the political subject. What concerns philosophy is not politics, it is not even justice and injustice in the city, but justice and injustice inasmuch as they are committed by someone who is an acting subject; acting as a citizen, or as a subject, or possibly as a sovereign. Philosophy's question is not the question of politics; it is the question of the subject in politics.

I will just add one word. In both of the cases referred to (that of the battle of the Arginuses and Plato's refusal to vote with the majority, and also in that of the order given by the Thirty tyrants to arrest someone) I said that Socrates made use of *parrēsia*. You could say that, all the same, it is a very discreet *parrēsia* since, precisely, he has not spoken. He did not come forward and explain to the people why it was unjust to condemn the generals of the Arginuses. No more did he say publicly to the Thirty tyrants that the arrest of Leon of Salamis was unjust. He confined himself to showing it. And the text, moreover, says this: I risked my life *ergō*, and not *logō* (not by discourse but in fact),[21] which as you know is an extremely common expression that contrasts what one does in words only and what one does in reality. Here then, Socrates wants to say that he is not satisfied with asserting that he risked his life, he really risked it. But we should note that actually this is not at all *logō*—and here I employ the expression in the strict sense—it is not at all by *logos* that he thus asserted the truth, it is *ergō*. What is at stake is *ergon*, that is to say, what he has done. In the first case he contents himself with voting against the majority. In the other case, when he is ordered to arrest someone, he simply returns home. He returns home, openly and publicly, no more and no less. And you see that there is another important element here. The first was the fact that philosophical *parrēsia* as it appears in Socrates is not a directly, immediately political *parrēsia*. It is a *parrēsia* which stands back in relation to politics. Second, it is a *parrēsia* in which what is at stake is the acting subject's, not the city's safety. Finally, the third point is that this philosophical *parrēsia* does not necessarily or exclusively go through *logos*, through the great ritual of language in which one addresses the group or even an individual. After all, *parrēsia* may appear in the things themselves, it may appear in ways of doing things, it may appear in ways of being.

And I think this is how the famous theme which will be so important throughout the history of thought, and especially of ancient philosophy, that is to say, the problem of the philosophical attitude, takes root. Being an agent of the truth, being a philosopher, and as a philosopher claiming for oneself the monopoly of *parrēsia*, will not just mean claiming that one can state the truth in teaching, in the advice one gives, and in the speeches one makes, but that one really is in fact, in one's life, an agent of the truth. *Parrēsia* as form of life, *parrēsia* as way of behaving, *parrēsia* even in the philosopher's style of dress, are constitutive elements of this monopoly that philosophical *parrēsia* claims for itself. You may recall that when we were talking about Epictetus last year we frequently came across that character, so typical of Epictetus, of the young man whose hair is a bit too curled, who is bit too perfumed, a bit too carefully got up, and who is always a rhetorician. He is a rhetorician and he is decked out because as a rhetorician he is precisely the man of embellishment. In his way of speaking, his clothing, his way of being, and in his tastes and pleasures, he is someone who does not speak the truth, who is other than himself; he is the man of flattery, the perfumed man, the effeminate boy.[22] By contrast, the philosopher will be precisely someone who not only tells the truth in this discourse—this *etumos* discourse—but also someone who tells the truth, who demonstrates the truth, and is the individual of truth in his way of being. And this truth will of course also be the bearded virility on the basis of [...*]. All of these themes of the parrhesiast philosopher— standing back in relation to politics, being concerned with the subject and not the city, and finally demonstrating the truth as much through what he is as by what he says (through *ergō* as much as through *logō*)— appear quite clearly in the *Apology*. So, in a moment I will finish what I wanted to say to you about the *Apology* and we will move on, if I have time, to the *Phaedrus*.

---

* Inaudible.

1. See, for example, *Gorgias* 463a, *Phaedrus* 240b, but also on this point see the lecture of 10 March 1982, first hour, in *L'Herméneutique du sujet*, pp. 363-364; *The Hermeneutics of the Subject*, pp. 379-381.

2. Plutarch, "How to Distinguish the Flatterer from the Friend" in *Plutarch's Moralia*, vol. I, trans. F.C. Babbit (Cambridge, Mass. and London: Harvard University Press and Heinemann, "Loeb Classical Library," 1969).

3. Tacite, "Dialogue des Orateurs," in *Œuvres complètes*, ed., P. Grimal (Paris: Gallimard, coll. "La Pléiade," 1990) pp. 65-105; English translation by M. Hutton, W. Peterson, revised by R.M. Ogilvie, E.H. Warmington, and M. Winterbottom as "A Dialogue on Oratory" in Tacitus, *Tacitus, I, Agricola. Germania. Dialogus*. (Cambridge, Mass.: Harvard University Press, "Loeb Classical Library," 1914).

4. Lucien, *Philosophes à l'encan*, trans. T. Beaupère (Paris: Les Belles Lettres, 1967); English translation by H.W. Fowler and F.G. Fowler as, Lucian, *Sale of Creeds*, in *The Works of Lucian of Samosata* (Oxford: The Clarendon Press, 1905), vol. 1. For another reference to this text, see *L'Herméneutic du sujet*, p. 89; *The Hermeneutics of the Subject*, p. 92.

5. Lucian, *Le Pêcheur ou les Ressuscités*, §29, in *Œuvres complètes*, trans. E. Chambry (Paris: Garnier, no date) p. 331: "As for me, when I became aware of the inevitable unpleasantness attached to the profession of advocate, of the deceitfulness, lying, impudence, shouting, pushing, and a thousand other inconveniences, I naturally saved myself from this hell and took refuge in your sanctuary, Philosophy, to pass there the rest of my days, like a man who hastens to escape from the storms and turmoil of the waves and enter the calm of the harbor"; English translation by A.M. Harmon as *The Dead Come to Life or The Fisherman* in Lucian, *Lucian III* (Cambridge, Mass.: Harvard University Press, "Loeb Classical Library," 1921) pp. 45-47: "As soon as I perceived how many disagreeable attributes a public speaker must needs acquire, such as chicanery, lying, impudence, loudness of mouth, sharpness of elbow, and what all besides, I fled from all that, as was natural, and set out to attain your high ideals, Philosophy, expecting to sail, as it were, out of stormy waters into a peaceful haven and to live out the rest of my life under your protection."

6. For a first analysis of these metaphors, see *L'Herméneutique du sujet*, lecture of 17 February 1982, first hour, pp. 238-239; *The Hermeneutics of the Subject*, pp. 248-249.

7. Platon, *Apologie de Socrate*, 17d, trans. M. Croiset (Paris: Les Belles Lettres, 1970) p. 141: "For as you know, today is the first time I have appeared before a court; now I am seventy years old. So I am a complete stranger to the language here (*atekhnōs oun xenōs ekhō tēs enthade lexeōs*)"; English translation by Hugh Tredennick, as *Socrates' Defense (Apology)* in Hamilton and Cairns, eds., *The Collected Dialogues*, p. 4: "This is my first appearance in a court of law, at the age of seventy, and so I am a complete stranger to the language of this place."

8. Ibid., 17c, French p. 140; English p. 4: "what you will hear will be a straightforward speech in the first words that occur to me."

9. Plato, *Le Banquet*, 199a-b, trans. L. Robin (Paris: Belles Lettres, 1929) p. 47: "However, if it is a question of truths this time, I am pleased to speak, if you want, as I know how and not so as to compete with your eloquence: I am not keen to be laughed at"; English translation by Michael Joyce, as Plato, *Symposium*, in Hamilton and Cairns, eds., *Collected Dialogues*, p. 551: "But I don't mind telling you the truth about Love, if you're interested; only, if I do, I must tell it in my own way, for I'm not going to make a fool of myself."

10. Ibid.

11. Ibid.

12. Platon, *Apologie de Socrate*, 17c, p. 140; English p. 4.

13. Platon, *Apologie de Socrate*, in *Œuvres complètes*, vol. I, trans. L. Robin (Paris: Gallimard, "La Pléiade," 1950) p. 147: "nor having, like them, all the drapery of vocabulary and style, but rather of things said..."; *Socrates' Defense (Apology)*, p. 4: "not...in flowery language like theirs, decked out with fine words and phrases. No, what you will hear will be a straightforward speech in the first words that occur to me, confident as I am in the justice of my cause."

14. Platon, *Phèdre*, 243a, in *Œuvres complètes*, IV-3, trans. L. Robin (Paris: Les Belles Lettres, 1944) p. 29: "There is no truth in this language (*ouk' est' etumos logos houtos*)!"—a quotation from Stesichorus which is taken up again at 244a, p. 31; English translation by R. Hackforth

as, Plato, *Phaedrus*, in Hamilton and Cairns, eds., *The Collected Dialogues*, p. 490: "False, false the tale" (and p. 491 for 244a: " 'False is the tale' ").

15. Platon, *Apologie de Socrate*, 31e, trans. L. Robin, p. 168; Plato, *Socrates' Defense*, p. 17: "if I had tried long ago to engage in politics, I should long ago have lost my life, without doing any good either to you or to myself."

16. Ibid., 32a, p. 169; English p. 17: "must necessarily confine himself to private life."

17. Ibid., 31d, p. 159; English p. 17.

18. Ibid., 32c, p. 169; English p. 18: "I thought that it was my duty to face it out on the side of law and justice rather than support you, through fear of prison or death."

19. Ibid., 32d, p. 170; English p. 18: "On this occasion, however, I again made it clear not by my words but by my actions that death did not matter to me at all."

20. Euripides, *Ion*, 595, trans. H. Grégoire, p. 208; English, *Ion*, trans. Philip Vellacott, p. 60.

21. Platon, *Apologie de Socrate*, 32a, trans. M. Croizet, p. 160: "I will give you strong proofs of what I say, not verbal proofs (*ou logous*), but those you set great store by, facts (*erga*)"; English pp. 17-18: "I will offer you substantial proofs of what I have said—not theories, but what you can appreciate better, facts."

22. Epictetus, *The Discourses as Reported by Arrian*, vol II, Book III, i, trans. W.A. Oldfather (Cambridge, Mass. and London: Harvard University Press, "Loeb Classical Library," 2000). For the analysis of this text, see the lecture of 20 January 1982, first hour, *L'Herméneutique du sujet*, p. 93; *The Hermeneutics of the Subject*, p. 96.

eighteen

2 MARCH 1983

Second hour

[
End of study of Socrates' Apology: parrēsia/*rhetoric opposition.* ⌒ *Study of the* Phaedrus: *general plan of the dialogue.* ⌒ *The conditions of good* logos. ⌒ *Truth as permanent function of discourse.* ⌒ *Dialectic and psychagogy.* ⌒ *Philosophical* parrēsia.
]

[I WOULD LIKE TO finish] very quickly what I wanted to say about the *Apology*, since [these are] things which are both well-known and [were already mentioned] last year. I wanted to show that Socratic *parrēsia* did not in any way consist in undertaking to tell the truth about and regarding political decisions in the political field, but that it is a function, as it were, of a break with political activity strictly speaking. This break is indicated by the *daimōn*'s prohibition, but also by the obligation to bring the truth into play with regard to this political field when the requirements of this field, of these political structures are such that someone caught up in them will be in danger himself of becoming the subject of an unjust action. This is clearly stated at 28b: a man of any worth is not to calculate his chances of life and death. "When he acts he should consider only whether his action is just or not, whether he is conducting himself as a good man or a vile one."[1] And at 28d: "Whoever occupies a post [precisely the post that Socrates occupied as prytanis, or the position of authority entrusted to him by the tyrants; M.F.]—whether he chose it himself or was placed there by a leader—has in my view the duty to remain firm in it whatever the risk, taking no account of death or any danger, rather than sacrifice his honor."[2] So the question now is whether *parrēsia* will be limited to marking this caesura in relation to the political field, and to marking it by a break through which the truth will appear either through *logō* (through discourse) or through *ergō* (through action, the facts, real behavior).

You know that there are a number of texts in the *Apology* which reply to this question by showing that there is a parrhesiastic role for the philosopher which is not that of intervening before the Assembly, but which is also different from the simple manifest and explicit refusal to become an unjust subject. There is a properly philosophical *parrēsia* which is described, as you know, when [Socrates] speaks of the task precisely entrusted to him, not by the *daimōn* (which confines itself to giving negative orders, to saying: don't do this or that), but by the god, the oracles, dreams, and all the means, he says, a divine power may employ.[3] This is the task he has decided to pursue until his last breath, the task to which he has bound his life, and for which he refuses any payment or reward. I am not one of those, he says, who speak only when they are paid and otherwise remain silent. He is at the disposal of anyone, rich or poor, provided that they wish to listen. And this pact of listening, of the listening which is necessary even before the philosophical task begins, and which has been agreed to before, is thus designated in this text. So how will the philosopher reply to this listening and to the request of others? On the god's command, he will reply by exhorting those he meets not to care about honor, wealth, or glory, but to care about themselves—this is the *epimeleia heautōn* as you know. And caring about oneself consists first and foremost in knowing whether or not one does know what one knows. Philosophical *parrēsia*, which is identified not just with a mode or technique of justice but with life itself, consists in practicing philosophy, caring about oneself, exhorting others to care about themselves, and doing this by examining, testing, putting what others do and do not know to the test. I must, he says, "live practicing philosophy [*zēn philosophounta kai exetasonta ematuton kai tous allous*: and examining, testing: M.F.], examining myself as well as others."[4]

This is philosophical *parrēsia*, and this test of oneself and others is useful to the city, since by being the parrhesiast within the city in this way [Socrates] prevents the city from sleeping. And, he says, you know very well that condemning me to death you will spend the rest of your life asleep. Philosophical *parrēsia* is characterized by this function, which is not at all a political office but a necessary function with regard to politics, not necessary for the working of the city, for its government, but necessary for its very life and for keeping it from sleeping (for its wakefulness, for keeping watch over the city).

You see that this philosophical *parrēsia* contrasts with rhetorical discourse on every point. Philosophical *parrēsia* is not a discourse which would be practiced in the political field, or on the political stage, in the assemblies or courts. It is a discourse which stands back and breaks with the scene of rhetorical discourse, and yet it is a discourse which may, and in some cases, has to take a stand in relation to political decisions. Second, it is a discourse which is not characterized by its objective of persuading others. From the point of view of its origin it is characterized much more by the fact that it is *etumos*, that is to say, has no other form than to be, in its simplicity and spontaneity, as close as possible to the reality to which it refers. It is a discourse which does not owe its strength (its *dunamis*) to the fact that it persuades. It is a discourse which owes its *dunamis* to the fact that it springs from the very being which speaks through it. Finally, third, philosophical discourse is not a discourse which claims to know and, claiming to know, seeks to persuade the other that he does not know. Rather, it is a discourse which is constantly testing itself at every moment in both the person who delivers it and the person to whom it is addressed. It is the test of itself, of the person speaking, and of the person being spoken to. This is, in broad terms, the theme of philosophical *parrēsia* which, you can see, matches up with some of the themes I touched on last year.

I am going through this quickly and would like now to come to the *Phaedrus*, which I would also like to look at to see how the contrast between philosophical discourse and rhetorical discourse is formulated and emerges in Plato. The *Apology* and the *Phaedrus* are certainly not the only places where these problems are discussed in Plato. In a sense, the philosophy/rhetoric problem runs through all of Plato's work. To go quickly, I am taking these two texts, chosen for the reasons I just mentioned: the former is, as it were, the practical discourse in which Socrates brings into play his own *parrēsia* in relation to his own life; in the latter, on the other hand, philosophy, the art of practicing philosophy will confront some of the most developed forms of what claims to be the art of rhetoric. So the issue is not the life and death of Socrates, it is love. You know—I'm sorry for reminding you of these trivialities—that the *Phaedrus* is organized, roughly, around four major focal points. First of all you have the speech of Lysias (the speech Phaedrus had in his pocket, or the folds of his cloak, and which had so enchanted him when he heard it that he wanted to learn it by heart). Intrigued, Socrates asks Phaedrus to read Lysias' speech, and its theme is that a boy should grant his favors to a man who does not love him rather than to one who does. Socrates, not without coaxing, will reply to this speech by saying that he, Socrates, is not really capable of speaking and making such fine eulogies. But he makes a speech which as it were backs up, complements, and up to a point is the pastiche of the one he has just heard from the mouth of Lysias. And in this speech, or imitation-pastiche of the speech, Socrates explains therefore—Lysias' speech said that a boy must grant his favors to the one who does not love him—that a boy should not grant his favors to the one who loves him because a lover only loves the basest, most shameful qualities in the one he is in love with, and in any case a lover, an old man in love with a young boy, is after all a bore. Another, third speech, Socrates' second, will then be given, and this will be the true speech, that is to say, a speech with very complex relations to the truth since, in the first place, unlike the first two speeches, in which there was praise only for those who do not love and disqualification of the lovers, here rather, the third speech (Socrates' second) is the praise of real love, of true love. Second, this praise of true love is not a rhetorical praise intended to persuade someone of a thesis which is quite difficult to sustain. It is the true speech which praises true love. The relationship to the truth therefore is double, since it is a matter of the true praise of true love, and it is here that this speech of truth becomes complex and problematizes its relations to the truth since, as you know, it goes through a series of what are called fables: the fable of the union of the charioteer and his team of steeds, the fable of love which fosters the growth of the soul's plumage, etcetera. That is the third element, the third focal point of the *Phaedrus*. And then the dialogue comes to its high point or draws to a close, if you like, precisely in a reflection directly devoted to the problem of the art of language, of what the true *tekhnē* is with regard to *logos*. Is it rhetoric or something else? Second, the second problem linked to this is the problem of writing: is writing to be included in the *tekhnē* of discourse?

I do not intend to go into the details of this fourth part and I would just like to consider it from the point of view of this history of the mode of being of true discourse and how it is distinguished from rhetoric. I would like to focus on the following points in this final part of the *Phaedrus*. First, in his endeavor to distinguish philosophical discourse and rhetorical discourse, to size up rhetoric's claim to be an art, the art (*tekhnē*) of discourse (*logos*), so in this endeavor to gauge the true value of rhetoric, we should note straightaway—for it is pointed out from the start of this fourth part of the *Phaedrus*—that Plato does not at all put oral discourse (*logos*) on one side and written discourse on another. We should note that throughout the text, throughout this fourth part, the word *logos* refers sometimes to written discourse, sometimes to oral discourse, and sometimes we cannot tell which of them it refers to. There is another passage which is much clearer and more explicit on the absence of a division, for the moment at least, between written and oral discourse. It is when Plato has made his second speech (the third of the series), which is the true speech on true love, and Phaedrus, who had been smitten by Lysias' speech, has the scales torn from his eyes or his ears unblocked. And he understands that Lysias' speech was of little value when compared with Socrates' speech. And Phaedrus says: Well yes, Lysias' speech is not worth much, but there is no doubt a reason for this. And the reason Phaedrus suggests is this: Lysias is only a logographer,[5] that is to say, someone who writes his speeches, and whose discourse does not come from his own *logos* in the present reality of speech. He is only one of those professionals hired for writing speeches for others. So, since he is a man of writing, we should not be surprised that his speech is so flat and poor beside the one just now improvised by Socrates beneath the cicadas singing overhead. Now Socrates replies to Phaedrus' hypothesis (that Lysias' speech is worthless because it is a written speech), and he replies sharply, saying: But why are logographers so despised? You know very well that famous politicians who claim that they do not make use of the good offices of a logographer and who claim to speak for themselves are in actual fact more attached to writing than anyone else, since they cannot wait to have their own speeches written and to boast of them. Do not despise the logographers, he says, for the difference is not between the written and the oral. There is nothing intrinsically wicked (*aiskhron*: shameful) in writing the speech, Socrates says. Where things start to be wicked (*aiskhron*) is when, whether in writing or orally, one does not speak well, but badly.[6]

The problem then which Socrates or Plato poses quite explicitly at the start of the fourth part of the *Phaedrus* is this: Let us leave to one side as irrelevant the oft' repeated classical opposition between the shoddy goods of the logographers' written discourse and the good, living *logos*. This is not what is important for Plato; it is not what is important for Socrates. It is something else: How can we tell good speech, written or oral, from bad? That is to say: What is the quality of the speech itself? Is it written or spoken well or badly? How should the distinction be made? The division is not therefore between written and oral. How is the division made between good or bad speaking or writing?

Phaedrus begins by proposing what immediately appears to be a satisfactory solution, and he says: In reality, for written or spoken discourse to be good, the speaker or writer must have knowledge of the truth (*to alēthes*)[7] concerning the things he is talking about. This seems to be all very simple and direct. It says everything, and this really is what is at issue, rhetoric precisely being completely indifferent to the truth since it boasts of being able to support any thesis and get the just be seen as the unjust. The best proof is that rhetoric can show that a boy should grant his favors to the man who does not love him rather than to the one who does. So, Phaedrus says, if the speaker knows the truth his discourse will be good. Now Socrates is not satisfied with this solution which would amount to saying: Give us the truth first of all, and the speaker having acquired the truth, rhetoric will be able to add to it. Socrates emphasizes this: If the truth could simply be known by the speaker before he speaks, as the prior condition, as it were, [of his discourse] (which is what Phaedrus suggests), then in that case his discourse will not be a discourse of truth. Knowledge of the truth, for Socrates, is not a precondition of the good practice of discourse. For precisely, if the truth were to be given prior to the practice of discourse, what would rhetoric be but the set of embellishments, transformations, constructions, and games of language through which what is true is forgotten, obliterated, hidden, or omitted?

For discourse to be a discourse of truth it is not necessary that knowledge of the truth be given to the speaker before he speaks; truth must be a constant and permanent function of the discourse. And Socrates quotes an apophthegm, which he calls a Spartan, Laconian apophthegm—whose origin is unknown, for it is quoted only one other time, by Plutarch in his *Sayings of the Spartans*, which follows the *Phaedrus* text however, so that we can say that there is only one quotation, that of the *Phaedrus*—which says this: a genuine art (*etumos tekhnē*: that is to say, an art which is closest to the being that it deals with through its own technique) does not exist and will not be able to exist in the future without being attached to the truth.[8] Discourse, the *etumos* art, the genuine art of speaking will only be a true art on condition that the truth is a permanent function of the discourse. Then the problem arises: How can this necessary and continuous relationship of discourse to the truth be assured so that, in this perpetual relation to the truth, the speaker will possess and put to work the *etumos tekhnē* (the genuine technique)?

It is at this point that Socrates develops his conception of the relationship between discourse and truth, showing how the truth is not the psychological precondition of the practice of the art of oratory, but must be that to which discourse refers at every moment. He shows this first of all by proceeding to a stark generalization, which will be held in suspense throughout part of the discussion and which we will see shortly how he takes it up again and relocates it. He says: At bottom, what is this art of rhetoric which wants to persuade? Well, he says, it is nothing other than a general form of what he calls *psukhagōgia dia tōn logōn* (psychagogy through discourse),[9] that is to say, rhetoric is no more than a way of conducting souls through the intermediary of discourse. Consequently he will not pose the problem in the framework of just rhetoric, but in the much more general framework of the category in which rhetoric is or should be placed, that of psychagogy (the conduct of souls) *dia tōn logōn* (by discourse).

So, after laying down this general principle and having shown that he is not going to talk about rhetoric in particular so much as about psychagogy in general, he returns to the definition that orators give of their art. Actually, when the orators want to define the *tekhnē* of their rhetoric, they say that it is an art which enables the same thing to appear just or unjust, or the same decision sometimes to appear good and at other times bad. Now, says Socrates, for the same thing to appear now good now bad, now just now unjust, one must be able to exploit an illusion which will persuade the individual that what is just is unjust, or the other way round. Now how can one produce the illusion? Is it merely by substituting the just for the unjust, by going from one extreme to the other, or from one opposite to another? Certainly not. The text says that to go from the just to the unjust one has to advance by small differences.[10] The true rhetorical art, if it really wants to present the ugly as beautiful, the unjust as just, etcetera, will have to progress from one to the other through small differences, and not by a sudden leap from the just to the unjust, from the beautiful to the ugly, or from the good to the bad, which would deceive no one. Now to be able to carry out this movement from one extreme to the other (from good to bad, just to unjust) through small differences, and so that the orator does not get lost in this progression, one must also be able to establish these differences and to establish them in the best way. Now how can one best establish the small differences and know them as they are so that one can obtain the effect of persuasion desired? And this is where the famous passage of the *Phaedrus* is found, at 265d-265e, in which he says that, in order to know a difference one must first be able to bring that which is disseminated and dispersed together in a vision of the whole. And when we have a vision of the whole, we must be able to divide this unity by kinds, into kinds (*eidē*), observing the natural articulations, like good carvers who do not hack brutally but follow the articulations as they are given.[11] I am not going back over this, it is a *topos* in the history of philosophy with which most of you, I think, are familiar. What is interesting, you see, is that in this way Socrates shows that what is needed to obtain the same end that rhetoric seeks— namely: to persuade of the just as well as the unjust, to make the just appear unjust and the other way round—is not a *tekhnē rētorikē*, but a *tekhnē dialektikē*.[12] It is simply the dialectic which will enable this result to be obtained. However, Socrates continues, one could grant this and say that, very well, rhetoric needs this dialectic and so prior knowledge of the truth (which Phaedrus proposed) is not enough for its purpose and one needs in addition all that dialectical knowledge which will support the discourse and so to speak articulate it in its details, but it nevertheless remains that—this is what the rhetoricians could say, the objection Socrates puts to himself—on top of this dialectic, and in order for this dialectical truth to arrive at its sought for effect of persuasion, one needs to employ methods which are precisely those of rhetoric strictly speaking.

The hypothesis envisaged here, which Socrates will not refute, amounts to saying: Agreed, one needs this permanent function of the relationship to the truth which is assured in discourse by the dialectic, but this dialectic must be complemented by a rhetorical art which is superimposed on it, which conveys as it were this dialectic and produces the effects of persuasion one seeks. And he lists the different parts, which the rhetoricians know well and present as their own art: the art of making introductions, of bringing in witnesses, clues, probabilities, the whole system of proofs, and the refutation—in short, you have here the whole passage in which Socrates lists the different parts of the rhetorical art of his time. Now, to this claim of the possibility at least of a *tekhnē rētorikē* on top of the dialectical function, Socrates will reply by saying that all these elements are in actual fact only rudiments of what is really the art and action of persuading. Because, what is it that persuades? It is not putting an introductory exposition at the head of one's speech, then witnesses, then emphasizing clues, probabilities, and then refuting, etcetera. Being able to persuade means knowing where, when, how, and under what conditions to apply these different methods. And here, of course, the reference is to medicine. Medical treatment is not the physician's knowledge of the list of medicines to be applied, but his knowing exactly to what patient, at what point in the development of the disease, and in what quantity medicine is to be applied. Now a good physician not only has to know the *dunamis* (power) of the medication, he also has to really know the body, the constitution of the bodies to which he applies medication—and here the reference is to Hippocrates,[13] and maybe to the exact text in which Hippocrates, or [a] Hippocratic [physician], boasts that he has completely changed the old conception of regimen and replaced the simple codification of recipes with a reflection on regimen in terms of the condition of the body which is itself considered in terms of climatic conditions and the state of the whole world.[14] Reference to these Hippocratic themes: it was Hippocrates who thus substituted or completed medical art, or enabled it to be not just the application of a recipe, but well and truly an art of curing through knowledge of the body. So, in the same way, even if we allow that the dialectic is necessary to discourse, rhetorical *tekhnē*, the ability to persuade for which rhetoric still claims to be the *tekhnē*, is no more than a body of recipes. And it is applicable and will have its effects only if we know the soul, just as the physician must know the body. One must know what it is that these techniques, [or rather] these rhetorical methods are applied to. At 270e it is said that one must know the soul itself. To equip someone technically with the art of speaking one must show him the nature (the *phusis*) in its essence (in its *ousia*) of that to which discourse is applied, that is to say, the soul.[15] And at 271c he says: "Since the specific function of discourse [the power of discourse: *logou dunamis*; M.F.] is to be [we return then to the theme raised earlier; M.F.] a psychagogy, someone who wishes to become a talented orator must know how many forms the soul may have."[16]

Here then it should be understood that when Socrates and Plato emphasize that truth must be a permanent function throughout discourse, and not just a precondition of knowledge, they do not mean that discourse must first be linked to truth through the knowledge of what one is speaking about and then through the knowledge or assessment of those to whom one is speaking. It is not a matter of saying that to give a discourse of truth one must first know the truth and then take into account the person to whom one addresses it. The double requirement of a dialectic and a psychagogy, of a *tekhnē dialektikē* and a knowledge of psychagogy (*psukhagōgia*), is not to be understood, once again, as a requirement on the side of the speaker and a function of those to whom one speaks. What is involved is a double condition, two absolutely interlinked conditions which must constitute the mode of being peculiar to philosophical discourse. Knowledge of Being through the dialectic and the effect of discourse on the being of the soul through psychagogy are linked. They are intrinsically linked and linked by an essential bond since it is through the movement of the soul that the latter will be able to accede to knowledge of Being, and since it is in the knowledge of what is that the soul will be able to know itself and recognize what it is, that is to say, related to Being itself. At this point we understand that the function in the dialogue of Socrates' great speech (the third speech, his second, but third in the *Phaedrus*) on true love, frenzy, the soul as union of the charioteer and his two steeds, the ascent to realities, the role of *erōs*, the feathers that grow, and the taking wing of the soul which remembers, etcetera, is not just to give an example of true discourse on true love in contrast with the devices of rhetorical discourses. Its function was already to anticipate the content shown in the fourth part. This speech showed in advance the bond existing between access to the truth and the soul's relation to itself. Who wishes to follow the path of the dialectic, which will establish a relation with Being itself, cannot avoid having a relation to his own soul, or to the other's soul through love, which is such that his soul will thereby be modified and rendered able to accede to the truth.

Dialectic and psychagogy are two sides of one and the same process, of one and the same art, of one and the same *tekhnē*, which is the *tekhnē* of *logos*. Like the philosophical *logos*, the philosophical *tekhnē* of *logos* is a *tekhnē* which makes possible at the same time both knowledge of the truth and the practice or ascesis of the soul on itself. The discourse of rhetoric, the mode of being of rhetorical discourse is such that, on the one hand, indifference to the truth means that it is possible to speak for or against, for the just as for the unjust. And, on the other hand, rhetorical discourse is marked by being concerned solely with the effect to be produced on the soul of the listener. In contrast, the mode of being of philosophical discourse is characterized by the fact that, on the one hand, knowledge of the truth is not just necessary to it, it is not just its precondition, but is a constant function of it. And this constant function of the relation to the truth in discourse, which is the dialectic, is inseparable from the immediate, direct effect which is brought about not just on the soul of the person to whom the discourse is addressed, but also of the person giving the discourse. And this is psychagogy.

The *tekhnē* peculiar to true discourse is characterized by knowledge of the truth and practice of the soul, the fundamental, essential, inseparable connection of dialectic and psychagogy, and it is in being both a dialectician and a psychagogue that the philosopher will really be the parrhesiast, the only parrhesiast, which the rhetorician, the man of rhetoric cannot be or function as. Rhetoric is an *atekhnia* (an absence of *tekhnē*) with regard to discourse.[17] Philosophy is the *etumos tekhnē* (the genuine technique) of true discourse. Then it remains to address the question of writing so far as it can be deduced from this, and as it appears at the end of the discourse. I will try to remind you of it next week.* […†]

---

* Foucault does not return to this problem in the lecture of 9 March. Fortunately there is a trace of what he wanted to add on this point at the end of the manuscript:

"On the basis of this, by reinserting it in this argument we can understand the problematic of writing which closes the dialogue. It should be understood that this development is in a symmetrical position in relation to the remarks made after the three speeches. The question was: was the bad quality of Lysias' speech due to it being written? This has no importance, Socrates had replied. The questions that must be posed concern oral speech as well as writing. And now that the genuine *tekhnē* with regard to discourse is revealed to be philosophy, how is the question of writing presented? The written text is not living; it cannot defend itself, it can only be a means of *hupumnēsia*. […]. There is no division between *logos* and writing, but between two modes of being of *logos*: a rhetorical mode of being, which lacks both the problem of Being to which it is indifferent and that of the being of the soul to which it only addresses itself through flattery; a philosophical mode of being bound to the truth of Being and the practice of the soul and which comprises the transformation of the soul. Logographic mode of being of rhetorical discourse and auto-ascetic mode of being of philosophical discourse."

† M.F.: Do you want a small meeting at a quarter to twelve, for those who are interested? Yes, no?

1. Platon, *Apologie*, 28b, trans. M. Croiset, p. 155; Plato, *Socrates' Defense (Apology)*, p. 14: "He has only one thing to consider in performing any action—that is, whether he is acting rightly or wrongly, like a good man or a bad one."

2. Ibid., 28d, French p. 155; English p. 15: "Where a man has once taken up his stand, either because it seems best to him or in obedience to his orders, there I believe he is bound to remain and face danger, taking no account of death or anything else before dishonor."

3. Ibid., 28e-29b, French pp. 155-157; English p. 15.

4. Ibid., 28e, French pp. 155-157; English p. 15: "God appointed me...to the duty of leading the philosophical life, examining myself and others."

5. Platon, *Phèdre*, 257c, trans. L. Robin, p. 58; Plato, *Phaedrus, The Dialogues of Plato*, Volume 2, trans. Benjamin Jowett, eds. R.M. Hare and D.A. Russell (London: Sphere Books Ltd., 1970) p. 274: "'speech-writer'."

6. Ibid., 258d, French: "In my view, things start to be wicked (*vilaine [aiskhron]*) when one neither speaks nor writes finely, but wickedly and badly (*all'aiskhrōs te kai kakōs*)"; English p. 276: "The disgrace, I assume, begins when a man speaks or writes not well, but badly."

7. Ibid., 259e, French p. 60: "Should it not be a quality of what one will want to say, at least well and finely, that in the speaker's thought there is knowledge of the truth (*talēthes*) of the subject on which he will have to speak?"; English p. 277: "Before there can be any question of excellence in speech, must not the mind of the speaker be furnished with knowledge of the truth of the matter about which he is going to speak?" It is Socrates, in fact, who proposes this hypothesis to Phaedrus.

8. Plutarque, "Apophtegmes laconiens," 260e, in *Œuvres morales*, t. III, trans. F. Fuhrmann (Paris: Les Belles Lettres, 1988) pp. 62-63: "A genuine art (*etumos tekhnē*) of speech, says the Laconian, if it is not attached to the Truth (*aneu tou alētheias*), neither exists nor will ever be able to arise in the future"; English translation by F.C. Babbit as *Sayings of the Spartans*, in *Plutarch's Moralia*, vol. III (London and Cambridge, Mass.: Harvard University Press, "Loeb Classical Library," 1931).

9. Platon, *Phèdre*, 261a, p. 64: "Well, is not the art of oratory, all in all, a psychagogy (*psukhagōgia*), a way of leading souls by means of discourse (*dia logōn*)"; Plato, *Phaedrus*, p. 278: "Is not rhetoric, taken generally, a universal art of enchanting the mind by arguments."

10. Ibid., 262b, French p. 65: "The art of bringing about a change, bit by bit, by using similarities (*tekhnikos estai metabibazein kata smikron dia tōn ōmoiotētōn*) in order in each case to pass from reality to its opposite"; English p. 280: "...a skilled artist in making the gradual departure from truth into the opposite of truth which is effected by the help of resemblances."

11. Ibid., 265e, French p. 72: "Being able to separate into kinds (*kat' eidē*), observing the natural articulations; making every effort not to break any part and avoid the ways of a poor carver"; English p. 284: "division into species according to the natural formation, where the joint is, not breaking any part as a bad carver might."

12. Ibid., 276e, French p. 92; English p. 296.

13. Ibid., 270c, French p. 80; English p. 289.

14. On the difficulty of referring this passage in Plato to a precise Hippocratic teaching, see R. Joly, "Platon, Phèdre et Hippocrate: vingt ans après," in *Formes de pensée dans la Collection Hippocratique. Actes du IVe Colloque international hippocratique* (Geneva: Droz, 1983) pp. 407-422.

15. Platon, *Phèdre*, 270e, p. 81: "On the contrary is its clear that the teaching of eloquence, if given with art, will reveal in its reality (*tēn ousian*), with exactness, the nature (*tēs phuseōs*) of that to which the student will apply his discourse. Now this object will no doubt be the soul"; English pp. 289-290: "The rhetorician, whose teaching of eloquence is scientific, will particularly set forth the nature of the being to which he addresses his speeches; and this I conceive to be the soul."

16. Ibid., 271c, French p. 82; English p. 290: "Since the power of speech is a guidance of the soul, he who proposes to become an orator must know what forms [or parts] the soul has."

17. Ibid., 274b, French p. 86; English p. 293.

nineteen

9 MARCH 1983

First hour

[
The historical turnaround of parrēsia: *from the political game to the philosophical game.* ⌒ *Philosophy as practice of* parrēsia: *the example of Aristippus.* ⌒ *The philosophical life as manifestation of the truth.* ⌒ *The permanent address to power.* ⌒ *The interpellation of each.* ⌒ *Portrait of the Cynic in Epictetus.* ⌒ *Pericles and Socrates.* ⌒ *Modern philosophy and courage of the truth.*
]

TODAY IS THE LAST session. My project was first of all to finish what I was saying to you about the parrhesiast philosopher in Plato. I have tried to examine profiles of this parrhesiast philosopher, first in the *Letters* VII and VIII, and then in the *Phaedrus*. Today I would like to do the same with regard to the *Gorgias*, which brings out, I think, a third aspect of the parrhesiastic function of philosophy. And then, of course, I was meaning and still mean to conclude. Only, you know me, I was likely to drag on indefinitely and not come to a conclusion. So I was wondering if we should not begin by concluding, before moving on to this third part, this third aspect, this third profile of the parrhesiast philosopher. I was hesitating about this when the photocopying [service] informed me that there was a problem and the text I wanted to distribute [from the *Gorgias*] would not be ready before ten at the earliest, if you will be able to have it at all. Consequently the order of things has determined the series of my statements. So there's no alternative but to begin by concluding. You will make a note of this, if you will, in a small corner of your mind, and then, in the second hour, I will come back once again to a certain aspect of philosophical *parrēsia* that I would nonetheless like to emphasize because it has its place in the table I would like to draw up. So forgive this inversion of chronologies and logics. So, to start with, let's conclude.

In the first part of my lectures, you recall, I tried to analyze a form of *parrēsia* as it appears in Euripides or Thucydides. And we can put this form of *parrēsia* under the sign, symbol, or mark of Pericles. Let's call this, if you like, the Periclean moment of *parrēsia*. And then I tried to outline something of what could be called the Socratic-Platonic moment of *parrēsia*. While the Periclean moment is situated, of course, in the second half of the fifth century, the Socratic and Platonic moment will be situated in the first half, even right at the start of the fourth century. It seems to me that philosophical practice will be taken up with this Platonic moment of *parrēsia* for some time, even for a long time. [...*] So the first part was the Periclean moment of *parrēsia*. The second was the Platonic moment, which sets off, I think, at least the history of philosophy considered as a certain practice of veridiction.

In short, I tried to show you that we see a sort of shift of the places and forms of the practice of *parrēsia*. With the Platonic moment I have tried to locate we see what happens when the main part of parrhesiastic practice no longer takes place on the political stage, no longer principally on the political stage—understood in the strict, institutional sense of the term, with the Assembly, courts, and all those decision making sites—but in philosophy. I do not mean at all—and we must be very clear about this—that *parrēsia*, truth-telling disappeared from the field of politics. The problem of the practice of *parrēsia* in the political field will continue to be posed, and in new terms, throughout the history of political institutions in Antiquity up to and including the Roman Empire. After all, the question of the emperor's counselor, the question of the freedom given by the emperor to his entourage to tell him or not tell him the truth, his need to listen to flatterers, or his

---

* M.F. [*a humming noise covers his voice*]: You can't hear? You can't hear, but neither can I. Well, I hear myself, but not what I am saying [*the noise stops*]. Good, so this Platonic moment of *parrēsia* seems to me to take up philosophical practice for a long time, or more exactly if you like... [*the same noise again*]. I quite like the idea that the project of illogicality on which I am resolved finds expression in such drastic sanctions...

courage in accepting being told the truth, will all continue to be a political problem. So I do not mean at all that this question of *parrēsia* is confiscated once and for all by philosophy. Nor do I mean that philosophy was born from the transfer of political *parrēsia* to a different site, which would be a serious historical error. Obviously philosophy existed before Socrates practices his *parrēsia*. I mean simply, and think that this is nevertheless not without significance, that there was a sort of gradual diversion of at least a part and a set of functions of *parrēsia* towards and into philosophical practice which induced, once again not by any means the very birth of philosophy, not at all as a radical origin, but a certain inflection of philosophical discourse, philosophical practice, and the philosophical life. It is the moment of this inflection of philosophical discourse, practice, and life by political *parrēsia* that I have tried to reconstruct. At the same time that philosophy becomes the site, or rather one of the sites of *parrēsia*—at least as important as that of politics and in a perpetual relationship of vis-à-vis, of challenge with political *parrēsia*—another actor of *parrēsia*, another parrhesiast appears. This is no longer the famous citizen of *Ion*, for example, or of Thucydides' account of how Pericles performed his political role at Athens. The parrhesiast who now appears is no longer the man who, as a citizen, has the same rights as everyone else, as every other citizen, that is to say, the right to speak, but with something extra which is the ascendancy in the name of which he can speak out and undertake to lead others. The parrhesiast is now someone else with a different profile, a different character. This is no longer simply, solely, or exactly that citizen among other citizens and a bit in the forefront of them. He is, you remember—we saw this with Socrates—a citizen, of course, like the others, who speaks like them, who speaks the language of everyone, but yet who holds himself, in a way, aside from them. This substitution, or rather this doubling of the political parrhesiast, who is a citizen in the forefront of the others, by the philosopher, who is a citizen like the others, speaking the same language as everyone else, but aside from the others, appears to me to be another aspect of the same transformation that I have tried to reconstruct.

So, if you like, political *parrēsia*, with all the problems it raises and will continue to raise until the end of Antiquity, does not disappear, and there is no sudden, radical birth of philosophy. But around philosophy, in philosophy, there is the formation of another focal point of *parrēsia*. So another focal point of *parrēsia* was lit up in ancient culture, in Greek culture, a focal point of *parrēsia* which did not undermine the first, but which will acquire increasing importance through its own strength and through the transformation of political conditions and institutional structures which will clearly reduce quite considerably the role of political *parrēsia* with all the dimensions, importance, value, and effects that it had in the field of democracy. The disappearance of democratic structures does not mean the total disappearance of the question of political *parrēsia*, but clearly it greatly restricts its field, effects, and problematic. And as a result, philosophical *parrēsia*, in its complex relationship with politics, can only assume greater importance. In short, *parrēsia*, the function of freely and courageously telling the truth, is gradually displaced, shifts its emphases, and increasingly enters the field of the practice of philosophy. Again, it should be understood that the daughter of *parrēsia* is certainly not the whole of philosophy, philosophy since its origin, philosophy in all its aspects, but philosophy understood as the free courage of telling the truth and, in telling the truth courageously, taking ascendancy over others so as to conduct them properly in a game in which the parrhesiast himself must accept a risk, even that of death. Philosophy thus defined as the free courage of telling the truth so as to take ascendancy over others and conduct them properly, even at the risk of death, is, I think, the daughter of *parrēsia*. Anyway, it seems to me that this is the form in which philosophical practice asserts itself throughout Antiquity.

As very early evidence of this I will just take what was already shown by a contemporary of Socrates. This is Aristippus, as described by Diogenes Laertius, who also appears straightaway as a parrhesiast, symmetrically to Socrates and Plato, in a different way for sure, but no doubt in the way that most philosophers of Antiquity will be parrhesiasts. Aristippus was also a philosopher who, like Plato, had dealings with the tyrant Dionysius. Moreover, Dionysius had great respect for him—well a relative respect, you will see. And, like Plato, Aristippus demonstrated his *parrēsia* in his stormy relationship with Dionysius, but obviously in a somewhat different way, since this is the anecdote reported by Diogenes Laertius: "Aristippus did not become angry when Dionysius spat in his face, and as he was censured for accepting

Dionysus' spit, he said: 'Look at the fishermen, if they let themselves get drenched by the sea in order to catch a gudgeon, am I, who wants to catch a whale, unable to bear some spittle?"[1] So you see this other kind of game, this other form of *parrēsia*, in which the philosopher is once again dealing with the tyrant, the governor, and having to play a certain game of truth in relation to him. But whereas Plato's dignity did not allow him to put up with insults, Aristippus accepts Dionysius' insults. He accepts them in order to be more certain of guiding him better, as one catches a whale. Is some spittle too much to bear when one is catching a whale, a big fish, that is to say, a tyrant? But—this taking place in the general framework of what for Aristippus, Socrates, Plato, and, it seems to me, all of ancient philosophy was the general function of philosophy, that is to say, the possibility of speaking courageously and freely, and telling one's truth courageously and freely—when asked "what benefit he had got from philosophy," Aristippus replied: "That of being able to speak freely to everyone."[2]

It seems to me, in fact, that ancient philosophy does appear as a *parrēsia* in different aspects. First, the fact that ancient philosophy is a form of life should be interpreted in the general framework of this parrhesiastic function which ran through, permeated, and sustained it. What is a philosophical life? It is, of course, a particular choice of existence entailing the renunciation of certain things. But if the philosophical life is the renunciation of some things, it is not so much, or at any rate it is not only in order to carry out a purification of existence—which is what Christian asceticism will be. This dimension of purification certainly existed in ascetic forms of the philosophical life, and it had its roots, moreover, in the old Pythagorean tradition, which should not be forgotten or its importance belittled. But it seems to me that if we look at things over the long term—that is to say, in the history of ancient philosophy up to the second century C.E.—then this Pythagorean [function] of purification, traces of which remain, of course, in Plato, was not the most constant or important function for defining the nature of the philosophical life or for the assertion that philosophy is inseparable from a certain form of life. The philosophical life is a manifestation of the truth. It is a testimony. Through the type of life one leads, the set of choices one makes, the things one renounces and those one accepts, how one dresses, and how one speaks, etcetera, the philosophical life should be from start to finish the manifestation of this truth.

So, on this theme we could return to the famous *Lives of Philosophers* recounted especially by Diogenes Laertius, and also by Philostratus. These *Lives of Philosophers*—I am sure many of you are familiar with them— are very interesting. What is interesting is seeing the very systematic way in which doctrinal elements, physical, material descriptions of the philosopher's *habitus*, his *ēthos*, and some anecdotes, little stories, scenes, fragments of dialogue, and retorts are linked and braided together as it were. In these *Lives of Philosophers*, these three elements (doctrine; physical bearing, *ēthos*; little scene) comprise the way in which the philosophical life makes itself known as a manifestation of truth. To live philosophically is to show the truth through the *ēthos* (the way one lives), the way one reacts (to a situation, a scene, when confronted with a particular situation), and obviously the doctrine one teaches; it is to show the truth in all these aspects and through these three vehicles (*ēthos* of the scene, *kairos* of the situation, and doctrine).

Second, it seems to me that throughout its history in ancient culture philosophy is also *parrēsia* not only because it is life, but also because, in one way or another, it never ceased to address those who govern. And it did so, of course, in very diverse ways. Addressing those who govern may take the form of Cynical insolence, of which I have given you some examples. It may take the form of the interpellation of the powerful in the form of the diatribe addressed directly or indirectly to those who exercise power, criticizing the way in which they exercise it. Obviously, this intervention, this way of addressing those who govern may take the form of the Prince's education; this is the case par excellence of Seneca. It may also take the form of membership of political circles which are often, if not always, circles of political opposition. Such was the role, for example, of the Roman Epicurean circles in the first century before and the first century after [Christ]. This was the case above all with the big Stoic circles of the first and second centuries, in which we find fundamental figures like Musonius Rufus.[3] It may also take the form of advice given to a particular sovereign in very particular circumstances. There is a very interesting passage in the *Life and Times of Apollonius of Tyana* by Philostratus[4] which tells how, for example, at the time of Vespasian's rebellion, when he is raising legions and undertaking to seize the Empire, he consults two philosophers, one of whom is Apollonius, to ask them what is the best regime he should strive for when he has taken power. Should it be an autocratic and above all hereditary monarchy? Should it be a sort of princedom tempered by the triumvirate? This is the type of advice that the philosopher considers himself authorized to give. So, philosophy is a form of life, and it is also a sort of both private and public office of political advice. This seems to me to be a constant dimension of ancient philosophy.

I think that ancient philosophy is also a *parrēsia* in a third way, in the sense that it is a perpetual interpellation addressed, collectively or individually, to persons, private individuals, and which may take the form of the great Cynic and Stoic type of preaching in the theater, the assemblies, at the games, or in the forum, and which may be the interpellation of an individual or of a crowd. There is also that rather curious structure of the ancient philosophical schools, which function quite differently from medieval schools (the monastic school or medieval university), and obviously from our schools. How the school of Epictetus functioned is very significant from this point of view, inasmuch as it was a sort of supple structure whose teaching or speech could be addressed, alternately or simultaneously, to permanent students who intended to become professional philosophers, to students who came to follow a course in order, so to speak, to complete their studies and training, and to people who needed some time to recover a sort of philosophical health—a sort of philosophical refresher course. And then there were those who, passing through on a journey, or simply because they had heard of the teaching and its value, came for a consultation.[5] Epictetus' *Discourses* should be read as addressing either all these categories of listeners at the same time, or, more frequently, this or that particular category of listener, so that they do not all have the same value and meaning inasmuch as they are not all inserted in the same pedagogical framework. And then again we should also cite the rarer, more closed communities like those of the Epicureans in which, here again, the game of truth-telling was so important. And it seems to me that it is in the Epicureans that we see the development of the practice of confession (*aveu*), of reciprocal confidence, of the detailed account of the faults one has committed which one recounts either to one's director or even to others, in order to get advice.[6] It seems to me that in these different aspects ancient philosophy can appear as a sort of great elaboration of this general form, this general project of *parrēsia*, of the courage of telling the truth to others in order to conduct them in their own conduct.

So if we look at ancient philosophy in this way, that is to say, as a sort of parrhesiastic practice, you can see that we cannot judge it by the standards of what Western philosophy later became, or at least by the standards of the way in which Western philosophy, from let's say Descartes to Hegel by way of Kant and the others, is represented today. Modern Western philosophy, at least if we take it as it is currently presented as an object of academic or university study, has relatively few points in common with the parrhesiastic philosophy I have tried to talk about. This ancient, parrhesiastic philosophy, in its different doctrines, sects, forms of intervention and expression—and here too the role played by letters, theoretical treatises, aphorisms, lectures, and sermons should be studied—should not be understood as a system given as a system of truths in a determinate domain, or a system of truths with regard to Being itself. Throughout Antiquity philosophy is really lived as the free questioning of men's conduct by a truth-telling which accepts the risk of danger to itself.

To that extent it seems to me that the most typical form of ancient philosophy is that described by Epictetus at the very end of the golden age of this ancient philosophy, in the famous discourse 22 of Book III of the *Discourses* in which he portrays the Cynic. This discourse and the way in which philosophy appears in it mark out a sort of boundary to the great history of ancient philosophy as *parrēsia*. It marks a boundary in two senses since, on the one hand, I think we arrive at a certain boundary of what ancient philosophy had been, and it is a boundary because one senses the emergence of something like the place in which Christian thought, Christian asceticism, Christian preaching, and Christian truth-telling will be able to make its entry.[7] I would just like to quote some passages from this discourse which show how the parrhesiastic function I have just schematized is seen in operation.

First, philosophy as way of life, as flagrant way of life, as perpetual manifestation of the truth. The Cynic, Epictetus explains, is someone who detaches himself from all artifice and ornament. He is someone who detaches himself from everything pertaining to the passions. Above all he is someone who does not seek to conceal his desires, passions, dependencies, etcetera, but who presents himself naked, in his destitution. "You should know this: other men make use of the shelter of their walls, their homes, and the dark to perform actions of this kind [that is to say: anger, resentment, envy, pity; M.F.], and they have a thousand ways of concealing them: one keeps his door shut, another posts someone outside his bedroom: 'if someone comes, say he's out, he's not free'. But the Cynic, instead of all these protections, should shelter behind his reserve [the word translated as 'reserve' is *aidōs*: this is that kind of relationship to himself by which the individual respects himself and has nothing to hide, and so has nothing of himself to hide; *aidōs* should not be understood as a kind of reserve like modesty, if you like, as we understand it, nor does it have anything to do with shame; *aidōs* is the kind of transparency by which the individual, when he has nothing to hide, actually hides nothing, this is *aidōs*; well, the Cynic therefore, instead of all these protections—these walls and servants which keep away the importunate, etcetera—should shelter behind his *aidōs*; M.F.]; otherwise, he will display his indecency in his nudity and in the open. His reserve is for him his house, his door, the guards outside his bedroom, and his dark. No, he should not wish to conceal anything that concerns him (or else he has disappeared, he has destroyed the Cynic in him, the man who lives in the open, the free man, he has begun to fear some external object, he has begun to need to hide), and when he wishes to conceal something, he cannot."[8] So, you see, the Cynic is someone who lives out in the open, and who lives in the open because he is a free man, without anything to fear from the outside. In his life he is the manifest truth.

The second characteristic of the Cynic, which confirms what I have told you, is the fact that to tell the truth he is ready to address even the powerful, even those to be feared, without thinking of the danger of losing his life if his truth-telling were to irritate them. And evoking the example of Diogenes, who addressed Philip in his well-known offhand way, Epictetus comments: "In reality, the Cynic is a scout for men, finding out what is favorable to them and what is hostile. He must explore accurately, then return to state the truth without letting himself be so paralyzed by fear that he designates as enemies those who are not, and without letting his mind be disturbed or confused in any other way by representations [which may come to him; M.F.]."[9] The Cynic, the philosopher, is therefore someone for whom stating the truth should never be held back by fear. The third aspect of this philosopher presented by Epictetus is that in this role as scout who states the truth without fear of danger, the Cynic, of course, saves himself. He not only saves himself, but on top of that, through this salvation and the courage with which he tells the truth, he is able to be of service to all humanity: "If it gives you pleasure, ask me too if the Cynic will take part in public affairs. Simpleton, can you imagine a more noble politics than the one with which he concerns himself? At Athens, will he mount the tribune to speak of revenues and resources, [absolutely not, the Cynic is—M.F.] the man who must argue with all men, with Athenians as well as with Corinthians or Romans [and he must discuss—M.F.] not resources or public revenues, nor peace and war, but [he must speak—M.F.] of happiness and unhappiness, of good and ill fortune, of servitude and freedom. When a man is actively engaged in such a politics, do you ask me if he participates in public affairs? Ask me if he will occupy an office and I will reply again: Fool, what more noble office is there than the one he is now exercising!"[10]

Basically, shortly after Epictetus, six or seven centuries after Socrates, I think the different forms of Christian teaching will take over from this parrhesiastic function and gradually divest it of philosophy. In the first place, new relations to Scripture and Revelation, new structures of authority within the Church, and a new definition of asceticism, no longer defined on the basis of self control, but on renunciation of the world, will, I believe, profoundly change the system of truth-telling. For a number of centuries it will no longer be philosophy that plays the role of *parrēsia*. What I would suggest is that after moving from politics to this philosophical focal point, philosophy's great parrhesiastic function was in fact transferred a second time from the philosophical focal point to what we can call the Christian pastoral.

Only, the question I would like to pose is this: could we not consider modern philosophy, at least the philosophy which reappears from the sixteenth century, as the reallocation of the main functions of *parrēsia* back within philosophy, and as the retrieval of *parrēsia*, which had been institutionalized and organized, and which had functioned in multiple, very rich, dense, and interesting ways in the Christian pastoral? Is this not what will now be retrieved, taken up again, and put back in play with different rules of the game in modern European philosophy? And to that extent, maybe the history of European philosophy from the sixteenth century should not be seen as a series of doctrines which undertake to say what is true or false concerning politics, or science, or morality. Maybe we could envisage the history of modern European philosophy as a history of practices of veridiction, as a history of practices of *parrēsia*. Could we not read modern philosophy, in at least some of its most fundamental aspects and significations, as a parrhesiastic enterprise? Is it not as *parrēsia*, much more than as doctrine about the world, politics, Nature, etcetera, that European philosophy is actually inserted in reality and history, or rather in the reality that is our history? Is it not as *parrēsia* to be continually taken up again that philosophy continually recommences? And to that extent is not philosophy a phenomenon which is unique and specific to Western societies?

If we see the way in which modern philosophy actually emerged in the sixteenth century from discussions which for the most part revolved around the nature of the Christian pastoral, its effects, structures of authority, and the relationship to the Word, to the Text, to Scripture it imposed, and if we want to look upon philosophy's emergence in the sixteenth century as criticism of these pastoral practices, then I think that we can consider that it was as *parrēsia* that it actually asserted itself anew. After all, if Descartes' *Meditations* are in fact an enterprise to found a scientific discourse in truth, [they are] also an enterprise of *parrēsia* in the sense that it is actually the philosopher as such who speaks in saying "I," and in affirming his *parrēsia* in that precisely scientifically founded form of evidence, and he does this in order first of all to play a particular role in relation to the structures of power of ecclesiastical, scientific, and political authority in the name of which he will be able to conduct men's conduct. The moral project, present from the start of the Cartesian enterprise, is not just something added on to an essential project of founding a science. It seems to me that in the great movement which goes from the statement in the first person of what Descartes thinks in the form of evidence up to the final project of conducting men in their life and in the life of their bodies, you have the great resumption of the parrhesiastic function that philosophy had in the ancient world. And in this sense I think that it would be difficult to find the equivalent to this in the philosophy of the Middle Ages when, organized according to theology, it left the parrhesiastic function to the Christian pastoral. Anyway, if I began this year's lectures with Kant, it is inasmuch as Kant's text on the *Aufklärung* is a certain way for philosophy, through the critique of the *Aufklärung*, to become aware of problems which were traditionally problems of *parrēsia* in antiquity, which will re-emerge in the sixteenth and seventeenth centuries, and which became aware of themselves in the *Aufklärung*, and particularly in Kant's text.

Anyway [...*], it was so as to suggest to you a history of philosophy which is not organized according to either of the two schemas which are so often prevalent today, that of a history of philosophy which would seek its radical origin in something like a forgetting, or the other schema which would consist in envisaging the history of philosophy as progress, avatar, or development of a rationality. I think we can also do the history of philosophy, neither as forgetting nor as the development of rationality, but as a series of episodes and forms—recurrent forms, forms which are transformed—of veridiction. The history of philosophy, in short, as movement of *parrēsia*, as redistribution of *parrēsia*, as varied game of truth-telling, philosophy envisaged thus in what could be called its allocutionary force. This, if you like, was the general theme I wanted to develop or suggest in this year's lectures.

I would now like to return a bit more precisely to what I have tried to say, reminding you of the two images that I tried to clarify. In the first place, there is the image of Pericles which appeared very indirectly in *Ion*, but very directly in Thucydides. You know what this image was. In the people's Assembly, where each has been able to give his views in turn and freely, this citizen gets up, takes the floor, and speaks with the authority of someone who is the foremost Athenian. And he speaks in the solemn, ritual, and codified forms of rhetoric. In this way he gives an opinion, which he reminds the audience is his own. But this opinion may become, should become, and will in fact

---

* Inaudible.

become the city's opinion. And, as a result, through this now shared opinion, the foremost citizen and the city itself must together take a risk, which will be that of success or failure. This character is Pericles. Well, some years later, we can make out another character, Socrates, who, while steadfastly refusing to go to the Assembly and address the people, speaks the everyday language of everyone in the streets of Athens. Why does he employ this common everyday language? So as to be able to look after himself by visibly and manifestly refusing the injustices that may be done to him, but also by encouraging others, questioning them casually [so as to] take care of them by showing them that, knowing nothing, they really should take care of themselves. And he takes upon himself the other danger that such an activity entails. He takes it upon himself till his last breath, even to the point of accepted death. So these are the two images on which I have tried to structure the lectures, and I have tried to show you the transition from one to the other.

But—and this is the other set of conclusions that I would like to draw—in revealing this transition, this transformation from one character to the other, it seems to me that we can reveal some of the three aspects in which ancient philosophy manifested and practiced the parrhesiastic functions. The first is the one I tried to extract from the Letters VII and VIII, that is to say, the relationship of philosophical *parrēsia* to politics, which I tried to show was one of exteriority, of both distance and correlation. This philosophical *parrēsia* was a particular non-political way of speaking to those who govern, and of speaking [to them] about the way in which they should govern others and govern themselves. This indirect relationship of exteriority and correlation with politics puts philosophy in a sort of vis-à-vis relationship to politics, a vis-à-vis defined by its exteriority as well as by its irreducibility; a sort of restive and insistent exteriority towards politics. And it seems to me that this is where both the courage peculiar to *parrēsia*, and the fact that philosophical *parrēsia*, you recall, tests its own reality in this relation to politics, become apparent.

The second aspect I wanted to show—I focused on this last week—is that with regard to rhetoric, philosophical *parrēsia* no longer stands in that relationship it has with politics of vis-à-vis or correlative exteriority, but in a relationship of opposition and exclusion.

This appeared clearly in the *Phaedrus*. The relationship of philosophy to rhetoric is very different from its relationship to politics. It is no longer a relationship of asserted exteriority and sustained correlation. It is a relationship of strict contradiction, of constant polemic, of exclusion. Where there is philosophy, there should be a relationship to politics. But where there is philosophy, there can be no rhetoric. Philosophy is defined in the *Phaedrus* as an alternative and opposition to rhetoric. If the politician is, in a way, an other in relation to the philosopher, he is an other to whom the philosopher speaks, and he is an other [with whom] the philosopher tests the very reality of his philosophical practice. The rhetor, on the other hand, is an other in relation to the philosopher in the sense that where there is the philosopher, the rhetor must be driven out. The two cannot co-exist; their relationship is one of exclusion. It is only by breaking with rhetoric that philosophical discourse, in the very act of expelling it, can constitute itself and affirm itself as a constant and permanent relationship to truth. You remember that we saw this in the *Phaedrus* when what appeared in the expulsion and disqualification of rhetoric was not at all the eulogy of a logocentrism that would make speech the form peculiar to philosophy, but the affirmation of the constant connection of philosophical discourse—no matter whether in written or oral form—to the truth, in the double form of the dialectic and pedagogy. So philosophy can exist only by sacrificing rhetoric. But, in this sacrifice philosophy demonstrates, asserts, and constitutes its permanent connection to the truth.

Finally the third aspect—and I will try to analyze this shortly, asking you to put it in its place, that is to say, before everything I have just been telling you—is one that can be found in many of Plato's dialogues, but in the *Gorgias* in particular. So, the *Letters*, if you like, would define the relationship of philosophy as *parrēsia* to politics. The *Phaedrus* would show the nature of philosophy as *parrēsia* as opposed to rhetoric. And then the *Gorgias*, it seems to me, shows the relationship of philosophy to action on souls, the government of others, the direction and conduction of the other person: philosophy as psychagogy. Anyway, parrhesiastic philosophy appears in this text in its essential relationship, no longer to politics, no longer to rhetoric, but to psychagogy, to the guidance and conduction of souls. Parrhesiastic philosophy in its psychagogic activity is no longer addressed to the politician or to the rhetor, but to the disciple, the other soul, the person one pursues, to the person whose soul and possibly whose body one pursues. And so we would have to deal with a third type of relationship. This is no longer the relationship in the form of vis-à-vis (philosophy vis-à-vis politics, as was the case in the *Letters*). It is no longer the relationship of exclusion with regard to rhetoric. It is a certain relationship of inclusion, reciprocity, and twinning, a relationship which is pedagogic and erotic, and this is what is defined in the *Gorgias* and what appears to me to be the third aspect, the third profile of the philosopher as parrhesiast. And we can say that philosophy in these three profiles (relationship to politics, exclusion of rhetoric, pursuit of the other soul) has taken up, in a way, the principal functions that we were able to outline concerning Periclean, political *parrēsia*.

After all, the great Athenian Pericles, you recall, also had the courage and the free courage to tell the truth in order to act on others. But Pericles exercised his free courage in the political field itself. Socrates, Plato, and the ancient philosophers will exercise their courage in relation to the political institutions, but no longer within the political institutions. Pericles told the truth on the sole condition that what he said was what he thought to be true. Socrates, Plato, and then all of ancient philosophy will be able to tell the truth only subject to more costly conditions. Their discourse will have to be organized according to the principles of the dialectic. In short, in the case of Pericles it was just a question of acting by persuading those who listened to him. In order to succeed in acting on the soul of others, Socrates, and then Plato, or the other philosophers, will have to deploy many other methods than those of pure and simple persuasion.

If in fact we see how the three functions of Pericles' political *parrēsia* are transformed in Socratic *parrēsia* and then in the philosophical *parrēsia* of Antiquity, then you see also taking shape in these three functions what appear to me to be the most fundamental elements and characteristics of modern philosophy in the historical mode of being that it defines for itself. Once again, what is modern philosophy if we read it as a history of veridiction in its parresiastic form? It is a practice which tests its reality in its relationship to politics. It is a practice which finds its function of truth in the criticism of illusion, deception, trickery, and flattery. And finally it is a practice which finds [the object of its] exercise* in the transformation of the subject by himself and of the subject by the other. Philosophy as exteriority with regard to a politics which constitutes its test of reality, philosophy as critique of a domain of illusion which challenges it to constitute itself as true discourse, and philosophy as ascesis, that is to say, as constitution of the subject by himself, seem to me to constitute the mode of being of modern philosophy, or maybe that which, in the mode of being of modern philosophy, takes up the mode of being of ancient philosophy.

Anyway, if it is possible to sustain this perspective you can well understand why philosophy, modern as well as ancient philosophy, is or at any rate would be wrong to want to say what must be done in the realm of politics and how one should govern. It would be wrong to want to say what is true or false in the realm of science. And it would equally be wrong to want to give itself the mission of the liberation or disalienation of the subject himself. It is not for philosophy to say what should be done in politics. It has to exist in a permanent and restive exteriority with regard to politics, and it is in this that it is real. Secondly, it is not for philosophy to divide the true and the false in the domain of science. It has to constantly practice its criticism with regard to deception, trickery, and illusion, and it is in this that it plays the dialectical game of its own truth. Finally, third, it is not for philosophy to disalienate the subject. It has to define the forms in which the relationship to self may possibly be transformed. I think that philosophy as ascesis, as critique, and as restive exteriority to politics is the mode of being of modern philosophy. It was, at any rate, the mode of being of ancient philosophy.

These were the things that I wanted to draw out somewhat from this history of *parrēsia* and of the transfer from political *parrēsia* to philosophical *parrēsia*. So you can see that there is a development missing from this schema, a gap. This is what should have been [devoted] to the *Gorgias*, that is to say, to the way in which Plato defines or describes philosophy, no longer therefore in its relationship to the governor, no longer therefore in its relationship to the rhetor, but in its relationship with the person in whom it takes an interest, that is to say, the other

---

* M.F.: the exercise of its practice.

person, the young man or anyone in whom it is interested, who it pursues, and whose soul it tries to form. It is this type of relationship—very different from [that] of vis-à-vis that we found with politics, very different from [that] of exclusion with regard to rhetoric—that I would like to try to analyze starting from one or two texts. So, if you like, we will break off there. [...*]

---

* M.F.: I will try to find the photocopy of the text I am talking about.

1. Diogène Laërce [Diogenes Laertius], *Vie, doctrines et sentences des philosophes illustres*, vol. 1, p. 128; English translation by R.D. Hicks, "Aristippus" in *Diogenes Laertius I. Lives of Eminent Philosophers*, Book II, §67 (Cambridge Mass. and London: Harvard University Press/William Heinemann Ltd., "Loeb Classical Library," 1925) p. 197: "He bore with Dionysius when he spat on him, and to one who took him to task he replied, 'If the fishermen let themselves be drenched with sea-water in order to catch a gudgeon, ought I not to endure to be wetted with negus in order to take a blenny?'"

2. Ibid.; English p. 197: "Being asked what he had gained from philosophy, he replied, 'The ability to feel at ease in any society.'"

3. Foucault referred several times to this author in *The Hermeneutics of the Subject*, but from an ethical point of view. However, there is a more political argument on Musonius Rufus and Rubellious Plautus in the manuscript for the lecture of 27 January 1982.

4. Philostrate, *Vie d'Apollonius de Tyane*, Book V, ch. 27-37, in P. Grimal, ed., *Romans grecs et latins* (Paris: Gallimard, La Pléiade, 1963) pp. 1194-1206; English translation by C.P. Eells as Philostratus the Elder, *Life and Times of Apollonius of Tyana* (Stanford: Stanford University Publications, 1923). Actually, this political debate involves three philosophers: Apollonius, Euphrates, and Dion.

5. On the operation of the school of Epictetus, see the lecture of 27 January 1982, first hour, *L'Herméutique du sujet*, pp. 133-137; *The Hermeneutic of the Subject*, pp. 138-142.

6. On this point see Foucault's analysis in the lecture of 10 March 1982, first hour (ibid., French pp. 373-374; English pp. 390-391) based mainly on the fragments of Philodemus' *Peri parrēsias*.

7. On Christian *parrēsia* one must refer to the 1984 lectures.

8. Epictetus (Épictète), *Entretiens*, Book III, 22, 14-16, trans. A. Jagu (Paris: Les Belles Lettres, 1963) pp. 71-72; English translation by W.A. Oldfather as *The Discourses as reported by Arrian*, vol. II, Book III, xxii, pp. 135-137: "For this you ought to know: Other men have the protection of their walls and their houses and darkness, when they do anything of that sort, and they have many things to hide them. A man closes his door, stations someone at the entrance to his bedroom: 'If anyone comes, tell him "He is not at home, he is not at leisure".' But the Cynic, instead of all these defences, has to make his self-respect his protection; if he does not, he will be disgracing himself naked and out of doors. His self-respect is his house, his door, his guards at the entrance to his bedroom, his darkness. For neither ought he to wish to keep concealed anything that is his (otherwise he is lost, he has destroyed the Cynic within him, the man of outdoor life, the free man; he has begun to fear something external, he has begun to need something to conceal him), nor can he keep it concealed when he wishes to do so."

9. Ibid., 24-25, French p. 73; English p. 139: "For the Cynic is truly a scout, to find out what things are friendly to men and what hostile; and he must first do his scouting accurately, and on returning must tell the truth, not driven by fear to designate as enemies those who are not such, nor in any other fashion be distraught or confused by his external impressions."

10. Ibid., 83-85, French p. 82; English pp. 159-161: "If you will, ask me also if he is to be active in politics. You ninny, are you looking for any nobler politics than that in which he is engaged? Or would you have someone in Athens step forward and discourse about incomes and revenues, when he is the person who ought to talk with all men, Athenians, Corinthians, and Romans alike, not about revenues, or income, or peace, or war, but about happiness and unhappiness, about success and failure, about slavery and freedom? When a man is engaging in such exalted politics, do *you* ask me if he is to engage in politics? Ask me also, if he will hold office. Again I will tell you: Fool, what nobler office will he hold than that which he now has?"

twenty

9 MARCH 1983

Second hour

[
Study of the Gorgias. ∽ *The obligation of confession (*aveu*) in
Plato: the context of liquidation of rhetoric.* ∽ *The three qualities
of Callicles:* epistemē; parrēsia; eunoia. ∽ *Agonistic game
against egalitarian system.* ∽ *Socratic speech:* basanos *and*
homologia.
]

I WILL REPEAT WHAT I have said: this is the last lecture. I assume you
know that this is the last lecture since I have already drawn the conclusions. So, as something of a supplement and to fill a gap, I would like to
return to two texts from the *Gorgias*, basically to one which appears to
me to set out quite well, or at least to outline the type of relationship
that should be established in philosophical *parrēsia*, again, not with the
politician or the rhetor, but with the disciple. This is the third aspect, the
third profile, the third field of activity or exercise of *parrēsia*. […] I had
it in mind to study in turn two texts from the *Gorgias*. I will pass more
quickly over one of these inasmuch as, despite the importance given to it,
it does not appear to me to correspond exactly to philosophical *parrēsia*.
In the other text Plato employs the word *parrēsia*, and this is the first
use of the word in what could be called the field of practices of spiritual
direction. Obviously, I would like to stick close to this second text.

Briefly, what I would like to say to you concerning the *Gorgias* is
this. As you know, in the post- or Neo-Platonist classification, the
Gorgias was given the sub-title of *Peri tēs rētorikēs* (On the subject of

rhetoric). And in fact it is a questioning of rhetoric, but it is completely different from that in the *Phaedrus*. As you know, the criticism of rhetoric in the *Phaedrus* is carried out through an imitation of rhetoric—a complex game inasmuch as rhetoric is itself an art of flattery—at the end of which it is shown that with regard to love it is not rhetorical discourse that can make the true eulogy of true love, but another type of discourse which must be permanently and continually linked with the truth in the form of the dialectic. The *Gorgias* raises the question of rhetoric, but it does so differently, and in two ways. There is a double difference.

In the first place, it is different because the *Gorgias* raises the question: "What is rhetoric?" And here we should refer, right at the start of the text, to a series of questions focused on this. While successive interlocutors, especially Gorgias and Polos, want to praise rhetoric, Socrates replies each time: But no, that is not the question, what we want to know is *tis an eiē tekhnē tēs rētorikēs* (what is the rhetorical art, what is the being of rhetorical technique)?[1] And at the end of a first discussion which shows that rhetoric is nothing, to the extent that it is an art of flattery, something happens which does not define but shows what in fact the other *tekhnē* is, that is to say, philosophy as the conduction of souls. [This will be] the transition from rhetoric to this other practice of the conduction of souls starting from a questioning of the being of rhetoric, and the barely theorized demonstration of what philosophical practice is. I say "barely theorized" precisely because there is nevertheless a short passage in which this is what is involved, and [in which] precisely the being of philosophical discourse is linked to the practice of *parrēsia*.

So the first part dealing with the question: "What is rhetoric, what is the being of rhetoric?" arrives at the conclusion that it is nothing, the [general] argument consisting in showing that rhetoric is not capable of attaining what it claims, that is to say, the good. What it does instead is suggest, in place of its own end, something else entirely, which is the imitation, pretence, and illusion of this end, in such a way that for the objective of the good it substitutes its semblance, which is pleasure. So it does not achieve its aim, and the end it attains is nothing. Rhetoric is nothing for these two reasons. And in fact after having acquired this result of the non-being of rhetoric, at least as *tekhnē* (the fact that it does not have the being of a *tekhnē*, of a true art), [having reached this point] at which rhetoric is already nothing, there is, in addition as it were, the text I have reproduced (480a), which is a highly, and, to my mind, unjustly famous text. Let's quickly read, if you like, this text: "But if it happens that either oneself or someone for whom one cares does wrong, one should hasten willingly to where one will be punished most quickly, to the judge, as one would go to the physician for fear that the injustice of evil is not caught in time and deeply corrupts the soul and renders it incurable."[2] And a bit further on (I am going quickly) he says: "When it is a matter of defending our own injustice, or our parents, friends, children, and country when they are guilty, rhetoric, Polus, can be of no use to us; unless on the contrary we accept that we should make use of it to accuse first ourselves, and then all those of our friends or family who have made themselves guilty, hiding nothing, but instead bringing the wrong out into the light so that the guilty be cured through expiation. Then one will strive and urge others not to weaken, to present themselves bravely to the judges, with eyes closed, as though to the physician's iron and fire, disregarding the pain, in love of the beautiful and the good, and, if the wrong deserves blows, advancing to meet them, meeting chains if it deserves chains, being ready to pay if fined, to go into exile if that be the penalty, to die if it is death, always being the first to accuse himself and his kin; orator for this sole purpose of making the wrong evident, the better to deliver himself from the greatest of evils, injustice."[3]

There's no need to tell you why this text interests me, since one of the aspects, one of the questions I would like to put to the history of *parrēsia* concerns the long and slow evolution over several centuries which led from a conception of political *parrēsia* as the right, the privilege of speaking to others in order to guide them (Periclean *parrēsia*) to, I was going to say post-antique *parrēsia*, the *parrēsia* we find after ancient philosophy, in Christianity, where it becomes an obligation to speak of oneself, to tell the truth about oneself, to tell everything about oneself, and to do so in order to be cured.[4] This kind of great mutation from *parrēsia* as "the privilege of free speech in order to guide others" to *parrēsia* as "the obligation of someone who has done wrong to tell everything about himself in order to be saved," is certainly one of the most important aspects of the history of parrhesiastic practice. And, in a sense, this is really what I would like to reconstruct. Now at first sight it seems clear that we have here something like the first expression of this inflection of *parrēsia* from "right to speak to others in order to guide them" to "obligation to speak about oneself in order to be saved." This long history is obviously very important if we want to analyze the relations between subjectivity and truth and the relations between government of self and government of others. And the question I would like to put is this: Can this text really be read as the first formulation of this inflection, of this turnaround? This would make it a paradoxical text, since it is the only recorded instance, it is almost unique here—you will see that this is not entirely the case—and half-foreshadows or seems to prefigure Christian confession five or six centuries in advance. For such a text—its formulations, precepts, and justifications—is very close to what you can find when the practice of penitence is effectively institutionalized—let's say after, or in the course of the third century—and then becomes a constant practice, at least in Christian asceticism or an aspect of Christian asceticism, from the fourth and fifth centuries. At any rate, in texts like those of Saint Cyprian,[5] you can already find again, almost word for word, this obligation, this formulation that when you have done wrong you must run to the person who can at the same time punish you like a judge and cure you like a physician, without, as far as I know—and subject to correction—any Christian author ever referring to this passage from the *Gorgias*, as if they were well aware that it did not involve the same thing at all. Anyway, it doesn't matter; I am putting some question marks here. Maybe we will find some references to the *Gorgias*, but it is absolutely true that at first sight the analogy is quite striking. In any case, in modern commentaries of the text this passage is generally interpreted as a serious model of good moral and civic conduct. We know that when you have committed a bad action it is best, after all, to go to the person who can sentence you and cure you, and this [...*].

Socrates refers twice to this idea moreover—you see, there are two paragraphs—thereby seeming to establish that, if one wishes to

---

* Inaudible.

transform oneself and become just after being unjust, the best way, the best mode of psychagogy would thus be to employ rhetoric on the judicial stage, which is its privileged (I was going to say natural, [rather] institutional) site, to accuse oneself and obtain one's cure through the subsequent punishment. Is not this the true psychagogy? And then, the commentators find confirmation that this is what Platonic psychagogy is, the acknowledged prefiguration, authenticated by Plato himself, of what will become a centuries and even thousand year old practice, in the fact that in a way this little schema seems to prefigure what Socrates himself had to do when he was accused and did not flee his judges. On the contrary, he faced up to things, recognized grievances against him, and accepted the punishment. It is also true that the theme that sin is a disease is frequently found in Plato, and it is of Pythagorean origin. Sin is a disease, which means that it should be understood on the double register of an impurity to be expelled and a disease to be cured. Purification and cure are mixed together in the Pythagorean tradition and it is clear that there is an echo of this here. Finally, in Greek tragedy too we quite frequently find the idea that sin being both disease and impurity, the sentence which punishes, the judgment delivered, the punishment imposed are cure and purification at the same time. We may therefore suppose that, supported by other confirmations and echoing other ideas, we have here the theme that the true transformation of the soul must take place through a rhetoric of confession (*aveu*) in a judicial setting where telling the truth about oneself and being punished by someone else will lead to one's transformation from unjust to just. We would therefore have a kind of kernel with a thousand years long destiny. Now if we give this text the kind of positive and immediate meaning that I have just suggested, I think it is of course because we allow our view to be obscured by two anachronistic schemas: the schema of Christian confession (*confession*), with its constant double, judicial and medical reference; and the schema of a penal practice which, since at least the eighteenth century, has always given a therapeutic justification for punishment.

[So,] I do not believe this text can be given this meaning. And nothing appears to me to be further from Platonic psychagogy than the idea that a rhetoric of confession (*aveu*) in a judicial setting could bring about the transformation of the unjust into the just.* Actually, if there are many references in Greek tragedy and other Greek texts to the therapeutic function of the tribunal, most of the time the therapy demanded from the tribunal does not concern the soul of the person who committed the offense. It is a therapy that must be applied to the city. Take the example of Oedipus: punishing the criminal does not cure him; it expels from the city an evil, which is actually seen as both an impurity and a disease. It is not psychagogical, it is political. It is a politics of purification which is brought into play by the idea that the tribunal cures; in no way is it a psychagogy of individual souls. Secondly, nor do I think we can invoke the example of Socrates, because, basically, Socrates does not accuse himself, he does something completely different when he is dragged before the court. Socrates does not run to the judge after committing an offense; he does not present himself to the judge at all. On the contrary, it was the judges who prosecuted him. And, on the other hand, if he lets himself be sentenced, this is not at all because he was guilty of an injustice and acknowledged the fact. In the texts, whether from the *Apology*, the *Phaedo*, a bit of the *Crito*, or a passage at the end of the *Gorgias* which alludes, by a sort of retrospective prefiguration, to Socrates' trial[6]—historically in the past, but in the future in the dialogue—Socrates absolutely does not appear as someone who says: I am guilty and that is why I submit to the laws. He says rather: Since citizens make use of just laws to sentence me unjustly, I myself would commit an injustice if I were to try to escape these laws. The recognition I owe the city, the respect due to the laws, means that even if I were prosecuted unjustly, I would hide neither from the proceedings nor from their consequences; that would be injustice. So Socrates' game with regard to his judges has nothing to do with confession; it is another game entirely. It is not a confession of the offense committed, but obedience to the laws so as not to commit an injustice by disobeying them. So let's not cite the example of Socrates to confirm the meaning of this so-called scene of therapeutic and psychagogic confession.

---

* [The French text has "la transformation du juste en injuste," but this seems to be a slip, either of Foucault himself or of his editors. Just before this sentence Foucault speaks of "la transformation du injuste en juste"; G.B.].

So why does Socrates refer here to the confession of misdeeds, and what meaning should we give this passage? It seems to me that first of all we should recall the context. This passage is at the turning point of the, as it were, preliminary discussion with Polus—in which, again, rhetoric is shown to be nothing, at least if one requires it to be a *tekhnē*—and so at the point of transition from this liquidation of rhetoric to philosophical *parrēsia* itself, which will be brought out through the discussion with Callicles in the second part. We should take this text as a sort of endpoint of the debate on rhetoric and, it rather seems to me, its historical reversal. Socrates presents a quasi farcical use of rhetoric. Well, I am putting "farcical" in scare quotes; we should be more prudent and moderate. What I mean is this. Socrates has established—this is how he demonstrated that rhetoric is nothing—that escaping the injustice of others is not what matters. The important thing is not to commit injustice oneself. And if this is what is important, what use is rhetoric? He has said it: rhetoric is of no use. Because, if it is important not to commit injustice, then it is important to see to it that the unjust person actually becomes just, and not that he merely appear to be just. So rhetoric serves no purpose. And, having reached this point, he simply says: If you really want to make use of rhetoric, if, notwithstanding the real non-use of rhetoric, you were to want to use it, of what use could it be to you? And then he imagines this paradoxical scene—an impossible scene, which, I think, would have no sense for a Greek—in which we see someone rush to the courts and—the text says it exactly—use all his art of rhetoric to say: I'm the guilty one, please, punish me. Socrates presents this use of rhetoric as a paradoxical, impossible scene in order to show the extent to which, in fact, rhetoric can do nothing. I think we have confirmation that this really is the meaning that Socrates presents—that of a paradoxical and literally impossible scene—in the immediately following passage in which, having analyzed this confessional use, this rhetorical use of confession, he says: There is another possible use of rhetoric, if you still want to use it after having accepted that the important thing is not to commit injustice. If you accept that, well you can use rhetoric either for the absolutely bizarre and unimaginable purpose of accusing yourself, or: "In the reverse situation, when it is a matter of someone, an enemy or anyone else, to whom you would like to do harm—on the sole condition that he is not the victim but the author of an injustice—then [one needs a—M.F.] different approach. You must make every effort in words and deeds to ensure that he does not have to give an account of himself or appear before the judges, and if he does appear before the judges, you must arrange things so that he escapes punishment; and if he has stolen a large sum, you must ensure that he does not surrender it but keeps it and spends it on himself and his friends in an unjust and impious way; and if he deserves death for his crimes, you must do as much as possible to ensure that he does not die but lives for ever in his wickedness or, at least, for as long as possible in this state."[7] It seems to me that this text clarifies perfectly the meaning of the immediately preceding one of which I have distributed the photocopy. The situation then is this: since what matters is not to commit injustice, from this we can deduce that rhetoric is nothing. It is nothing in itself and has no use. But—starting from the principle that the important thing is not to commit injustice—if you really were to want to make use of rhetoric, of this thing which is nothing and serves no purpose, what could you do with it? Well, you could make two grotesque uses: one, of running to the judge and deploying your rhetorical talent to accuse yourself; and the other, if you were to have an enemy against whom you have a solid grudge, you would defend him in the courts and strive to see to it that he is not punished and so not find through punishment the source of his transformation from an unjust man into a just one. You would keep him in his injustice, you would see to it that he does not make amends, and in this way you, his enemy, would be able to do him the worst harm. These are the two paradoxes of the impossible and ridiculous use of rhetoric when one has accepted the previous principles. There is no psychagogy of confession; there is no judicial psychagogy. It is not by revealing the truth of oneself before a judge who punishes that you would be able to transform yourself from an unjust man into a just man. And therefore it seems to me that this is the meaning we should keep in mind when speaking about this text.*

On the other hand—here we move on to the other text I would like to talk to you about—there is a passage in which we see what mode of

---

* The manuscript contains here a very long exposition on the difference between the position expressed by Socrates here with regard to the function of punishment and that of Protagoras in the dialogue named after him, at 324a.

being of discourse really will be able to bring about the psychagogy in question. Psychagogy will not be brought about by rhetoric, through the judicial offense, in the game of offense, confession, and punishment. The passage I am quoting [...*] is at 486d: "If my soul, Callicles, were made of gold, can you doubt that I would be happy to find one of those stones which are used to test gold? A stone as perfect as possible which I would apply to my soul so that, if it was [...] in agreement with me on the opinions of my soul, this, then, will be true. I consider, in fact, that to correctly judge whether a soul lives well or badly, one must have three qualities and that you possess all three: knowledge (*epistemēn*), benevolence (*eunoian*), and frankness (*parrēsian*). I often meet people who are unable to test me, not being learned as you are; others are learned, but they do not want to tell me the truth, because they do not care for me as you do. As for these two strangers, Gorgias and Polus, they are both learned and my friends, but an unfortunate timidity prevents them from *parrēsia* with me. Nothing is more obvious: this timidity is so great that out of false modesty each is led to contradict himself before a large audience [...]. You, however, have all these qualities."[8] And he lists the three qualities that Callicles possesses: he is *epistēmōn* (he has *epistemē*); he has friendship, affection for Socrates;[9] and "as for your frankness (*parrēsiazesthai*) and absence of timidity, you strongly affirm them and your last speech has not disappointed me. So the question is settled: whenever we agree on a point, this point will be considered as sufficiently proven by both sides and there is no need to examine it further."[10] A bit further on, right at the end at the bottom of the page, you see, on the basis of what could be called this parrhesiastic pact of the test of souls, this short paragraph, these lines which actually refer to the conduct and conduction of souls: "As for me, if in my conduct I commit some fault, be sure that I do not do so intentionally but that it is out of pure ignorance on my part, and since you have begun to advise me, do not abandon me therefore, but point out to me the kind of activities to which I should devote myself and how best to prepare myself for them; later, if after having agreed with you today you find me doing something other than what I agreed to, consider me vile and henceforth unworthy to receive your advice."[11]

---

* M.F.: it is the other photocopy.

You can see that this passage indirectly but fairly clearly conflicts with the one I just read to you. In both cases the question is what is to be done when an offense has been committed. The farcical, absurd hypothesis for someone who would believe in rhetoric is: run to the judge to accuse oneself. And now here is the other formula, which is precisely that of philosophical action on the soul, in which, if an offense has been committed, one should accept that it was not committed voluntarily, and that consequently the person who committed it is once again in need of advice. But if, after this advice, and after having been enlightened as to the nature of the offense, he commits it again, then the only punishment will be to be abandoned by the person who is guiding him. You see that we are in a completely different setting, with completely different procedures, in a completely different context, and with a game that is completely different from that of judicial scene of the confession. I would like to go back over the elements present in this passage.

It seems to me that in this passage the mode of being of philosophical discourse and its way of binding the soul to, at the same time, truth, Being (what is), and the Other are defined, albeit rapidly and in a, so to speak, purely methodological way (as rules of the discussion). I think this passage is interesting because it takes up and theorizes, in an obviously fleeting but nonetheless very clear way, what has been at stake throughout the dialogue, since—those of you who have read it will recall—Socrates hasn't ceased saying to his interlocutor: I do not want you to give me a big speech, I do not want you to sing me the praises of rhetoric, I simply want you to answer my questions. And I want you to answer my questions, not—as will be said in the *Meno* or in other dialogues—because deep within yourself you know the truth. [Or rather] this proposition is actually implicit in this, but the theme of "I want you to answer my questions" which runs through the *Gorgias* is not focused on this. "I want you to answer my questions" signifies in the *Gorgias*: I want you to be the witness of the truth. By answering the questions I put to you with exactly what you think, exactly what you have in mind, without dissimulating anything out of interest, rhetorical embellishment, or shame—[which] again plays a big role in this—by saying exactly what you think, in this way we will have a genuine test of the soul. The dialogue is not justified here as an instrument of memorization, as a dialectical game with the memory. It is justified as a permanent test of the soul, a *basanos* (a test) of the soul and its quality through the game of questions and answers.

This text is interesting also because, while theorizing in this way, or at least grouping together some themes running through the dialogue, which are a sort of pact that Socrates evokes throughout the dialogue, we find here the word *parrēsia* which, for sure, is employed with its everyday meaning outside of its precise political, institutional field we have talked about. That is to say, it is a matter here purely and simply of free-spokenness, of speaking one's mind, of freedom of speech and saying exactly what one thinks without limits or shame. But if this meaning of *parrēsia* is the traditional one, the word is employed here in a reflection on what philosophical dialogue should be and, consequently, on what the game of truth and the game of testing played by the philosopher and his disciple should be—what the game played by questioner and questioned, pursuer and pursued should be. To that extent, I believe that we have here a first use—there are no others at any rate in the literature of this epoch, and there were none prior to this—of the word *parrēsia* in what is already the context, the practice of spiritual direction. Much later you will find texts which fully, or in part anyway, accord an important part to the theory of *parrēsia*. There is, for example, a treatise by Plutarch which is devoted to identifying flatterers: How can one recognize a flatterer, how can one unmask a flatterer?[12] In reality this text is a very technical discussion of the nature of flattery as opposed to *parrēsia*. It contains if not a theoretical, then at least a technical, almost technological discussion of *parrēsia*. It is not yet a question of this in Plato, but the word is already employed in the context of the practice of the conduction of souls, of the philosophical, individual conduction of souls, and it is the first time it is used in this context. For this reason we should devote some attention to this text.

You recall that this passage is situated in a very simple context. It comes shortly after the passage we read on the confession, of which it seems to me to be precisely almost a caricature. Polus, then, has been discredited as an interlocutor, since in the discussion he got it all wrong as it were. He has been forced to admit that if in fact the just is better than the unjust, then rhetoric is of no use. At this point Callicles enters the discussion, and he has clearly seen the weak point in Polus' speech, namely that Polus tried to maintain two propositions at the same time: first, that rhetoric is useful; second, that the just is better than the unjust. Socrates has shown that it was not possible to maintain both propositions, and, holding that the just is better than the unjust, he thus demonstrated that rhetoric is useless, and not only that it is useless, but that it is nothing. Consequently, from this it is very easy to deduce the tactic Callicles will adopt in the discussion. Callicles will take up the other position which consists in saying: It is not true that the just is preferable to the unjust, and so rhetoric exists, and is useful. This famous passage, on the just not being preferable to the unjust, has been analyzed and interpreted as not only the sketch of the view taken by Thrasymachus in the *Republic*—which is correct—but also as a sort of prefiguration of Nietzschean man, a sort of first affirmation of the will to power. This interpretation, however, seems to me to be utterly rash and as completely anachronistic as the one that gave the earlier passage we examined as a prefiguration of confession. What is staged in the dialogue of the *Gorgias* is not a contrast between a morality of confession and punishment and a morality of the will to power. For obvious historical reasons, it would be astonishing if this were the case.

You will see that I emphasize Callicles for a simple reason. Just to situate things, because we must be quick, I would like to say that, at bottom, Callicles is a good, decent and, all in all, completely normal young man. For in his speech on the just and the unjust, how does he justify his statement that it is not true that the just are to be preferred to the unjust and on what grounds does he base this? He justifies it by saying: One should not do as slaves do, for slaves suffer injustice without being able to defend themselves (this is at 483b). At 483c: One should belong to the stronger, more capable part, those who are *dunatoi pleon ekhein* (able to excel more than others). One should seek to prevail over the *hoi polloi*, the many (483d), one should be among the *dunatōteroi* (those more powerful than the others). 483e: The stronger (*kreittōn*) should command the less strong, the weaker (*hēttōn*), one should be part of the *beltistoi*, the best.[13] Now all of these are the most banal expressions that can be found in any Greek who belongs to the category of fully-fledged citizens and to that class of people who claim to govern the city by virtue of their status, birth, and wealth. There is nothing extraordinary in Callicles' project. The only thing he comes up against and which means that this absolutely normal attitude—wanting to be among the best, as best, someone who commands the weaker and less good—[encounters a resistance], is that he is faced with a *nomos* (a law), which is precisely the law of Athenian democracy which aims to give the same status to everybody, and especially to prevent anyone prevailing over the others. And—there is something here which means that Callicles is not a young aristocrat exactly like all the others—faced with what for him is a scandal (this law of equality), he uses an argument that we know comes directly from the Sophists, from Gorgias, from Protagoras, etcetera, and which consists in saying that the *nomos* is only a matter of convention and that legal constraint does not derive from Nature. He thus reinterprets this situation which is intolerable for him. Callicles, who wants to play the aristocratic game of the best in the usual way, who belongs to an agonistic world in which the stronger should prevail over the weaker, uses this type of reasoning. And so we should see that Socrates is not dealing with a premonitory representative of a quasi-Nietzschean aristocracy unable to yield to any law which would like to curb its appetite for power. With Callicles, Socrates is dealing with a young man who wants to play a traditional agonistic game in a system which has become egalitarian. His advantages of wealth and his traditional status can no longer place him among the best, and the fact of being among the best does not give him any real authority. How will he be able to acquire such authority? Well, quite simply by rhetoric. Rhetoric will thus be the instrument that will enable him to play the old traditional game of pre-eminence and privileged status in the egalitarian system. Rhetoric is the instrument for restoring inequality to a society on which an attempt to impose an egalitarian structure had been pursued through democratic laws. Rhetoric must therefore no longer be indexed to the law, since rhetoric must work against this law. Rhetoric must therefore be indifferent to the just and the unjust and is justified as a pure agonistic game. This is the context in which the passage I would like to analyze is situated.

So, confronted with this use of rhetoric without any indexation to the just and the unjust, what will Socrates propose to Callicles? Well, he will propose an entirely different discursive game, different in every respect. Actually first of all, in the traditional or conflictual situation, in which members of the elite or those who want to play the agonistic game are dealing with an egalitarian or democratic structure, rhetoric is a discourse which to Callicles' mind, as to the minds of the rhetors, has only one use: it is a matter of prevailing over one's rivals and so of addressing oneself to the many (*hoi polloi*) and thereby persuading them. One will be able to outmatch one's rivals by obtaining the conviction and support of the many. Rhetoric is, if you like, a discursive practice involving three categories of characters: there is the many who must be convinced; there are the rivals over whom one must prevail; and then there is the person who uses rhetoric and wants to become the foremost.

Socrates proposes to Callicles a discourse which does not operate in this three stage game, or which does not operate in this agonistic space with the many, the rivals, and the one who wants to prevail. It is a discourse one uses as a *basanos*,[14] as the test of one soul by another. Throughout the preceding discussion with Polus the interlocutor was to be used as a *martur*,* a witness.[15] Here, the word *basanos* means that the discourse goes from one soul to the other as a test. In what sense is it a test? The use of the metaphor of the touchstone is interesting. What does the touchstone actually show? What is its nature and function? Its nature is that it has something like an affinity with what it tests which means that it reveals the nature of what it tests. Second, the touchstone operates on two levels: on the level of reality and on the level of truth. That is to say, the touchstone enables one to know the reality of the thing one wants to test, and by demonstrating the reality of the thing it tests one shows whether it really is what it claims to be, and consequently whether its discourse or appearance really does conform to what it is. So the relationship between souls will no longer be that agonistic type of relationship involving prevailing over others. The relationship between souls will be a test relationship, this relationship of *basanos* (touchstone), in which there will be a natural affinity and, through this natural affinity, a demonstration of reality and truth, that is to say, of what the soul is and the degree to which it is *etumos* (authentic). You remember that we have already come across

---

* [The French text has *martyr* (martyr), but this seems to be a slip, since there is no reference to martyrdom in the text. I have assumed that what was intended was the Greek *martur* (witness, from which the word "martyr" derives); G.B.]

this notion of the authentic (the *etumos*) with regard to *logos*.[16] And inasmuch as a soul manifests itself through what it says (through its *logos*, [through] the test, in dialogue, of the *logos*: knowing what it is in reality and whether what it is in actual fact conforms to reality and whether it tells the truth), then what is valid for the *logos* is also valid for the soul. The game therefore is no longer agonistic (one of superiority); it is a game between two souls of the test of the soul's reality-truth through natural affinity and manifestation of authenticity.

Second, in this test of truth, a distinctive element is pointed out several times as what will ensure that one really will undertake the test and that it will give a result. This is what the text calls *homologia*. This term *homologia* is repeated several times and refers to the identity of the discourse of both participants in the dialogue.[17] One will have a criterion of truth when there is a *homologia* in the two souls tested through natural affinity, which means that what is said by one can be said by the other. The criterion of truth of philosophical discourse is not to be sought therefore in a sort of internal connection between the person who thinks and what is thought. The truth of philosophical discourse is not obtained therefore in the form of what we will later call evidence, but through something called *homologia*, that is to say, the identity of the discourse between two persons. On one condition however, and it is here that we meet with the three terms that I would like to analyze and in which we find "*parrēsia*." For this *homologia*, that is to say, this identity of discourse, really to be what we want it to be, namely a test of the soul's quality, not only the discourse, but the soul, and the individual whose discourse it is—and to tell the truth these three things coincide—must meet certain criteria. These three criteria [are]: *epistemē*, *eunoia*, *parrēsia*.[18] We should look at other texts which are found a bit further on concerning flattery, but unfortunately I don't have time.[19] What actually is flattery? It too seems to be a *homologia*. What is it to flatter? To flatter is to take what the listener already thinks, formulate it for his benefit as my own discourse, and give it back to the listener, who is thereby all the more easily convinced and seduced since it is what he says.

We have here, in appearance if you like, a *homologia*. But this will never be called *homologia*, because this apparent identity is only an appearance. It is not the *logos* itself which is identical; it is the passions, desires, pleasures, opinions, and everything illusory and false. This is what flattery reconstructs and repeats. On the other hand, the *homologia* of dialogue is a true criterion of truth. And the fact that both interlocutors deliver the same *logos* will not make it flattery, on condition that they are endowed with *epistemē*, *eunoia*, and *parrēsia*. I say "the listeners are endowed with," and we will have to come back to this, but let's leave it for the moment. *Epistemē*, that is to say, it is necessary that they know: "knowledge (*savoir*)" as opposed to that flattery which is thus dismissed here, since it is of use only for opinion. Here, *epistemē* refers not so much to the knowledge the interlocutor or interlocutors might possess of a form of knowledge they have learned, as [to the fact] of only ever saying what they say when they really know that it is true. Second, *homologia* will not be flattery on condition that—here again in contrast with the practice of flatterers—the interlocutors are not looking for their own good, their advantage, a good reputation among their listeners, their political success, and so on. For *homologia* actually to have value as the locus of the formulation and test of the truth, the interlocutors must have a feeling of benevolence for each other which comes from friendship (*eunoia*). And finally, the third thing required to be sure that *homologia* is not just that adaptation of the flatterer's discourse to the other's opinions is that both must use *parrēsia*, that is to say, [that nothing], not fear, timidity, or shame will limit the expression of what one thinks is true. Parrhesiastic courage is necessary. *Epistemē*, which means that one says what one thinks is true, *eunoia*, which means that one speaks only out of benevolence for the other, and *parrēsia*, which gives one courage to say all that one thinks despite rules, laws, and customs, are the three conditions on which *homologia*, that is to say, the identity of *logos* in both interlocutors, will be able to play the role of *basanos* (of test, touchstone). If you really want to make some philosophical comparisons, you may well say that in a philosophical practice defined by dialogue and the action of one soul on another, *epistemē*, *eunoia*, and *parrēsia* occupy exactly, well, in a way, the place occupied by Cartesian evidence when Cartesian discourse puts itself forward and asserts itself as the site where truth appears and manifests itself.

Then obviously we should complicate things a little, even quite a bit; unfortunately I don't have the time... For in fact this is a game of two people, that is to say, the *epistēmē*, *eunoia*, and *parrēsia* of Callicles are not the same as the *epistēmē*, *eunoia*, and *parrēsia* of Socrates. And precisely, everything in the rest of the dialogue involves the way in which, by effectively working with his *epistēmē*—with what he knows and what he knows as true—with his friendship—somewhat limited but, even so, with his good will toward Socrates—and then with his *parrēsia*-which is well defined as the ability to say even scandalous and shameful things—so working with all this and applying these rules to his own dialogue, Callicles is gradually led to let Socrates' discourse prevail. And it is at that point, in the silence of Callicles who gives up speaking, that an *epistēmē* of Socrates is asserted which manifests itself in the formulation of the three great principles concerning the body and the soul, life, death and the afterlife, and which are like the very core of philosophical knowledge; Socrates' *eunoia*, which is his affection for Callicles; and Socratic *parrēsia*, the *parrēsia* he had tested throughout the dialogue, but which will actually be evoked at the end, when, by a retrospective anticipation, the dialogue calls to mind Socrates' trial and death, and the courage with which he will tell the truth before his judges.[20]

You can see that this is how *epistēmē*, *eunoia*, and *parrēsia* function as the effective agencies of truth. Through a pact into which Socrates invites Callicles, *homologia*, which will develop and articulate the rest of the dialogue, will be the proof of the truth of what is said, and so of the quality of the souls who say it. You see that in this conception of the touchstone, of *homologia*, and of their internal condition which culminates in *parrēsia*, we have the definition of the bond through which the *logos* of one can act on the soul of the other and lead it to the truth. And this is how *parrēsia*—which, in its political use according to, let's say, the Periclean model, made it possible to bind the plurality of the others around the person in command within the unity of the city—will now bind master and disciple to each other. And, binding them to each other, [it will] no longer bind both of them to the unity of the city, but to the unity of knowledge, which is the unity of the Idea, the unity of Being itself. Socrates' philosophical *parrēsia* binds the other, the two others, master and disciple, in the unity of Being, unlike the Periclean type of *parrēsia* which bound the plurality of citizens brought together in the city to the unity of command of the person who assumes ascendancy over them. You understand why Periclean *parrēsia* necessarily had to lead to something like rhetoric, that is to say, to that use of language that enables one to prevail over others and bring them together, by persuasion, in the unity of this command, in the form of this asserted superiority. In contrast, philosophical *parrēsia*, which in this dialogue operates between master and disciple, leads not to rhetoric, but to an erotics. That's it, and many thanks.

1. Plato (Platon), *Gorgias*, 448e, trans. L. Bodin, p. 111: "*Tis eiē hē Gorgiou tekhnē*"; Plato, *Gorgias*, trans. W.D. Woodhead, p. 232: "But no one is asking in what kind of art Gorgias is engaged but what it actually is and what we should call Gorgias."

2. Ibid., 480a, French p. 158; English p. 263: "But if he or anyone of those for whom he cares has done wrong, he ought to go of his own accord where he will most speedily be punished, to the judge as though to a doctor, in his eagerness to prevent the distemper of evil from becoming ingrained and producing a festering and incurable ulcer in his soul."

3. Ibid., 480b-d, French p. 158; English p. 264: "Then for the purpose of defending one's own guilt or that of his parents or friends or children, or his country when guilty, Polus, rhetoric is of no use whatever—unless we should on the contrary assume that a man ought to accuse himself first and foremost, and then his kinsfolk and any friend who at any time is guilty of wrongdoing, and that he ought not to hide the evil away but bring it to light in order that the culprit may be punished and regain his health. And he should prevail upon himself and the others not to play the coward but to submit as a patient submits bravely with closed eyes to the knife or cautery of the surgeon, ever pursuing what is good and honorable and heeding not the pain, but if his guilty deeds be worthy of flogging, submitting to the lash; if of imprisonment, to bonds; if of a fine, to the payment thereof; if of exile, to exile; if of death, to death. He should be the first to accuse himself and his kinsmen, and should use rhetoric for the sole purpose of exposing his own misdeeds and ridding himself of the greatest of all evils, wickedness."

4. These dimensions of Christian *parrēsia* will be studied in the lecture of 7 March 1984.

5. See especially the letters. Saint Cyprian, *The Letters of St. Cyprian of Carthage*, trans. G.W. Clarke (New York: Newman Press, "The Works of the Fathers in Translation" 43, 1984).

6. Plato, *Gorgias*, 521c, French p. 216: "CALLICLES: You appear to be strangely confident, Socrates, that nothing similar will happen to you, that you are protected and could not be dragged before the court by some possibly wicked and contemptible man"; English p. 302: "How confident you seem, Socrates, that you can never experience any of these troubles whatever, as if you dwelt apart and could never be haled into court by, it may be, some utterly mean and vile creature." See also the subsequent exchanges 521d-522e.

7. Ibid., 480e-481b, French p. 159; English p. 264: "Then conversely again, if after all it is right to injure anybody, whether it be an enemy or whoever it may be—always provided that you have not been yourself the victim of injury by him, for this you must guard against—but if your enemy injures another, you should contrive by every possible means, both by word and by deed, that he escape punishment and come not before the judge. But if he does appear, you must see to it that your enemy be not sentenced and punished, but that if he has robbed others of a large sum of money, he shall not pay it back but shall keep it and squander it, in defiance of god and man, upon himself and his friends; and, if his crimes are worthy of death, that, if possible, he shall never die but live forever in his wickedness, or, if not this, shall at any rate live as long as possible in this character."

8. Ibid., 486d-481b, French pp. 166-167; English p. 269: "If my soul were wrought of gold, Callicles, do you not think I should be delighted to find one of those stones wherewith they test gold—the best of them—which I could apply to it…I consider that in meeting you I have encountered such a godsend…that if you agree with the opinions held by my soul, then at last we have attained the actual truth. For I observe that anyone who is to test adequately a human soul for good or evil living must possess three qualifications, all of which you possess, namely knowledge, good will, and frankness. Now I encounter many who cannot test me because they are not wise like you, and others are wise but unwilling to tell the truth because they do not care for me as you do, and our two guests here, Gorgias and Polus, while they are wise men and friends of mine, are more deficient than they ought to be in outspokenness and somewhat too bashful. How could it be otherwise, when their bashfulness is so great that out of sheer timidity each of them ventures to contradict himself in the presence of many people…But you possess all the qualifications lacking in the others."

9. Ibid., 487b, French p. 167: "You are well educated (*pepaideusai te gar hikanōs*), as a host of Athenians can testify, and you have friendship for me (*emoi ei eunoūs*)"; English p. 269: "You have received a good education, as many Athenians would agree, and you are well disposed toward me."

10. Ibid.; English pp. 269-270: "Moreover, that you are inclined to be frank and not bashful is borne out by your own statement and confirmed by the speech you made a short time ago. Evidently, then, the case at the moment is this. If at any point in our discussion you agree with me, that matter will already have been adequately tested both by you and by me, and there will no longer be any need to refer it to any other touchstone."

11. Ibid., 488a-b, French p. 168; English p. 270: "As for me, if I act wrongly at all in the conduct of my life, you may be assured that my error is not voluntary but due to my ignorance. Now that you have begun to admonish me, therefore, do not give it up, but reveal to me clearly what course I must follow and how I may achieve it; and if you catch me agreeing with you now but later not doing what I agreed to, you may consider me an utter dolt and refuse to admonish me any more as a worthless creature."

12. Plutarch, *How to Distinguish the Flatterer from the Friend*, in *Plutarch's Moralia*, vol. I, trans. F.C. Babbit (Cambridge Mass. and London: Harvard University Press and Heinemann, "Loeb Classical Library," 1969).

13. Plato, *Gorgias*, 483b-e, French p. 162: "The law, however, is made by the weak and the many (*hoi polloi*). They therefore make the law with regard to their own interest and accordingly apportion praise and blame. To frighten the stronger, the more able from prevailing over them (*ekphobountes te tous errōmenesterous tōn anthrōpōn kai dunatous ontas pleon ekhein*) [...]. But in my view nature herself proves to us that in justice the better should prevail over the worse, the capable over the incapable (*pleon ekhein kai ton dunatōteron tou adunatōterou*) [...] the mark of the just is the domination of the weak by the strong (*ton kreittō tou hēttonos arkhein*) [...] we fashion the best (*tous beltistous*) and the most vigorous among ourselves"; English p. 266: "But in my opinion those who framed the laws are the weaker folk, the majority. And accordingly they frame the laws for themselves and their own advantage, and so too with their approval and censure, and to prevent the stronger who are able to overreach them from gaining the advantage, they frighten them [...]. But in my view nature herself makes it plain that it is right for the better to have the advantage over the worse, the more able over the less [...] right is recognized to be the sovereignty and advantage of the stronger over the weaker [...] We mold the best and strongest among ourselves."

14. Ibid., 486d, French p. 160: "One of those stones which are used to test gold (*tina tōn lithōn hē basanizousin ton khruson*)"; English p. 269: "one of those stones wherewith they test gold." In Greek *basanos* means touchstone.

15. Ibid., 472b, French pp. 144-145: "As for me, on the contrary, if I do not get your own testimony, and it alone (*an mē se auton hena onta martura*) in favor of my assertion, I reckon I have done nothing"; English p. 254: "But if I cannot produce in you yourself a single witness in agreement with my views, I consider that I have accomplished nothing worth speaking of."

16. See the lecture of 2 March, second hour, and the reference to the *Phaedrus* 243a, p. 331 above.

17. *Gorgias*, 486d, "*Homologēseien*"; 486e and 487e, "*homologēsēs*."

18. Ibid., 487a, French p. 166; English p. 269: "knowledge, good will, and frankness."

19. Ibid., 502d-e and 522d, French pp. 190-191 and p. 218; English p. 285 and p. 303.

20. See above, note 6.

COURSE CONTEXT

Frédéric Gros*

WRITING PROJECTS AND NEW DEPARTURE

THE TITLE OF THE lectures Michel Foucault delivered at the Collège
de France in 1983 is "The Government of self and others." This is also
the title of a book Foucault planned to publish with the Éditions du
Seuil in the new series "Des Travaux."[1] That year Foucault undertook
research which should have formed the chapters of this work that never
appeared, completing the analyses of the previous years which were
also constructed as a series of expositions which were to be included in
the same volume. Foucault in fact envisaged the publication, alongside
his *Histoire de la sexualité*,[2] of a series of studies of the ethical and political dimensions of ancient governmentality. The lectures are therefore
an extension of those of 1982. He frequently refers to them moreover,
recalling earlier analyses here and there as a matter of interest.[3] In
1982 Foucault had set out the historical study of the relations between
subjectivity and truth as the general framework of his work.[4] For him
this involved starting from the study of the notion of "care of self"
(*epimeleia heautou, cura sui*) in Greek and Roman philosophy to describe
the historically situated "techniques" by which a subject constructs
a definite relationship to self, gives form to his or her own existence,

* Frédéric Gros is professor of political philosophy at the university of Paris-XII. He also
teaches at the Paris Institut d'études politiques (Master "Histoire et Théorie du politique").
His most recent book was *États de violence. Essai sur la fin de la guerre*, Paris: Gallimard (coll. "Les
Essais"), 2006.

and establishes a well-ordered relationship to the world and to others. It then became apparent fairly quickly that this care of self could not represent a spontaneous attitude, a natural movement of subjectivity, except in debased forms (egoism, narcissism, hedonism). One had to be called to the correct care of self by another person.[5] The figure of the ancient master of existence was thus called upon, who represented at least since the lectures at the Collège de France of 1980[6] a major historical alternative to the Christian spiritual director.[7] For this master of existence speaks rather than listens, instructs rather than confesses, induces positive construction rather than sacrificial renunciation. The question of what it is that structures this utterance addressed to the person receiving direction entails precisely a first study, in 1982, of the theme of *parrēsia* as free-spokenness, courage of the truth, within the framework of the ancient direction of existence.[8]

The transition from the government of self (*epimeleia heautou* in 1982) to the government of others (*parrēsia* in 1983) was therefore coherent. However, Foucault seems to stress that he wanted to mark a new departure in 1983. He begins his lectures with a commentary on Kant's text on the Enlightenment which is itself preceded by an ambitious methodological preamble.[9] The first words of the lectures thus quickly take on the appearance of an overall reevaluation and balance sheet of his work since *Histoire de la folie*, Foucault endeavoring to scan the whole of his work in three moments (veridiction/governmentality/subjectivation), to clarify the major conceptual shifts carried out each time, and to avoid misunderstandings.

The first lecture will focus essentially on Kant's text however. The short work on the *Aufklärung*[10] had already been the object of a communication to the Société française de philosophie on 27 May 1978 ("Qu'est-ce que la critique?").[11] Despite surface repetitions, the difference between the commentaries is nonetheless clear. In 1978 Kant's text was situated in the perspective of a "critical attitude" that Foucault dates from the beginning of the modern age and in opposition to the requirements of a pastoral governmentality (directing individuals' conduct by the truth). Posing the question of Enlightenment involved rediscovering the question: *how not to be governed in that way?* The problem posed was that of a "desubjectification" in the framework of a "politics of truth."[12] Modernity was then defined as a privileged historical period for studying the subjecting/subjectifying forms of knowledge-power.[13] In 1983 the question of Enlightenment will be thought of as the reinvestment of a requirement of truth-telling, of a courageous speaking the truth that appeared in the Greeks, and as giving rise to a different question: What government of self should be posited as both the foundation and limit of the government of others? The meaning of "modernity" also changes: it becomes a meta-historical attitude of thought itself.[14] On the other hand, in places there remains the opposition between two possible Kantian legacies: a transcendental legacy to which Foucault refused to subscribe (establishing universal rules of truth in order to avoid the misuses of a dominating reason); on the other hand, a "critical" legacy in which he wants to situate himself (challenging the present on the basis of the diagnosis of "what we are"). From the first lecture Foucault wants therefore to define his own place within a philosophical heritage, as if he was declaring that through these studies of *parrēsia* he was problematizing the status of his own speech and the definition of his role. Moreover, Foucault was never so much looking down on himself from above as in this lecture.[15]

ETHICS AND POLITICS OF *PARRĒSIA*[16]

Foucault will devote the whole of 1983 to the historical problematization of the ancient notion of *parrēsia*. Before embarking on this study, setting off from an exemplary parrhesiastic scene reported by Plutarch (Plato speaking out freely before the tyrant Dionysius and risking his life in doing so), Foucault begins by formalizing the notion on the basis of a contrast with the *speech act* of the English pragmatists (the essential references here seem to be Austin and Searle[17]). The dialogue with the analytical tradition had already begun in *The Archeology of Knowledge*.[18] In 1969 however, it was a matter of contrasting two definitions of the "statement (*énoncé*)": either, for analytical philosophy, the statement as a sequence of a possible combination of language (*langage*) for which one defines the rules of production, or, for archeology, the statement as a sequence really inscribed in the cultural archive for which one defines the conditions of reality. In 1983 it is the subject's ontological commitment in the act of enunciation that distinguishes *parrēsia* from speech acts, the former being characterized as the public and risky expression of a personal conviction. This speaking the truth, exposing its enunciator to a risk, nevertheless covers very different situations: the public orator addressing the assembled people, the philosopher acting as the Prince's counselor, etcetera.

In 1982, with the first analyses, it was simply a matter of *parrēsia* describing the master of existence's frankness, his willingness to shake up his disciple and arouse his anger by bluntly exposing his faults, vices, and bad passions. Foucault had then studied in particular Galen's treatise *On the Passions and Errors of the Soul* and some of Seneca's letters to Lucilius in which the Stoic teacher praises transparent speech.[19] He had also stressed the specificity of Epicurean *parrēsia* within the framework of the direction of existence, which involved a community of friends freely confiding in each other in order to mutually correct each other, rather than the face to face relationship of director and disciple.[20] The lectures of 1984 will extend the problematization of a specifically ethical *parrēsia* beyond the lectures of 1983 by taking the examination back to the test of souls in Socrates and the Cynics.[21] But if the objective remains the same from Socrates to Seneca (to transform the *ēthos* of the person one is addressing), the way in which this is done is no longer the same. The *parrēsia* studied in the lectures of 1984 is no longer practiced within an individual relationship of direction but is instead an address in a public arena, taking the form of Socrates' ironic, maieutic discourse or the Cynic's brutal, rough harangue. For all that, all these forms of *parrēsia* (Socratic, Cynic, Stoic, or Epicurean) remain relatively irreducible to the political relationship.

In 1983 Foucault basically studies a political *parrēsia*, although the final lectures of March set off on new tracks starting from the opposition between philosophy and rhetoric.[22] This political *parrēsia* comprises two major historical forms: that of a discourse addressed to the Assembly, to all the citizens by an individual concerned to make his conception of the general interest prevail (democratic *parrēsia*); that of the philosopher's private discourse intended for the prince's soul in order to encourage him to follow the right path and to get him to hear what flatterers conceal from him (autocratic *parrēsia*).

The study of democratic *parrēsia* is constructed on the basis of two sets of texts: the tragedies of Euripides and the speeches of Pericles as "reported" by Thucydides in his *History of the Peloponnesian War*.

A large part of January will be devoted to a very detailed study of Euripides' *Ion*.[23] The tragedy recounts how Ion (legendary ancestor of the Ionians), the hidden son of Apollo and Creusa, obtains the secret of his birth and, discovering his mother is Athenian, can found democratic right at Athens. In this play *parrēsia* is not considered as either a basic right of the citizen or as a technical ability peculiar to political leaders. It is that free exercise of speech operating in a rivalry between peers which will have to designate who is best to govern. It is rooted in that dimension of politics as "experience" (provisionally designated by Foucault by the term *dunasteia* as opposed to *politeia*[24]) rather than as the organizational rule of multiplicities: what is examined here is what political involvement requires in terms of the subject's construction of a relation to self.

What is involved therefore is reading Euripides' tragedy as the legendary founding moment of truth-telling of Athenian democracy, by which a citizen commits his free speech in order to intervene in the city's affairs, inasmuch as this truth-telling is irreducible to the simple equal right to speak (*isēgoria*). However, in conclusion, Foucault is very careful to identify, through the study of two speeches by Creusa, the tentative emergence of two parrhesiastic modalities which are destined to further consolidation and development: the inferior's speech of imprecation to her superior in order to denounce his injustice, which will become the philosopher's courageous speech before the Prince; the confession of a misdeed to a confidant, which will be found in a Christian *parrēsia* redefined as the transparent opening of the heart to the spiritual director.[25] The first modality will be studied throughout February 1983. As for the second, it is only in 1984 that it will be the object of an inventory drawn up in the urgency of the last lectures.[26] However, in 1980 Foucault actually devoted the year to the analysis of the formation of Christian confession on the basis of the rites of penitence,[27] but at that time it was not a question of *parrēsia*.

In Euripides' *Ion*, democratic *parrēsia* was the object of a legendary foundation. The speeches of Pericles reconstructed by Thucydides then make it possible to consider it in its concrete practice. The close study of these speeches, evidence of what Foucault calls the "golden age" of democratic *parrēsia*, enables him to construct the difference between egalitarian speech (*isēgoria*), on the one hand, and the courageous and singular speech which introduces the difference of a truth-telling into the debate, on the other. It is this tension between a constitutional equality and an inequality stemming from the actual exercise of democratic power that interests Foucault. In fact, this inequality introduced by *parrēsia* (the exercise of an ascendancy), far from calling into question the democratic foundation, is supposed to guarantee its concrete exercise. At any moment formal egalitarianism may turn back against this difference introduced by the true discourse of the person who courageously commits his speech in order to defend his point of view on the common interest. This is the demagogic moment criticized by Isocrates and Plato, when *parrēsia* is submerged by *isēgoria*. The parrhesiast is then rejected and disparaged by a fickle rabble ceaselessly flattered by demagogues. Democratic *parrēsia* is distorted and transformed: it becomes the publicly recognized right to say anything to anyone in any way.

Parrēsia re-emerges in its positivity, but within a different framework: that of the philosopher's confrontation with the Prince. It is in order to study this new truth-telling that Foucault sets off on the second major reading exercise of 1983: after Euripides' *Ion*, Plato's seventh letter. Here again, Foucault quickly goes beyond the strict framework of an historical description of the modalities of *parrēsia*, using this reading to define, on the basis of an astonishing interpretation of Plato, the very identity of the philosophical enterprise. Foucault had already raised the problem of the relationship between philosophical discourse and reality in 1981 (the lecture of 18 March). Classically, he recalled, philosophy is thought to reflect, obscure, or rationalize reality. According to Foucault, the particular example of the great philosophical texts on marriage of the Hellenistic period enable one to reconsider this relationship: philosophy may actually be defined as an enterprise of theoretical elaboration and proposal of subjective postures conducive to the stylizing of certain social practices. In 1983 Foucault will pose the problem in a different way in terms of the "reality" of philosophy. He does not mean by this some extra-linguistic referent but that which an activity must confront in order to test its own truth. Letter VII, in which Plato explains his reasons for going to Sicily, enables Foucault to define this reality. We learn that philosophical activity must not confine itself solely to discourse, but must put itself to the test of practices, conflicts, and deeds. Philosophy's reality will be found in this active confrontation with power. Philosophy finds a second reality in a constant practice of the soul. According to the same letter philosophy could not be understood as a constituted system of contents of knowledge (*mathēmata*) but is practice of self, a constant exercise of the soul. Here Foucault rediscovers some paths he had already followed in 1982. But at the same time he is thereby able to reply to Derrida's famous readings which denounce Plato's "logocentrism." For Foucault in fact, we do not find in Plato a Platonic rejection of writing in the name of the pure *logos* but a silent work of self on self which disqualifies all *logos*, written or oral. This criticism of the key Derridean theses is continued in March with the analysis of the *Phaedrus* when Foucault shows that, here again, the essential division is not between the written and the oral but, to take up the terms of the manuscript, between "a logographic mode of being of rhetorical discourse and an auto-ascetic mode of being of philosophical discourse."[28] To conclude, the close examination of the detailed political "advice" given by Plato to Dion's friends at the end of Letter VII enables Foucault to reconsider the Platonic figure of the "philosopher king." He refuses to see in this the theme of legitimacy through knowledge (*savoir*), as if, by virtue of its speculative superiority, philosophical science could inform political action. What should coincide is rather a mode of being, a relationship of self to self: the philosopher does not have to get political claims recognized by virtue of his speculative abilities, but rather bring the philosophical mode of subjectivation into play within the exercise of power. In an interview in April 1983 at the University of Berkeley, Foucault extends these analyses by refusing to compare the "theories" of intellectuals by reference to their "practical politics": "The key to the personal political attitude of a philosopher is not to be sought in his ideas, as if it could be deduced from them, but rather in his philosophy, as life, in his philosophical life, his *ethos*."[29]

The last two sessions at the Collège de France in 1983 point already to 1984. In these lectures Foucault studies successively Plato's the *Apology*, the *Phaedrus*, and the *Gorgias*. The analysis of the *Apology* will be taken up again in 1984, supported by that of the *Phaedo* and the *Laches* (and also, to a lesser extent, the *Crito*). But if the same text is taken up again, it is not in the same perspective: in 1984 Foucault will describe Socratic *parrēsia* as the ethical test of his own and the other's life by a discourse of truth. This will involve raising the problem of the "true life."

But in 1983 Foucault devotes himself above all to constructing the opposition between philosophy and rhetoric in the framework of what he calls an "ontology of discourses."[30] Philosophical truth-telling in the *Apology*, through its direct and forthright character, is opposed to judicial rhetoric. With the *Phaedrus* the stress is put on the implications of a complete philosophical truth-telling (a genuine ontological initiation, a metaphysics of the bond between the soul and Being), which will condemn in advance the impostures of rhetoric. Finally, for Foucault the *Gorgias* establishes more classically the divorce between a Socratic *parrēsia* as test of the soul (psychagogy) and, with Callicles, a rhetorical art fed by political ambition.

METHODS

The analysis of the Greek texts is always rigorous and very analytical. The manuscript for 1983 contains in the margins passages re-translated from the Greek, which shows the importance and meticulousness of this work close to the original text. Most of the time Foucault follows his written text when giving his lecture and there is little improvisation. Only the manuscripts of the final sessions, concerning the *Phaedrus* and especially the *Gorgias*, contain long expositions which will not be delivered for lack of time. In 1983, more than in previous years, one feels that Foucault is aware of work in progress: sometimes he feels his way, or marks time, at other times he quickly outlines and tries out syntheses. Frequently there is the very strong impression of being present at the gestation of a line of research, and the tone is never dogmatic (Foucault multiplies the use of "I think," "we could say," "it seems that," "maybe"...). This dimension of a laboratory of ideas, of theoretical trial runs, of lines of research being marked out, finally had some difficulty withstanding the conditions Foucault met with at the Collège de France: a huge, silent, captivated public ready to receive a magisterial discourse with unwavering reverence and admiration. No exchanges, no discussion. Foucault frequently complained about this ambiance and about the attitude it imposed on him. As he said, he is

condemned to "theater," to playing the role of the great professor offici-
ating alone from his chair. He frequently expresses his regrets and his
willingness to meet students or teachers working on related subjects,
so as to be able to exchange perspectives. He organizes meetings and
reserves rooms in an attempt to reconstruct a small working group.
This nostalgia for group work will be felt again in 1984.

Foucault makes explicit reference to the few critical sources he was
able to use, here and there, to problematise *parrēsia*: he cites Scarpat's
book[31] and especially the articles in major encyclopedias or dictionar-
ies of theology.[32] However, Foucault will never look for theses or even
interpretative frameworks in this secondary literature, but only for
references which are very quickly worked on again in the original text
and situated within the framework of a specific problematization. The
commentaries on Euripides, Thucydides, and Plato are thus entirely
original. His procedure is the same as in 1982: very precise textual
commentaries, with great attention given to the Greek text (at several
points he corrects the existing translation), interspersed with moments
of sudden and wide-ranging overview. But Foucault had already accustomed us to this sharp contrast between painstaking analyses of a few
lines of Greek and a sudden widening and opening out onto a centuries old history of subjectivity. As he put it in the second lecture of
19 January: "That the main, fundamental part of history takes place
through the fine, slender thread of events is something [to which] I
think we should reconcile ourselves, or rather that [we should] bravely
confront. History, and the main part of history, passes through the
eye of a needle." Overall the method remains the same as the one he
used the previous year regarding the care of self: starting from a notion
(here, *parrēsia*), locating key texts, describing the strategies of usage,
plotting lines of evolution or rupture.

The examination of Euripides' *Ion* nevertheless presents some nota-
ble particularities: Foucault here deploys a structural analysis of the
work which extends widely beyond the initial framework of study (the
notion of *parrēsia*). He thus tests a series of reading grids first developed
with the reading of Sophocles' *Oedipus the King* (a tragedy on which he
had commented several times: in 1971, 1972, 1973, 1980, and 1981).[33]
The dramatic progression can be described as a series of interlocking parts of the truth fitting together in pairs (the structure of the

sumbolon). And the tragic scene itself is understood as the site of confrontation between competing regimes of veridiction (the truth-telling of the gods, of men, etcetera),[34] of the emergence of new structures of veridiction (the judicial testimony in *Oedipus*, the imprecation and confession in *Ion*), and finally of the disqualification (tyrannical knowledge in *Oedipus*) or legitimation (democratic speaking-the-truth in *Ion*) of political speech. Moreover, in the framework now of an analysis of the great mythological themes, Foucault explicitly follows the tracks of Dumézil in studying the figure of Apollo, god of the voice, of gold, and of fecundity. In 1984, this time with regard to Plato's *Phaedo*, Foucault will continue to put Dumézil's studies to work in his own lectures.[35]

THE STAKES

The lectures given in 1983 are especially precious, the studies they contain not having given rise to any publication while Foucault was alive (the six lectures given at Berkeley in October 1983, appearing as an unauthorized publication after his death, pick out quite succinctly what was developed more fully from January to March).[36] The 1982 lectures at the Collège de France (*The Hermeneutics of the Subject*) already made it possible to see how the ancient problematization of sexuality had to be only one chapter of a larger history of those practices by which a subject constitutes itself in and on the basis of a definite relationship to the truth (the techniques of self). The 1983 lectures make it clear, as far as Foucault was concerned, the extent to which this historical study of practices of subjectivation did not turn him away from politics.[37] In fact, at the center of the lectures we find the assertion of an essential and structuring relationship between philosophy and politics. But this relationship is considered in an absolutely original way. Classically this relationship took the form in fact of "political philosophy": either the description of an ideal city governed by a set of perfect laws (the problem of the best regime), or the rational foundation, the metaphysical deduction, or more modestly the conceptual analysis of the political relation. We have already said how much Foucault's reading of Plato's seventh letter led to a remarkable reevaluation of this relation. With politics, in fact, philosophy will encounter its "reality": it can only test its truth in this confrontation with politics. This means that philosophy does not have to state the truth of politics, but to confront politics in order to test *its* truth.

For philosophy, encountering its "reality" would mean either putting to work the difference of its speech, its discourse, in an otherwise autonomous political field (the example of the *parrēsia* of Pericles in Thucydides), or informing the "political will,"[38] that is to say, proposing structuring elements of a relation to self suited to arousing political commitment, adherence, or action.

In this the 1983 lectures do something very different from raising the question of the "care of others" after having raised that of the "care of self" the previous year. It is a question rather of understanding how philosophical discourse in the West constructs a fundamental part of its identity in this fold of the government of self and others: what relation to self is constructed in the person who wants to direct others and in those who will obey him? This fold was already at the heart of the Kantian questioning of the Enlightenment as Foucault understood it.

The political stakes of the lectures go far beyond the context of their delivery, even if retrospectively we cannot fail to emphasize coincidences between the terms of the debates of the time and the theoretical positions defended by Foucault with regard to the relationship between philosophy and politics.[39] But it is not this context that clarifies Foucault's positions; rather what he shows in these years is that it is his reading of the Ancients which helps him in a political ethos of problematization whose exercise he demonstrates during these years. If philosophy must find its reality in a relationship to politics, this relationship must remain that of a "restive exteriority."[40] The action taken by Foucault alongside the C.F.D.T. from December 1981 in response to events in Poland,[41] or his interventions in French debates of the time (whether it is a matter of the case of the Irish of Vincennes[42] in August 1982, or the problem of social security[43]) may well serve to illustrate this ethical stance. This new way of engaging in politics, proceeding by problematization rather than by dogmas, counting on individuals' ethical capacities rather than on their blind adherence to doctrines, in July 1983 was again behind the "Académie Tarnier," a group of personalities and friends meeting together to consider the international political situation.[44]

More generally, these lectures are an important contribution to the major theoretical debates on democracy, and even more generally, on the very nature of politics. By starting from the Greek example (from Thucydides to Plato), Foucault adopts an original approach towards the tension inherent in every democracy: on the basis of constitutional equality, it is the difference introduced by a truth-telling that makes democracy work; but, in return, democracy is always a recurrent threat for this truth-telling. We see this in the lectures: Foucault no more belongs to the camp of cynical detractors of democracy than he does to that of its blind flatterers. He simply problematizes it.

One of the most astonishing dimensions of these lectures stems from the way in which Foucault, with great clarity and serenity, affirms in them his relationship to philosophy as free and courageous discourse of truth. We can review here the general movement of the lectures. With Kant, Foucault started from a new definition of modern philosophy: modern philosophy was philosophy which agreed to think, not on the basis of a reflection on its own history, but on the basis of a summons by the present. What is it in the present moment that calls for us to think? This question of what in the present moment must be the object of thought, insofar as it calls for us to think and this summons is part of the process in which the thinker takes part and which he carries out, this question was defined by Foucault as the point which opens up a specifically modern philosophy in whose tradition he wanted to insert himself.

The study of ancient *parrēsia* leads Foucault to the patient description of a philosophical truth-telling, of a discourse in a real social setting which combines courage with ethical power and provocativeness, from Pericles to Plato. At the end of the course,[45] he notes that a feature of modern philosophy, from the Cartesian *cogito* rejecting authorities of knowledge up to the Kantian "*Sapere aude*," is a reactivation of this parrhesiastic structure. This bridge thrown for the first time between ancient and modern philosophy may finally open up in Foucault a trans-historical, perennial characterization of philosophical activity: this is the practice of courageous and free speech which constantly asserts the difference and force of truth-telling in the political game and which aims to disturb and transform the mode of being of subjects.

Many thanks to Daniel Defert for his constant generosity and to Jorge Davila for his magnanimity.

1. The series was launched in February 1983, edited by Michel Foucault, François Wahl, and Paul Veyne. See the "Chronologie" of Daniel Defert in Michel Foucault, *Dits et Écrits, 1954-1988*, ed., D. Defert and F. Ewald with the collaboration of J. Lagrange (Paris: Gallimard, 1994), Vol. 1, p. 61.

2. *Histoire de la sexualité II. L'usage des plaisirs* (Paris: Gallimard, 1984); English translation by R. Hurley, *The Use of Pleasure* (New York: Random House, 1985 and Harmondsworth: Viking, 1986), and *Histoire de la sexualité III. Le souci de soi* (Paris: Gallimard, 1984); English translation by R. Hurley, *The Care of the Self* (New York: Random House, 1985 and Harmondsworth: Viking, 1986).

3. See the lectures of 12 January, first hour; 16 February, first hour; 23 February, first hour; and 2 March, first hour.

4. *L'Herméneutique du sujet. Cours a Collège de France, 1981-1982*, ed. F. Gros (Paris: Gallimard-Le Seuil, "Hautes Études," 2001) pp. 3-4; English translation by Graham Burchell, *The Hermeneutics of the Subject. Lectures at the Collège de France, 1981-1982*, English series editor Arnold I. Davidson (New York and Basingstoke: Palgrave Macmillan, 2005) pp. 2-3.

5. *L'Herméneutique du sujet*, p. 130; *The Hermeneutics of the Subject*, p. 134.

6. See the final lecture of 1980 (26 March).

7. *L'Herméneutique du sujet*, pp. 389-390; *The Hermeneutics of the Subject*, pp. 407-409.

8. See *L'Herméneutique du sujet*, the end of the lecture of 3 March and the two hours of 10 March, pp. 348-391; *The Hermeneutics of the Subject*, pp. 366-409.

9. See above, pp. 2-6, the beginning of the lecture of 5 January, first hour.

10. It may be recalled for the record that Kant's and Mendelssohn's texts are answers to the question "What is Enlightenment?" which was first posed by the pastor Zöllner in 1783, in a note to an article published in the same *Berlinische Monatsschrift* and which bore on the question of the civil or religious dimensions of marriage (for further clarifications see J. Mondot's book, *Qu'est-ce que les Lumières?* Presses universitaires de Saint-Étienne, 1991).

11. Published in the *Bulletin de la Société française de philosophie* of 27 May 1978; English translation by Kevin Paul Geiman, "What is Critique?" in James Schmidt, ed., *What is Enlightenment? Eighteenth-Century Answers and Twentieth-Century Questions* (Berkeley and Los Angeles: University of California Press, 1996) pp. 382-398.

12. Ibid., p. 39; English p. 386.

13. Ibid., p. 46; English p. 392.

14. See above, lecture of 9 March, first hour.

15. This work on the Enlightenment may also be read as a way of situating his own relationship to Kant differently from that of Jurgen Habermas who the same year was invited by Paul Veyne to give some lectures at the Collège de France (from 7 to 22 March; see Daniel Defert's "Chronologie," p. 62). We recall that in 1981, when the university of Berkeley proposed the creation of a Foucault-Habermas seminar, which could have become permanent, Habermas proposed "modernity" as its theme (see what Foucault said about this in *Dits et Écrits, IV*, pp. 446-447).

16. In the absence of a "Course summary" like those Foucault wrote in previous years for the Collège administration, we give here a description of the basic structure of the year's lectures.

17. See the examples given ("the meeting is open," "I apologize") in the lecture of 12 January, second hour.

18. *L'Archéologie du savoir* (Paris: Gallimard, 1969), see, for example, pp. 118-120 et passim; English translation by A. Sheridan, *The Archeology of Knowledge* (London: Tavistock, and New York: Pantheon, 1973) pp. 82-84.

19. *L'Herméneutique du sujet*, lecture of 10 March 1982, second hour, pp. 378-394; *The Hermeneutics of the Subject*, pp. 395-411.

20. Ibid., 10 March 1982, first hour, pp. 372-374; pp. 389-391.

21. Lectures of February and March 1984.

22. See above, lectures of 2 and 9 March 1983.

23. In the lecture of 2 February 1983, first hour (see above), Foucault studies the appearances of the term *parrēsia* in Euripides' tragedies, *The Phoenician Women, Hippolytus, The Bacchae, and*

Orestes. In the lectures at Berkeley in the autumn of 1983 he will add a study of *Electra* (see
M. Foucault, *Fearless Speech*, Los Angeles: Semiotext(e), 2001, pp. 33-36).

24. See above, lecture of 2 February, first hour.

25. See above, lecture of 26 January, second hour.

26. Lecture of 28 March, 1984, second hour.

27. See the lectures of February and March 1980.

28. Manuscript of the lecture of 2 March 1983.

29. "Politique et éthique: une interview," in *Dits et Écrits*, IV, 341, pp. 585-586; English transla-
    tion of Foucault's replies by Catherine Porter in P. Rabinow, ed., *The Foucault Reader* (New
    York: Pantheon Books, 1984) p. 374. [The English translation has "the personal *poetic* atti-
    tude of a philosopher"; G.B.]

30. See above, lecture of 2 March, first hour.

31. G. Scarpat, *Parrhesia. Storie del termine et delle sue traduzioni in Latino* (Brescia: Paideia Editrice,
    1964).

32. For example: H. Schlier, "Parrēsia, parrēsiazomai," in G. Kittel, ed., *Theologisches Wörterbuch
    zum Neuen Testament* (Kohlhammer Verlag: Stuttgart, 1949-1979).

33. He proposed a study of the tragedy in 1971 at the Collège de France (in the lectures "La
    Volonté de savoir"), in 1972 in the United States (in a seminar at Buffalo on "La Volonté
    de vérité dans la Grèce ancienne" including an analysis of Sophocles' tragedy and a lecture
    on "Le Savoir d'Œdipe" at the University of Cornell), in 1973 (in the first of the lectures
    delivered in May in Rio de Janeiro on "La Vérité et les formes juridique), in 1980 (lectures
    at the Collège de France, 16 and 23 January), and 1981 (first of the six lectures given at
    Louvain in May, "Mal faire, dire vrai. Fonctions de l'aveu").

34. It should be noted here that, more broadly, in the first series of lectures given by Foucault
    in 1970 at the Collège de France, it is judicial practices which appear as the frameworks of
    veridiction.

35. The interpretation of the final words of Socrates ("Crito, we owe a cock to Asclepius" in
    Phaedo, 118a) based on Dumézil's *Moyne noir en gris dedans Varennes* (Paris: Gallimard, 1984);
    English translation by Betsy Wing as Georges Dumézil, *The Riddle of Nostradamus. A Critical
    Dialogue* (Baltimore and London: Johns Hopkins University Press, 1999).

36. M. Foucault, *Fearless Speech*.

37. Through this refocusing on the study of Greek political thought, the 1983 lectures echo
    the first course of 1971 ("La Volonté de savoir") devoted to the judicial practices of Ancient
    Greece and already proposing the analysis of crucial concepts of Athenian democracy like
    that of *isonomia*.

38. The lecture of 16 February, first hour (the illustration in this case is that of the Platonic
    figure of the Prince's philosopher advisor).

39. The Left was in power in France from May 1981, with Mitterand as head of state. Soon
    after the liberal turn in Mitterand's policies, the "intellectuals of the left," formerly so
    active in protest, were deplored for their present lack of energy for making concrete pro-
    posals or defending the new reforms. In *Le Monde* of 26 July 1983, Max Gallo, who at the
    time wanted to provoke a debate on these breaks, published an article on "the silence of
    the intellectuals" in which, noting "the resurgence of right wing ideas," he regretted that
    a "large part" of the new generation of intellectuals had " 'withdrawn' onto the Aventine"
    at a time when one should reflect on the country setting off on the path of an active "mod-
    ernization." Some days later, in the same newspaper, Philippe Boggio extended the debate
    (still under the same heading: "The silence of the intellectuals") and commented: "There
    is hardly a rush on the part of the Collège de France, publishers, or the CNRS to make
    their contribution to the fabric of the Left in power, particularly when the wind of polemic
    with the opposition is blowing." As he wished to recall with them "their relations with the
    State," he noted that "some, like Simone de Beauvoir or Michel Foucault, have refused to
    take part in this inquiry" (Foucault actually did not think that these criticisms concerned
    him, in view of his numerous concrete commitments). These articles appeared in July (to
    be complete we should refer to J.-M. Helvig's reply to Max Gallo in *Libération*, that of
    P. Guilbert in *Quotidien de Paris*, etcetera) and so long after Foucault had given his lectures
    at the Collège de France on political *parrēsia*. But some of the lectures could sound like an
    advance reply to these criticisms. Foucault had actually never ceased to emphasize that it is

not the philosopher's office to tell politicians what they should do. It is not for the philosopher to legislate in their place, nor even to present himself as the intellectual guarantor of their action, as if he should support the well-founded nature of their decisions with his knowledge.

40. See above, lecture of 9 March, first hour.
41. On this point see Daniel Defert's "Chronologie," in *Dits et Écrits*, I, p. 60.
42. On this point see "Le Terrorisme ice et là," in *Dits et Écrits*, IV, 316, pp. 318-319.
43. On this point see "Un système fini face à une demande infinie," ibid., 325, pp. 367-383; English translation, "The Risks of Security" in *Power. Essential Works of Foucault 1954-1984*, *Vol. Three*, ed., James D. Faubion, trans., Robert Hurley and others (New York: The New Press, 2000).
44. On this point see Daniel Defert's "Chronologie," p. 62.
45. The first hour of the lecture of 9 March.

INDEX OF NAMES

INDEX OF CONCEPTS AND NOTIONS

Printed in the United States
By Bookmasters